World Politics
and International Economics

Originally published as the Winter 1975
special issue (Volume 29, Number 1) of
International Organization,
a journal sponsored by the World Peace Foundation,
edited at Stanford University, and published by
the University of Wisconsin Press.

C. FRED BERGSTEN AND LAWRENCE B. KRAUSE
Editors

World Politics
and International Economics

Contributions by
C. Fred Bergsten, Robert O. Keohane, and Joseph S. Nye, Jr.
Robert Gilpin
Richard N. Cooper
Robert E. Baldwin and David A. Kay
Charles R. Frank, Jr., and Mary Baird
Robert O. Keohane and Van Doorn Ooms
Carlos F. Díaz-Alejandro
H. Jon Rosenbaum and William G. Tyler
Franklyn D. Holzman and Robert Legvold
Lawrence B. Krause and Joseph S. Nye, Jr.

THE BROOKINGS INSTITUTION
Washington, D.C.

Copyright © 1975 by
THE BROOKINGS INSTITUTION
1775 Massachusetts Avenue, N.W., Washington, D.C. 20036

Library of Congress Cataloging in Publication data:
Main entry under title:
World politics and international economics.

 Originally published as the winter 1975 special issue
(v. 29, no. 1) of International organization.
 Bibliography: p.
 Includes index.
 1. International economic relations—Addresses,
essays, lectures. 2. International finance—Addresses,
essays, lectures. 3. World politics—1955-
—Addresses, essays, lectures. I. Bergsten, C. Fred,
1941- II. Krause, Lawrence B.
HF1411.W66 338.91 75-15684

ISBN 0-8157-0916-1
ISBN 0-8157-0915-3 pbk.

9 8 7 6 5 4 3 2 1

THE BROOKINGS INSTITUTION is an independent organization devoted to nonpartisan research, education, and publication in economics, government, foreign policy, and the social sciences generally. Its principal purposes are to aid in the development of sound public policies and to promote public understanding of issues of national importance.

The Institution was founded on December 8, 1927, to merge the activities of the Institute for Government Research, founded in 1916, the Institute of Economics, founded in 1922, and the Robert Brookings Graduate School of Economics and Government, founded in 1924.

The Board of Trustees is responsible for the general administration of the Institution, while the immediate direction of the policies, program, and staff is vested in the President, assisted by an advisory committee of the officers and staff. The by-laws of the Institution state: "It is the function of the Trustees to make possible the conduct of scientific research, and publication, under the most favorable conditions, and to safeguard the independence of the research staff in the pursuit of their studies and in the publication of the results of such studies. It is not a part of their function to determine, control, or influence the conduct of particular investigations or the conclusions reached."

The President bears final responsibility for the decision to publish a manuscript as a Brookings book. In reaching his judgment on the competence, accuracy, and objectivity of each study, the President is advised by the director of the appropriate research program and weighs the views of a panel of expert outside readers who report to him in confidence on the quality of the work. Publication of a work signifies that it is deemed a competent treatment worthy of public consideration but does not imply endorsement of conclusions or recommendations.

The Institution maintains its position of neutrality on issues of public policy in order to safeguard the intellectual freedom of the staff. Hence interpretations or conclusions in Brookings publications should be understood to be solely those of the authors and should not be attributed to the Institution, to its trustees, officers, or other staff members, or to the organizations that support its research.

Foreword

In recent years the world economy has suffered major shocks and undergone rapid change. The fixed exchange rates built into the international monetary system designed at Bretton Woods in 1944 have given way to flexible rates. Trading relations that were for many years disturbed only by changes in the tariffs and quotas imposed by importing nations have been disrupted by embargoes and other controls imposed by exporters. Long-standing bilateral aid relations between donors and recipients have been substantially altered. Overseas direct investment has become of major significance, and it is no longer dominated by American corporations.

These economic changes stem in part from political factors, such as the shift in power relations that followed the erosion of U.S. economic predominance and the ebbing of the cold war. They have also been influenced by the emergence of new actors on the international economic stage, such as multinational enterprises. Change has often followed crises, some of which have arisen from the politicizing of international economic issues, which in turn reflects the politics of domestic economic affairs and the blurring of traditional distinctions between domestic and international concerns.

All these developments have added to the complexity of current international economic relations, and it is the purpose of those who contributed to this book to sort them out and analyze them. The task requires interdisciplinary expertise, especially that of economists who understand politics and of political scientists familiar with economics. The research that went into this book was designed to extract the lessons of the past, to make sense of the present, and to formulate recommendations for improving international economic relations with particular emphasis on the role of international organizations.

The papers presented here set forth an analytical framework and alternative models of future international economic arrangements. They analyze the four main functional areas of international economics—money, trade, investment, and aid; describe interactions among groups of variously situated countries; and consider alternative future roles for international institutions.

This book was first published as the Winter 1975 special issue of the journal *International Organization*, which is sponsored by the World Peace Foundation, edited at Stanford University, and published by the University of Wisconsin Press. The journal's board of editors asked C. Fred Bergsten and Lawrence B. Krause, both members of the board and Brookings senior fellows in Foreign Policy Studies and Economic Studies, respectively, to serve as editors and to organize and supervise the research effort. In order to focus the requisite analytical skills, the editors paired economists and political scientists as authors of most of the chapters. The remaining chapters were assigned to single authors whose professional breadth embraces both disciplines.

The Winter 1975 special issue of *International Organization* was copyedited by Irene D. Jacobs, executive editor of the journal, and is here reproduced in its entirety and without textual change other than the addition of an index prepared by Annette H. Braver and the correction of minor errors. The Brookings Institution and the editors are grateful to the University of Wisconsin Press for making the original reproduction proofs available for the publication of the Brookings edition.

As the authors state in their preface immediately following, the project received financial assistance from the Johnson Foundation and the Ford Foundation, as well as the Brookings Institution. The views expressed in this book are solely those of the authors and should not be ascribed to either of those foundations, to the World Peace Foundation, to the University of Wisconsin or its press, or to the trustees, officers, or other staff members of the Brookings Institution.

KERMIT GORDON
President

April 1975
Washington, D.C.

Editors' preface

The primary objective of this volume is an integrated analysis of the economic and political factors that together determine international economic arrangements. The international economic order of the first postwar generation has eroded badly, if not totally collapsed. The search for replacements is well under way, but has not progressed far.

In our view, this lack of progress is partly due to an inadequate intellectual understanding of sweeping changes in the key elements that underlie any international economic arrangements. Some of these changes are economic, some are political. Yet most analyses of the problem, and proposals for reform, focus almost entirely on either the economic or, to a far lesser extent, the politics of the issues. This volume is predicated on the view that only an integrated approach can adequately explain the bases of international economic arrangements and thus provide solid policy proposals. It represents an effort to provide such an integrated analysis as a basis for proposing directions for the future evolution of the international economic order.

The second objective of the volume is the methodological consequence of this substantive focus on international political economy. Such integrated analysis can be performed only by individuals who can systematically handle both economic and political issues, or by teams that combine experts from each discipline. The volume uses both approaches. Four of the essays have a single author, three of whom are economists and one of whom is a political scientist. The other six essays are jointly authored by an economist and a political scientist (or, in one case, an economist and two political scientists). One of the objectives is to see how well the two methods will work in integrating economic and political analysis, which we feel is an essential component of most policy-oriented research on international economics.

The third objective is to carry the substantive analyses of international economic arrangements through to their institutional conclusions. Most analyses stop short of this point. Yet institutions—defined broadly to include informal and ad hoc arrangements as well as the formalities of permanent organizations—are a central element in the functioning of any international economic system. Indeed, they can help resolve substantive problems or, if they are inadequate, impede solutions. And institutional successes have intrinsic merit through their impact on the development of international law and orderly conduct. Thus, this volume seeks to explore the institutional implications of its substantive conclusions, with respect both to specific issues and to overall international economic policies.

The volume comprises four sections. The first essay introduces the subject by analyzing the interaction between economics and politics in providing a basis for international economic arrangements. It then examines the economic and political criteria against which any system can be judged—the objectives it seeks, and against whose achievement its success can be measured. The succeeding essays were to apply these criteria to the operation of the arrangements in the functional or geographic area on which they focus.

The second essay in Section I presents three alternative models of international economic arrangements for the future, against which the analyses of specific topics in the subsequent essays can be compared. Section I was originally to have also included an analysis of world economic arrangements from a "radical" perspective, but the tragic death of Stephen Hymer in February 1974 precluded the completion of that essay. In tribute to his constant effort to integrate economic and political factors in the analysis of international economic issues, and his path-breaking studies of multinational corporations, we dedicate this volume to Stephen Hymer.

Section II includes politicoeconomic analyses of the four main functional areas of international economics: international monetary relations, international trade, foreign direct investment, and foreign aid. The authors describe existing arrangements and some of the proposals for reform in each area, analyzing each in terms of criteria such as those discussed in the introductory essay. To assure adequate attention to the political variables, the authors were asked to look at the impact of different arrangements on *world* welfare, *individual countries* or groups of countries, and key *sectors* within individual countries.

Section II was thus intended to present a three-dimensional grid: the impact of alternative international economic arrangements within (1) four functional categories on (2) the world, on different countries and different sectors, and (3) on a given set of economic and political criteria. Its primary emphasis, however, was the global effect of alternative arrangements on those criteria.

Section III, in turn, was to present a geographical focus through the perspective of relations within the industrialized non-Communist world, between the industrialized and Communist countries, among the developing countries, and between the industrialized and developing countries. The authors were to assess the priorities attached to the different objectives by key countries within each grouping and the way they view international economic policy within their array of policy instruments. The essay intended to cover the first of these geographical foci, by Robert Gilpin, instead turned out to cover other areas as well and fit better into Section I. However, relations among the industrialized countries are treated extensively in the functional essays of Section II and in the introductory essay.

Finally, the single concluding essay in Section IV pulls together the functional and geographic analyses of the earlier essays and sets forth alternative international economic arrangements for the future, including their institutional implications. It concludes that the essays do not make a case for sweeping institutional reform, but instead opt for basic changes in national attitudes toward international economic arrangements—especially regarding the quest for collective economic security, pursuing the joint gains that are available from international economic relationships, and in developing new systemic leadership to supplement the previous role of the United States—and incremental improvements in the existing institutional foundation.

This project was conceived at the annual meetings of the Board of Editors of *International Organization* in May 1972 and May 1973, at which the coeditors presented their perspectives on international economic problems and the need for rigorous politicoeconomic analysis that married the talents of economists and political scientists. Authors were chosen in early 1973, held an organizational meeting at Wingspread (the Johnson Foundation conference facility in Racine, Wisconsin) in May 1973, and discussed advanced drafts of the essays at a conference at the Brookings Institution in January 1974. Final drafts of all essays, except the first and the last, were completed by June 1974.

Throughout, the project was directed by an informal steering group composed of the coeditors, Robert Keohane, and Joseph Nye. Our thanks go to the members of the Board of Editors of *International Organization* and to the several nonauthors who participated in the Wingspread and Brookings conferences, especially Benjamin J. Cohen, Theodore Geiger, and Morton H. Halperin, whose comments as the volume progressed were exceedingly valuable. The project was made possible through the financial assistance of the Brookings Institution, the Johnson Foundation, and the Ford Foundation.

C. Fred Bergsten
Lawrence B. Krause
November 1974

Contents

Section I

International economics and international politics: a framework for analysis

C. Fred Bergsten, Robert O. Keohane, and Joseph S. Nye

Until August 1971, the United States categorically rejected any notion of devaluing the dollar and championed an international monetary system based on fixed but adjustable exchange rates. From August 1971 through February 1973, the United States aggressively sought massive devaluation of the dollar, and since early 1973, it has actively promoted the adoption of highly flexible exchange rates.

From 1962 until November 1967, the British government borrowed billions of dollars and adopted dozens of policy measures to avoid devaluing sterling. In June 1972, the British government floated sterling—to a sure depreciation—after just two days of speculative attack on the currency.

Until late 1971, Japan adamantly refused to consider revaluation of the yen and adopted numerous policy measures to avoid it. In 1973, Japan sold at least $6 billion from its reserves to keep the yen from depreciating back toward its earlier level.

Since the early 1960s, the United States pressed Europe and Japan to lower their barriers to US agricultural exports. In June 1973, the United States totally embargoed its exports to Europe and Japan (and everywhere else) of some of those very same agricultural products.

In the early 1960s, Brazil and other producing countries pleaded with consuming countries to negotiate the International Coffee Agreement to keep coffee prices from declining. By the middle 1970s, those coffee producers let the agreement lapse because they felt sufficiently strong to force prices up on their own.

What were the objectives of these international economic policies of some of the leading countries in the world economy? Did these objectives change as dramatically, over both longer and shorter periods of time, as appears to be the

C. Fred Bergsten is a senior fellow at the Brookings Institution in Washington, D. C., and is coeditor of this volume. Robert O. Keohane is an associate professor of political science at Stanford University in Stanford, California. Joseph S. Nye is a professor of political science at Harvard University in Cambridge, Massachusetts.

case? If so, was this because the countries' preferences changed? Or because the nature of the problem they faced changed? Or because their power to achieve ends they had sought all along changed? Or because they were forced to alter their views by other countries or by nonnational actors such as transnational enterprises? Or were the objectives relatively constant, with the changes only in the means used to pursue desired outcomes?

Indeed, why did the international order that had effectively structured world economic relationships for the first postwar generation begin to collapse in the late 1960s and early 1970s? Did it no longer address the issues most critical to its member countries? Did it no longer comport with the world economic environment it sought to order? Did it no longer accurately reflect the constellation of national power that must underpin any international system?

This volume seeks to answer such questions, and, in doing so, assist in the construction of a new international economic order. This introductory essay presents a conceptual framework for such analysis, and it examines the relationship between international economic policies and international politics more generally, discusses postwar United States predominance and its partial decline, and analyzes the economic goals sought by governments in international relations. Governmental economic policies and transnational behavior do not take place in a vacuum; the political order strongly affects national decisions about economic goals and the leeway given to transnational actors. It is appropriate, therefore, to begin with an analysis of the impact of world politics on the international economic order, rather than, as is too often done, introducing politics merely as a constraint on the attainment of independently determined economic goals.

The international political context of world economics

Politics and economics in the contemporary system

Politics and economics are interwoven strands in the fabric of world order. Two world wars, a depression, and the cold war have made us well aware of the important causal effects of each on the other. Unless definitions of *politics* and *economics* are arranged so that one category necessarily includes all fundamental phenomena, neither economic nor political determinism can explain events successfully.

Debates about the origins of imperialism or about postwar United States foreign policy, between analysts who stress security motivations and power competition and those who emphasize economic incentives, are inconclusive. The energetic globalism of United States policy can be explained by either a genuine fear of widespread totalitarian resurgence if it were not checked at all points, analogous to contemporary perceptions of the lessons of Munich, or by a desire to make the world safe for American commerce, or both. Indeed, the security and economic motives were inextricably linked: the breakdown of the international economy in the 1930s was widely viewed as a central element in the national economic catastrophes, especially in Europe, which led to the installation of totalitarian governments, which in turn produced World War II. Monocausal arguments founder on the fact that policymakers usually have more than one set of reasons for their actions and see intimate linkages between the different categories, which are often isolated in scholarly writing.[1]

On the motivational level, therefore, political and economic factors are frequently so closely intertwined that they cannot be disentangled. In addition, regardless of motivations, politics and economics are almost inevitably linked at the systemic level. An international economic system is affected by the international political system existing at the time, and vice versa. The behavior of governments on economic issues will be affected by their political calculations, which will in turn be determined in part by the structure of world politics. At the same time, political steps by governments must often rest on economic capabilities and, as we will see shortly, are increasingly taking economic form.

The fact that a particular economic activity is characterized by nonpolitical behavior (for instance, when transactions are carried on through a market system) does not imply that politics is unimportant. Indeed, politics may have been crucial in establishing the setting within which the activity took place, the *structure* of relations in the overall system. This second "face of power" is extremely important in determining what issues are raised for political decisions and what issues are not.[2]

The importance of this aspect of power leads us to distinguish between two levels of analysis: a process level, dealing with short-term behavior within a constant set of institutions, fundamental assumptions, and expectations; and a structure level, having to do with long-term political and economic determinants of the systemic incentives and constraints within which actors operate. At this structural level, we are interested in how the institutions, fundamental assumptions, and rules of the game are created and how they support or undermine different patterns of short-term economic activity.[3]

---

[1] For an attempt to argue that economic considerations were paramount in United States foreign policy after World War II, see Joyce and Gabriel Kolko, *The Limits of Power: The World and United States Foreign Policy, 1945-54* (New York: Random House, 1972). The authors choose references to economic purposes as indicating "real" motivations, and ignore or discount references to security purposes. The limitations of their analysis are most graphically revealed by their failure even to mention the psychic effects of Munich—in over 700 pages about the first postwar decade of US foreign policy! Conservative historians have taken the opposite approach of regarding economic motivation as simply derivative from security concerns. In our view this represents an artificial and ultimately fruitless search for the "essential" element in an inextricably intertwined set of reasons and rationalizations.

[2] See Peter Bachrach and Morton Baratz, "Decisions and Nondecisions: An Analytical Framework," *American Political Science Review* 57 (1963): 632-42.

[3] See Robert O. Keohane and Joseph S. Nye, "World Politics and the International Economic System," in C. Fred Bergsten, ed., *The Future of the International Economic Order: An Agenda for Research* (Lexington, Mass.: D.C. Heath, 1973). The following six pages draw heavily upon this essay.

In some systems at some times, the levels of structure and process are relatively well insulated from one another. Basic institutions and practices are accepted as legitimate by all major parties. Economic activity in these systems may involve very little direct political intervention. On the international level, only minor and infrequent attention may be paid to economic affairs by top government officials. At other times, however, the rules of the game themselves are called into question by major participants. The system becomes politicized as controversy increases. In highly politicized systems, attention of top-level decision makers is focused on the system, and nonroutine behavior dominates routine behavior. Insulation between the structure of the system and particular processes breaks down; specific quarrels become linked to arguments about appropriate institutions and permanent arrangements.

It is when accepted structures, with their associated rules of the game, are called into question that controversy, and therefore politicization, are likely to increase most rapidly. During these periods, questions of who will exercise political control, and how, become dominant. Thus one observes increasing disagreements between a larger number of important contenders, over a greater number of specific issues, with more direct linkage between immediate problems (e.g., the exchange rate of the yen) and systemic issues (e.g., fixed versus more flexible exchange rates), and an increase in the attention devoted to these issues by heads of government and cabinet ministers. In recent years, we have witnessed increased politicization of international economic affairs.

To some extent, this increased politicization is the result of secular trends towards more governmental intervention in the economy as governments accept responsibility for an increasing array of policy targets. The dramatic increase in international economic interpenetration heightens the external threat to successful pursuit of these government objectives, and thereby produces a tendency for countries to seek to shield themselves from it. But, at the same time, outside forces offer additional policy instruments, often of very high value, to governments that can harness them effectively, which produces a tendency for countries to welcome international exchange as long as they can assure that it points in desired directions.

Thus the increased policy role of national governments combines with the increased internationalization of the world economy to force a blurring of the lines between domestic and foreign policy, and an increase in the number of issues relevant to foreign policy. International economic issues rise toward the top of national policy agendas and become increasingly politicized in the process.

Economic power and military force

The increased politicization of international economics, however, is also a product of other long-term changes that have affected the relations among states, the effective means at their disposal, and other aspects of their political-economic milieu. One of these important long-run changes has been in the relative utility of force and economic power for major states.

Political scientists for the past three decades have generally emphasized the role of force, particularly organized military force, in international politics. Force dominates other means of power in the sense that *if* there are no constraints on one's choice of instruments (a hypothetical situation that has only been approximated in the two world wars), the state or states with superior military force will prevail. Thus, American economic sanctions against Japan in 1940-41 were countered by Japanese military action; to the military challenge, the United States had to answer in military terms. If the security dilemma for all states were extremely acute, military force and its supporting components, which, of course, include a large economic dimension, would clearly be the dominant source of power. Survival is the primary goal of all states, and in the most adverse situations, force is ultimately necessary to guarantee survival. Thus military force is always a central component of national power.

But insofar as the perceived margin of safety for states widens, other goals—such as economic welfare, political autonomy, and status—become relatively more important. This is in fact the situation at present, as widespread perceptions of détente have rendered quite low most countries' fear of any use of force by the major military powers. This situation is not necessarily permanent: the cold war could reappear, or nuclear proliferation could again raise deep national insecurities. But, at least for now, economic issues have become far more salient in international affairs than at any point since the beginning of World War II, both because of their increased importance in their own right and because of the decline in concerns about survival and the traditional forms of security.

It is unlikely that military force will be an appropriate tool to achieve these nonmilitary goals. Furthermore, as the nature of military force and the consequence of its use change, it has become less efficacious even for achieving the goals that it formerly served. The disproportionate destructiveness of nuclear weapons limits the utility of this type of force for achieving positive goals, as opposed to deterrent objectives. In addition, prevailing norms and the costliness of ruling alien populations that have become socially mobilized increase the cost of using conventional force.[4] As these changes in goals and in the nature of force take place, the roles of other instruments of power and influence tend to increase.

It is important to notice, however, that the effects of these increasing constraints on the use of force are not felt equally by all actors in world politics, nor are the constraints the same for all potential uses of force by the same actors. It may be useful briefly to discuss the effects on three sets of actors: (1) the superpowers—the US and the USSR, (2) other developed countries, and (3) other actors, particularly Third World states and transnational organizations.

The superpowers have continued to use force or the threat of force to control events within certain other states. The threat of force is probably most effective

[4] See Stanley Hoffmann, *Gulliver's Troubles, or The Setting of American Foreign Policy* (New York: McGraw Hill, 1968).

where it remains in the background. Military power based on undeterred local preponderance and occasional military intervention helps to explain the high degree of conformity of the economic systems of the states in the Council for Mutual Economic Cooperation (COMECON) to that of the Soviet Union, and the substantial trade preferences between those states. Similarly, the threat of open or covert US military intervention has played a role in limiting revolutionary regime changes in Latin American countries over the past three decades, and has therefore tended to keep their economies more closely tied to that of the United States than might otherwise have been the case. In some cases the *use* of force has been effective, as in the United States intervention in the Dominican Republic in 1965 and the Soviet intervention in Czechoslovakia three years later. In others, such as the United States support of the Bay of Pigs invasion in 1961 or the American intervention in Indochina, the policy of force led to disastrous results. On some disputes on which force might have been used in the past, such as the Arab oil embargo against the United States in 1973-74 or the Chilean expropriation, without significant compensation, of American-owned enterprises under the Allende government in 1971, the United States has resorted to other means of influence. "Gunboat diplomacy" is widely regarded as dangerous and often counterproductive; force is seen as an undesirable means of intervention, except as a last resort.

Force, however, can be used not only for intervention but for deterrence, and here its utility does not seem to have diminished so sharply. Since each superpower continues to use the threat of force to deter attacks by the other superpower on itself or on its allies, the importance of these nuclear weapons for deterrence remains a valuable resource that can be used by alliance leaders in their own bargaining on other issues with their allies. This is particularly important for the United States, whose allies are concerned about potential Soviet threats, and which has fewer other means of influence over its allies than does the Soviet Union over its Eastern European partners. The United States has, accordingly, taken advantage of the Europeans' (particularly the Germans') desire for American protection with regard to the issue of troop levels in Europe and their links to trade and monetary negotiations. Sometimes this has taken place through calculated executive actions, sometimes through congressional initiatives contrary to executive preference. Thus, although the first-order effect of deterrent force is essentially negative—to deny effective offensive power to a superpower opponent—the state within the alliance controlling this force can gain positive political influence from its possession. Since neither Europe nor Japan seems willing to undertake the expense and risk of developing a major nuclear second-strike capability in the immediate future, this form of militarily based power remains significant for the United States.

For other developed countries, in general, force is of less utility than for the superpowers. Indeed, in relations between many developed countries, force is of negligible importance, for instance, between Germany and Japan, Italy and Holland, or New Zealand and the United Kingdom. Intense relationships of mutual influence are developing in which force is irrelevant as an instrument of policy, and these are not limited to common markets or members of a close-knit politico-military bloc. Since economic instruments have largely supplanted the use or threat of force in these relationships, the implications for the political relevance of economic ties between these countries are considerable.

For the superpowers and developed countries generally, we have stressed the declining role of force. For other actors in world politics, however, force remains valuable. Indeed, in areas such as the Persian Gulf from which British or American force has been partially withdrawn, force may be becoming more important than formerly as a means of influence for small or middle powers. It is clear that force remains important on the Indian subcontinent, in southeast Asia, and in the eastern Mediterranean. National liberation movements, sometimes operating transnationally, often rely heavily on force; witness the recently successful movement in Mozambique and the various Palestinian paramilitary operations.

Yet limits on the use of force, although they operate unevenly, are frequently important. To some extent, economic instruments are used in reaction to this situation as a substitute for force, to achieve similar purposes when force is unavailable or its use is deemed too costly. Using economic instruments in this way is a well-established practice in world politics. Examples include the Allied blockade against Napoleon, the League of Nations oil embargo against Italy, the near total US embargo of exports to Cuba, and United Nations sanctions against Rhodesia, as well as the recent embargo of oil sales to the United States and the Netherlands by Arab states in 1973-74 in pursuit of a favorable political settlement in the Middle East. The most sustained effort in this direction in the postwar period has been the US effort to restrict trade in some strategic materials, and to limit Soviet access to advanced technology. Here economic sources of power allow governments to carry on "war by other means."

But there is a more straightforward function served by economic instruments: to exercise influence on questions arising out of patterns of economic interdependence, for the sake of affecting economic transactions and benefits to be derived from them. The monetary negotiations of the last decade, as well as negotiations on trade and on foreign investment, have primarily reflected competition for economic benefits, as well as to some extent for political influence or status within the context of relatively intense economic intercourse. Where transactions are economic, economic instruments are likely to be used first. They can be wielded by the same bureaucracies that deal with the economic transactions, and they often appear more legitimate to other governments than instruments that appear to "escalate" the controversy to the political-military plane.

Yet much of the complexity, as well as much of the interest, in international political-economic relations derives from the fact that linkages between issue areas, both within the broad arena of economics itself and between economic and security concerns, frequently do take place. In 1971, for instance, the United States linked trade and monetary negotiations together for the sake of getting a better monetary agreement, and there were also references to the need to attain a trade surplus to permit the United States to maintain its worldwide political and military position. About the same time, the United States linked the reversion of Okinawa to Japan to Japanese agreement to limit its textile exports to the United States; and US troop levels in Germany have for fifteen years been linked, at least implicitly, to German willingness to offset the costs of those troops to the US balance of payments. The Arab oil producers' actions on behalf of their political goals of a favorable Middle East settlement have often been almost indistinguishable from their economic goals of increasing revenue from their petroleum resources. Within the European Common Market, complex linkages and trade-offs between issues are commonplace.

In general, whenever there is less than perfect congruity between various sources of power for states involved in close and complex relations with one another (for instance, where one set of states is stronger militarily, but the other controls a valuable economic resource that is at issue), linkages between issue areas are likely to be drawn. Arab oil producers used economic power—their only source of major international leverage—to pursue their most urgent national security objectives in 1973-74; and the United States has attempted to counter this by implicitly threatening military force, and by linking high petroleum prices to the world food issue, where it is *American* resources (food surpluses for export) that are sought by other governments.

In a period such as the present, with interdependence high, rapid shifts taking place in governmental policies, and vast asymmetries between the economic and military power of numerous states, linkages between issue areas are likely to become particularly pronounced. One linkage breeds another, as the states disadvantaged by the first linkage seek to bring their sources of strength to bear upon the problem at hand. In the immediate future, world economics will be increasingly politicized, and vice versa.

New actors

In addition to changes in the relative utility of force and economic power as instruments for major states, the international economic order must now encompass two new sets of major actors that have emerged because of their economic power: a number of countries that were unimportant to world economics when the postwar world was organized, or even ten years ago; and transnational economic actors, of which multinational enterprises are the most important and well known.

The postwar economic system was organized primarily by, and for, the United States, Canada, and Western Europe, with some participation from Latin America (and the Soviet Union, which soon dropped out). Many countries that play a central role in today's world, including some of the oil-exporting countries, were not even independent at that time.

But Japan, which entered the core group of international economic decision makers in the early 1960s, and the oil countries have made the set of major economic powers more heterogeneous. In addition, other states, largely from the Third World, have become more important and more active. The participation, or at least acquiescence, of many of these countries is necessary in at least some aspects of any new international economic structure, not only because of their possession of many key primary products but also because of their new awareness of their needs and opportunities, which will prompt them to attempt to block international economic reform unless their interests are taken into account.[5] Indeed, this new "middle class" has left behind a "Fourth World," which remains the hard-core international welfare problem of the 1970s and beyond.

With regard to multinational enterprises, some incautious or enthusiastic observers have gone too far in proclaiming the death of the nation state in a world of interdependence.[6] The nonstate actors do not supersede states, although they do affect the system—particularly the monetary and trading systems, via the growth of the Eurocurrency market and intracorporate trade—and create new problems for governments. Outcomes in these issue areas can no longer be understood solely as results of state action and policy.

It is clear that, at a minimum, these transnational actors have greatly speeded the transmission of economic events from one country to another. The Eurocurrency and Eurobond markets provide a truly international center for financial and capital transactions. Multinational firms increasingly scan the globe for production and marketing opportunities and hence speed shifts in national comparative advantage. As a result of this acceleration of the pace of international economic change, the threats and opportunities generated for national policies by external events have become much more acute. Questions arise as to whether the pace should be deliberately slowed, perhaps by placing restraints on the growing economic interdependence of nations, including these very transnational forces that have promoted its acceleration.

The emergence of new international economic issues

Reference to these transnational actors leads us to the final key change in the political milieu for international economic relations: the emergence of important

---

[5] For one of the coauthors' views on these issues, see C. Fred Bergsten, "The Threat from the Third World," *Foreign Policy*, no. 11 (Summer 1973): 102-24; and Bergsten, "The Response to the Third World," *Foreign Policy*, no. 17 (Winter 1974-75).

[6] In 1969 Charles Kindleberger argued in a much-quoted (and probably much-regretted) phrase that "the nation-state is just about through as an economic unit" (*American Business Abroad* [New Haven, Conn.: Yale University Press, 1969], p. 207). The most trenchant criticisms of this view can be found in the works of Kenneth N. Waltz, particularly, "The Myth of National Interdependence," in Charles Kindleberger, ed., *The International Corporation* (Cambridge, Mass.: Harvard University Press, 1970); and Robert Gilpin, particularly, "The Politics of Transnational Economic Relations," in Robert O. Keohane and Joseph S. Nye, eds., *Transnational Relations and World Politics* (Cambridge, Mass.: Harvard University Press, 1972). For an assessment of the controversy, see the essay by Keohane and Ooms in this volume, and Robert O. Keohane and Joseph S. Nye, "International Interdependence and Integration," in Nelson Polsby and Fred Greenstein, eds., *Handbook of Political Science*, vol. 7 (forthcoming in 1975).

new international economic issues that were ignored, or inadequately covered, in the postwar structure, such as nontariff barriers to trade, agriculture, business and government cartels, the variety of issues relating to multinational enterprises, and adjustment assistance to domestic groups adversely affected by international transactions.

The most important new issue is access to supplies. When the postwar economic order was constructed, the attention of virtually all countries was riveted on the fear of unemployment. Hence, the International Monetary Fund (IMF), the General Agreement on Tariffs and Trade (GATT), and the World Bank systems aimed to avoid national efforts to export unemployment (through competitive depreciations of exchange rates, import controls, and export subsidies), as had occurred with such devastating effect in the 1930s, and in fact to maximize national opportunities to expand production and to sell to other countries.

In the 1970s, however, inflation has emerged in virtually all countries as an economic (and hence political) problem at least as severe as unemployment, if not more so. Indeed, in recent years numerous countries have been seeking to insulate their economies against imported inflation and even export their inflation to others by *up*valuing their exchange rates, unilaterally *liberalizing* their import controls, and instituting *export* controls. Access to supplies has come to rival, if not surpass, access to markets as a major issue of international economics. But because of the previous focus on unemployment, by both governments and outside analysts, there exist no effective international rules and arrangements to govern these new policy approaches and few ideas for developing them.[7] Thus the international economic agenda has broadened at the same time that it has become more complex due to underlying political and economic changes.

United States predominance and the distribution of power

A number of essays in this volume refer loosely to shifts in the distribution of power among states. Positing that power abhors a free market, Díaz-Alejandro argues that multipolar deterrence has now made free markets more plausible than before. Gilpin speaks of the need for the United States to adjust to "the shifting balance of power." Clearly, there is a relationship between the distribution of states' military power and international economic order, but the discussion of this relationship is often marked by confusion resulting from failure to make necessary distinctions.

A simple reductionist theory of international economic affairs could hold that they are merely reflections of political-military developments. Changes in international economic relations would therefore be explained by shifts in military

---

[7] For one effort, see C. Fred Bergsten, *Completing the GATT: Toward New International Rules to Govern Export Controls* (Washington, D.C.: British–North American Committee, November 1974).

power. This explanation, however, does not hold up well against the pattern of recent events. The United States position in the world economy and its dominance in policymaking have clearly declined since 1944. At Bretton Woods the United States could construct the system largely according to its specifications; now it can only veto proposals it dislikes. Yet during this period, the United States has remained, militarily, the most powerful state in the world, and its lead in this respect over its major economic partners, Japan and Europe, has been maintained. Although it has become more costly for the United States to intervene effectively in other countries over the past 30 years, American deterrent power has remained intact.

Thus, although the distribution of military power is an important underlying factor affecting the international economic order, by itself it provides only a partial explanation. Two other major factors particularly must be taken into account to explain changes in international economic relations: changes in perceptions of the threat of military aggression, and changes in the relative economic strength of countries within US-led alliances.

Perceptions of threat are important. Many of the major advances in international economic relations came during the long period of maximum cold-war tension, between 1947 (Truman Doctrine) and 1963 (Test Ban Treaty). In these years, the IMF, the World Bank, the GATT, and the Organization for Economic Cooperation and Development (OECD) began to function, currency convertibility was achieved and major tariff cuts were implemented, and the Common Market was established. United States security leadership was prized by its allies, and the American perception of high threat from the Soviet Union encouraged United States policymakers to grant a variety of economic concessions to the Europeans and to the Japanese in the interest of systemic progress. The sharp reductions in perceived threats in recent years have reduced the ability of the United States to translate its military leadership of the alliance into economic leaderhip without resorting to overt and highly resented linkages between economic and military issues. American allies became less inclined to accept the roles of junior partners once they had perceived the external threat as diminished.[8] At the same time, United States willingness to accept trade barriers against American goods, or exchange rates that had similar effects, was also declining.

These changes in perceptions were reinforced by increases in European and Japanese economic capabilities relative to those of the United States. In the early postwar period, Europe was largely supine, and, although it was able to bargain and resist on particular issues, it usually complied with US leadership, particularly on the overall economic structure. In later years, the European economies had recov-

[8] For evidence of this in the case of Canada, see Joseph S. Nye, "Transnational Relations and Interstate Conflicts: An Empirical Analysis," *International Organization* 28 (Autumn 1974): 961-96. It should be noted that a serious future threat—not necessarily from the Soviet Union and not necessarily military—could restore greater cohesion. The steps taken in late 1974 toward an oil consumers organization provide an indication that events might move in this direction.

ered tremendously. Indeed, their recovery alone, and the confidence it gave them at least on economic issues, provide the primary explanation for the closely related advent of the Dillon Round tariff cuts, currency convertibility and subsequent reduced reliance on the dollar, and the construction of the Common Market. The latter steps were also motivated by a desire to boost the relative strength of Europe, politically as well as economically, so that it could better stand on its own against the Soviet Union (and later, the United States).

In the United States, the increased difficulties encountered in exercising leadership also reflected the increased relative economic strength of Europe and Japan. As the economic strength of America's partners grew, so did the price paid for a leadership role. European and Japanese exports did not significantly threaten American jobs in the 1950s, but they certainly did so by 1971; and domestic American interest groups reacted accordingly.[9] Earlier, the ability of the executive to persuade Congress and resist the demands of disadvantaged groups had been enhanced by the shared perception of a serious external threat to national security. Thus, perceived threat diminished while the costs of leadership were rising.

As the preceding discussion indicates, we reject an interpretation of contemporary international economic relations that attributes changes solely, or even primarily, to the declining military hegemony of the United States. Even in a simple model, changes in relative economic situation and perception of threats would have to be taken heavily into account. Too often, furthermore, the concept of hegemony is loosely defined and used largely as a pejorative term for preponderance or a leadership style of which the author disapproves.[10]

Nevertheless, hegemony can be a useful concept, since it focuses on the political structure of an international economic system, and since it draws attention to inequality, which tends to be a pervasive condition of international systems. Yet it is necessary to specify quite precisely to what range of phenomena an analysis of hegemony is meant to apply. Some writers use the term to imply dictation by one country on *all* issues. At the other extreme, the term is applied to any situation where one state has more influence than others. We will regard a hegemonic system as one in which one state is able and willing to determine and maintain the essential rules by which relations among states are governed. The hegemonical state not only can abrogate existing rules or prevent the adoption of rules that it opposes but can also play the dominant role in constructing new rules. A distinguishing characteristic of a hegemonical system, therefore, is that the preponderant state has both positive and negative power.

When changes take place requiring adjustments by actors in the system, the hegemonic power is in a particularly strong position, since it can change the rules rather than being forced to adjust its policies to the existing rules. This is well

---

[9] For two views of this problem, see C. Fred Bergsten, "Crisis in U.S. Trade Policy," *Foreign Affairs,* July 1971, pp. 619-35; and Raymond Vernon, "A Skeptic Looks at the Balance of Payments," *Foreign Policy,* no. 5 (Winter 1971-72).

[10] See, for instance, David P. Calleo and Benjamin M. Rowland, *America and the World Political Economy* (Bloomington, Ind.: Indiana University Press, 1973). Their first section, on "interdependence and American hegemony" (pp. 3-8), fails to define either term.

illustrated by Britain's position as a defender of "freedom of the seas" in the nineteenth century. Britain played a dominant role in determining and maintaining rules guaranteeing freedom of the seas, but this did not deter it from interfering with neutral shipping when a war occurred in which it was a belligerent.

Yet the inference should not be drawn that a hegemonical power is never required to compromise, or that it never loses on specific issues. Possession of dominant rule-making power does not necessarily imply control over every political process taking place within those rules. Furthermore, degrees of dominance can vary from issue area to issue area, or between geographical regions. United States dominance in the petroleum-supply issue area has eroded more rapidly than it has on issues of international monetary policy; such dominance was never so complete in Europe as in Latin America. Finally, the alliance leader is always subject to special demands by client states, which may have a variety of techniques at their disposal for persuasion or pressure, particularly within the context of active superpower competition.[11]

With these caveats in mind, we use the concept of hegemony with particular reference to the international monetary system of the postwar world. In this analysis, a hegemonical system serves as an ideal type against which one can view changes in the extent of United States dominance. As a way of analyzing changes in the international monetary system since Bretton Woods, it leads to some revealing insights. The centrality of the international monetary system for overall international economic relations provides a sound reason for concentrating our attention there.

Hegemonic systems have certain advantages. As Charles Kindleberger has argued, during the last century monetary systems in which there has been sufficient preponderance of power to enable one state to claim leadership have tended to be more stable than systems where this was not the case, and have been associated with more prosperous economic conditions.[12] Although not a necessary condition for leadership, hegemony certainly facilitates it. In the nineteenth century, the financial strength of Great Britain provided the basis for a monetary system that was largely managed by the Bank of England through the key-currency role of sterling. From World War II until the 1960s, the economic preponderance of the United States enabled it to manage monetary relations among non-Communist countries through the Bretton Woods system, largely through the key-currency role of the dollar. By contrast, the unhappy international monetary experiences of the interwar period took place in a context of United States unwillingness to exercise strong leadership and British inability to do so.

[11] See Robert O. Keohane, "The Big Influence of Small Allies," *Foreign Policy*, no. 2 (Spring 1971).
[12] See Charles Kindleberger, *The World in Depression 1929-1939* (Berkeley, Calif.: University of California Press, 1974). A parallel argument is found in the literature on regional economic and political integration, in which it is often held that either clear preponderance by one power or relative equality between several may be conducive to integration but that an intermediate situation is less auspicious. See Joseph S. Nye, *Peace in Parts* (Boston: Little, Brown & Co., 1971), for a full discussion of these issues.

It should also be pointed out that hegemonical powers do not necessarily exploit secondary powers economically. During the heyday of the sterling standard, industrial production in France, Germany, Russia, and the United States increased from 50 percent to 400 percent faster than in Britain.[13] Under the United States–dominated monetary system of the postwar period, Europe and Japan grew more rapidly than the United States. Even so severe a critic of US hegemony as David Calleo admits that "it was difficult to argue that the [dollar] system was causing economic harm to its members."[14]

Ironically, it is the benefits of a hegemonical system, and the extent to which they are shared, that may bring about its collapse. As their economic power increases, the assumptions of secondary powers change. No longer do they have to accept a one-sided dependence that, no matter how prosperous, adversely affects their national autonomy and political status. As the possibility of gaining autonomy and status evolves, these values are taken from the closet of "desirable but unrealizable goals" and made operative. At least for some leaders and for some countries (good examples are provided by the international monetary policies of France in the 1920s and 1960s), prosperity is no longer enough.[15]

These changes in state policy are complemented by the natural cycle of a reserve currency system. As Fred Hirsch has described it:

> In an expanding world economy with an upward trend to the price level, accruals of gold to monetary reserves tend to diminish, leaving the system increasingly dependent for incremental liquidity on the further expansion of reserve-currency balances. Since such expansion involves a further deterioration of the reserves-to-liabilities ratio of the reserve center, the process cannot be sustained and must eventuate in suspension of convertibility.[16]

Before convertibility is suspended, however, there may be a period of time during which the reserve currency country is dependent on decisions of foreign central banks: since liquid liabilities so far exceed liquid assets, central bank decisions to convert holdings of the reserve currency into gold could force suspension of convertibility. Of course, if the benefits they receive from the system are high enough, secondary powers may fear system collapse as much as the hegemonic

---

[13] For the figures, see John P. McKay, *Pioneers for Profit: Foreign Entrepreneurship and Russian Industrialization, 1885-1913* (Chicago: University of Chicago Press, 1970), table 2, p. 5.

[14] David P. Calleo, "American Foreign Policy and American European Studies: An Imperial Bias?," in Wolfram Hanreider, ed., *The United States and Western Europe* (Cambridge, Mass.: Winthrop, 1974).

[15] See particularly Charles P. Kindleberger, "The International Monetary Politics of a Near-Great Power: Two French Episodes, 1926-1936 and 1960-1970," *Economic Notes* (Siena) 1, no. 2-3 (1972); or Kindleberger, *The World in Depression.*

[16] Fred Hirsch, *An SDR Standard: Impetus, Elements, and Impediments,* Princeton Essay in International Finance No. 99 (Princeton, N.J.: International Finance Section, Department of Economics, Princeton University, June 1973), p. 3.

state, or even more so since the hegemonic state may rely less on international economic transactions than do the secondary powers. However, insofar as the secondary powers are willing to run the risk of forcing a change in the system, they can gain some political leverage from the weak balance-sheet position of the dominant state.

Thus, as hegemony begins to erode, the policies of secondary powers are likely to change. But so are the policies of the leading state. An atmosphere of crisis and a proliferation of ad hoc policy measures will be found not only undignified but unsettling to many; dissenters will begin to wonder about the costs of leadership. Further, this leadership will less and less appear to guarantee attainment of economic and political objectives, as other states become more assertive. In the particular case of leadership of a key-currency monetary system, the prohibition against devaluation of the key currency will loom increasingly large if domestic unemployment becomes a major problem (as in Britain in the middle 1920s and the United States in the early 1970s). The renewed emphasis of these secondary governments on status and autonomy will add a further complication, since these values have a zero-sum connotation that is much less pronounced where economic values are involved. More status for secondary states means relatively less for the dominant power; increases in the autonomy of weaker powers bring concomitant declines in the positive influence of the system leader.

Thus the systemic orientation natural to hegemonic power, which identifies its interests with those of the system it manages, is challenged by a more nationalistic perspective. The alternatives of bilateralism and autarky, formerly rejected on political as well as on efficiency grounds, are once again considered. Their adherents stress the benefits of economic security, or risk aversion. Where power seems to assure that risks are minimal, this argument carries little weight; but where cracks appear in the hegemonical construction, prudence now counsels what efficiency formerly proscribed.

When this point is reached on both sides, the hegemonic equilibrium has been broken and a spiral of action and counteraction is likely to set in. As the system changes, assumptions change. Considerations of risk aversion on one side and greater independence on the other counsel policies that are less international, or less systemic, in their implications. The uncertainty thus created may be difficult to stop.

Yet there is no inevitability in the process. In the leading state, interests in maintaining systemic leadership and in paying its costs will persist, particularly among the transnational actors based there, in the financial elite, and in governmental bureaucracies charged with maintaining economic order and good relations with allies. In the governments of secondary powers as well, no firm consensus is to be expected: the benefits of dependency may provide comforts for some interests, necessities for others. Leaders may not wish to embark on a perilous adventure into a newly plural world. Thus the analysis cannot predict confidently that hegemony, once its bases begin to erode, will necessarily decline, although there will certainly be serious pressures in that direction. Indeed, inertia and resistance to change play a major role, at least in international monetary affairs, as indicated by the continued, and even growing, roles played by sterling and the dollar long after their underlying relative strength clearly turned down.

This indeterminancy is reinforced if the perceived erosion in position in an issue area is based on a decline in indices of power whose importance can be minimized by systemic change itself. In 1971, the decline in US international monetary power was symbolized most vividly by the sharp decline in US monetary reserves, relative to US international needs, in relation to the reserves of most other countries. But reserves are of cardinal importance only in a monetary system based on fixed exchange rates where they have to be used to defend a given parity. In a world of flexible exchange rates, other indicators of monetary power become far more important than reserves, and it so happens that the United States outstrips all other countries on those indicators.[17] Thus the preponderant power still had enough clout to change the de facto rules of the game, but it lacked hegemonic power sufficient to compel agreement on a new set of rules. In this situation of uneven erosion, we are confronted with the politics of linkage between issue areas internationally, and the ambiguities of changing symbols and perceptions in the domestic politics of foreign policy.

Domestic politics and leadership symbols

It has become fashionable to refer to protectionist policies in advanced industrial nations as *mercantilist*. However, the implicit analogy with seventeenth century economic policies is misleading. By and large, the major political source of the recent resurgence of economic nationalism, particularly in the United States, has not been governmental elites concerned with using foreign economic policy to enhance the relative power positions of their states, but relatively immobile domestic groups pressing the government for protection of their share of welfare in the competition with transnational competitors. It is not a situation in which foreign economic policy is used to enhance state power but in which short-term problems of the distribution of economic welfare, particularly for groups whose interests are hurt by increasing international transactions, exert strong pressure on foreign economic policy, *regardless* of the implications for interstate power or even the aggregate welfare of the national society.

The recent upsurge of economic nationalism is partly a response to the disruptive challenge of rising transnational interdependence. But as we indicated earlier, it is also a function of changing perceptions of military security.

Demands by domestic groups for government protection against transnational disturbance have existed throughout the postwar period. Under the two-track

---

[17]C. Fred Bergsten, *The Dilemmas of the Dollar: The Economics and Politics of United States International Monetary Policy* (New York: Council on Foreign Relations, forthcoming 1975), which also covers in depth some of the points discussed in this section.

Bretton Woods–GATT system, however, economic and security issues were usually handled quite separately.[18] This absence of linkage in the international arena was the product of a *hierarchical* linkage of security and economic issues in the domestic US political arena. During the cold war, *national security* was used by American political leaders to generate support for their policies of bolstering the economic, military, and political structure of "Free World" systems for which the United States worked so hard and on which it spent so much. National security justified international cooperation in economic and functional areas and support for the United Nations, as well as providing the rationale for alliances, foreign aid, and extensive military involvements around the world. It became the favorite symbol of those who favored increased United States involvement in world affairs. The intellectual ambiguity of national security became more pronounced as varied and often contradictory forms of involvement were sheltered under a single rhetorical umbrella.

The pervasiveness of the national security symbolism profoundly affected American foreign policy: through linkage to this symbol, certain sectoral economic interests were suppressed and controlled. The Truman administration used the alleged Soviet threat to American security to push the loan to Britain and then the Marshall Plan through Congress; the Kennedy administration employed the argument that an Atlantic partnership would strengthen United States security to promote the 1962 Trade Expansion Act. Congressmen who protested adverse economic effects on their districts or increased taxes could be assured, and could in turn explain to constituents, that the national security interest required their sacrifice.

This is not to argue that national security symbolism was always used against special interests. Powerful industries were frequently able to manipulate the symbolism for their own purposes, as in the case of the petroleum import quotas justified on national security grounds. Similarly, Glenn Snyder concluded that a major theme in the stockpiling of strategic materials between the end of World War II and the early 1960s was "the gradual and increasing corruption or distortion of a national security program by the pressures of subnational interests."[19]

Yet the postwar mood of internationalism—in the service of which national security symbolism was used by leaders—did have an effect on policy. It was not simply a facade behind which interests hid. Bauer, Pool, and Dexter concluded that self-interest and internationalism in the 1950s were "independent forces operating on tariff attitudes."[20] National security symbolism helped to construct a favorable global environment for transnational economic actors as well as for the large governmental bureaucracies of the Agency for International Development, the

---

[18] Richard N. Cooper, "Trade Policy is Foreign Policy," *Foreign Policy,* no. 9 (Winter 1972-73).

[19] Glenn H. Snyder, *Stockpiling Strategic Materials: Politics and National Defense* (San Francisco: Chandler Publishing Co., 1966), p. 267.

[20] Raymond A. Bauer, Ithiel DeSola Pool, and Lewis Anthony Dexter, *American Business and Public Policy: The Politics of Foreign Trade,* 2nd ed. (Chicago: Aldine-Atherton, 1972), p. 144.

Central Intelligence Agency, and the military services. National security was an ambiguous symbol, but it was also a force.[21]

As the cold-war sense of security threat slackened, foreign economic competition and domestic distributional conflict increased. National security symbolism became even more ambiguous in policy terms. Secretary of the Treasury Shultz proclaimed that Santa Claus was dead, but his pronouncements were mild compared to those of his predecessor, John Connally. The question of whether the United States should aspire to lead others or merely provide for itself came to the fore. United States policies on monetary questions were subject to divergent interpretations: they could be seen as bold attempts to lead the world toward a beneficial future of more flexible exchange rates with changes to be based on objective indicators, or as brazen unilateral moves to establish a dollar standard or to launch a "total economic offensive" against the Europeans.[22]

As the ambiguity of national security has increased, its power as a symbol has declined. This presumably reflects not only the increased ambiguity itself, but also the reaction in the United States to Vietnam and détente. National security has become a secondary symbol. The prime symbolism of the internationalists now focuses on *interdependence.* When used by analytical scholars, interdependence focuses on sensitivities of societies and policies to one another, and on the vulnerabilities that patterns of transactions may create.[23] Since it may be asymmetrical, it does not imply equality; since both sensitivity to external economic events and vulnerability to changes in the world economic system can be painful, it does not guarantee a reduction of conflict. From a policy viewpoint, the analysis of interdependence may even yield the conclusion that "systems should be designed consciously to reduce interdependence at politically sensitive points as a means of protecting not only national autonomy in the short term, but adverse politicization as a result of the actions of disgruntled groups."[24]

The use of interdependence rhetoric by policymakers is quite different. Here overtones of equality are clear, and the plea is for greater cooperation with other governments and greater openness to the world. Interdependence is viewed as a natural necessity, as a fact to which policy must adjust, rather than as a situation partially created by policy itself. Furthermore, it is held that conflicts of interest are reduced by interdependence, and that cooperation alone holds the answer to

[21] Arnold Wolfers developed the seminal discussion of this issue in "National Security as an Ambiguous Symbol," in *Political Science Quarterly* 67 (December 1952), which was later reprinted in Wolfers, *Discord and Collaboration* (Baltimore: The Johns Hopkins Press, 1962), chapter 10.

[22] For the constructive interpretation, see a variety of official reports, including particularly the *International Economic Report of the President,* February 1974, transmitting the second annual "International Economic Report" of the Council on International Economic Policy (Washington, D.C.: Government Printing Office, 1974). For representative adverse reactions, see the essays by Calleo and by Cohen in Hanreider, ed., *The United States and Western Europe.*

[23] For a fuller discussion, see Robert O. Keohane and Joseph S. Nye, "World Politics and the International Economic System"; and the works cited in footnote 6.

[24] Keohane and Nye, "World Politics and the International Economic System," p. 138.

world problems: "We are all engaged in a common enterprise. No nations or group of nations can gain by pushing its claims beyond the limits that sustain world economic growth. No one benefits from basing progress on tests of strength."[25]

These words are clearly the statesman's rhetoric rather than objective reality, and they are composed for the legitimate purpose of influencing public attitude. For those who wish to maintain United States leadership, interdependence has become the new symbolism, to be used both against economic nationalism at home and assertive challenges abroad. One may well approve the general tone. Yet one must also recognize that, as in the case of national security, noble purposes are subject to corruption by particular interests: no political symbol remains pure for long.

Interdependence symbolism suggests that conflicts of interest are passé. Traditional balance of power models of world politics, by contrast, regard such conflicts as fundamental; and the political-military focus of these models tends to lead analysts into stressing the severity of the resulting conflicts. Gains in military power in a balance of power system are sought for the relative advantages a state may thereby gain over its potential adversaries.

Neither of these views is fully satisfactory as a framework for the analysis of international political-economic relations. Interdependence rhetoric erroneously suggests that conflicts of interest do not exist because of a common threat: we are all involved, it is alleged, in a kind of grand "game against nature." The conclusion would only follow if three conditions were met: if the "single international economic system on which all of our national economic objectives depend"[26] were in danger of collapse; if all countries were significantly vulnerable to such a catastrophe; *and* if there were only one unique solution to the problem (so that no room would be left for bargaining about *how* to solve it). Merely to list the conditions for the assertion to be correct indicates its fallaciousness.

Balance of power imagery is little better for analyzing political-economic questions. It is correct in pointing to the permanence of conflict, but it fails to account for a crucial difference between economic and military competition. Economic gains are generally sought not merely or even chiefly for the advantages they bring relative to others, but are desired primarily for their absolute benefits (greater income, increased economic security, etc.). Thus a chief prediction of classical balance of power theory—that states will act to protect themselves by limiting the capabilities of strong states or coalitions[27] —may not hold where states pursue a substantial gain in wealth or employment. Domestic political pressures will frequently lead governments to approve international economic arrangements that will help others as much as, or even more than, themselves, as long as they stand to

[25] Henry A. Kissinger, Address before the Sixth Special Session of the United Nations General Assembly, 15 April 1974, Department of State, Office of Media Services, News Release, 15 April 1974, p. 2; reprinted in *International Organization* 28 (Summer 1974): 573-83.

[26] Ibid., p. 1.

[27] See Morton Kaplan, *System and Process in International Politics* (New York: Wiley, 1957).

benefit as well. Thus the politics of economic relations resemble a mixed-motive game with incentives for both cooperation and conflict.

Economic objectives and world order

We now turn to an analysis of the different economic objectives that individual countries, and different groups within countries, may seek either through cooperation or through conflict. For there is a wide array of "purely" economic goals, which can be sought through a variety of domestic and international means. The creation of any set of international economic arrangements presupposes fairly wide agreement between countries on the hierarchy of economic objectives, and how the different economic objectives are ranked.

The theory of economic policy

Before turning to a detailed discussion of the individual economic criteria, however, it is necessary to outline the theory of economic policy. As developed by Tinbergen[28] and others, this theory posits that the number of economic policy instruments must at least equal the number of policy targets that can be met; it is usually impossible to achieve a greater number of policy targets than one has available policy instruments. In view of the vast proliferation over the last few decades in the number of policy objectives, this means that governments are actively seeking additional policy instruments, notably including those that can influence external economic events, in order to block unwanted effects and to actively promote domestic goals. At a minimum, they actively seek to limit external constraints on their pursuit of internal economic (and social) objectives.

The original theory of economic policy, however, related to a single country. New problems arise when one opens the model to include external events that can be influenced by the country being considered, which in turn feed back on the probability of successful use of its own policy instruments.[29] Country A may be able to force a depreciation (appreciation) of its exchange rate and thereby transmit some of its unemployment (inflation) to country B. If so, country A obviously possesses a valuable additional policy instrument.

But what about country B? It must turn one or more of its policy instruments either to countering directly the change effected by country A in the exchange rate or to offsetting the induced change in the level of unemployment (e.g., through expansive fiscal policy). Its choice will be determined by the relative effectiveness of its policy tools. But whichever tool it chooses, the ratio of policy instruments to policy targets in country B has been adversely affected. It has been

---

[28] Jan Tinbergen, *On the Theory of Economic Policy*, 2nd ed. (Amsterdam: North Holland Publishing Co., 1963).
[29] See Richard N. Cooper, "Macroeconomic Policy Adjustment in Interdependent Economies," *Quarterly Journal of Economics* 83 (February 1969): 1-24.

forced either to adopt a new economic target (avoiding the induced change in its exchange rate) or to assign at least one more of its policy instruments to the target upset by the action of country A.

This example leads us back into the political thicket. The relative success of countries A and B in attaining their goals will depend not only on the structure of their economies and the intelligence of their economic policies but also on their relative power. If country B happens to be the world's premier military power, whose armed forces are protecting A from potential aggression, it may be able to prevent A from using a policy instrument that would be damaging to B, or at least to compel compensating adjustment of policy by other dependent countries or by A itself in other areas. On the other hand, country B may have a strong national interest in seeing a strong economy in country A, to shore up their alliance and reduce the risk that B will ever have to actually fight for A, and may let A get away with its effort to export its economic problem even when B has the power to block such a step.

By contrast, if B is a peripheral, minor state, it may not have such leverage and indeed might be afraid to offend powerful states upon which the security and prosperity of its governmental elite may depend. Equally plausible, it may be able to get away with aggressive economic actions simply because it is small and does not much matter. Whichever outcome occurs in each case, the politics of the situation have at least as important an impact as the economics.

In a securely hegemonical international system, extremes of power are very great, but the stability of the system is likely to be high. One fears repression and inequity more than protracted and damaging international economic conflict. In a system of eroding hegemony, as in the present, on the other hand, conflict becomes more likely as weaker states are increasingly able and willing to oppose the wishes of the leading power.

In the real world, there are well over 100 countries, at least two dozen of which are relevant to most major international economic issues. Thus the opportunity, indeed the likelihood, of such external upset of internal economic policies is very great. No country, including the United States,[30] is immune from such upsets. It would thus be desirable, from the global standpoint, to devise an international economic system that avoided such upsets, especially if they result from aggressive actions by individual countries, as in the universally scorned beggar-thy-neighbor

---

[30] Numerous examples beyond the obvious US dependence in imports of oil and other raw materials can be cited. The overvaluation of the dollar was probably costing the United States 500,000 jobs by mid-1971, raising the rate of unemployment by 0.7 percentage points (from near 5 percent to about 6 percent), a jump of great political as well as economic importance. Conversely, the dollar devaluations of 1971-73 contributed at least one-fourth of the rise in the US inflation rate during that period, and growing foreign demand for US agricultural goods added to this total. About one quarter of all investment by US-based firms now takes place in other countries. These foreign direct investments provide a like share of US corporate profits, and well over one-half of the profits of many major US firms. Over one quarter of US farm output is exported.

policies of competitive exchange rate depreciations and adoption of new trade barriers in the 1930s. The traditional risks that countries will seek to export unemployment to each other through import controls and exchange rate depreciations have now been joined by risks that countries will seek to export inflation to each other through export controls and exchange rate appreciations, and they use their policies toward foreign direct investment to do both.[31]

A long line of observers, from David Ricardo forward, have proposed systems that would avoid such international economic conflict. The doctrine of free trade would in essence assign to trade policy the objective of maximizing global efficiency, which should in turn both help counter inflation and, at least over the longer run, boost growth and employment. (Whether it can achieve that goal in practice is examined by Baldwin and Kay in their essay in this volume; it depends, inter alia, on the existence of market imperfections such as business and labor oligopolies.) Free trade would eschew any conscious efforts at distributing that enhanced global welfare, though it should help raise living standards at all income levels by maximizing aggregate output. In a more recent formulation, based on the view that the dollar dominates world finance and the restoration of fixed exchange rates, Mundell would assign to the United States the responsibility for restraining world inflation and to other major countries the responsibility for providing adequate but not excessive growth of world reserves (through gold transactions with the United States when US payments imbalances, either surpluses or deficits, become excessive).[32]

It is too early in this volume to discuss the merits of these, or other, particular approaches. Yet they reveal three significant (and closely related) elements that are germane to the present discussion. First, they ignore such issues as income distribution and economic security, which, as we will shortly see, are among the criteria against which any international economic order must be judged. Second, they ignore the fact that the world is not a decision-making unit and that the pursuit of global welfare, however appealing to many economists, is an extremely difficult concept to implement in practice. Third, they ignore the innate tendencies of virtually all states to try to use their power to seize an increased share of the benefits of any order, in some cases through subtle identification of world welfare with their own welfare rather than through any crude seizure of benefits which their power might permit, and the resulting high probability of conflict in international economic relations.

Since the political dimensions of international economic relations are so significant, essential elements of the situation and necessary analytical distinctions are often obscured by symbolism, rhetoric, and ideology. The theory of economic policy indicates that we must distinguish clearly, for instance, between economic

---

[31] On the last point, see C. Fred Bergsten, "Coming Investment Wars?," *Foreign Affairs,* October 1974, pp. 135-52.

[32] Robert A. Mundell, *International Economics* (New York: MacMillan Co., 1968), especially pp. 282-88.

objectives and economic instruments. The president of the United States announces that he wants to devalue the dollar or the prime minister of Japan professes a desire to reduce his country's trade surplus, but the underlying objectives of these actions remain unstated or are deliberately concealed. Thus a trade surplus or deficit, or a devalued or revalued exchange rate, often comes to be regarded, erroneously, as an end in itself. When certain economic indicators (such as a trade surplus or a "strong currency") become regarded as sources of internal or external prestige for government or nation, the confusion of instruments with objectives becomes even more pronounced.

The failure to distinguish between independent and instrumental variables—ends and means—has confused much of the debate over alternative international economic arrangements. Differences in viewpoints can occur at two levels. First, there can be differences about the goals themselves, the independent variables. Rich countries (and rich groups in poor countries) may seek a system that maximizes economic efficiency, while poor countries (and less affluent groups in rich countries) may seek a system that redistributes income in their direction. Second, there can be disagreement about the means for achieving agreed goals, the instrumental variables. A small country quite open to the world economy may view free trade as the best route to full employment, while a large country relatively closed to the world economy may view import barriers as best achieving the very same goal. Since the nature of any international economic arrangements (fixed or flexible exchange rates, free trade or protectionism) greatly influences the likelihood of alternative outcomes, these disagreements produce very different views on what systemic arrangements should prevail.

The charters of the major postwar international economic institutions perhaps surprisingly dwelt primarily on instrumental rather than independent objectives. All six of the purposes in Article I of the IMF charter, for example, are instrumental; the basic goal "to contribute thereby to the promotion and maintenance of high levels of employment and real income" appears only as a derivative clause in one of the six. The six purposes of the World Bank as stated in Article I of its charter are similarly instrumental, again with the exception of a single derivative clause—"assisting in raising . . . the standard of living and conditions of labor. . . ." The GATT was much more explicit, advocating trade relations that would be effective in ". . . raising standards of living, assuring full employment and a large and steadily growing volume of real income and effective demand. . . ."[33] None of these documents revealed whether their authors confronted (much less, made) the hard choices between the different economic objectives, although their references to full employment were certainly more explicit than their references to price stability (*"real* income").

---

[33] The charter of the abortive International Trade Organization provided a far clearer statement of objectives than did the charters cited in the text. It included a full chapter on "employment and Economic Activity" as well. See Raymond Mikesell, "The ITO Charter," *American Economic Review* 37 (June 1947): 353-56.

It is quite natural to find designers of new international regimes concentrating on instrumental rather than on fundamental purposes. Practical results may thereby be achieved and sterile conflict over abstractions avoided. In the later essays of this volume, there is much discussion of instruments. This would, however, be relatively fruitless except in the context of an appreciation of the independent variables—the economic criteria in light of which policy instruments must be chosen and evaluated. We therefore turn next to an analysis of those criteria, and how they relate to one another.

The economic criteria

In this section we consider, in turn, seven criteria against which to judge the effectiveness of any international economic system: efficiency, growth, full employment, income distribution, price stability, quality of life, and economic security. In each case we examine the nature of the objective, how its pursuit is affected by the international economy, and how important it has been in the international economic arrangements that have existed through the postwar period. It will become apparent both that it may be difficult to achieve any of these objectives and that there may be sharp conflicts between them.

Efficiency

The standard focus of positive economic analysis is the degree to which existing arrangements achieve the most efficient possible allocation of economic resources. The objective is to maximize welfare, defined as maximizing consumption of goods and services.[34]

Reliance on market forces—free trade, freedom for international capital movements, and equilibrium exchange rates—is the traditional approach of international economic policy to pursuing this goal. Several complications arise immediately, however.

First, reliance on the market may not always promote economic efficiency. Economics has long recognized the existence of market imperfections. At the macroeconomic level, for example, imperfections in the international capital market may distort output. At the microeconomic level, oligopolists and oligopsonists (such as many multinational corporations, state enterprises, and producer country cartels) may pervert the market mechanism and require countervailing checks if efficiency is to be maximized. Harry Johnson has indicated that "the scientific issue is whether observed deviations of fact from assumptions are empirically significant·

---

[34] *Welfare* can of course have several different meanings, in terms of both economics per se and at the broader societal level. Indeed, each of the goals described in this article represents a different aspect of welfare, broadly defined. For a useful comparative analysis of the different concepts of economic welfare, see Hla Myint, *Theories of Welfare Economics* (New York: Sentry Press, 1965), especially chapter 12.

enough to destroy the validity of the conclusion of the (traditional) theory,"[35] and no one has yet answered the question.[36]

Second, the pursuit of efficiency through reliance on market forces often produces dislocations that themselves reduce total output and even produce declines in efficiency elsewhere. Free trade, for example, generates dislocations that idle plants and workers and reduce output by suppliers of the affected plants and workers. In addition, many modern societies accept a responsibility for helping these idled factors adjust, which in turn requires spending by the government (and perhaps by the private sector), which may divert resources from uses that are more efficient, at least in the short run.

Third, long-run efficiency may be maximized by introducing short-run inefficiencies. This is because optimum allocation may never eventuate unless consciously promoted by policies that admittedly depart from optimum allocation for a while to get there. (For such an approach to represent "rational" policy, increases in efficiency over the long run, suitably discounted, must exceed the reduction in efficiency in the short run.) The classical case for tariff protection of infant industries is based on this notion. The modern importance of economies of scale in achieving optimum allocation of resources has probably heightened the importance of the argument. For any single country, however, this focus can suggest policies either of (1) trade protectionism (to promote exploitation of a sufficiently sizeable domestic market by limiting foreign competition), or (2) free trade, at least within a regional grouping, and undervalued exchange rates (to help smaller countries exploit foreign markets). Its implications for the international economic order as a whole are indeterminate.

Hence, even the pursuit of economic efficiency as the chief objective of international economic policy does not necessarily call for total devotion to the judgment of the marketplace. Such considerations as the need to check excessive concentrations of market power (e.g., through global antitrust policies), the transformation costs of adjusting to new patterns of production, and economies of scale may both dominate the static maximization of efficiency from a given set of factors of production (including technology) and suggest that even static maximization may require intervention. On the other hand, it may often prove more efficient to deal with these considerations through direct government subsidies or other domestic devices than through changes in international economic policy. Thus, their existence by no means rules out an essentially liberal international economic system.

A final consideration is the quantitative importance of international economic considerations for the efficiency of national economies (and hence the world

---

[35] Harry G. Johnson, *Comparative Cost and Commercial Policy Theory for a Developing World Economy*, Wicksell Lectures 1968 (Stockholm: Almquist & Wicksell, 1968), p. 10.

[36] For an enumeration of these deviations and a subjective judgment that their quantitative impact is not large, see Richard N. Cooper, "Economic Assumptions of the Case for Liberal Trade," in C. Fred Bergsten, ed., *Toward A New World Trade Policy: The Maidenhead Papers* (Lexington, Mass.: D.C. Heath, 1975).

economy). The gains from trade (and, presumably, from free capital movements as well) are usually deemed to be quite small relative to gross national products. But they may be quite significant for small countries and even for a few big ones, such as Japan. Conversely, big countries can best improve their national positions through optimum tariffs or other controls over international economic flows simply because they are sufficiently important in the world economy to reap monopoly/ monopsony gains through unilateral action. In addition, most countries can probably achieve greater efficiency gains (in static terms) from changes in their international economic policies than from virtually any other policy instruments at their command.[37] International economic policy is thus a highly significant issue for virtually all countries, and its importance may be growing in view of the increasing share of external transactions in the economies of virtually all countries.

The postwar economic system placed a relatively high emphasis on efficiency. Despite deep concerns that massive unemployment might recur, the IMF-GATT machinery relied heavily on the market, though with a few exceptions, as for capital movements in general and import flows for countries with balance-of-payments problems. The most plausible explanation for this outcome is its virtual dictation by the United States, which believed that barriers to international economic transactions produced major tensions between countries and hence international conflict, which was devoted to free markets ideologically, and which was fully confident of its ability to maximize its national economic interests in such a world.

The trend toward freeing markets continued into the middle 1960s, with successive trade liberalizations, the freeing of capital flows, and the elimination of exchange controls attendant to the advent of widespread currency convertibility. But from the middle 1960s into the middle 1970s, controls over capital movements again proliferated and, after the conclusion of the Kennedy Round, trade controls began to emerge once more. In addition, most home and host countries began to levy explicit controls on foreign direct investment, which was rapidly becoming one of the major engines of international economic exchange. The erosion of US hegemony was an important factor in this shift away from a focus on efficiency and market forces,[38] and we will see shortly that other criteria were now being given greater priority, relative to efficiency. But again in the middle 1970s, a notable liberalization of some kinds of controls, frequently on a unilateral basis, began to occur once more due to concerns for more efficiency, to help fight inflation.[39]

[37] Harry G. Johnson, "The Probable Effects of Freer Trade on Individual Countries," in Bergsten, ed., *Toward a New World Trade Policy: The Maidenhead Papers.*

[38] It is true that the United States tolerated discrimination against it in the early postwar period, which detracted from global economic efficiency. This was done for reasons of national security, however, rather than to meet any other economic criteria (except, perhaps, for an application of "infant industry" reasoning to the postwar reconstruction of Europe and Japan). In addition, many of the discriminatory steps were viewed by the United States as necessary but temporary way stations en route to a world of multilateral free trade and payments, which proved correct at least in the monetary area where the European Payments Union paved the way for European convertibility.

[39] The shift from fixed parities to managed flexibility of exchange rates resulted from the

Growth

A second criterion against which to judge international economic systems is their impact on economic growth. Growth obviously raises total future output, and is thus likely to be the chief criterion of success for those who seek maximum output over time above all else.

Just as efficiency can contribute to growth, growth can contribute to efficiency. It can minimize the costs of adjustment to an improved allocation of existing resources by providing new opportunities for dislocated plants and workers. It contributes to the achievement of economies of scale, and hence to more efficient production processes. It often provides scope for new entrants and may thus even help break down undue market concentration. Growth contributes to the possibility for better distribution of income, both among and within countries, since it is politically far easier to divide up a growing pie than a static one. It may also contribute directly to income inequality by raising the share of savings in national income, although income inequalities have diminished in most countries during the unprecedented period of growth since World War II.

On the other hand, it has now been widely recognized that growth may entail significant costs, which economists often call external diseconomies. Some world resources are limited, and unbridled growth may jeopardize life itself, or at least life as we know it now, within a relevant period of time. The costs of environmental pollution should be explicitly considered as a cost of some kinds of growth. And excessive growth can trigger rapid inflation, which generates many costs directly and can in turn stunt growth itself.

International economic arrangements can contribute to growth in two ways. They can help countries avoid restrictive economic policies by reducing the constraints of external events, such as balance-of-payments deficits, on internal policies. Going further, they can provide opportunities for rapid growth by positively facilitating expansive policies, for example, through reductions in trade barriers that promote growth via world trade and through reductions in barriers to capital flows that promote infusions of savings.

Like all postwar economic policies, the international economic structure was heavily oriented toward growth. Generous financing for balance-of-payments deficits in the IMF and through foreign aid programs, and the automatic financing accorded reserve currency countries, tended to reduce the need for restrictive internal policies, and indeed permitted excessively expansionary policies at least in the United Kingdom in the early 1960s and in the United States in the late 1960s. Trade and investment barriers were steadily reduced through the middle 1960s, opening world goods and factor markets for increased expansion. The system paid virtually no attention to the adverse manifestations of growth: the possible deple-

---

widespread conclusion that markets could set equilibrium exchange rates better than governments, more than from any shift in notions about which system was more efficient. We will see shortly, however, that changes in the views of key countries about the relative importance of the different criteria had a major impact on that change.

tion of resources, environmental pollution, possible maldistribution of income, and the build-up of inflationary pressures from steadily rising demand and the resulting, even faster, rise in popular expectations.

Full employment

Closely related to the criterion of growth is full employment, which has been elevated to a (if not *the*) top spot in the hierarchy of national policy goals since the Great Depression. However, rapid growth and full employment are not identical; developing countries are now learning that one can have rapid growth with rising unemployment.

One can also have full employment without rapid growth. This can be done at the price of relatively high inefficiency, as is apparently the policy of the People's Republic of China at present, which reduces the welfare of some portion (presumably a majority) of the population in order to avoid excessive hardship for any portion. Or full employment can be achieved without rapid growth in a society not experiencing much growth in productivity, as in Britain during much of the postwar period. The cost in that case is the concomitant loss in real income in the future, and possibly also a deterioration in the country's international competitiveness, which will eventually force depreciation of its exchange rate and losses of real income relative to a situation in which its productivity grew more rapidly. Nevertheless, sufficient attachment to the goal of full employment could render either aspect of relative inefficiency acceptable.

The same kinds of international policies that foster growth, as just cited, also foster full employment. In addition, external policies can be used by individual countries to try to export unemployment via exchange rate depreciations, import controls, and export subsidies. Such policies were widely pursued in the 1930s, with the resulting lesson that they would quickly feed back negatively—via reduced world incomes and hence reduced exports for every country, as well as direct policy emulation and retaliation—even on countries that gained from them in the very short run. Therefore, the postwar arrangements sought to erect barriers against national efforts to export unemployment.

These efforts succeeded, on the whole, in blocking destructive actions. But they did not compel constructive actions. Thus, part of the postwar success of such countries as Germany and Japan in maintaining full employment was due to their maintenance of undervalued exchange rates (and, in the case of Japan, a number of residual import controls). From August 1971, when the United States concluded that a significant share of its unemployment had been imported as a result, it took drastic unilateral action both to restore exchange rate equilibrium immediately and to create a monetary system that would maintain equilibrium for the future. Nor did the system compel policies that would enable developing countries to escape increasing unemployment, despite impressive growth rates in some cases.

Another gap is the absence of international rules to govern shifts in jobs resulting from government policies toward foreign investment, which are becoming increasingly important.[40] Given the obvious continuing importance of the unemployment criterion, it will be a major consideration in the construction of any new international economic arrangements.

Income distribution

Income distribution has two key aspects: distribution within individual countries, and distribution among different countries. The two can vary inversely. The income gap between developed countries (DCs) and less developed countries (LDCs) could be reduced while internal disparities within both were growing. And internal redistribution within individual developing countries could slow their overall national progress in reducing the DC-LDC gap (though it need not do so). Hence, the criterion must be further defined before one can use it operationally.

Another fundamental conceptual problem with income distribution is its basic objective. What is a better distribution of income? Does it seek *equal* income for all (countries or people)? Or simply a *reduction* in the disparities that currently exist? If the latter, how much better is enough? When the issue is extended to the international plane, it becomes increasingly complicated: Should below-average earners in DCs transfer part of their income to above-average earners in LDCs who earn less in absolute terms? Should the resource-rich and/or successfully industrializing countries of the Third World transfer to the resource-poor countries of the Fourth World, now additionally faced by the heavily increased costs of energy and food? In short, what is the optimum distribution of income?[41]

This final question in turn raises the link between policies to redistribute income and policies to increase total (world or national) income. Many (though not all) policies that seek primarily to redistribute also cut growth, and many policies that pursue growth exacerbate income disparities. Thus an individual (country or person) may be better off, *in absolute terms,* with a smaller share of a bigger pie. The time dimension is of critical importance in answering this question: Are societies, or sectors of societies, willing to forego income redistribution *now* in order to generate larger total incomes for all sectors, and hence more to redistribute, in future generations?

On the other hand, income distribution has become more equal in several rapidly growing developing countries, such as Taiwan, and may even have boosted their rates of growth. Thus, it may be quite possible to find policies that simultaneously foster growth and better income distribution.

In pursuing this issue, we cannot avoid a question that probes beneath economics: Do people seek (1) the highest possible standard of living, *in absolute terms,* or (2) the least possible disparity in income vis-à-vis their neighbors, even if

---

[40] Bergsten, "Coming Investment Wars?"

[41] Jan Pen presents a "non-exhaustive" list of 21 alternative objectives of income distribution in his *Income Distribution* (New York: Praeger, 1971), pp. 291-316, a lucid and witty presentation particularly useful for noneconomists.

their resulting income is *lower* in absolute terms than under (1)? The answer to the question may change as the size of the pie grows. The search for absolute improvement may dominate at lower levels of income, but the quest for equality may become ascendent at more comfortable absolute levels. Whatever the answer, it obviously mixes psychology and sociology with economics, and is probably not amenable to any simple generalizations.

International economic relations can have a major impact on income distribution both within and among countries. Trade and investment flows affect both importantly. International aid flows are analogous to transfer payments within an economy, and there have been proposals for a minimum world income as well as guaranteed annual incomes for all citizens of individual countries. Indeed, a major complaint of the LDCs throughout the postwar period has been that the international economic system was biased against them and exacerbated the North-South gap through such devices as high effective tariffs against their products, terms of trade that steadily turned against them, and distribution of the major share of new international liquidity (whether via dollar balances, special drawing rights, or gold revaluation) to those already rich. In the recent past, of course, the oil exporters and some other commodity-rich developing countries have sharply improved their terms of trade and redistributed world income dramatically in their favor.

The postwar economic system ostensibly placed income redistribution high on its priority list. The World Bank was created to reconstruct Europe. Foreign aid programs from the Marshall Plan forward sought to promote living standards in the contemporary developing countries. Germany and several other European countries now approximate the US level of per capita income, and Japan will do so within a few years. The relatively liberal regimes for trade and capital flows supported the rapid progress of scores of countries, from Japan through Brazil, in cutting the gap between their national products and those of the United States and Europe.

On the other hand, the international dollar standard enabled the richest country, the United States, to appropriate at least some real resources from the rest of the world. The ongoing maintenance of an increasingly overvalued dollar artificially inflated US living standards (as American tourists abroad have now painfully learned). The absolute DC-LDC gap has continued to grow. Therefore, the effects of the present international economic order on international income distribution are ambiguous.

Its effects on income distribution within countries are equally unclear. Freedom for foreign investment probably raises the income share of labor in capital-importing countries, and cuts it in capital-exporting countries. Fixed exchange rates subsidize the foreign sector of an economy at the expense of the domestically traded sector,[42] but the controls often undertaken on external transactions to preserve such rates tax the foreign sector itself directly. Free trade generally helps the most efficient, and thus increases the existing wage disparities between groups

---

[42] Assuming that the rate itself reflects long-term equilibrium conditions, and by contrast with a rate fluctuating around that same equilibrium point.

(such as skilled versus unskilled labor). But it also promotes consumer welfare, which is generally most valuable to the least efficient (and hence lowest paid).

Price stability

Price stability is a complex economic goal because, in our terminology, it is both an independent and an instrumental variable. It is an independent variable because some observers fear that excessive inflation can itself destroy fundamental institutions of society, including existing political structures. They point to historical instances, particularly in Europe in the interwar period, as evidence for this view.[43]

Economists, however, without necessarily regarding inflation as any less serious, primarily view it as an instrumental variable. It clearly redistributes income to those able to keep their money incomes rising faster than prices (some businessmen, workers whose contracts encompass escalator clauses, and countries whose terms of trade can be kept rising over time) and away from those whose incomes are relatively fixed in money terms (such as private pensioners and some salaried workers). In addition, it can distort factor markets, particularly the financial system. Hence, it can lead to restrictive economic policies, which will still further undermine efficiency, growth, and full employment. The likelihood of such an outcome is increased to the extent that high rates of inflation are unstable, inevitably spiraling into hyper-inflation unless quickly restored to relatively modest levels. The problem is reduced to the extent that societies can accommodate to inflation, through such devices as widespread indexation.

International economic policy could be oriented primarily toward maintaining price stability. This is easiest to see for individual countries. Revaluations, reductions in import barriers, and export controls help a country fight inflation, at least in the short run. Germany has in fact consciously used exchange rate policy to fight inflation in recent years, and Japan used massive sales of its dollar reserves to do so throughout most of 1973. A number of countries have unilaterally cut their import barriers, and even eliminated some of them entirely, to help fight inflation.

At the systemic level, competitive revaluations and export controls could in fact replace competitive devaluations and import controls as the primary sources of international economic conflict, if rapid inflation became endemic. And international economic arrangements can accelerate world inflation through such means as excessive creation of international liquidity and promotion of rising commodity prices.

On the other hand, the international economic order could incorporate joint policies to fight inflation. For example, the level of world reserves could be reduced through a cancellation of special drawing rights. Sales of gold by central banks could reduce the price of gold in the free market, which might lead to reductions in

---

[43] Such a view can be found in Irving S. Friedman, *Inflation: World-Wide Disaster* (Boston: Houghton Mifflin Co., 1973), especially chapter 5.

other commodity prices as well. The trading community could adopt new rules to limit export controls, and perhaps retaliate against them, as in the GATT they developed rules to limit import controls and sanctioned retaliation against them. Even more ambitiously, better coordination of domestic policies—including incomes policies, as well as monetary and fiscal policies—could improve the effectiveness of the individual national efforts against inflation.

The existing international economic system pays virtually no explicit attention to inflation. Indeed, the dollar-based monetary system that emerged from Bretton Woods came to be widely viewed as an engine of inflation, because it placed no control over the growth of world liquidity and no meaningful external constraint on inflationary policies in the United States, the most important single country in determining the rate of world inflation.[44] As already noted, the postwar economic order aimed primarily to foster growth and combat unemployment, and thus its inattention to inflation is understandable. Nevertheless, its absence of effective rules and institutions to govern the means through which countries seek to export inflation, such as export controls, represents a major gap in its intellectual and political structure.

The quality of life

A further economic criterion encompasses the increasing array of issues generalized under the heading "improving the quality of life." We have already mentioned the external diseconomies of untrammeled economic growth. Indeed, new measures of "gross national welfare" have been devised to take account of such qualitative factors as the value of leisure time and of interesting jobs, and the costs of pollution and job dislocation. The most important single aspect of the issue is probably environmental management: pollution of both air and water can occur both through the processes of production and through consumption of final products.[45]

Attention to such concerns probably rises with the level of income. It is thus generally higher in the affluent industrialized countries than in the developing world, and is an issue over which there is wide disagreement between different countries. There has been very little effort at international regulation of these issues in the past, partly because of these differences in national views and partly because ecological concerns have only been raised at all quite recently.

Economic security

The final economic criterion is economic security. In its international manifestations, the concept encompasses a wide variety of specific interests: assured

---

[44] On the other hand, some observers view the present system of managed flexibility of exchange rates as equally, if not more, inflationary.

[45] For a comprehensive analysis, see Ingo Walter, "Environmental Management and the International Economic Order," in Bergsten, ed., *The Future of the International Economic Order: An Agenda for Research.*

access to foreign supplies, especially of needed foodstuffs and raw materials; assured access to foreign markets, so that exports and hence domestic employment are not suddenly jeopardized; protection against dislocations stemming from rapid penetration by foreign goods, labor, or capital. Like the other economic issues, it has an important time dimension. For example, the US import quotas on oil may have enhanced US economic (and military) security in the short run by keeping higher levels of domestic capacity in operation, but they clearly undermined that security in the longer run by depleting US resources and hence increasing US vulnerability to foreign suppliers.

All of these issues have already been considered under the discussions of price stability and full employment and in other sections. In some senses, the search for economic security is thus not a separate objective at all but represents an effort to increase the probability that other objectives will be achieved.

Nevertheless, we single out the issue for separate treatment for three reasons. First, it has become a major concern of many governments. The oil crisis dramatized the vulnerability of most of the world, including the United States, to supply interruptions of a single key commodity. The various suggestions of physical or artificial (i.e., cartelized) shortages of other commodities has broadened that concern. Short-term food shortages, and an uncertain outlook for world food supplies for the longer run, have led to famine conditions in a few places and real risks of starvation (an issue that is not part of any of our other criteria) and hence call for new arrangements for world security.

Second, economic security is closely related to traditional military security and thereby links economic and political considerations even more closely than do the other economic objectives.[46] Oil and other raw materials are obviously needed to avoid excessive inflation, unemployment, and constraints on military capabilities. Food shortages could lead to such severe domestic political outbursts that they could cause major international security problems. Barriers against steel (or oil, or electronic) imports may be adopted both to protect workers and to preserve a national economic capability to produce goods needed by the military. Some countries, most notably China and the Soviet Union, have consciously pursued policies of autarky to shield themselves against virtually all economic disturbances from abroad.

Third, the international economic order could play an important role in improving the economic security of nations, through new arrangements to govern trade, commodity flows, investment, and other international economic transactions. This is because assurances of many kinds of economic security for all countries require sacrifices on the part of other countries, sacrifices that are, by comparison, quite marginal. The United States could cut back on its consumption of food or fertilizer sufficiently to alleviate substantially world shortages of those products, and several of the Arab states could guarantee adequate oil for the world at marginal cost to their total earnings (and even less cost to their real needs, since their earnings already so far exceed those needs). This is not to say that such

---

[46] See also the discussion in this volume in the last essay by Krause and Nye.

international arrangements would be easy to negotiate; we know that they would not. But we can also see the bases for new arrangements, to promote an objective to which previous international economic orders have given little attention.

Summary and conclusions

We have now reviewed the criteria against which any international economic system must be judged.

There are sharp conflicts between the criteria. A focus on efficiency or price stability may create unemployment, at least in the short run; there is an international dimension to the Phillips curve, which economists sometimes use to describe trade-offs between inflation and unemployment, as when a depreciating exchange rate (or import controls) helps combat unemployment but at the same time raises prices. A focus on income redistribution, or economic security, may create inefficiency. A focus on the quality of life may reduce growth, which in turn may generate unemployment. A focus on any of the political criteria, whether currying favor with a particular domestic interest group or denying trade to a foreign adversary, will almost by definition run counter to at least some of the economic criteria. Numerous other conflicts have been mentioned. The essays in Section II of this volume judge how both the existing functional systems (monetary, trade, etc.) and possible new systems reconcile, or fail to reconcile, some of these conflicts. Those in Section III analyze differences in national policy preferences, and national situations, that affect attempts to reach collective international judgments on economic issues. But even the cryptic analysis presented here illustrates the complexity of the problem.

This essay has not presented a comprehensive analysis of international economic policies and institutions; it is, after all, only an introduction. Yet enough has been said to indicate both the complexity of the issues and the pervasiveness of conflicts between objectives both at the political and economic levels and between the two levels. Simple solutions are unlikely to be found to such complex problems. Plans that focus on only a few objectives would generate vociferous objections from groups whose cherished values had been ignored. Amidst this complexity, the challenge is to develop economic policies that are both effective in attaining the desired economic objectives when applied and politically feasible, so that they can be applied in the first place and maintained. If one wills the economic end, one must also will the political consequences as well as the political and economic means.

Yet it is obvious that the present difficulties of the international economic order will not be dispelled by generalities. If only complex solutions are likely to be feasible, detailed technical work and specific proposals will be necessary. The suggestions in the essays that follow represent a series of attempts to work toward the construction of feasible regimes for ordering international economic relations and of specific means for implementing them, taking into account the conflicts that necessarily arise in a politically diverse and decentralized world.

Three models of the future

Robert Gilpin

Edward Hallet Carr observed that "the science of economics presupposes a given political order, and cannot be profitably studied in isolation from politics."[1] Throughout history, the larger configurations of world politics and state interests have in large measure determined the framework of the international economy. Succeeding imperial and hegemonic powers have sought to organize and maintain the international economy in terms of their economic and security interests.

From this perspective, the contemporary international economy was the creation of the world's dominant economic and military power, the United States. At the end of the Second World War, there were efforts to create a universal and liberal system of trade and monetary relations. After 1947, however, the world economy began to revive on the foundations of the triangular relationship of the three major centers of noncommunist industrial power: the United States, Western Europe, and Japan. Under the umbrella of American nuclear protection and connected with the United States through military alliances, Japan and Western Europe were encouraged to grow and prosper. In order to rebuild these industrial economies adjacent to the Sino-Soviet bloc, the United States encouraged Japanese growth, led by exports, into the American market and, through the European Economic Community's (EEC) common external tariff and agricultural policy, also encouraged discrimination against American exports.[2]

Today, the triangular relationship of the noncommunist industrial powers upon which the world economy has rested is in disarray. The signs of decay were visible as early as the middle 1960s, when President John F. Kennedy's grand design failed to stem the coalescence of an inward-looking European economic bloc and to

Robert Gilpin is a professor of politics and international affairs at Princeton University in Princeton, New Jersey.

[1] Edward Hallet Carr, *The Twenty Years' Crisis 1919-1939* (London: Macmillan and Co., 1951), p. 117.

[2] This theme is developed in Robert Gilpin, "The Politics of Transnational Economic Relations," *International Organization* 25 (Summer 1971): 398-419. This article was part of a special issue of the journal, entitled "Transnational Relations and World Politics," which was edited by Robert O. Keohane and Joseph S. Nye, Jr., and was subsequently published under the same title as a book by Harvard University Press in 1972.

achieve its objective of an economic and political community extending from Scandinavia to Japan and pivoted on the United States.[3]

Believing that the world trading and monetary system was operating to America's disadvantage, the administration of Richard Nixon took up the challenge with a completely different approach. On 15 August 1971, former President Nixon announced a new foreign economic policy for the United States. In response to the first trade deficit since 1893 and to accelerating attacks on the dollar, the president imposed a surcharge on American imports, suspended the convertibility of the dollar, and took other remedial actions. Subsequently the dollar was devalued twice (December 1971 and February 1973); the world moved toward a system of flexible exchange rates; and intense negotiations were initiated to create a new international monetary and trading system.

A new economic policy was necessary for several reasons. The United States believed an overvalued dollar was adding significantly to its unemployment rate.[4] American expenditures abroad for military commitments, foreign direct investment, and goods and services required, in the 1970s, greater outlays of foreign exchange than the United States could earn or wished to borrow. The US rapprochement with China, its moves toward détente with the Soviet Union, and President Nixon's announcement of the New Economic Policy appeared to signal the end of the political order that American economic and military supremacy had guaranteed; this political order had been the foundation for the post–World War II world economy. All these policy initiatives were efforts to adjust to the growing economic power of America's partners, Europe and Japan, and to the growing military power of its primary antagonist, the Soviet Union. In terms of the present article, these economic and political changes raised the question of whether the interdependent world economy could survive in the changing political environment of the 1970s and beyond.

In this brief article I make no attempt to give a definitive answer to this question. Rather, my purpose is to present and evaluate three models of the future drawn from current writings on international relations. These models are really representative of the three prevailing schools of thought on political economy: liberalism, Marxism, and economic nationalism. Each model is an amalgam of the ideas of several writers who, in my judgment (or by their own statements), fall into one or another of these three perspectives on the relationship of economic and political affairs.

Each model constitutes an ideal type. Perhaps no one individual would subscribe to each argument made by any one position. Yet the tendencies and assumptions associated with each perception of the future are real enough; they have a profound influence on popular, academic, and official thinking on trade,

---

[3] Ernest Preeg, *Traders and Diplomats* (Washington, D.C.: The Brookings Institution, 1970), p. 1.

[4] C. Fred Bergsten, "The New Economics and U.S. Foreign Policy," *Foreign Affairs* 50 (January 1972): 199-222.

monetary, and investment problems. One, in fact, cannot really escape being influenced by one position or another.

Following the presentation of the three models, I present a critique that sets forth the strengths and weaknesses of each. On the basis of this critique, I draw some general conclusions with respect to the future of international economic organization and the nature of future international relations in general.

The sovereignty-at-bay model

I label the first model *sovereignty at bay,* after the title of Raymond Vernon's influential book on the multinational corporation.[5] According to this view, increasing economic interdependence and technological advances in communication and transportation are making the nation state an anachronism. These economic and technological developments are said to have undermined the traditional economic rationale of the nation state. In the interest of world efficiency and domestic economic welfare, the nation state's control over economic affairs will continually give way to the multinational corporation, to the Eurodollar market, and to other international institutions better suited to the economic needs of mankind.

Perhaps the most forceful statement of the sovereignty-at-bay thesis is that of Harry Johnson—the paragon of economic liberalism. Analyzing the international economic problems of the 1970s, Johnson makes the following prediction:

> In an important sense, the fundamental problem of the future is the conflict between the political forces of nationalism and the economic forces pressing for world integration. This conflict currently appears as one between the national government and the international corporation, in which the balance of power at least superficially appears to lie on the side of the national government. But in the longer run economic forces are likely to predominate over political, and may indeed come to do so before the end of this decade. Ultimately, a world federal government will appear as the only rational method for coping with the world's economic problems.[6]

Though not all adherents of the sovereignty-at-bay thesis would go as far as Johnson, and an interdependent world economy is quite conceivable without unbridled scope for the activities of multinational corporations, most do regard the multinational corporation as the embodiment par excellence of the liberal ideal of an interdependent world economy. It has taken the integration of national economies beyond trade and money to the internationalization of production. For the first time in history, production, marketing, and investment are being organized on a global scale rather than in terms of isolated national economies. The multinational

[5] Raymond Vernon, *Sovereignty at Bay* (New York: Basic Books, 1971).
[6] Harry G. Johnson, *International Economic Questions Facing Britain, the United States, and Canada in the 70's,* British-North American Research Association, June 1970, p. 24.

corporations are increasingly indifferent to national boundaries in making decisions with respect to markets, production, and sources of supply.

The sovereignty-at-bay thesis argues that national economies have become enmeshed in a web of economic interdependence from which they cannot easily escape, and from which they derive great economic benefits. Through trade, monetary relations, and foreign investment, the destinies and well-being of societies have become too inexorably interwoven for these bonds to be severed. The costs of the ensuing inefficiencies in order to assert national autonomy or some other nationalistic goal would be too high. The citizenry, so this thesis contends, would not tolerate the sacrifices of domestic economic well-being that would be entailed if individual nation states sought to hamper unduly the successful operation of the international economy.

Underlying this development, the liberal position argues, is a revolution in economic needs and expectations. Domestic economic goals have been elevated to a predominant position in the hierarchy of national goals. Full employment, regional development, and other economic welfare goals have become the primary concerns of political leadership. More importantly, these goals can only be achieved, this position argues, through participation in the world economy. No government, for example, would dare shut out the multinational corporations and thereby forgo employment, regional development, or other benefits these corporations bring into countries. In short, the rise of the welfare state and the increasing sensitivity of national governments to the rising economic expectations of their societies have made them dependent upon the benefits provided by a liberal world-economic system.

In essence, this argument runs, one must distinguish between the creation of the interdependent world economy and the consequences of its subsequent dynamics.[7] Though the postwar world economy was primarily a creation of the United States, the system has since become essentially irreversible. The intermeshing of interests across national boundaries and the recognized benefits of interdependence now cement the system together for the future. Therefore, even though the power of the United States and security concerns may be in relative decline, this does not portend a major transformation of the international economy and political system.

The multinational corporation, for example, is now believed to be sufficiently strong to stand and survive on its own. The flexibility, mobility, and vast resources of the corporations give them an advantage in confrontations with nation states. A corporation always has the option of moving its production facilities elsewhere. If it does, the nation state is the loser in terms of employment, corporate resources, and access to world markets. Thus the multinationals are escaping the control of nation states, including that of their home (source) governments. They are emerging as sufficient powers in their own right to survive the changing context of international political relations.

[7] Samuel Huntington, "Transnational Organizations in World Politics," *World Politics* 25 (April 1973): 361.

On the other hand, it is argued that the nation state has been placed in a dilemma it cannot hope to resolve.[8] It is losing control over economic affairs to transnational actors like the multinational corporation.[9] It cannot retain its traditional independence and sovereignty and simultaneously meet the expanding economic needs and desires of its populace. The efforts of nation states to enhance their security and power *relative* to others are held to be incompatible with an interdependent world economy that generates *absolute* gains for everyone. In response to the growing economic demands of its citizens, the nation state must adjust to the forces of economic rationality and efficiency.

In the contemporary world, the costs of disrupting economic interdependence, of territorial conquest, and of risking nuclear warfare are believed to be far greater than any conceivable benefits. The calculus of benefits and risks has changed, and "the rational relationship between violence as a means of foreign policy and the ends of foreign policy has been destroyed by the possibility of all-out nuclear war."[10] In contrast to the nineteenth century, the cost of acquiring territory is viewed as having simply become too great. In the contemporary world, there is more to be gained through economic cooperation and an international division of labor than through strife and conflict. Thus, in the opinion of Saburo Okita, formerly president of the Japan Economic Research Center, the exercise of force for economic gain or to defend economic interests is an anachronism:

> We are living in a century when such military action is no longer viable. To build up military power just to protect overseas private property is rather absurd in terms of cost-benefit calculations. The best course for the Government in case of nationalization or seizure of overseas private Japanese assets is to compensate Japanese investors directly in Japan rather than to spend very large amounts of money to build up military strength.[11]

Just as the nuclear revolution in warfare now inhibits the exercise of military power, the revolution in economic relations now inhibits the national exercise of economic power by increasing the cost. Advances in transportation and communications have integrated national economies to the point where many believe it is too costly to threaten the severance of economic relations in order to achieve particular political and economic goals. Economically as well as militarily in the contemporary world, nations are said to be mutually deterred from actions that would disrupt the interdependent economy. This mutual vulnerability of necessity limits and moderates the economic and political struggle among nation states. It provides the necessary minimum political order where the multinational corporations of all the major industrial powers can flourish and bring benefits to the whole of mankind.

---

[8] Edward L. Morse, "Crisis Diplomacy, Interdependence, and the Politics of International Economic Relations," *World Politics* 24, supplement (Spring 1972): 123-50.

[9] Keohane and Nye.

[10] Hans Morgenthau, "Western Values and Total War," *Commentary*, October 1961, p. 280.

[11] Quoted in *New York Times Magazine*, 29 October 1972, p. 58.

The sovereignty-at-bay view also envisages a major transformation of the relationships among developed and underdeveloped countries. The multinational corporations of the developed, industrial economies must not only produce in each other's markets, but the locus of manufacturing industry will increasingly shift to underdeveloped countries.[12] As the economies of developed countries become more service oriented, as their terms of trade for raw materials continue to deteriorate, and as their labor costs continue to rise, manufacturing will migrate to lesser-developed countries. United States firms already engage in extensive offshore production in Asia and Latin America. Western Europe has reached the limits of importing Mediterranean labor, which is the functional equivalent of foreign direct investment. Japan's favorable wage structure and undervalued currency have eroded. With the end of the era of cheap energy and of favorable terms of trade for raw materials, the logic of industrial location favors the underdeveloped periphery. Increasingly, the multinational corporations of all industrial powers will follow the logic of this manufacturing revolution. Manufacturing, particularly of components and semiprocessed goods, will migrate to lesser-developed countries.

This vision of the future has been portrayed most dramatically by Norman Macrae, in an issue of *The Economist,* who foresees a world of spreading affluence energized perhaps by "small transnational companies run in West Africa by London telecommuters who live in Honolulu?"[13] New computer-based training methods and information systems will facilitate the rapid diffusion of skills, technologies, and industries to lesser-developed countries. The whole system will be connected by modern telecommunications and computers; the rich will concentrate on the knowledge-creating and knowledge-processing industries. More and more of the old manufacturing industries will move to the underdeveloped world. The entire West and Japan will be a service-oriented island in a labor-intensive global archipelago. Thus, whereas the telephone and jet aircraft facilitated the internationalization of production in the Northern Hemisphere, the contemporary revolution in communications and transportation will encompass the whole globe.

"The logical and eventual development of this possibility," according to management consultant John Diebold, "would be the end of nationality and national governments as we know them."[14] This sovereignty-at-bay world, then, is one of voluntary and cooperative relations among interdependent economies, the goal of which is to accelerate the economic growth and welfare of everyone. In this model, development of the poor is achieved through the transfer of capital, technology, and managerial know-how from the continually advancing developed lands to the lesser-developed nations; it is a world in which the tide of economic growth lifts all boats. In this liberal vision of the future, the multinational corporation, freed from the nation state, is the critical transmission belt of capital, ideas, and growth.

[12] John Diebold, "Multinational Corporations—Why be Scared of Them?," *Foreign Policy,* no. 12 (Fall 1973): 79-95.

[13] "The Future of International Business," *The Economist,* 22 January 1972.

[14] Diebold, p. 87.

The dependencia model

In contrast to the sovereignty-at-bay vision of the future is what may be characterized as the *dependencia* model.[15] Although the analysis underlying the two approaches has much in common, the dependencia model challenges the partners-in-development motif of the sovereignty-at-bay model. Its Marxist conception is one of a hierarchical and exploitative world order. The sovereignty-at-bay model envisages a relatively benevolent system in which growth and wealth spread from the developed core to the lesser-developed periphery. In the dependencia model, on the other hand, the flow of wealth and benefits is seen as moving—via the same mechanisms—from the global, underdeveloped periphery to the centers of industrial financial power and decision. It is an exploitative system that produces affluent development for some and dependent underdevelopment for the majority of mankind. In effect, what is termed transnationalism by the sovereignty-at-bay advocates is considered imperialism by the Marxist proponents of the dependencia model.

In the interdependent world economy of the dependencia model, the multinational corporation also reigns supreme. But the world created by these corporations is held to be far different from that envisaged by the sovereignty-at-bay school of thought. In the dependencia model the political and economic consequences of the multinational corporation are due to what Stephen Hymer has called the two laws of development: the law of increasing firm size, and the law of uneven development. The law of increasing firm size, Hymer argues, is the tendency since the Industrial Revolution for firms to increase in size "from the *workshop* to the *factory* to the *national* corporation to the *multidivisional corporation* and now to the multinational corporation."[16] The law of uneven development, he continues, is the tendency of the international economy to produce poverty as well as wealth, underdevelopment as well as development. Together, these two economic laws are producing the following consequence:

> . . . a regime of North Atlantic Multinational Corporations would tend to produce a hierarchical division of labor within the firm. It would tend to centralize high-level decision-making occupations in a few key cities in the advanced countries, surrounded by a number of regional sub-capitals, and confine the rest of the world to lower levels of activity and income, i.e., to the status of towns and villages in a new Imperial system. Income, status, authority, and consumption patterns would radiate out from these centers

---

[15] The literature on dependencia, or underdevelopment, has now become legend. One of the better statements of this thesis is Osvaldo Sunkel, "Big Business and 'Dependencia': A Latin American View," *Foreign Affairs* 50 (April 1972): 517-31. For an excellent and critical view of the dependencia thesis, see Benjamin J. Cohen, *The Question of Imperialism—The Political Economy of Dominance and Dependence* (New York: Basic Books, 1973), chapter 6.

[16] "The Multinational Corporation and the Law of Uneven Development," in *Economics and World Order—From the 1970's to the 1990's*, ed. Jagdish Bhagwati (New York: The Macmillan Co., 1972), p. 113 and passim.

along a declining curve, and the existing pattern of inequality and dependency would be perpetrated. The pattern would be complex, just as the
structure of the corporation is complex, but the basic relationship between
different countries would be one of superior and subordinate, head office and
branch office.[17]

In this hierarchical and exploitative world system, power and decision would
be lodged in the urban financial and industrial cores of New York, London, Tokyo,
etc. Here would be located the computers and data banks of the closely integrated
global systems of production and distribution; the main computer in the core
would control subsidiary computers in the periphery. The higher functions of
management, research and development, entrepreneurship, and finance would be
located in these Northern metropolitan centers. "Lower" functions and labor-
intensive manufacturing would be continuously diffused to the lesser-developed
countries where are found cheap pliable labor, abundant raw materials, and an
indifference to industrial pollution. This global division of labor between higher and
lower economic functions would perpetuate the chasm between the affluent northern one-fifth of the globe and the destitute southern four-fifths of the globe.

The argument of the dependencia thesis is that the economic dependence of
the underdeveloped periphery upon the developed core is responsible for the
impoverishment of the former. Development and underdevelopment are simul-
taneous processes; the developed countries have progressed and have grown rich
through exploiting the poor and making them poorer. Lacking true autonomy and
being economically dependent upon the developed countries, the underdeveloped
countries have suffered because the developed have a veto over their development:

> By dependence we mean a situation in which the economy of certain
> countries is conditioned by the development and expansion of another
> economy to which the former is subjected. The relation of interdependence
> between two or more economies, and between these and world trade, assumes
> the form of dependence when some countries (the dominant ones) can
> expand and be self-sustaining, while other countries (the dependent ones) can
> do this only as a reflection of that expansion, which can have either a positive
> or negative effect on their immediate development.[18]

Though this particular quotation refers to trade relations, much of the
dependence literature is addressed to the issue of foreign direct investment. In
content, most of this literature is of a piece with traditional Marxist and radical
theories of imperialism. Whether because of the falling rate of profit in capitalist
economies or the attraction of superprofits abroad, multinational corporations are
believed to exploit the underdeveloped countries. Thus, Paul Baran and Paul
Sweezy see the multinationals necessarily impelled to invest in lesser-developed

[17] Ibid., p. 114.
[18] Quoted in Cohen, pp. 190-91.

countries.[19] Constantine Vaitsos has sought to document the superprofits available to American corporations in Latin America.[20] The message conveyed by this literature is that the imperialism of free investment has replaced the imperialism of free trade in the contemporary world.

The mercantilist model

A key element missing in both the sovereignty-at-bay and the dependencia models is the nation state. Both envisage a world organized and managed by powerful North American, European, and Japanese corporations. In the beneficial corporate order of the first model and the imperialist corporate order of the second, there is little room for nation states, save as servants of corporate power and ambition. In opposition to both these models, therefore, the third model of the future—the mercantilist model—views the nation state and the interplay of national interests (as distinct from corporate interests) as the primary determinants of the future role of the world economy.[21]

According to this mercantilist view, the interdependent world economy, which has provided such a favorable environment for the multinational corporation, is coming to an end. In the wake of the relative decline of American power and of growing conflicts among the capitalist economies, a new international political order less favorable to the multinational corporation is coming into existence. Whether it is former President Nixon's five-power world (US, USSR, China, the EEC, and Japan), a triangular world (US, USSR, and China), or some form of American-Soviet condominium, the emergent world order will be characterized by intense international economic competition for markets, investment outlets, and sources of raw materials.

By *mercantilism* I mean the attempt of governments to manipulate economic arrangements in order to maximize their own interests, whether or not this is at the expense of others. These interests may be related to domestic concerns (full employment, price stability, etc.) or to foreign policy (security, independence, etc.).

This use of the term *mercantilism* is far broader than its eighteenth-century association with a trade and balance-of-payments surplus. The essence of mercantilism, as the concept is used in this article, is the priority of *national* economic and political objectives over considerations of *global* economic efficiency. The mercan-

---

[19] *Monopoly Capital—An Essay on the American Economic and Social Order* (New York: Monthly Review Press, 1966).

[20] Constantine Vaitsos, "Transfer of Resources and Preservation of Monopoly Rents," Economic Development Report No. 168, Development Advisory Service, Harvard University, 1970. (Mimeographed.)

[21] See, for example, David Calleo and Benjamin Rowland, *America and the World Political Economy* (Bloomington, Ind.: Indiana University Press, 1973). Mercantilism is also the real theme of Ernest Mandel's *Europe vs. America—Contradictions of Imperialism* (New York: Monthly Review Press, 1970).

tilist impulse can take many forms in the contemporary world: the desire for a balance-of-payments surplus; the export of unemployment, inflation, or both; the imposition of import and/or export controls; the expansion of world market shares; and the stimulation of advanced technology. In short, each nation will pursue economic policies that reflect domestic economic needs and external political ambitions without much concern for the effects of these policies on other countries or on the international economic system as a whole.

The mercantilist position in effect reverses the argument of the liberals with respect to the nature and success of the interdependent world economy. In contrast to the liberal view that trade liberalization has fostered economic growth, the mercantilist thesis is that several decades of uninterrupted economic growth permitted interdependence. Growth, based in part on relatively cheap energy and other resources as well as on the diffusion of American technology abroad, facilitated the reintroduction of Japan into the world economy and the development of a closely linked Atlantic economy. Now both cheap energy and a technological gap, which were sources of rapid economic growth and global interdependence, have ceased to exist.

International competition has intensified and has become disruptive precisely because the United States has lost much of its technological lead in products and industrial processes. As happened in Britain in the latter part of the nineteenth century, the United States no longer holds the monopoly position in advanced technologies. Its exports must now compete increasingly on the basis of price and a devalued dollar. As was also the case with Great Britain, the United States has lost the technological rents associated with its previous industrial superiority. This loss of industrial supremacy on the part of the dominant industrial power threatens to give rise to economic conflict between the rising and declining centers of industrial power.[22]

From the mercantilist perspective, the fundamental problem of modern international society has been how to organize an industrial world economy. This issue arose with the spread of industrialism from Great Britain and the emergence of several competing capitalist economies in the latter part of the nineteenth century.[23] In the decades prior to the First World War, the issue of how to organize a world economy composed of several competing industrial economies was at the

[22] Vietnam-generated inflation was also a factor in the decline of American competitiveness in the late 1960s. But mercantilists and others (such as Richard Nelson and Michael Boretsky) respond that it is precisely because the US has lost much of its technological lead in products and industrial processes that pure competition has become so important. For an analysis of this debate, see Philip Boffey, "Technology and World Trade: Is There Cause for Alarm?," *Science*, 2 April 1971.

[23] I have benefited very much from the as yet unpublished writings of Kendall Myers on this subject. Myers's manuscript entitled "Appeasement and Nazi Germany—Regional Blocs or Universalism" was the basis of a seminar held at the Lehrman Institute in New York. See also the reflections of Simon Kuznets, *Modern Economy Growth* (New Haven, Conn.: Yale University Press, 1966). The issue, of course, is fundamental to the radical and Marxist critique of capitalism.

heart of international politics. The resulting commercial and imperial struggle was a major factor in the subsequent outbreak of the First World War.

The issue was never resolved during the interwar period. During the Second World War, the organization of the world economy was regarded, at least in the United States, as a central question for the postwar era. Would it be a universal liberal system or a fragmented system of regional blocs and preference arrangements? With the outbreak of the cold war and the undisputed hegemony of the United States over other capitalist economies, however, the issue faded into the background. Former President Nixon's 15 August 1971 speech signaled to mercantilist writers that with the easing of the cold war the issue has once again moved to the fore.

These mercantilist writers tend to fall into the two camps of malevolent and benign mercantilism. Both tend to believe the world economy is fragmenting into regional blocs. In the wake of the relative decline of American power, nation states will form regional economic alliances or blocs in order to advance their interests in opposition to other nation states. International trade, monetary arrangements, and investment will be increasingly interregional. This regionalization of economic relations will replace the present American emphasis on multilateral free trade, the international role of the dollar, and the reign of the American multinational corporation.

Malevolent mercantilism believes regionalization will intensify internationl economic conflict.[24] Each bloc centered on the large industrial powers—the United States, Western Europe, Japan, and the Soviet Union—will clash over markets, currency, and investment outlets. This would be a return to the lawlessness and beggar-thy-neighbor policies of the 1930s.

Benign mercantilism, on the other hand, believes regional blocs would stabilize world economic relations.[25] It believes that throughout modern history universalism and regionalism have been at odds. The rationale of regional blocs is that one can have simultaneously the benefits of greater scale and interdependence and minimal accompanying costs of economic and political interdependence. Though the material gains from a global division of labor and free trade could be greater, regionalism is held to provide security and protection against external economic and political forces over which the nation state, acting alone, has little influence or control. In short, the organization of the world economy into regional blocs could provide the basis for a secure and peaceful economic order.[26]

Benign mercantilism derives from the view of John Maynard Keynes and other Englishmen who were highly critical of an increasingly interdependent world economy. The loss of national self-sufficiency, this more benign view of mercan-

---

[24] Ernest Mandel, in his *Europe vs. America,* is more malevolent mercantilist than Marxist in his argument.

[25] Calleo and Rowland.

[26] For a recent analysis of this issue, see Ernest Preeg, *Economic Blocs and U.S. Foreign Policy* (Washington, D.C.: National Planning Association, 1974).

tilism holds, is a source of economic-political insecurity and conflict.[27] Liberalism, moreover, is detrimental to national cultural and political development. Therefore, this benign mercantilist position advocates a regionalization of the world economy as the appropriate middle road between a declining American-centered world economy and a global conflict between the capitalist economies. An inevitable clash between industrial economies can be prevented through the carving out of regional spheres of influence and the exercise of mutual self-restraint among them.

In the opinion of benign mercantilism, the thrust of much domestic and international economic policy, especially since the end of the First World War, has in fact been away from interdependence. Nations have placed a higher priority on domestic stability and policies of full employment than on the maintenance of international links; they have sought to exert national control over their monetary and other economic policies. This is what the Keynesian revolution and its emphasis on management of the domestic economy is said to be all about. The same desire for greater latitude in domestic policy underlies the increasing popularity today of flexible over fixed exchange rates and the movement toward regional blocs. Mercantilists point out that in many industrialized economies there is, in fact, a renewed questioning of whether the further benefits of trade liberalization and interdependence are worth the costs. Interdependence accentuates domestic economic adjustment problems as economic instabilities in one economy spill over into others. It causes labor dislocations, may accentuate inequalities of income distribution, and makes national planning more difficult. In short, according to these mercantilists, the world has reached the limits of interdependence and loss of national self-sufficiency.

A critique of the three models

In this section of the article, I evaluate the three models and draw from each what I consider to be important insights into the nature of contemporary international economic relations. This critique is not meant to cover all the points of each model but only those most directly relevant to this essay.

Sovereignty at bay

Fundamentally, the sovereignty-at-bay thesis reduces to a question of interests and power: Who has the power to make the world economy serve its interests? This point may be best illustrated by considering the relationship of the multinational corporation and the nation state. In the writings I identified with the sovereignty-at-bay thesis, this contest is held to be most critical.

On one side of this contest is the host nation state. Its primary source of power is its control over access to its territory, that is, access to its internal market,

---

[27] This paradox is analyzed by Eugene Staley, *World Economy in Transition* (New York: Council on Foreign Relations, 1939), chapter 6, especially p. 15.

investment opportunities, and sources of raw material. On the other side is the corporation with its capital, technology, and access to world markets.[28] Each has something the other wants. Each seeks to maximize its benefits and minimize its costs. The bargain they strike is dependent upon how much one wants what the other has to offer and how skillfully one or the other can exploit its respective advantages. In most cases, the issue is how the benefits and costs of foreign investment are to be divided between the foreign corporation and the host economy.

The sovereignty-at-bay thesis assumes that the bargaining advantages are and always will be on the side of the corporation. In contrast to the corporation's vast resources and flexibility, the nation state has little with which to bargain. Most nation states lack the economies of scale, indigenous technological capabilities, or native entrepreneurship to free themselves from dependence upon American (or other) multinational corporations. According to this argument, the extent to which nation states reassert their sovereignty is dependent upon the economic price they are willing to pay, and it assumes that when confronted with this cost, they will retreat from nationalistic policies.

In an age of rising economic expectations, the sovereignty-at-bay thesis rests on an important truth: A government is reluctant to assert its sovereignty and drive out the multinational corporations if this means a dramatic lowering of the standard of living, increasing unemployment, and the like. But in an age when the petroleum-producing states, through cooperation, have successfully turned the tables on the multinational corporations, it becomes obvious that the sovereignty-at-bay thesis also neglects the fact that the success of the multinational corporation has been dependent upon a favorable political order. As this order changes, so will the fortunes of the multinationals.

This political order has been characterized by an absence of unity on the part of the economies that have been host to American and other corporations. The divisions between and within the host countries themselves, and the influence of the American government, left the host countries with little power to bargain effectively or to increase their relative benefits from foreign investments in their countries. Thus, in the case of Canada, the competition between the provinces and particularly between English Canada and Quebec greatly weakened Canada's position vis-à-vis American investors. Similarly, nationalistic competition for investment has weakened attempts, such as the Andean Pact, that have tried to develop a common policy toward foreign corporations. But the importance of political factors in the overseas expansion of American corporations may be best illustrated by the case of Western Europe and Japan.

American corporations coveted both the Japanese and Western European markets; they have been able to establish hundreds of subsidiaries in the latter but only a few in the former. The reason for this difference is largely political. Whereas the former has one central government controlling access to Japan's internal market

---

[28] For an excellent examination of this relationship, see Huntington.

of 100 million population, six (now nine) political centers have controlled access to the European Common Market. By interposing itself between powerful American corporations and intensely competitive Japanese firms that desired American capital and technology, the Japanese government has been able to prevent the latter from making agreements not desired by the government. As a consequence, the Japanese home market has been protected as the almost exclusive domain of Japanese industry. American firms have had, therefore, a strong incentive to license their technology to the Japanese or to form corporate arrangements in which the American firms were no more than a minor partner.

What the Japanese succeeded in doing was to break up the package of capital, technology, and entrepreneurship that foreign direct investment entails. The Japanese did not need the capital; they got the technology without managerial control by American corporations; entrepreneurship remained in the hands of Japanese. This Japanese example of untying the package and obtaining the technology, and in many cases the capital, required for development without loss of control has become an inspiration for economic nationalists in Latin America, Canada, and elsewhere.

In Western Europe, on the other hand, an American firm denied the right to establish a subsidiary in one Common Market country has had the option of trying another country and thereby still gaining access to the whole Market. Moreover, the strong desire of individual European countries for American investment has enabled American corporations to invest on very favorable terms. In certain cases, the firms have followed a divide-and-conquer strategy. Denied permission by President de Gaulle to invest in France, General Motors established in Belgium one of the largest automobile assembly plants in the Common Market. Through this route, the corporation gained access to the French market as well as to other European markets.

In response to this situation, de Gaulle sought to obtain West German cooperation against American investment in EEC countries. Together these two most powerful of the Six could dictate a policy the others would be forced to accept. Through the instrumentality of the Franco-German Friendship Treaty of 1963, therefore, de Gaulle sought to form a Bonn-Paris axis directed against American hegemony in Western Europe.

Although there was sentiment in West Germany favorable to taking measures to limit the rapidly growing role of American subsidiaries in EEC countries, the West German government refused to take any action that might weaken the American commitment to defend Western Europe. The United States government not only reminded the West Germans that a continued American military presence was dependent upon West German support of measures to lessen the American balance-of-payments deficit, but it also pressured West Germany to increase its military purchases from the United States and to avoid competitive arrangements with France. Largely as a result of these American pressures, the Friendship Treaty was, in effect, aborted. The first serious counteroffensive of the nation state against the multinational corporation collapsed. It is clear, however, that the outcome of this tale would have been altogether different if West Germany had desired greater military and economic independence from the United States. In short, the American corporate penetration of the European Common Market has been dependent upon the special security relationship of the United States and West Germany.

One could extend this type of analysis for the whole of American overseas investment. American investment in the Middle East, Africa, Latin America, Canada, and elsewhere has benefited from America's dominant position in the world. This position is now seriously challenged not only by the Soviet Union but by Japan, Western Europe, China, the Arabs, and Brazil in Latin America. Throughout these areas, economic nationalism is on the rise, threatening American investments and the income they bring to the United States. The thrust of this attack has been to break up the package of capital, technology, and management in order to acquire the first two without the third; the goal is greater local control through joint ventures, nationalization, and other policies. While the host countries are unlikely to "kill off" the American multinational corporations, they will increasingly make them serve local interests. This in turn will undoubtedly make direct investment abroad less attractive to American corporations.

A reversal of fortunes has already been seen in the case of the oil multinationals. The significance of the offensive by the oil-producing states against the large international oil companies is not merely that the price of oil to the United States and to the rest of the world has risen but also that the United States may lose one of its most lucrative sources of investment income. The oil crisis and Arab oil boycott which followed the 1973 Arab-Israeli war was a profound learning experience for Europe, Japan, and even the United States. The oil boycott and the behavior of the oil multinationals set into motion a series of events that cannot help but transform national attitudes and policies toward the oil multinationals. The sudden appreciation of how vulnerable governments were to the policies of the oil multinationals and how far their "sovereignty" had been compromised awakened them to the inherent dangers of overdependence on the corporations and their policies.

The French and, to a lesser extent, the Japanese responses to this experience have received the most attention. But perhaps more noteworthy was the reaction of the West German government—after the United States the nation most committed to a liberal world economy. It was the West German representative at the February 1973 Washington conference of oil-consuming nations who demanded that the United States and Western Europe undertake "a joint analysis of the price policies, profits, and taxes of oil-multinationals." While the proposal, which became part of the Washington Declaration, does not mean demise of the oil multinationals, it does suggest that the policies of nation states will increasingly impinge on the freedom of action of these particular multinational corporations.

This change in attitude toward the oil multinationals can be witnessed in the United States itself. The role of the companies as instruments of the Arab boycott has had a significant impact on American perceptions. Prior to that time, few probing questions about the oil multinationals had been raised in the press or in Congress. Other than a few "radicals," few had challenged the fact that Exxon, Gulf, and other oil multinationals paid virtually no taxes to the United States government and that they acted as sovereign entities in their dealings with the oil-producing countries. When the tables were turned, however, and the oil companies became the instruments of the Arab boycott against the United States, then even their staunchest defenders began to raise questions about tax avoidance. More importantly, the United States government took into its own hands some of the task of negotiating with the oil-producing states. Thus, when the multinationals were perceived as no longer supportive of the national interests of the United States, there was a reassertion of national sovereignty.

The case of oil and the oil multinationals is perhaps unique. Yet it does suggest that nation states have not lost their power or their will to act when they believe the multinational corporations are threatening their perceived national interests and sovereignty. The experience of the oil boycott and the role of the multinationals in carrying it out reveal the extent to which the operators and the success of these corporations have been dependent upon American power. With the relative decline of American power and the rise of governments hostile to American interests and policies, this case history at least raises the question of how the weakening of the Pax Americana will affect the status of other American multinational corporations throughout the world.

Dependencia

The weakness of the dependencia, or ultraimperialism, model is that it makes at least three unwarranted assumptions. In the first place, it assumes much greater common interest among the noncommunist industrial powers—the United States, Western Europe, and Japan—than is actually the case. Secondly, it treats the peripheral states of Asia, Africa, Latin America, Canada, and the Middle East solely as objects of international economic and political relations. Neither assumption is true. As the first assumption is considered in more detail in the next section, let us consider the second for a moment.

After nearly two centuries, the passivity of the periphery is now past. The Soviet challenge to the West and the divisions among the capitalist powers themselves have given the emerging elites in the periphery room for maneuver. These nationalist elites are no longer ignorant and pliable colonials. Within the periphery, there are coalescing centers of power that will weigh increasingly in the future world balance of power: China, Indonesia, India, Iran, Nigeria, Brazil, and some form of Arab oil power. Moreover, if properly organized and led, such centers of power in control over a vital resource, as the experience of the Organization of Petroleum Exporting Countries (OPEC) demonstrates, may reverse the tables and make the core dependent upon the periphery. For the moment at least, a perceptible shift appears to be taking place in the global balance of economic power from the owners of capital to the owners of natural resources.[29]

The third unwarranted assumption is that a quasi-Marxist theory of capitalist imperialism is applicable to the relationship of developed and lesser-developed economies today. Again, I illustrate my argument by considering the role of the multinational corporation in the lesser-developed countries, since its allegedly exploitative function is stressed by almost all dependencia theorists.

The dependencia theory undoubtedly has a good case with respect to foreign direct investment in petroleum and other extractive industries. The oil, copper, and other multinationals have provided the noncommunist industrial world with a plentiful and relatively cheap supply of minerals and energy. The dramatic reversal of this situation by the oil-producing countries in 1973-74 and the steady rise of prices of other commodities support the contention that the producing countries were not getting the highest possible price and possibly not a just price for their nonrenewable resources. But what constitutes the just price for a natural endowment that was worthless until the multinationals found it is not an easy issue to resolve.

With respect to foreign direct investment in manufacturing, the case is far more ambiguous. Even if technological rents are collected, does the foreign corporation bring more into the economy in terms of technology, capital, and access to world markets than it takes out in the form of earnings? The research of Canadian, Australian, and other economists, for example, suggest that it does. They find no differences in the corporate behavior of domestic and foreign firms; on the contrary, foreign firms are given higher marks in terms of export performance, industrial research and development, and other economic indicators.[30] Nonetheless, it would be naive to suggest that no exploitation or severe distortions of host economies have taken place.

On the other hand, it may not be unwarranted to suggest that a strong presumption exists for arguing that in terms of economic growth and industrial development, foreign direct investment in *manufacturing* is to the advantage of the host economy. A major cause of foreign direct investment is the sector-specific nature of knowledge and capital in the home economy.[31] In order to prevent a fall in their rate of profits through overinvesting at home or diversifying into unknown areas, American corporations frequently go abroad to guard against a lower rate of profit at home rather than because the superprofits abroad are attractive. Insofar as this is true, and there is sufficient evidence to warrant its plausibility, foreign direct investment benefits both the corporation and the host economy at a cost to other

---

[29] See C. Fred Bergsten, "The Threat From The Third World," *Foreign Policy*, no. 11 (Summer 1973): 102-24.

[30] See, for example, A. E. Safarian, *Foreign Ownership of Canadian Industry* (Toronto: University of Toronto Press, 1973).

[31] This point is developed in US Congress, Senate Committee on Labor and Public Welfare, *The Multinational Corporation and the National Interest* (report prepared for the Committee), 93rd Cong., 1st sess., 1973, Committee print.

factors of production in the home economy. Thus, though the Marxists may be right in saying that there is an imperative for capitalism to go abroad, the effect is not to exploit but to benefit the recipient economy—a conclusion, by the way, that Marx himself would have accepted.[32]

While it is true that, in general, lesser-developed countries are economically dependent upon developed countries, the conclusions to be drawn from this fact are not self-evident. Are the countries underdeveloped because they are dependent, as dependencia theorists assume, or are they dependent because they are underdeveloped? China is underdeveloped, but it is not dependent upon any external power (though one could argue a historical case). As Benjamin Cohen has pointed out, the critical question is whether the poor are worse off economically because of this dependence.[33] Does dependence upon the developed countries entail a new loss, or foreclose opportunities of greater benefit to the economy of the undeveloped country? While the opportunity to exploit may be there, is it exercised? These are empirical questions to which no general answers can be given. Whether foreign direct investment is exploitative or beneficial depends on the type of investment, its terms, and the policies of the recipient economy itself.

The dependencia argument that foreign direct investment by multinational corporations preempts the emergence of an indigenous entrepreneurial middle class and creates a situation of technological dependence provides a clue to what is the central concern of dependence theory. Though most frequently couched solely in economic terms, the concepts of underdevelopment and dependence are more political than economic in nature. They involve an assessment of the political costs of foreign investment. They refer both to the internal political development of the recipient country and its external relations. As one of the better dependence theorists has put it, the problem "is not so much growth, i.e., expansion of a given socio-economic system, as it is 'development,' i.e., rapid and fundamental politico-socio-economic transformation."[34] In other words, foreign direct investment fosters an international division of labor that perpetuates underdevelopment and politico-economic dependencia.

This distinction between *growth* and *development* is crucial.[35] Economic growth is defined by most development economists simply as an increase in output or income per capita; it is essentially a positive and quantitative concept. The concepts of development and underdevelopment as used by dependence theorists are primarily normative and qualitative; they refer to structural changes internal to the lesser-developed economy and in external relations with the developed world. Dependencia theory really calls for a change in the current international division of

---

[32] Karl Marx, "The Future Results of British Rule in India," in *Karl Marx on Colonialism and Modernization,* ed. Shlomo Avineri (Garden City, N.Y.: Doubleday, 1968), pp. 125-31.

[33] Cohen, chapter 6.

[34] This distinction is developed by Keith Griffin, *Underdevelopment in Spanish America* (Cambridge, Mass.: The M.I.T. Press, 1969), p. 117.

[35] For a more detailed analysis of the distinction, see J. D. Gould, *Economic Growth in History* (London: Methuen and Co., 1972), chapter 1.

labor between the core and the periphery of the international economy, in which the periphery is a supplier of raw materials and whose industries are branch plants of the core's multinational corporations.

Whatever its economic merits, the dependencia model will continue to generate opposition against the structure of the contemporary world economy and the multinational corporation throughout the underdeveloped periphery of the world economy. As these peripheral societies grow in power, one can anticipate that they will undertake initiatives that attempt to lessen their dependence upon developed countries.

Mercantilism

It seems to me that mercantilists either ignore or ascribe too little significance to certain primary facts. Although the relative power of the United States has declined, the United States remains the dominant world economy. The scale, diversity, and dynamics of the American economy will continue to place the United States at the center of the international economic system. The universal desire for access to the huge American market, the inherent technological dynamism of the American ecnomy, and America's additional strength in both agriculture and resources—which Europe and Japan do not have—provide a cement sufficient to hold the world economy together and to keep the United States at its center.[36]

Furthermore, the United States can compensate for its loss of strength in one issue area by its continued strength in another. For example, the American economic position has indeed declined relative to Europe and Japan. Yet the continued dependence of Europe and Japan on the United States for their security provides the United States with a strong lever over the economic policies of each.

Thus, the fundamental weakness of the mercantilist model is the absence of a convincing alternative to an American-centered world economy. Western Europe, the primary economic challenger to the United States, remains internally divided; it is as yet unable to develop common policies in such areas as industry and energy or with respect to economic and monetary union. It is merely a customs union with a common agricultural policy. Moreover, like Japan, it continues to be totally dependent upon the United States for its security. As long as both Europe and Japan lack an alternative to their military and economic dependence on the United States, the mercantilist world of regional blocs lacks credibility.

The so-called energy crisis has affirmed this assessment. In the first place, the Arab oil boycott revealed the fragility of European unity. Threatened with the loss of vital supplies of Middle Eastern oil, every nation fended for itself. But subsequently, despite their reluctance, both Europe and Japan participated in the American-sponsored Washington energy conference. The American purpose in calling the conference was in part to reinforce its Middle Eastern diplomacy. But the purpose was also to reassert America's influence over its allies and to forestall

[36] A forceful statement of this position is Raymond Vernon's "Rogue Elephant in the Forest: An appraisal of Transatlantic Relations," *Foreign Affairs* 51 (April 1973): 573-87.

policies such as competitive currency depreciation, creation of new trade barriers, and bilateral deals that would tend to fragment the world economy. No doubt, too, as the French and others charge, the United States hoped to find a solution to the energy crisis that did not threaten the position of the American oil multinationals.

Calling for cooperation from its European and Japanese allies, the United States reminded them that their security still rested on American goodwill. Moreover, in the event of a conflict over oil, America's economic weapons were far superior. Thus chastened and reminded where power continued to rest, all but the French fell into line. For the time being at least, the United States demonstrated that it retained sufficient power to maintain intact an American-centered world economy.

Yet sufficient tensions and conflicts of interests remain within this world economy to prevent one from dismissing so quickly the mercantilist thesis. Undoubtedly, the interstate conflict that will be the most vexing is the growing demand and competition for raw materials, particularly petroleum.[37] The loss of energy self-sufficiency by the United States and the growth in demand for petroleum and other raw materials have already shifted the terms of trade against developed economies, and commodity prices have become major factors in world inflation. In the longer term, these changes have put the industrial powers in competition for these limited resources. They are also competing for export markets in order to finance these vital imports and for the capital the oil-producing states now have to invest. Thus, whereas in the past America's virtual control over the noncommunist world's supply of petroleum was a source of unity, today the United States is struggling with other industrial powers to insure its own position in a highly competitive environment.

In fact, one witnesses in the contemporary world the reemergence of the neo-Malthusian and Social Darwinist fears that swept industrial society and were so disruptive in the latter part of the nineteenth century. A common factor in the several imperialisms that burst forth after 1880 and fragmented the world economy was the growing fear of the potential consequences of exclusion from resources and markets. With expanding populations and productive industries believed to be dependent on foreign sources of food and raw materials, the insecurity of European states was magnified by the loss of their former relative self-sufficiency. The paradox of an interdependent world economy is that it creates sources of insecurity and competition. The very dependence of one state on another and the necessity for access to external markets and sources of raw materials cause anxieties and suspicions that exacerbate international relations.

The other reason for believing that there may be some validity in the mercantilist vision of the future is the weakening of political bonds between the United States, Western Europe, and Japan. During the height of the cold war, the foreign economic policies of these three countries were complementary. Potential conflicts over economic matters were subordinated to the necessity for political

---

[37]See Helmut Schmidt, "The Struggle for the Global Product," *Foreign Affairs* 52 (April 1974): 437-51.

unity against the Soviet Union and China. The United States encouraged export-led growth and accepted anti-American trade discrimination in order to enable Japan and Europe to rebuild their shattered economies. Reciprocally, Japan and Europe supported the international position of the dollar. Through foreign direct investment, American corporations were able to maintain their relative share of world markets. Neither the Europeans nor the Japanese challenged America's dominant position with respect to the industrial world's access to vital raw materials, particularly Middle Eastern petroleum.

Until the early 1970s, the political benefits of this arrangement were regarded as outweighing the economic costs to each partner. With the movement toward détente and with the revival of the European and Japanese economies, however, the political benefits have receded in importance and the concern over costs has increased. As a consequence, the United States and its industrial partners now desire reforms of the world's trading and monetary systems that would enable each to pursue its own particular set of interests and to limit that of the others. For example, the United States has proposed reforms of the trade and monetary systems that would limit the ability of the Europeans and the Japanese to run up huge trade surpluses. Europe and Japan, for their part, desire to preserve this scope and to limit the privileges of the United States as world banker.

Regardless of the outcome of the negotiations over the future of the international monetary system, one thing is certain: whatever privilege is retained by the dollar will not be sufficient to enable the United States to behave as it has in the past. Gone are the days when the United States could run an immense balance-of-payments deficit in order to support foreign commitments, to buy up foreign assets, and at the same time pursue a full employment policy at home. It will no longer be able to expand overseas at a relatively low cost to the American standard of living. Having already lost its technological superiority and technological rents, the United States will have to finance its economic and military position abroad through currency devaluation and a current account surplus. Thus the cost of any effort to maintain US political and economic hegemony will bear upon the American people themselves. The weight and popular appreciation of this cost will profoundly alter American attitudes toward America's world role and toward its European and Japanese allies. These changes in political interests and perceptions cannot but help to push the world in a mercantilistic direction.

Implications for international organization

What then do these three models and their relative merits tell us about the future of international economic organizations? As a consequence of the relative decline of American power and of other developments treated in this article, there is little reason to believe that many new international institutions will be created, but it is likely that the nature and functioning of existing institutions will be profoundly altered.

In a world of national states, international organizations tend to reflect the power and interests of the dominant states in the international system. From this perspective, the international organizations founded at the end of the Second World War reflected the then predominant states in the system. As the structure of the United Nations reflected the distribution of power between the United States and the Soviet Union, so the so-called Bretton Woods system and the institutions associated with it—the International Monetary Fund (IMF), the World Bank, and subsequently the General Agreement on Trade and Tariffs (GATT)—reflected the power and interests of the dominant world economy, the United States.

In both cases, the relative decline of American power over the past several decades has led to profound modifications of these political and economic institutions. Thus, with the growth of Soviet power in the United Nations Security Council and of the so-called nonaligned bloc in the General Assembly, the United Nation's role in American foreign policy and as an institution have been altered significantly. In terms of the major political issues of the world, the United Nations has moved from center stage to the sidelines. A similar transformation can be seen in the area of international economic institutions. This can be witnessed, for example, in the case of the IMF and the negotiations for the reform of the international monetary system which have taken place outside its aegis.

The transformation of the IMF began in the late 1950s with the gradual weakening of the dollar as an international currency. After 1958 the American balance-of-payments deficit began to assume major proportions. The moderate deficits of the previous decade became severe. A drain began on the large gold hoard the United States had accumulated before and during the Second World War. Between 1957 and 1963, US gold holdings fell from $22.8 billion to $15.5 billion, and foreign dollar holdings (official and private) rose from $15.1 to $28.8 billion. By 1968, American gold holdings fell to $10.9 billion, and foreign dollar holdings rose to $31.5 billion.

As Europeans and others began to turn dollars into gold, it became obvious that the United States could not continue to meet all gold claims. The immediate American response was to initiate numerous makeshift expedients—the gold pool, currency swap arrangements, the General Arrangements to Borrow, etc.—to reinforce the position of the dollar. Additionally, the United States undertook unilateral measures such as the Interest Equalization Tax (1963), "voluntary" controls on the export of capital (1965), and, eventually, mandatory controls on foreign direct investment (1968) to stem the outflow of dollars.

Despite these and other measures, monetary crises continued to mount throughout the 1960s. In response to these crises, demands mounted for a fundamental reform of the international monetary system. In the ensuing monetary negotiations, as in trade negotiations, the Western powers divided into three positions. On one side were ranged the United States and Great Britain. On the other stood France. In the middle was West Germany, which attempted to reconcile the Common Market and the Atlantic powers.

Whereas the United States wanted a reform that would ensure the continued privileged position of the dollar, France under de Gaulle wanted a reform that would dethrone the dollar and thus would redistribute economic power in the West. This would allegedly be achieved if the world returned to what de Gaulle believed was the true measure of wealth and guarantor of political independence, namely, gold. A return to the gold standard would not only enhance the power of France, which had replenished its gold reserves, but the United States would have to expend real wealth in order to maintain and/or expand its hegemony. If other nations refused to accept any more dollars and demanded gold, the United States would be forced to bring its payments into balance and to liquidate its global economic and military position. In short, a shift from the dollar to gold as the world's reserve currency would mean a retrenchment of American power in Europe, Asia, and around the globe.

At the same time that the United States desired to maintain the privileged position of the dollar, the basic instability of the system was appreciated by all. An international monetary system and an expanding trade system that depended upon the deficits of the United States were prone to crisis. From the perspective of most countries, a return to gold was both politically and economically undesirable, however. In the late sixties, therefore, extensive IMF negotiations produced an "international money" called special drawing rights (SDRs).

The United States had desired the SDRs to relieve the pressure on the dollar while preserving its ultimate reserve role. France wanted nothing less than the reimposition of monetary restraints on the United States. Between the two of them stood West Germany and its desire to hold together the European and Atlantic powers. Due largely to German initiatives, a compromise solution was finally reached, which gave the Americans their SDRs in exchange for greater European voting power in the International Monetary Fund. Thus, while the IMF would have the power to "issue" SDRs as an international reserve on a limited scale, Europe (if it were united) could exercise a veto over American policy in the IMF.

In short, the internal structure and functioning of the IMF was reconstituted to reflect the redistribution of world economic and monetary power. The United States no longer ran the organization. Control over it was now shared by the European powers. Similarly, one can anticipate that the immense growth of Arab monetary balances will lead to a further internal transformation of the IMF. By one method or other, this redistribution of monetary power will be given an institutional form.

In the areas of trade and investment, the continuing redistribution of power among nation states will find a response in the nature and functioning of international economic organizations. In trade this has already begun to happen, as the United States and other industrial nations ponder the future of the GATT. Perhaps the German initiative at the Washington energy conference in calling for an international investigation of the oil multinationals presages what many have long advocated—a GATT for investment. If so, it too will reflect the changes that have taken place in the world's distribution of economic and industrial power.

Conclusion

In conclusion, what does this redistribution of world power imply for the future of the interdependent world economy? Today, the liberal world economy is challenged by powerful groups (especially organized labor) within the dominant economy; the dominant economy itself is in relative decline. With the decline of the dominant economic power, the world economy may be following the pattern of the latter part of the nineteenth century and of the 1930s and may be fragmenting into regional trading and monetary blocs. This would be prevented, of course, if the United States, as it is presently trying to do, were to reassert its waning hegemony over Western Europe, Japan, and the rest of the noncommunist world economy.

In the wake of the decline of American power and the erosion of the political base upon which the world economy has rested, the question arises whether the wisest policy for the United States is to attempt to reassert its dominance. May not this effort in the areas of trade, money, investment, and energy exacerbate the conflicts between the United States, Western Europe, and Japan? If so, a future that could be characterized increasingly by benign mercantilism could well be transformed into its more malevolent relative. If this were to happen, the United States and its allies would be the losers.

This admonition suggests that the United States should accept a greater regionalization of the world economy than it has been wont to accept in the past. It implies greater representation and voice for other nations and regional blocs in international economic organizations. While such a policy of retrenchment would no doubt harm the interests of American corporations and other sectors of the American ecnomy, the attempt to hold on to rather than adjust to the shifting balance of world power could be even more costly for the United States in the long run.

In a world economy composed of regional blocs and centers of power, economic bargaining and competition would predominate. Through the exercise of economic power and various trade-offs, each center of the world economy would seek to shift the costs and benefits of economic interdependence to its own advantage. Trade, monetary, and investment relations would be the consequence of negotiations as nation states and regional blocs sought to increase the benefits of interdependence and to decrease the costs. This in fact has been the direction of the evolution of the international economy, from a liberal to a negotiated system, since the rise of large and rival economic entities in the latter part of the nineteenth century.

Therefore, debate and policy planning today should not focus on economic independence or dependence but on the nature and consequences of economic interdependence. Economic interdependence may take many forms; it may affect the welfare of nations in very different ways. Some will emphasize security; others, efficiency, low rates of inflation, or full employment. The question of how these benefits and costs will be distributed is at the heart of the increasingly mercantilistic policies of nation states in the contemporary world.

Section II

Prolegomena to the choice
of an international monetary system

Richard N. Cooper

The international monetary system—the rules and conventions that govern financial relations between countries—is an important component of international relations. When monetary relations go well, other relations have a better chance of going well; when they go badly, other areas are likely to suffer too. Monetary relations have a pervasive influence on both domestic and international economic developments, and history is strewn with examples of monetary failure leading subsequently to economic and political upheaval. Recent years have seen considerable turmoil in international monetary relations, and a marked deterioration in relations between Europe, Japan, and America. Ideally, monetary relations should be inconspicuous, part of the background in a well-functioning system, taken for granted. Once they become visible and uncertain, something is wrong.

As a consequence of this recent turmoil, intense official discussions on the nature and the future of the monetary system were belatedly begun in late 1972, under the auspices of the International Monetary Fund (IMF). A year later, little real progress in these discussions could be recorded (official press releases to the contrary notwithstanding). De facto monetary relations between countries were on a radically different course from the official discussions.

Many intricate details attend consideration of alternative monetary arrangements, and the details are often vitally important. It is not possible, however, to discuss them all in an essay charged with covering a broad spectrum of possible monetary arrangements and the broad implications of alternative monetary arrangements for the world as a whole, for groups of particular countries, and for particular groups within countries.

This essay has a somewhat more limited purpose. It attempts to survey systematically various possible types of international monetary regimes, to identify criteria for choice between alternative monetary regimes, and to discover the

Richard N. Cooper is a professor of economics at Yale University in New Haven, Connecticut.

reasons for disagreement between nations and between groups within nations on the choice of an international monetary regime. It draws on recent monetary history and on current discussions of reform of the monetary system for illustrations, and tries to suggest why cost-benefit analysis, while an appropriate framework in principle, is in practice so difficult to execute in this area. If the essay carries any principal message, it is that sources of disagreement do not generally derive from divergent interests, but rather from diverse perspectives and hence different conjectures about the consequences of one regime as compared with another. In short, disagreement arises mainly from ignorance about the true effects, so that we must use reasoned conjecture rather than solid fact to guide our choices, and reasonable people may and do differ with respect to their conjectures. The essay concludes with some brief observations on the appropriate role of international organizations in the international monetary arena and on the broad directions I believe the international monetary system should take.

I define a *regime* as any particular set of rules or conventions governing monetary and financial relations between countries. *Regime* seems preferable to *system* or *order*, both of which are sometimes used in this context, since it encompasses arrangements that are neither orderly nor systematic. A monetary regime specifies which instruments of policy may be used and which targets of policy are regarded as legitimate, including of course the limiting cases in which there are no restrictions on either.[1] I propose here to outline a number of international monetary regimes in terms of their major features, and to offer some brief comments on their costs and benefits. Each regime has many variants, variants that may either aggravate or mitigate the disadvantages, so that the distinctions between them are not in fact as sharp as I sometimes make it appear. Moreover, each regime may operate in many different ways, and a given regime may either be resoundingly successful or totally stymied, depending on how the participants operate within it. Some regimes lack the technical requisites for success and are bound to fail; others, internally consistent, can work effectively in one political milieu but not in another. Students of international relations too often focus on the political milieu to the neglect of requirements of internal consistency and technical proficiency; economists are prone to the opposite error.

One possible regime would be to have no rules or conventions at all—to allow each country to do what it thinks best, without any form of coordination. This may be called a free-for-all regime, with the understanding that in international monetary affairs governments and central banks are principal actors, so that the term *free-for-all* refers primarily to their actions, not merely to those of private

---

[1] A particularly poignant example of the severe limits a given regime can impose on the use of instruments of policy, and of the psychological hold a regime of long standing can have on even well-informed observers, is the surprised anguish of Fabian socialist Sidney Webb when, in 1931, in the face of enormous unemployment, Britain abandoned the fixed price of gold and allowed the pound to float: "No one told us we could do this." (A. J. P. Taylor, *English History, 1914-1945* [New York: Oxford University Press, 1965] p. 297, cited in Fred Hirsch, *Money International* [Garden City, N.Y.: Doubleday, 1969], p. 4.)

transactors. In contrast, a regime of freely floating exchange rates and no controls on private international transactions, that is, a regime in which governments agree not to interfere either with transactions or with the foreign exchange market in any way, is definitely not a system without rules; indeed, it involves extraordinarily stringent proscriptions.

A free-for-all regime does not commend itself. It would allow large nations to try to exploit their power at the expense of smaller nations. It would give rise to attempts by individual nations to pursue objectives that were not consistent with one another (e.g., inconsistent aims with regard to a single exchange rate between two currencies), with resulting disorganization of markets. Even if things finally settled down, the pattern would very likely be far from optimal from the viewpoint of all the participants.

A well-analyzed sequence from the realm of trade policy that encompasses all three of these disadvantages illustrates the possibilities. A large nation attempts to exploit its monopolistic position at the expense of other nations by imposing an optimum tariff. Other things being equal, it can gain by imposition of a tariff, the appropriate size of which depends on the monopoly position of the country. But other things do not generally remain equal, for other countries can also gain through the imposition of tariffs. Such retaliation creates a new situation for the first country, which should then alter its tariff, perhaps by raising it, to exploit fully its monopoly position. And so the tariff war goes, creating much turmoil with trade during the process, until a point is reached at which no country can gain further through unilateral action. Furthermore, the resulting pattern of tariffs will almost certainly leave all countries worse off than they would have been if the first country had not attempted to exploit its advantage.[2] A regime that prohibits or limits tariff warfare would be mutually beneficial.

Similar examples can be found in the monetary realm. For instance, a general shortage of liquidity under a gold standard regime might lead various countries to devalue their currencies in terms of gold in order to improve their payments positions for the purpose of adding to their stocks of money. This behavior would lead to competitive depreciation all around, with an ultimate write-up in the value of gold in terms of all currencies and possibly some stimulation of new gold production, but only after a painful and acrimonious transition. It would be far better to agree together on a "uniform change in par values" (in the language of the Bretton Woods Agreement) of currencies against gold, thus avoiding the needless change in relative currency values and the disruptions to national economies that would obtain under the hypothesized circumstances. It would be better still to abandon reliance on a commodity in short supply and create, by agreement, some

---

[2] Harry G. Johnson has pointed out that in the final equilibrium it is possible for one country to be left better off than in the free trade situation; but both countries taken together will certainly be worse off, and I judge that in most circumstances each country taken separately would be left worse off. See his "Optimum Tariffs and Retaliation," in his *International Trade and Economic Growth: Studies in Pure Theory* (Cambridge, Mass.: Harvard University Press, 1967).

form of fiduciary asset, such as domestic paper money within economies and special drawing rights at the international level.

Moreover, a free-for-all regime ignores the vital point that money, including international money, is a social convention, a collective human contrivance of the highest order. One after another during the nineteenth and early twentieth centuries, nations evolved domestic monies and then endowed them with legal tender status. At the international level, some kind of international money has also evolved. First came the commodity monies, silver and gold, then the national monies, sterling and the dollar. All served better than nothing but all fell short of an optimal solution. International agreement is required to do better.

Types of international monetary regimes

Perceiving that some form of order is necessary does not determine *what* kind of order. Many are possible, indeed, too many to discuss comprehensively. I thus confine the following discussion to three broad features, or dimensions, of a monetary regime, and to various possible stopping points along each dimension. The choice of these particular dimensions among many is influenced by the fact that they are the most prominent in current discussions of reform of the monetary system. The dimensions are (1) the role of exchange rates, (2) the nature of the reserve asset(s), and (3) the degree of control of international capital movements.

These features can be viewed as varying along a continuum, but for purposes of discussion it is perhaps more useful to specify particular points in each of these dimensions. Thus table 1 sets out an array of possible monetary regimes, drawing one element from each of the columns. Logically there would be 45 regimes (5x3x3) on the basis of the elements in table 1, but *freely* floating exchange rates strictly would require no reserve asset, so that in fact only 39 different regimes are described there—still too many to discuss comfortably, even before allowing for the many variants of each.

The textbook gold standard, which still provides the historical basis for comparison in many discussions of the international monetary systems, is entry I.A.1. in table 1: fixed exchange rates (except for modest variation within the gold points), gold reserves, and full freedom of capital movements. The original Bretton Woods system is entry II.A.3. in table 1, although the requirement that capital movements be controlled was implicit rather than explicit in that agreement. During the 1950s and again since 1970, Canada adopted the system IV.C.1., that is, a regime of managed flexibility in exchange rates and reliance on the United States dollar as its principal reserve asset.

The last example illustrates the important point that not all countries need abide by the same conventions within a given international monetary regime. Thus the European Community countries have set themselves the objective of adopting I.D.1. (where D stands for the as yet undetermined new European reserve asset),

Table 1. Several possible international monetary regimes (choose one from each column)

Role of exchange rates in balance-of-payments adjustment	Reserve asset	Degree of market convertibility for capital movements
I. Fixed exchange rate	A. Gold	1. Full
II. Adjustable parities	B. SDRs*	2. Dual market
III. Gliding parities	C. US dollars and other national currencies	3. Controlled
IV. Managed float		
V. Free float		

*Refers to special drawing rights, first created in 1970 by the International Monetary Fund.

regardless of the practices that obtain in the rest of the world. Many small countries may prefer II.C.1. with respect to a "mother country" (e.g., the Sterling Area) even though large countries are on a different regime. But to function, the mixed international regime must still meet certain consistency requirements: the different components must be compatible with one another.

Just specifying a regime in these gross dimensions does not indicate how well it will work. That depends, among other things, on how countries behave *within* the rules and conventions of a particular regime, not merely on the choice of regime. This fact greatly complicates the choice of a regime, since how countries will behave once it is adopted cannot be forecast with certainty. However, some regimes do have technical weaknesses as compared with others. An adjustable peg regime with uncontrolled capital movements will evoke large movements of funds whenever a change in exchange rates is in prospect, for example, and a gold standard requires balance-of-payments adjustment to take place through variations in domestic employment. To point to these difficulties shifts the discussion from *possible* regimes to the desirability of alternative regimes.

Criteria for choosing a monetary regime

Choice between alternative regimes requires a specification of objectives, with relative weights to indicate which ones must govern when a conflict arises between them. It is the liberal Western tradition to place as the ultimate objective the well-being of individual members of society (rather than the power of the state, the wealth of the ruling autocracy, etc.). Individual well-being has both an economic dimension, taken in its broadest terms, and a security dimension, also taken in its broadest terms. The first involves the economic capacity of an individual to pursue his own aims, and the second involves his liberty to do so without unnecessary interference from the state or from other individuals.

At this high level of generalization, there is little dispute between major participating countries over objectives of the international monetary system or over any other set of conventions governing relations among nations or men. Disputes, rather, arise over the best way to obtain these objectives, over means rather than over ends. It is nonetheless useful to state the ultimate objectives from time to time, for it frequently happens that means become proximate ends, and in the pursuit of these proximate or intermediate objectives in ever greater technical detail, actors may lose sight of the ultimate objectives and even compromise them for the sake of achieving some instrumental objective. Restrictive balance-of-payments measures by all major nations during the 1960s illustrate the point all too vividly.

By what criteria should we judge an international monetary system, having in mind its ultimate purpose of improving the economic well-being and the security of mankind? Four come to mind: (1) economic efficiency, (2) its scope for accommodating local diversity in objectives, (3) its contribution to harmony in international relations beyond monetary relations, and (4) its ability to achieve a desired distribution of the gains, both between countries and within countries, that arise from one regime over another. Economists have tended to focus their attention on the first of these criteria, with some attention to the second and the fourth. They have also devoted considerable attention to the technical workability of the numerous variants of alternative regimes.

Economic efficiency concerns the effectiveness with which we use the world's limited natural and human resources to make possible the improvement of economic well-being. The single most frequently used measure is per capita national product, although economists recognize that the figures they actually use to represent this concept can be misleading if not appropriately interpreted. In the context of international monetary reform, economic efficiency has been considered under three broad categories: (1) macroeconomic management, or the degree to which the international monetary system facilities or impedes the full employment of resources and the attainment of price stability; (2) microeconomic efficiency in the use of resources, especially as it is influenced by exchange rates as prices that guide the allocation of resources; and (3) microeconomic efficiency in the use of money as a lubricant for efficient resource allocation. The last of these categories has received the least systematic attention (partly because it cannot now be handled by conventional economic theory) yet, as I discuss below, represents an important area of reservation about a regime of flexible exchange rates.

Controversy over the choice of a monetary regime

Simply stating the criteria by which alternative international monetary regimes should be judged is not the same as determining which one dominates the others, even if the criteria could be fully quantified. Controversy over the choice of an international monetary regime arises in five separately identifiable categories: (1) understandably different preferences over the different distributional implications, actual or perceived, of alternative regimes, (2) different weights attached to the various criteria when compromises must be made between them, (3) different national economic circumstances, even when preferences regarding the criteria are similar, (4) disagreement over the effectiveness of alternative means to achieve agreed ends, and (5) uncertainty about the trustworthiness of other countries with regard to their behavior within any chosen regime. Each of these sources of controversy deserves extended comment, but it is only possible to touch on them lightly here.

Distribution

Disagreements arising from different distributional implications are perhaps the most straightforward source of controversy, although even here there is much disagreement about what actually are the distributional implications of alternative regimes. Several kinds of gain arising from alternative monetary regimes can be identified.

First, there is the question of seigniorage. Traditionally, seigniorage is the gain that accrues to the mint arising from any difference between the commodity value of the materials going into a coin and the monetary value of the minted coin. Strictly speaking, seigniorage is the difference *net* of the costs of minting, and under a competitive regime of free access to the mint seigniorage will be zero. In the course of time, governments asserted a monopoly over the power to coin money and restricted coinage, and seigniorage—in effect, monopoly rents—accrued to national governments.

By analogy, we can ask what happens to the seigniorage, if any, arising from the use of a particular reserve asset under alternative international monetary regimes.[3] The seigniorage under a gold standard regime accrues to the owners of gold mines, in the form of greater intramarginal rents on the production of gold than would be the case in the absence of monetary demand for that metal. Not surprisingly, among nations the Union of South Africa and the Soviet Union have been the two most consistent supporters of returning to gold as the principal international reserve asset; these two countries are the first and second largest

---

[3] Herbert G. Grubel, "The Distribution of Seigniorage from International Liquidity Creation," and Harry G. Johnson, "A Note on Seigniorage and the Social Saving from Substituting Credit for Commodity Money," in R. A. Mundell and A. K. Swoboda, eds., *Monetary Problems of the International Economy* (Chicago: University of Chicago Press, 1969), pp. 269-82, 323-29.

producers of gold in the world, and stand to gain the most in seigniorage from reliance on gold.

The seigniorage question has recently been raised in connection with the use of national currencies, mainly the US dollar, as international reserve assets. It has been alleged that the United States gains substantial seigniorage by virtue of international use of the dollar, and that this particular distribution of the gains from a monetary system to the world's richest country is perverse.

The debate is too complicated to explore thoroughly here, but the presence of seigniorage in this case is not in fact self-evident. It is undeniably true that international use of the dollar is a convenience to the American traveler, who does not always have to buy foreign money because his dollars are widely acceptable. In that respect, international use of a national currency is like international use of a national language: it confers benefits of convenience on the residents of the home country. But that is not seigniorage. And in any case, utilitarian calculation would suggest that international use of both the dollar and of English as the money and the language of convenience is optimal, since Americans represent by far the largest group of world travelers. (Where, as in southern Europe, Germans or others are the dominant group, their currency is similarly usable.)

Foreign holdings of US currency notes represent an inconsequential portion of foreign dollar holdings. Most *official* dollar holdings, those that constitute international reserves, are held as interest-bearing securities, such as Treasury bills and certificates of deposit. To the extent that the markets in these securities are competitive, and in fact financial markets for large transactors are among the most competitive markets anywhere, no seigniorage exists, i.e., no special gains arise from a privilege of currency issue. The gains from financial specialization are of course present, but they are diffused widely to all users of the financial system, foreign as well as domestic, partly in the form of interest payments. It simply represents another form of international specialization, such as that associated with commodity trade, leading to mutual gain. This is true even when it is observed that overall the United States has borrowed short and lent long, earning the difference in yield between short-term and long-term assets. Under competitive conditions, this difference merely represents the costs and risks associated with financial intermediation; again no special gain arises, and again it represents just another form of mutually beneficial specialization.[4]

Finally, it has been suggested that the United States has reaped a special gain by "borrowing" extensively abroad (international use of the dollar, looked at from the other side of the transaction, represents borrowing by the United States from the rest of the world, just as a checking account represents borrowing by the bank

---

[4] These arguments require some qualification. If competitive banks are subject to non-interest-bearing reserve requirements, as they are in the United States, then the interest rate on their certificates of deposit will be correspondingly reduced, and some seigniorage does arise. Furthermore, from 1963 to 1974, the United States imposed taxes (the Interest Equalization Tax) and other restrictions on capital outflow from the United States, with the encouragement and approval of many European countries, and such restrictions on financial intermediation would again give rise to some seigniorage.

from the depositor) and then depreciating the real value of its extensive debt by generating inflation. Thus the United States can allegedly impose an inflation tax on the rest of the world. But this assertion presupposes that interest rates do not adjust fully to compensate for the expected rate of inflation. The fact that US Treasury bill rates carried an average yield of 7.02 percent in 1973 compared with only 3.95 percent in 1965, both boom years, is surely explainable largely by an expectation in the latter period of more rapid inflation. If the adjustment in interest rates is complete, the inflation tax can be levied only on non-interest-bearing dollar assets, of which central banks hold relatively little. A gain of course can arise during a period of *changing* expectations when interest rates have not adjusted fully to the new situation, and during such a period this version of the seigniorage argument has some merit. But otherwise it is not compelling.

The seigniorage question arises most explicitly in a regime with an international fiduciary asset such as the IMF's special drawing rights (SDRs), for they represent a form of costless money that carries purchasing power. How they are allocated seems to confer real benefits directly on the recipients, and the complaint has been voiced that allocation according to the present IMF quotas, over 70 percent of which are assigned to the industrial countries, represents an undesirable and even an unfair system of distribution. The issue has been brought forward in current discussions of international monetary reform as a proposal to link SDR creation and development assistance by shifting the allocation of new SDRs heavily toward the less developed countries. Indeed, the latter countries as a group have all but made some movement in this direction a precondition for their approval of any monetary reform. (Again the issues are too complicated to be discussed fully here.[5]) Many observers fear that such a link would undermine the success of the SDR as a reserve asset, and thereby nullify its principal purpose, which most countries, at least at the level of rhetoric, purport to share, for the sake of a secondary distributional objective. Moreover, even the issue of whether there is true seigniorage here at least requires some further analysis, since the IMF quota formula for allocating SDRs purports to measure, with admitted imperfection, the liquidity needs of different nations; to the extent that it does so accurately, allocation of SDRs results in no net transfer of resources over time, and thus in no real seigniorage (i.e., no greater consumption or investment than otherwise).

Seigniorage as a source of distributional gain has drawn the greatest attention from economists, although in practice it is perhaps the least important of the distributional effects. Several other distributional effects arising from a reserve currency standard based on some national currency (formerly the pound sterling, more recently the dollar) can be mentioned. First, it has been claimed that the dollar exchange standard gave the United States much wider scope to pursue its preferred domestic economic and other policies, even its foreign policies, than was available to other countries. The United States could simply cover any resultant

---

[5]For a convenient summary of the debate, with extensive references to the literature, see Y. S. Park, *The Link Between Special Drawing Rights and Development Finance,* Essays in International Finance, no. 100 (Princeton, N.J.: Princeton University, September 1973).

balance-of-payments deficit by issuing more IOUs, which other countries would add to their reserves, whereas other countries would be sharply limited by the amount of reserves they had available.

This contention, which has adherents in the United States as well as abroad, is interesting for its implicit acceptance of a regime of fixed exchange rates, or alternatively its implicit assumption that a depreciation of the currency of a country pursuing expansionist economic or high-spending foreign policies would be unacceptable to the public and would compel retrenchment of those policies. The latter assumption is exceedingly doubtful, at least as applied to the United States. Indeed, the improvement in international competitiveness resulting from devaluation of the dollar is more likely to be welcomed in our still mercantilistic world, and was indeed even hailed as a victory when the Nixon administration achieved a devaluation in late 1971. And the assumption of fixed exchange rates is of course unwarranted in today's world.

It is arguable that far from gaining greater room for maneuver for its policies, the United States in the 1960s was, if anything, inhibited in its policies by the reserve currency role of the dollar, for the government ruled out devaluation as an acceptable measure (partly on grounds that because of the reserve currency role of the dollar, an effective devaluation could not be achieved, since other countries would simply devalue their currencies as well) and instead took a number of steps to protect the dollar that actually ran against its domestic economic or foreign policy aims. This was true of such measures as maintaining relatively high interest rates during the 1960-61 recession, reducing and tying foreign aid, and restricting outflows of capital from the United States.[6] This much can be conceded to the point, however: the reserve currency country can never find itself in the financially desperate straits that other countries can, with no alternative but to cut expenditures abroad quickly and drastically; it always has automatic access to short-term credit.

A more subtle distributional effect arises under a reserve currency regime, with possibly powerful effects *inside* the reserve currency country as well as inside other countries. With foreign acquisitions of the dollar, the United States could run a larger balance-of-payments deficit (measured in conventional terms) than would otherwise be the case. Or to put the same point a different way, the dollar could command more units of foreign currency than would otherwise be the case. By the standards of any alternative regime, the dollar would be overvalued and other currencies would be undervalued. Overvaluation of the dollar means that American exports are less competitive (and imports more competitive) than they would otherwise be, and this in turn implies that factors of production heavily engaged in the foreign trade sector would experience a smaller demand for their services than

[6] As James Tobin, writing in 1964, put it: "if the financial ship has weathered the storm [of the dollar crisis], it has done so only by jettisoning much of the valuable cargo it was supposed to deliver." See his "Europe and the Dollar," *Review of Economics and Statistics* 46 (May 1964): 123.

would otherwise be the case. The factors used relatively intensively to produce nontraded goods and services, on the other hand, would be relatively better off, assuming that conditions of full employment are maintained. For an economy as complex as the American one, it is not entirely clear which segments of society constitute these different groups. But it is a fair conjecture that an overvaluation of the dollar would penalize American farmers and the skilled workers in American manufacturing. It is no coincidence that organized labor in the United States became more protectionist during the period of growing deficits (financed by foreign "lending" to the United States through the acquisition of dollars) around 1970, and that this protectionist sentiment diminished somewhat after two devaluations of the dollar.

By the same token, a reserve currency regime with fixed exchange rates permits other currencies to be undervalued and thus permits other countries to enjoy export-led growth.[7] For the same reason as that given above, those factors of production engaged relatively heavily in the foreign trade sector, both producing exports and producing goods that compete with imports, will benefit from this arrangement, while others will suffer. Little can be said in general about this, except that the owners of land from which primary products are produced in exporting countries will generally benefit from such undervaluation of their currency.

Yet another distributional effect arising under a reserve currency regime involves the special status it is thought to confer upon the reserve currency country. Considerations of status leave economists somewhat baffled, since it is not clear what tangible or intangible benefits flow from it, apart from the feeling of high status itself.[8] But there is little doubt that the reluctance of some Britons to shed the reserve currency role of sterling arose from status considerations as well as from the business they thought sterling brought to the City of London, and President de Gaulle and his followers both coveted and resented the special status they thought the international role of the dollar conferred upon the United States.[9]

Other regimes also have distributional effects, but it is not always clear what they are. For example, inflation tends to redistribute real income away from those whose incomes do not respond fully to the rate of inflation, so that any influence of an international monetary regime on the rate of world inflation would have distributional effects, at least in the medium run. But there is no general agreement on whether a regime of fixed or of flexible rates is likely to be more conducive to inflation, or even on whether the substitution of SDRs for gold as international reserve assets will in practice be more conducive to inflation. Thus little specific can be said about these effects.

[7] For an explanation of how this occurs, see Richard N. Cooper, "Dollar Deficits and Postwar Economic Growth," *Review of Economics and Statistics* 46 (May 1964): 155-59.
[8] But see the discussion of status in a related context in Frank and Baird's essay in this volume.
[9] With evident resentment, de Gaulle wrote of the "monumentally overprivileged position that the world had conceded to the American currency" (*Memoirs of Hope: Renewal and Endeavor* [New York: Simon & Shuster, 1971], p. 371).

Different preferences

The second broad source of controversy involves different preferences between objectives where some compromise is necessary, because articulation of the objectives leads to some conflict between them. The classic trade-off in economic analysis is between efficiency and distributional considerations.[10] Different parties may disagree on the desirable lines of compromise. Actually, this type of disagreement has been relatively absent in the debate on international reform. But it can be found lurking below the surface in several areas. Discussion of the link between SDRs and development assistance has so far given full preference to efficiency considerations in the generation of international liquidity. But some opponents of the link suspect that in a regime in which dependence on SDR creation as a source of development assistance has become heavy, it would be exceedingly difficult to sustain a negligible increase in SDRs even when that is what liquidity requirements dictate. That is, they worry that distributional considerations will dominate efficiency considerations when the hard choices have to be made. Similarly, in their pursuit of monetary unification, European countries have resisted the choice of a single, existing European currency as the basis for a future European currency, even though on balance that would probably be the most efficient thing to do, because of the special status and other alleged advantages this would confer on the country whose currency was chosen. The drive for a system of multiple currency intervention at the global level reflects a similar willingness to forgo efficiency for the sake of symmetry. Surprisingly, no country seems to oppose this change, perhaps because none yet appreciates fully the operational complexities it involves.

A second, and major, area in which different preferences are a source of disagreement concerns the extent to which the international monetary system should "discipline" national economies. Since the 1940s, under the dual influence of the Great Depression and the Keynesian revolution in economic theory, democratic governments have accepted the obligation to maintain national full employment. Ideally, nations would pursue macroeconomic policy so balanced that, apart from external influences, a reasonable degree of price stability would be achieved along with full employment. In fact, however, a number of countries have a history of excessive government spending, a practice now legitimized by the desire to maintain full employment. Some experts look to the international monetary system to provide the necessary restraint on expansionist economic policies, attempting to impose this discipline through a balance-of-payments constraint. Others find the achievement of balance between domestic macroeconomic objectives difficult enough without adding an additional constraint, and they desire, therefore, an

---

[10] In certain circumstances, these broad objectives need not conflict: social organization can be arranged to achieve maximum economic efficiency, and then the fruits of that efficiency can be distributed through lump-sum transfers to satisfy the desired distribution. But in practice lump-sum transfers are difficult to achieve, and other forms of redistribution almost inevitably impinge adversely on efficiency. Thus a trade-off arises and compromises must be made.

international monetary system that at a minimum is neutral as regards the domestic objectives of macroeconomic policy and preferably provides some help in reconciling them.

This difference of view, which to some extent arises from differences in national historical experience, underlies the present impasse in official discussions on the monetary system. It takes the technical form of different views on the exchange rate regime, on the degree of compulsion in the use of exchange rates, and on the severity of the requirements for settlement of deficits. I return to this issue below, and suggest an interpretation in terms of divergent views *within* countries, especially the continental European countries.

Different national circumstances

Yet another source of disagreement on the features of the monetary regime is the very different character of national economies, as distinguished from differences in preferences between objectives. A single individual averse to rain may behave quite differently in different objective environments, always carrying his umbrella in Norway and never carrying it in Egypt. Similarly, two countries with similar preferences among the overall objectives may elect different monetary regimes because of their different objective environments. A small, high-income country may be highly dependent on foreign trade for its welfare and hence be reluctant to sanction any measures that restrict trade. It may also be extremely open, so that it is sensitive to economic developments abroad and at the same time has little monetary-fiscal leverage over its own macroeconomic developments because of the high leakages abroad. Under these circumstances, the country is likely to oppose exchange rate flexibility and trade restrictions for balance-of-payments reasons (and perhaps also restrictions on capital movements, depending on its dependence either on foreign capital inflows or on earnings from its own foreign investments); it will favor a regime that imposes a moderate degree of discipline on its major trading partners so as to minimize imported inflation or depression. A large, relatively closed economy, in contrast, will desire to maintain the maximum freedom of domestic monetary management and thus will oppose a system that restrains its freedom on domestic economic policy; it will also be more receptive to the use of trade restrictions as a balance-of-payments measure, and more hospitable to flexible exchange rates.

The position of the small, open economy on exchange rate flexibility is governed in part by the perception that residents under a flexible rate regime, which exhibits a high degree of openness and has no controls on capital movements, may hold a high proportion of their money balances in foreign currencies (so as to stabilize the value of money balances in terms of commodities, a high proportion of which, by assumption, come from outside the country), thus denying the country both the seigniorage gains arising from the creation of domestic currency and the little freedom it may still retain to influence macroeconomic events through domestic monetary management. It is this consideration that leads to the notion of an *optimal* currency area, one that achieves the appropriate balance between the scale economies of a single monetary unit, on the one hand, and the seigniorage gains and advantages of national monetary management, on the other.[11]

A game-theoretic formulation

The above sources of disagreement among countries on the choice of a monetary regime can be characterized in game-theoretic terms by specifying a payoff matrix (the net rewards) to each country arising from alternative choices of regime. This construction represents a necessary step if a quantitative cost-benefit analysis is to be done for alternative monetary regimes. For simplicity, consider only two countries (A and B) choosing between two international monetary regimes (I and II). Suppose, in correspondence with the arguments put earlier about the disadvantages of a free-for-all regime, that both countries gain substantially by agreeing on a regime: *some* rules of behavior are better than none, and we suppose that no agreement leads to a free-for-all regime.[12] A hypothetical "payoff" to each of the countries under the four possible configurations of regime is shown in figure 1.

Figure 1. Payoffs to choice of regime

A \ B	I	II
I	5(B) 3(A)	0(B) 0(A)
II	0(B) 0(A)	3(B) 5(A)

Each box represents a choice of regime by each country. Thus the southeast box represents the choice of regime II by both countries. Each box contains two numbers, one representing the net gain (after allowance for disadvantages) to

---

[11] For an analytical summary of the discussion on optimal currency areas, see Herbert G. Grubel, "The Theory of Optimum Currency Areas," *Canadian Journal of Economics* 3 (May 1970): 318-24.

[12] This, of course, need not actually be the case. Countries may implicitly agree on certain conventions governing behavior even when they are unable to reach explicit agreement, thus avoiding the disadvantages of a complete free-for-all.

country A, and the other representing the net gain to country B. Thus, in the southeast box A gains 5 and B gains 3.[13]

As the payoff matrix is constructed, both countries gain by reaching agreement, whether the gain be subjective or objective. Country A clearly prefers that both countries agree on regime II, while B prefers that both countries agree on regime I. The differences in reward may arise from any of the three broad sources of disagreement discussed above—straight distribution of system gains, different preferences between objectives that are differentially served by the alternative regimes, and different environmental circumstances in the two countries. The first and third of these sources of difference may be commensurable (e.g., measurable by impact on GNP), while the second clearly is not. For this reason alone, it would be virtually impossible to construct such payoff matrices corresponding to any actual set of choices. Moreover, the payoff matrix would in any case have to be enlarged (1) to allow more regimes between which to choose (no conceptual problem), (2) to enlarge the number of countries choosing regimes (much more of a conceptual problem, especially when coalitions are possible),[14] (3) to allow for uncertainty in the payoffs (one source of which is considered below), and (4) to allow for divergent factions *within* countries, which may form coalitions across national boundaries.

Allowing for all these factors would impose formidable if not insurmountable difficulties for comprehensive analysis of the negotiations on international monetary reform. But, in fact, the discussions have not gotten to the point at which these are the serious obstacles to analysis. For there remains fundamental disagree-

[13] Several interpretations are possible for the numbers entered in the payoff matrix. If the gains are commensurable, they can be added together according to some common unit of measurement and compared. Net increase in GNP would be an example. It is clear from the discussion above, however, that not all the advantages and disadvantages of alternative monetary regimes can be expressed in commensurable units. Status and maneuverability of action would be examples. In that case, each country must weigh for itself the various advantages and disadvantages of each configuration according to some utility index, and the entries in figure 1 then represent a scaling for each country according to its own utility index. But in that case, the gains to A as perceived by A, while comparable with one another, are not comparable with the gains to B as perceived by B. Entries for B in the four boxes can be compared with one another, and those for A can be compared, but entries for B cannot be compared with entries for A. Indeed, it is quite possible that country B will perceive the gains to A differently from the way A perceives them, and vice versa. For example, on B's utility scale the entry for A in the southeast box might be 8 instead of 5. This kind of difference is especially likely if status is an important consideration for B.

The payoff matrix is also drawn showing no net gain for either country in the case of disagreement on regime. If the payoffs to each country are commensurable, the payoff need not be the same for both countries in cases of disagreement. For example, B might actually *lose* in comparison with A, so that the entries for B in the northeast and southwest boxes would be negative. B would then have a stronger incentive to reach agreement than would A. If the payoffs are not commensurable, then the possibility of loss is merely a matter of choice of scale for each country. The lowest entry for *each* country can be arbitrarily chosen to equal zero, and the other entries for that country are then scaled to it.

[14] For a brilliant exploratory treatment of many similar decision units confronting binary choices, see Thomas C. Schelling, "Hockey Helmets, Concealed Weapons, and Daylight Savings: A Study of Binary Choices with Externalities," *Journal of Conflict Resolution* 17 (September 1973): 381-427.

ment on the relationship between particular features of a monetary regime and the costs and/or benefits associated with it. Most of the technical work aims at narrowing the still substantial differences of view on what may be called the "technology" of international monetary relations, the relationship between means and ends. Thus, it is not possible to fill in even the subcomponents of a payoff matrix to the satisfaction of most observers. This represents yet a fourth category of controversy.

Disagreement over means-ends relationships

Even with similar objectives and similar circumstances, honest men may and do disagree over the best way to achieve those common objectives, especially when the relationships are as complex and indirect as they are in international monetary affairs. Based on their own training and experience, and in the face of frustratingly ambiguous evidence, accomplished technicians form their own judgment about what is the best way to do this or that. Sometimes technicians disagree among themselves. At least as often, however, they share a view that is at variance with "outsiders" who have taken a broader but less detailed look at the issue or with politicians who suspect, sometime justifiably, that technicians are really trying to influence objectives by pressing their views on a particular means-ends relationship. This last case develops not so much because technicians have ultimate objectives at sharp variance with those of society as because they have implicitly substituted in their own thinking proximate, instrumental objectives for the ultimate objectives, and thus lose sight of the latter when considering issues as broad as reform of the monetary system.

Several examples of divergent views over means-ends relationships can be cited, although they often comingle differences in objectives as well. The most fundamental difference of view in contemporary discussions on monetary reform concerns the extent to which there should be governmental controls on private economic transactions, especially capital movements between nations. By and large, the American government has taken a stance of extreme liberalism in this regard, and in this it has been joined by Germany. At the other extreme stands France, joined by a few of the smaller European countries. The French government holds that a high degree of control on international capital movements is necessary to protect national economies from capricious financial disturbance from abroad.

This difference of view stems from deeply rooted philosophical differences between the liberal Anglo-Saxon tradition and the tradition of centralized France, running from Colbert through Napoleon to the present day. To some extent it involves a difference in objectives, for the Americans place a higher value on economic freedom than do the French government and bureaucracy (though not higher than the French people, who have traditionally taken strong pride in their individualism, including their ability to thwart government directive). And to some degree it reflects a genuine difference of view, rooted in the traditions and experience of each area, concerning the best way to maximize economic well-being.

Anglo-Saxons have generally accepted the competitive model of Adam Smith, who showed that under certain circumstances private pursuit of gain results in the social good, and that most of the weaknesses of the economic system arise from government interference, often for the private gain of particular individuals or groups. French thought, steeped in syndicalism, has never been deeply moved by this model of economic behavior, and French policy has never (except briefly during the nineteenth century) attempted to put it into practice.

Not surprisingly, each country tends to extend its own proclivities to the international arena. The difference becomes operational in considering the degree of flexibility that should be accorded to exchange rates (greater flexibility implying greater trust in the ability of the market to produce an acceptable result) and in the degree of freedom that should be accorded to private international capital movements. The two issues interact, in that the urgency felt by France and several other governments to control capital movements increases with the flexibility allowed to exchange rates. These governments fear that capital movements will lead to an "inappropriate" exchange rate, i.e., one that will deprive the country of employment in the export industries, or that capital movements will lead to high variability in exchange rates, with capricious consequences for domestic output and employment. The Anglo-Saxon view, to employ an inadequate shorthand for a complex issue, denies that a properly functioning market will lead to these results, and observes that the international relocation of capital guided by profitability will generally raise incomes, that is, improve economic welfare, all around.

A second area of technical disagreement concerns the efficacy of changes in exchange rates in influencing trade and service flows between nations in the modern world. Some observers contend that the highly technological nature of contemporary trade greatly reduces the sensitivity of trade and investment flows to changes in currency values, and that even when such sensitivity is present, it takes such a long time to become manifest that changes in exchange rates cannot be relied upon to equilibrate international payments. Other observers reject this elasticity pessimism and argue that changes in exchange rates (whether the adjustable parity or more flexible versions) are so far superior economically to alternative modes of correcting payments imbalances—trade controls or deflation of domestic economies—that heavy reliance should be placed on this mode of correction.

The difficulty in casting discussions of international monetary reform into a quantitative cost-benefit framework at the present time is specifically illustrated by the controversy over the merits of a regime of flexible exchange rates (free float, no reserve asset required, full convertibility for capital movements—V.1. in table 1). Conventional economic theory suggests that a system of freely flexible rates would be highly desirable, compared with alternatives, essentially on the grounds that under competitive conditions economic efficiency is best achieved by allowing prices, including the exchange rate, to respond to market forces. A regime of flexible exchange rates is quite consistent with the active use of macroeconomic measures to assure full employment, and it provides maximum freedom to economic transactors. Thus it would seem to dominate all alternative regimes.

This conventional view of flexible exchange rates is under challenge, although it has not yet been challenged decisively either on the theoretical or on the empirical plane. The theoretical objections that have been raised to a regime of flexible exchange rates indicate the range and complexity of argument about this particular regime, and hence implicitly about other regimes.

It is contended, first, that a regime of flexible exchange rates is subject to abuse by governments, that they will be tempted to engage in competitive depreciation in order to generate domestic employment by exporting their unemployment to other countries. Brief experience with flexible exchange rates during the 1930s supports this fear.[15] The counterargument is that: (1) governments now have more effective instruments for influencing aggregate demand than they did in the 1930s, so that they do not have to engage in competitive depreciation; (2) competitive depreciation is a game two (or more) can try to play, and if all attempt it, none will succeed; (3) the absurdity of the above situation will quickly become apparent, and nations will cease to engage in fruitless and absurd activity; and (4) concern with competitive depreciation is a thing of the past, the problem of the present and future is world inflation, and this will lead to greater domestic opposition to currency depreciation.

Second, it is contended that a system of flexible rates will reduce the balance-of-payments discipline on national governments and thereby remove a major restraint on inflationary spending.[16] The counterargument is that inflationary policies will quickly lead to a depreciation of the currency, and that this will become evident to the public more quickly than does inflationary spending that has as its initial impact the depletion of foreign exchange reserves. Depreciation raises prices, whereas use of reserves in the short run benefits the public by temporarily permitting a rise in consumption. Thus political pressures against inflationary policies are likely to be greater, not less, under a regime of flexible exchange rates. Moreover, it is a will-of-the-wisp to suppose that a system of fixed exchange rates really imposes discipline on governments in the modern world, since they know they can devalue if it ultimately proves necessary.

It is contended, third, that flexible exchange rates do not really achieve their objective of balancing international payments, because they rely for their effect on money illusion on the part of the public, and money illusion is rapidly disappearing as publics become more sophisticated about functioning in an inflationary environment.[17] The counterargument is that while money illusion helps, the effects of changes in exchange rates are not totally vitiated in the absence of

---

[15] The standard source is League of Nations [Ragnar Nurkse], *International Currency Experience* (New York: League of Nations, 1944).

[16] Henry Wallich, "Why Fixed Rates?," Committee for Economic Development, New York, 1973. (Mimeographed.)

[17] Robert A. Mundell, "Monetary Relations between Europe and America," in Charles P. Kindleberger and A. Shonfield, eds., *North American and Western European Economic Policies* (London: Macmillan & Co., 1971; New York: St. Martin's Press, 1971).

money illusion, and that in any case money illusion in all its possible forms has not yet disappeared and is not likely to.

Fourth, it is contended that money is not neutral in the economic system, as the conventional theory underlying flexible exchange rates supposes, and that too much fluctuation in the price of one money in terms of another will lead to real losses in economic efficiency that have not been reckoned in the calculation.[18] The counterargument is that this point is conjectural, and that at worst the efficiency losses will be small compared with those of alternative regimes.

It is contended, fifth, that currency speculation will not always be stabilizing, that destabilizing currency speculation may disrupt real economic activities and thereby impose efficiency losses, and that some destabilizing speculation may nonetheless become self-justifying because of exchange rate-induced changes in money wages and other factor prices.[19] The modern wage-standard economy has no natural or equilibrium price level, and arbitrary movements in the exchange rate may set off a round of disruptive cost inflation. The counterargument is that destabilizing speculation is a bugaboo and that private speculation is likely to lead the exchange rate far closer to its equilibrium than is official intervention.

Sixth, it is contended that a system of flexible exchange rates fails to promote international cooperation; by conferring greater autonomy on national governments, it removes a pressure for cooperation and introduces a divisive element into international relations. The counterargument is: What alternative is less divisive? Moreover, actually operating a system of flexible exchange rates will require a high degree of coordination of the exchange market intervention that will inevitably take place, and therefore may actually foster international cooperation.

Just to enumerate these points conveys some sense of the continuing debate— and its inconclusiveness. Until the costs of a regime of flexible exchange rates are clear, it is impossible to compare it definitively with other regimes. And the technical controversy over the costs and benefits of other regimes is only slightly less acerbic and inconclusive. We are still a long way from reaching professional— and hence official—agreement on the entries in the payoff matrix.

Lack of trust in other countries

A final source of disagreement over alternative monetary regimes concerns the varying extent to which their smooth functioning depends on relations of trust among countries, and the presence or absence of such trust. In particular, a regime

[18] Charles P. Kindleberger, "The Case for Fixed Exchange Rates, 1969," in *The International Adjustment Mechanism* (Boston: Federal Reserve Bank of Boston, 1970); and Arthur Laffer, "Two Arguments for Fixed Rates," in Harry G. Johnson and A. Swoboda, eds., *The Economics of Common Currencies* (London: Allen & Unwin, 1973), pp. 25-34.

[19] Richard N. Cooper, *The Economics of Interdependence* (New York: McGraw-Hill, 1968), chapter 9; and Cooper, "Issues in the Balance of Payments Adjustment Process," Committee for Economic Development, New York, 1973 (mimeographed).

may be attractive to one country if other countries behave within the regime in certain ways but not if they behave in other ways. Can they be counted upon to behave in the desired ways? The resolution of this uncertainty depends upon the commitments other countries make, their past record in honoring such commitments, the extent to which failure to honor commitments automatically carries penalties, the "hostages" the first country holds over the other countries both inside and outside the monetary arena, the general feeling of friendship and goodwill other countries have toward the first country, and a host of other factors.

The problem can be posed in terms of the type of payoff matrix introduced above. Suppose that the choice of regime I, instead of giving rise to a certain payoff to each country as shown in figure 1, produces benefits that depend on the particular policies adopted by each country within the framework of regime I. The payoff matrix thus might look like that shown in figure 2, where each country is assumed to be able to choose between two policies, P_1 and P_2, and the outcome for each country depends upon the choice of each. For simplicity, assume that regime II yields the certain payoff (5,3) shown in figure 1. The payoff structure shown in figure 2 is that of the classical prisoner's dilemma. The joint-maximizing policy for both countries is P_2, but if either country chooses P_2, the other can do still better by choosing P_1. Unless there is a high degree of mutual trust between the countries, each country will end up choosing P_1, the loss-minimizing policy. But if that is the case, it would have been better for both to choose regime II in preference to regime I, for on the assumption in this essay, both countries would be better off than they are in the northwest corner of regime I. Without mutual trust, both countries would prefer regime II; with mutual trust, they would prefer regime I.

Figure 2. Contingent payoffs in regime I: symmetric case

The payoff matrix is symmetric in figure 2, but of course in general it will not be. Thus the payoffs might have the asymmetry shown in figure 3, whereby in regime I country B loses substantially if country A chooses the first policy, P_1, but A loses only slightly if B chooses P_1 when A has chosen P_2. Under these circumstances, B's trust in A must be very high for it to prefer regime I, whereas A will always prefer regime I over regime II, in contrast to the case in figure 2 in which mutual distrust would lead to a stable choice of regime II by both countries.

Figure 3. Contingent payoffs in regime I: asymmetric case

A \ B	P_1	P_2
P_1	2(B) 2(A)	0(B) 13(A)
P_2	5(B) 9(A)	10(B) 10(A)

Under these kinds of circumstances, in which there is high reward for cooperation and mutual confidence but in which some distrust lingers, attempts may be made to redefine the regime, for example by ruling out P_1 as a legitimate instrument of policy in figure 2, or by ruling it out for A in figure 3 but not necessarily for B. Exemptions of less developed countries from some of the General Agreement on Tariffs and Trade (GATT) trading rules can be interpreted in this light: the damage that the less developed countries can inflict on others is negligible, while the industrial countries can inflict considerable damage on them, and on one another, through use of restrictive trade actions. Where trust is not complete, some form of international organization may be helpful to police the rules and supervise the imposition of penalties for violation of the rules. Both the GATT and the International Monetary Fund contain these features.

In the context of monetary reform, a functioning dollar standard has many positive aspects from many points of view, *provided* that the United States manages its domestic economy in such a way that it exerts a stabilizing influence on the rest of the world economy, e.g., provided that it does not inflate excessively, as it did in the late sixties.[20] But as with country A in figure 3, the United States has some

[20] R. I. McKinnon, *Private and Official International Money: The Case for the Dollar*, Essays in International Finance, no. 74 (Princeton, N.J.: Princeton University, April 1969); also Mundell.

incentive to inflate, since during the period in which expectations have not yet adjusted fully to the new situation under a regime in which dollars are extensively used as international reserves, it can in effect borrow from the rest of the world at subsidized interest rates; it imposes an inflation tax on outstanding dollar holdings. Loss of confidence in American macroeconomic management is one of the major sources (but not the only source) of dissatisfaction with the international monetary system as it had evolved by the early 1970s.

To sum up, the costs and benefits of international monetary reform must be decomposed in a number of ways: between countries, between divergent groups within countries, according to differences in preferences and in objective circumstances. Even then substantial uncertainty remains in the payoffs, for the analytical relationships between the technical features of each monetary regime and the attainment of objectives are only imperfectly understood, and there is the further uncertainty of how participating nations will actually behave within any given monetary regime. It would be nice if we could write down payoff matrices for alternative monetary regimes of the types shown in figures 1, 2, 3, suitably complicated to allow for the many relevant facets of the problem. But in the present state of knowledge, it simply cannot be done.[21]

The high degree of ignorance and uncertainty regarding the payoffs from alternative regimes has two consequences for discussions on international monetary reform. First, advocates of particular regimes may "fudge" the alleged payoffs to make them seem as believably attractive as possible to all parties, which is standard procedure in any advocacy process. Second, many parties simply do not know where their real interests lie; thus they pursue aggressively those few dimensions of the problem where they see their interests clearly to the neglect of what in fact may be far more important aspects of the problem, or they adopt a bargaining stance in the monetary area that may serve them well in bargaining with the same countries on quite different issues. A timely and graceful concession in the monetary arena, a concession that may in fact benefit the country making it, may be rewarded with a counterconcession by other countries in other areas of negotiation. There seems little doubt that the positions of France in international monetary discussions of the mid-sixties and of the less developed countries in the early 1970s were influenced by these considerations, for the positions they took on monetary questions were surely not in their national interests in the monetary arena alone.

---

[21] Bold and interesting attempts for the United States have been made by Robert Z. Aliber, *Choices for the Dollar* (Washington, D.C.: National Planning Association, 1971), and C. Fred Bergsten, *The Dilemmas of the Dollar: The Economics and Politics of United States International Monetary Policy* (New York: Council on Foreign Relations, forthcoming 1975). A more formal attempt at one component of the payoff is in K. Hamada, "Alternative Exchange-Rate Systems and the Interdependence of Monetary Policies," in Robert Z. Aliber, ed., *National Monetary Policy and the International Financial System* (Chicago: University of Chicago Press, 1974).

A brief history of monetary regimes[22]

The monetary regime reflected in the Bretton Woods Agreement of 1944 was a reaction to but also reflected deeply what had gone before it: the gold standard as it was understood; and the monetary chaos that prevailed on those occasions, immediately following the First World War and again in the Great Depression, in which the gold standard broke down.

The principal feature of the gold standard that made it unattractive to all countries following the Great Depression was that strict adherence to its canons required the domestic economy to be governed by balance-of-payments considerations, regardless of how inflationary or deflationary that might be. A secondary objection was that reliance on new gold production (minus private demand) for additions to international reserves left such additions to the caprice of technological change, new discoveries or exhaustion of mines, variations in private gold hoarding, and other irrelevant developments, which were at best inconvenient and at worst could work real hardship on the world economy. International discussion of these difficulties began in the nineteenth century, barely after the gold standard had become established, and resulted in international discussions in 1922 to economize on the use of gold by concentrating it in the hands of central banks and gradually replacing public circulation of gold money with fiduciary money.

The Bretton Woods Agreement asserted the primacy of domestic economic policy aimed at the maintenance of full employment and at the same time established the responsibility of each nation to the community of nations in the realm of international financial policy—a reaction to the self-serving, defensive, and ultimately destructive free-for-all of the 1930s. Domestic economic policies were to be protected from the strictures of the balance of payments through a double screen: *temporary* imbalances were to be financed, if necessary by drawing on lines of credit at a newly established lending institution, the International Monetary Fund (IMF); and *fundamental* imbalances were to be corrected by an alteration in the country's exchange rate. Responsibility to the community of nations was to be assured through a new set of agreed rules, policed by the IMF, that among other things (1) required each country to establish a fixed value (par value) for its currency, (2) forbade restrictions on payments for goods and services, and (3) required international approval of any change in an exchange rate that ultimately had to be made to correct a fundamental disequilibrium in the balance of payments.

In formulating the above regime, the British and American architects had to reach some balance between liberty to pursue domestic economic objectives and license to run payments deficits at the expense of the rest of the world. The final

[22] Some interpretations of postwar international monetary history can be found in Stephen D. Cohen, *International Monetary Reform, 1964-69: The Political Dimension* (New York: Praeger, 1970); Richard N. Cooper, *The Economics of Interdependence,* chapter 2; Keith Horsefield and others, *The International Monetary Fund 1945-1965,* 3 vols. (Washington, D.C.: IMF, 1969); Fritz Machlup, *Remaking the International Monetary System* (Baltimore, Md.: The Johns Hopkins Press, 1968); Bergsten, *The Dilemmas of the Dollar,* chapters 2-3.

agreement was an unsatisfactory compromise between an earlier American plan to involve the IMF in closer scrutiny and even direction of each nation's domestic and exchange rate policies and a British plan to permit large-scale borrowing if necessary but which was subject to increasing penalties. The resulting IMF had too little authority for the first and too little lending capacity for the second. Thus the Bretton Woods regime could not fulfill its assignment. Moreover, the distinction between temporary and fundamental imbalance proved less sharp in practice than it was in theory, so that countries procrastinated in changing their exchange rates. When changes finally did come, their need was clear, and they were large, providing an opportunity for large profits from private speculation on a change in the exchange rate. As the mobility of capital increased over time, this last feature developed into a fatal flaw in the Bretton Woods conception. To work, the agreement implicitly required effective control of international capital movements, something that cannot be assured.

A second weakness of the system was its failure to provide in any realistic way for steady increases in international reserves, since the mechanism for this implied by the system would have called for steady increases in the price of gold, which involved both political and conceptual difficulties.

The consequence of these two weaknesses was that the regime that actually functioned during the 1950s and 1960s was rather different from the Bretton Woods system, even though the latter was formally in force. After the major devaluations of 1949, changes in exchange rates by major countries were virtually unknown until the late 1960s. This was not because imbalances in payments did not arise. Rather, it was because the alteration of a par value was fraught with both political and economic risks. Thus, alternative mechanisms were found—adjustments in domestic economic policy, and the introduction or removal of restrictions on foreign trade and other foreign transactions—both of which were sharply out of keeping with the origins and the stated objectives of the Bretton Woods Agreement. The potential pain of these measures for many countries was relieved by the undervaluation of their currencies relative to the US dollar, so that balance could be maintained during the fifties through gradual removal of the postwar trade restrictions, and the surpluses of the sixties (the counterpart of the US deficit) could be ignored so long as they remained moderate.[23]

Similarly, the problem of augmenting international liquidity was "solved" through a process whereby countries added US dollars, earned through balance-of-payments surpluses, to their international reserves, a development for which there was no real place in the Bretton Woods system. This emergence of a dollar exchange standard was fraught with difficulties of its own, however, and proved to be only modestly more durable than the Bretton Woods system. The use of dollars as international reserves had two consequences: it permitted the United States to run deficits by borrowing from other countries to the extent of their buildup of dollar

[23] Richard N. Cooper, "Dollar Deficits and Postwar Economic Growth," *Review of Economics and Statistics* 46 (May 1964): 155-59.

reserves; and it gradually undermined the assumption that led to a willing acquisition of dollars in the first place, viz., that the dollar was as good as gold because it was convertible into gold, the primary reserve asset of the Bretton Woods system. As the outflow of dollars associated with United States direct investment abroad and then with the war in Vietnam grew steadily, foreign restlessness at the first consequence grew correspondingly. And as the total volume of foreign-held dollars grew, the credibility of their convertibility into gold diminished, until the inevitable inconvertibility was made formal in August 1971.

Thus the Bretton Woods system had an imperfect balance-of-payments adjustment mechanism and an imperfect method for satisfying world liquidity needs. Both deficiencies were filled pragmatically through unsystematic adaptation, but the resulting regime was also unsatisfactory. Dissatisfaction mounted rapidly when in the late 1960s what had been moderate US payments deficits threatened to become, and then in 1970 actually became, insupportably large. Major countries began to adjust their exchange rates as called for by the Bretton Woods system, and this proved to be highly disruptive of financial and foreign exchange markets, as well as to general confidence in the smooth functioning of the international monetary system and the capacity of governments to manage international financial matters successfully. Finally, governments abandoned any attempt to maintain fixed exchange rates, and in March 1973 (earlier for Canada and Britain) they allowed their currencies to float in exchange markets, several European countries cooperating sufficiently so that their currencies would float together.

It is fair to say that no government willed this result, although some found it less inconvenient than others. It resulted from lack of adequate foresight among governments regarding important trends in international finance and from an inability to agree on corrective measures.

Governments perceived the difficulties of the regime regarding international liquidity earlier than they saw the difficulties regarding the adjustment mechanism. After prolonged and laborious negotiation, they propounded a solution to the international liquidity problem involving special drawing rights (SDRs), which were created to relieve both gold and dollar of the burden of providing future international liquidity. The solution was in principle an adequate one, but it did not deal with the other weaknesses in either the Bretton Woods or the dollar exchange regimes.

Disaffection with the evolving international monetary system was expressed in several ways. Several European (and Latin American) countries resented what they considered to be Anglo-Saxon dominance of the International Monetary Fund. Britain and the United States together had over 50 percent of the original IMF votes, under a system of weighted voting reflecting their relative dominance of the world economy immediately before and after the Second World War; their shares diminished with the passage of time but remained large. When special arrangements to augment the resources of the IMF were established in 1961, at continental European insistence they were governed outside the IMF by the newly established Group of Ten, where the proportionate weight of continental European countries was higher. And when SDRs were established in 1969, Europeans insisted on a further shift in decision-making authority, which gave them an effective veto over all major SDR decisions (if they acted together).

Second, Gaullist France ostentatiously adopted a policy in 1964 of converting all the dollars it acquired, and previously had been willing to hold as dollars, into gold. This move was partly motivated by broader political considerations aimed at reducing general United States influence in Europe, but it was also partly motivated out of a genuine concern with the emerging weaknesses of the dollar exchange standard and an attempt to restore the original conception of the Bretton Woods system. It was, indeed, on these latter grounds that the French moves received some applause from others who did not share de Gaulle's political motivations.

Murmurs of dissatisfaction abroad became a chorus with the marked deterioration of the US trade balance in 1968 and 1969, which was generated directly and indirectly by the Vietnam War, by the masking of this deterioration in 1969 and early 1970 by very tight money in the United States, transmitted unwelcomely to European and other countries, and by the huge US payments deficits of late 1970 and of 1971. Official dissatisfaction with the evolving state of affairs grew rapidly, but agreement on a particular alternative arrangement, or even on what possible alternative arrangements there were, remained elusive. In September 1972 the Committee of Twenty, drawn from the membership of the IMF, was finally established to examine possible lines of reform and to make proposals.

Discussions by the Committee of Twenty

Work through the end of 1973 by the Committee of Twenty succeeded in clarifying the broad range of issues that required improvement and also in revealing how fundamental are the disagreements on fundamental issues. It is not possible here to dissect in detail the issues that have been considered by the Committee of Twenty, the various national positions on each of them, and the possible reasons for these divergent positions. The fundamental differences of view underlying disagreement on what seem to be mere technical details have already been discussed earlier in this essay. They revolve around the degree of autonomy countries should be permitted in pursuit of domestic economic policy, the efficacy and desirability of relying principally on exchange rates for balance-of-payments adjustment, the future role of the US dollar in the international monetary system and its relationship to freedom of action by the United States, and the possible use of the international monetary regime for the direct provision of aid to poor countries.

A number of European countries want the international monetary regime to provide a bulwark against inflation by imposing discipline on the spending and monetary policies of national governments. This is partly to correct what they perceive to be the abuses of the dollar exchange standard, under which there was little restraint on US policies, especially after gold convertibility of the dollar became tenuous. But it is partly also, I believe, to provide an external source of support (the international financial community and the international rules of the game) to domestic financial officials in their continuing struggle with pressures at home which they view as excessively expansionist. Thus, to an important extent, the international monetary negotiations, whose participants are drawn heavily from relatively conservative financial communities within each country, are being used as a piece in a competition between those urging restraint and those urging expansion within each of several important countries. To the extent that the members of the financial group can succeed in implanting *their* preferences (e.g., regarding the trade-off between inflation and unemployment) in the rules of the international monetary regime, they strengthen their hand later in the domestic debate by being able to invoke on their behalf the need to adhere to the international rules and the need to preserve harmony with other countries, considerations that rightly carry weight in any domestic debate over policy. Viewed in this way, it is a mistake to conceive the debate over international monetary reform entirely in terms of opposition of one national position to another.

The United States has taken the position that balance-of-payments adjustment should be prompt, symmetrical as between countries in deficit and surplus, relatively obligatory, and (reading between the lines) achieved if necessary, and often preferably, through changes in exchange rates. The focus on external measures (such as the exchange rate) to correct payments imbalances takes the pressure off adjustment of domestic demand, desired by some Europeans. The insistence on obligatory adjustment (backed by sanctions) is designed to deny the option to countries in surplus of simply deferring action and allowing their surpluses to continue, which the United States fears would be the case if the more discretionary, judgmental, and nonobligatory approach favored by the Europeans were adopted. Thus, in terms of the earlier discussion of distrust, the United States is fearful that under the regime favored by the Europeans, surplus countries (cast in the role of country A in figure 2) will elect policy P_1, no action, when the time comes for decisions, even though at the present time they verbally accept the principle that surplus countries should also take adjustment measures, P_2. The United States would like to specify the regime so as to exclude the policy of no action by surplus countries.

An analogous distrust exists on the question of settlement of balance-of-payments deficits. The United States agrees that convertibility of the dollar into some reserve asset (presumably SDRs) should be restored as a part of overall monetary reform. But some Europeans would like to go further and require that the United States settle *all* of its payments deficits in reserve assets other than the dollar, whereas the United States would have convertibility take place only at the request of the countries acquiring dollars. This would leave open the possibility, Europeans fear, that the United States would pressure countries into holding more dollars than they really desire, thereby restoring the US capacity to finance its deficits by issuing its own currency. A regime with obligatory settlement in nondollar assets would deny this possibility to the United States.

For its part, the United States points to the need of a well-functioning monetary regime for elasticity in reserve creation, which would be provided by the continued use of dollars not converted into SDRs. But the United States has supported a particular solution (among many possible solutions) to this legitimate problem that inevitably gives rise to suspicion and distrust at unexpressed US motives.

During the first year and a half of discussion in the Committee of Twenty, the eight representatives from less developed countries acted more or less as a group, having coordinated their positions ahead of time (as did the European representatives, though they broke rank more often). They strongly advocated a link between SDR creation and development assistance for understandable reasons, and in a form that had the least possible restraint on use of the funds. This form of the link was not in the interests of such major developing countries as India, Indonesia, Pakistan, and Bangladesh, which would stand to gain from channeling resources through the international lending agencies, but was necessary to maintain cohesion among the group. On other issues, such as the adjustment process, representatives of less developed countries have taken some surprising positions not obviously in their economic interests. For example, they have given strong support to restoration of a system of fixed and infrequently changed exchange rates. This was the global adjustment mechanism we had previously, and it resulted in tied aid, reduced aid, controls on capital movements, and eventually even restrictions on travel and imports, not to mention policy-induced economic recessions in some countries—all measures that have damaged the economies of developing countries.

An explanation for the position of these countries, if it is rational, must go outside the arena of economics.[24] If these countries have an economic interest in maintaining some relatively fixed currency relationship with their major trading partners (rather than let their own currencies float freely), as many of them do, then a regime involving a high degree of flexibility in exchange rates between leading currencies (even if it falls short of floating exchange rates) will compel developing countries to choose one of several currencies to which to tie their own. This choice, it may be feared, will not be devoid of political implications, even if only symbolic ones, for it smacks of the reestablishment of spheres of influence and neo-colonialism. Thus they would prefer a world in which this choice can be avoided by having all the leading currencies tied to one another in a relatively fixed relationship. They then go on to attempt to safeguard the economic position of developing countries in such a regime by asserting that the regime should give special consideration to the problems of developing countries, both as regards application of the rules directly to those countries (e.g., they can float their own currencies if that seems the best thing to do) and as regards exemption from the more harmful effects of any adjustment measures (e.g., controls on capital outflows or restrictions on imports) that industrial countries feel compelled to adopt. They cannot, of course, be exempt from the deleterious effects on their exports of recessions in industrial

---

[24] See also the views on this issue of Carlos Diaz-Alejandro in this volume.

countries induced by balance-of-payments problems. But this concern may be muted at the present time of world inflation.

Finally, the position of less developed countries on balance-of-payments adjustment may be subject to similar influences noted above for the European countries: financial officials desire the sanction of the international regime in dealing with their own more expansionist colleagues at home. But if that is the case, the possibility of their exemption from the rules should be played down.

General observations

A clear-cut cost-benefit analysis from the viewpoint of particular nations or groups within nations is not possible for alternative monetary regimes, given our present uncertain state of knowledge about the role of money, about the effects of changes in exchange rates on expectations and on economic behavior, and about the influence of international liquidity on national policymakers. Useful observations can, however, be made about the prospects of failure of certain international monetary regimes in terms of broad, generally agreed objectives.

Some possible regimes, such as the gold standard, can readily be rejected. Others that probably ought to be rejected still command attention, however, and the grounds for attention are to be found less in a clear perception of national or sectional interest by the proponents than in a muddled and partial appreciation of the capacity of these regimes to attain the generally agreed objectives. Just as agreement on international measures of public health was not finally achieved until the technical nature of the source and transmission of diseases was fully understood, after which controversy virtually ceased, so full agreement in the monetary area is not likely to be achieved until we have much more knowledge about the technical economic relationships involved. Even after that point controversy will remain, for the objectives and national interests in the monetary arena are far more complex than was true for public health.[25] But these differences are not yet the principal obstacles to agreement.

Two further observations can be made. First, an international monetary regime, like law, should not be changed frequently. Change creates transitional uncertainty and also reopens former political compromises, even when they work satisfactorily. Expectations and economic values become keyed to a particular regime, and changes in it, or even the prospect of changes, can prove highly disruptive of normal economic intercourse. One of the confusions of 1973 was that the old regime was clearly breaking up but no new regime was yet agreed. Currencies floated in the meantime, and some of the uncertainties associated with a change in regime were erroneously attributed to the flexibility of exchange rates.

---

[25] John F. Kennedy feared that the gold issue could be successfully used against him by political opponents, and this view led to his conservative approach to international financial questions. See Theodore C. Sorensen, *Kennedy* (New York: Harper and Row, 1965), pp. 405-8.

Moreover, it is difficult to alter one part of a regime without reopening discussion on many other parts, questions which were often settled earlier through agonizing negotiation. During the mid-1960s reform of the monetary system focused rather narrowly on the problem of international liquidity, but even then a condition for agreement was a host of amendments to the Bretton Woods Agreement, mainly aimed at altering the process of decision making (with the effect of giving greater weight to continental European views without the corresponding increase in quotas, which would have been the normal and appropriate way to achieve such reweighting under the original agreement) and at altering several other features that were thought to involve status. Reform of the process for generating international liquidity proved to be insufficient (as a number of analysts warned at the time), but when other dimensions of the monetary regime were opened for revision, the occasion was also taken to reopen the provision of international liquidity, especially the formula for SDR distribution.

Second, a word should be said about the relationship of the international monetary system to domestic economic policy. International finance is an arcane subject and normally attracts little attention. The public ordinarily does not have strong feelings about it, so long as things go well, although a possible exception resides in the residual public attachment to gold as a monetary metal, an attachment that is much stronger in some countries than in others and that acts as a constraint on governmental freedom of action. The public, at least in the United States, is likely to accept any reasonable sounding proposal, unlike in the area of foreign trade policy where much more is at stake for particularistic interests.

On the other hand, precisely because the public does not perceive much stake in the international monetary system, it will not be willing to make many sacrifices to preserve it once its dictates conflict sharply with the requirements of domestic economic policy. The same is true in most other major countries. During the 1950s and 1960s, it is true, the British government imposed considerable hardships on the British public for the sake of preserving the international position of sterling. But those days are over, and in any case can be interpreted as protecting a factional interest within Britain, not with preserving an international regime per se. Germany's revaluations, when they came, were made primarily for domestic (anti-inflationary) reasons; and at various times Canada, Britain, France, and the United States all abandoned the international rules when a sharp conflict with domestic interests developed. Thus it is neither realistic nor, I would add, desirable to ask of the international monetary system that it impose strong conditions on domestic economic policy. Rather, the regime should strive for harmonious diversity.

International organizations and the desirable directions for reform

This essay has attempted to lay out in systematic fashion the possible sources of disagreement on reform of the international monetary system and some of the reasons for those disagreements. While it has here and there identified special interests that may well be expected to urge particular aspects rather than others, its general message is that the sources of disagreement are *not* to be found, by and large, in divergent interest groups of the type so often examined by political scientists. The sources of disagreement are less rooted in divergent interests than in divergent perspectives arising out of history and ideology, perspectives that economic theory and the lessons of recent experience have thus far failed to bring together. In addition to these divergent perspectives, some mutual distrust and some old-fashioned divergence of interest also contribute to the disagreements, but they are relatively minor partners.

The nature of this volume requires addressing two further issues: where international organizations fit into the picture, and how the international monetary system should be reformed. These are each large topics, they do not fit comfortably into this essay, and I have written extensively elsewhere on both these topics, especially on the second.[26] Nonetheless, it is necessary to say something about each of them.

I regard the role of international organizations as derivative from the task to be performed. Therefore, in the monetary arena, the presence and the appropriate form of international organization depends on the regime actually selected.

A different view is possible. It is that international organizations should exist to provide a sense of participation for many or all nations, not merely to perform certain tasks. Other things being equal, providing a sense of participation is a good thing. But sometimes it can be accomplished only by diminishing the efficiency with which essential tasks are performed or even by jeopardizing the performance altogether. In the international monetary arena, this possible conflict between participation and efficient task performance is perhaps more acute than it is in many other arenas, for quick and decisive action is often the key to preventing an unruly financial situation from getting out of hand.

In practice, the IMF has been one of the most proficient of the great panoply of extant international organizations. It is true that the IMF (meaning its executive board and its senior staff, not of course all staff members) has been slow to acknowledge the need for reform. It resisted for many years the notion that there was a world liquidity problem, but it eventually became an enthusiastic supporter of SDRs. It also resisted for years the notion that there was an adjustment problem requiring greater flexibility in exchange rates, and it is still not clear whether the IMF will become an enthusiastic supporter of greater flexibility of exchange rates in the international monetary system. But these observations only suggest that this international organization should not be left with the sole responsibility for initiative. By and large, it has performed well.

[26] See "Flexing the International Monetary System: The Case for Gliding Parities," in Federal Reserve Bank of Boston, *The International Adjustment Mechanism,* reprinted in Harry G. Johnson and A. K. Swoboda, eds., *The Economics of Common Currencies* (London: Allen & Unwin, 1973), pp. 229-43; US Congress, Joint Economic Committee, *International Monetary Reconstruction, Hearings before the Joint Economic Committee, February 22, 1973,* 93d Cong., 1st sess.; and *Towards a Renovated World Monetary System,* a report to the Trilateral Commission, the Triangle Papers, no. 1, New York, 1973.

It is interesting to speculate on whether its good performance has been related to its almost unique decision-making apparatus among international organizations, whereby its 126 member countries are represented by only twenty individuals sitting on their behalf. There is here the beginning of representative government at the global level, with constituencies being nations rather than individuals. The twenty members of the executive board operate under a system of weighted voting (and while formal votes are rarely taken, the weights nonetheless play an informal role in the decision making), where the weights depend on IMF quotas, which in turn depend roughly on a measure of economic importance in the world economy. Twenty is a far more manageable group than 126.

Despite its relative proficiency, the IMF has had to be supplemented by other formal and informal modes of international economic cooperation. The formal economic reviews of the IMF were too far removed from responsible officials to be of immediate use in coordinating economic policies or even in allowing the actions of other countries to influence constructively each country's actions. Therefore, the Economic Policy Committee of the Organization for Economic Cooperation and Development (OECD) and its various subcommittees, especially Working Party Three with its mere ten members and top-level representation, came to play a much more important role. Moreover, because IMF machinery for making a loan was too clumsy to deal quickly with immediate flare-ups in financial markets, a series of "swap" arrangements was established between the Federal Reserve System and other central banks, and later between European central banks, to provide immediate short-term credit on a no-questions-asked basis.

Success or failure in the international monetary arena depends on agreement and cooperation between a dozen or so countries, in the important sense that other countries could violate agreements without undermining the regime. That is why this essay focuses on the main industrial countries of North America, Western Europe, and Japan. The Soviet Union and China, of great importance in the arena of national security and military strategy, are inconsequential in the international monetary arena because both are so withdrawn from the world economy in their national economic policies. Similarly, while less developed countries have a strong interest in the character and performance of the international monetary regime, their adherence to its rules is not critical to its success. But, in fact, many of them will find it advantageous to adhere to the rules much of the time.

Relative importance, of course, changes with time, and any regime should be flexible enough to adapt to such changes. Moreover, the monetary system may be subject to shocks of a magnitude and character that were not anticipated at all. The huge drain on reserves caused by the steep increase in oil prices in late 1973 will drastically alter ownership of the world's foreign exchange reserves. But the behavior of the oil-exporting countries is not likely to be influenced much by whether they are members of the IMF. Just as they abandoned solemnly sworn contracts when they found they could gain thereby, they would certainly exempt themselves from any rules under a drastic change in circumstances.

Thus, the reasons for more universal forums than a group of ten rest on an appreciated desire for participation by most countries and on a conscious awareness of the problems of small countries, as well as on an expressed intention that they not be overlooked. The price paid for these two benefits involves greater unwieldiness in decision taking, even when all participants are of good will, plus the complications for decision taking that arise when some participants for which the stakes in this arena are or seem to be low threaten to withhold agreement here in bargaining for improvements in their position in other arenas. Bargaining across areas of interest, of course, is not limited to marginal participants, but any failure to reach agreement arising from unwillingness of the marginal participants to agree reflects a very unfavorable cost-benefit ratio for the world economy.[27]

I believe that in the monetary arena wide participation is desirable, but not so desirable as to allow it to hold up important cooperative steps between the key nations. Translated into institutional terms, discussions on reform of the monetary system are appropriately held within the framework of the IMF. But if they threaten to bog down because of that organization's (near) universalism, discussions should be withdrawn from that forum to one in which progress can be made more quickly. So far, however, progress has been blocked by fundamental disagreements between the major participants, not with the marginal ones.

Another point about international organizations especially germane in the monetary arena is that any formal organization and body of rules typically requires formal equality for the participating nations. A state is a state, large or small. Limited deviation from this principle can be found in weighted voting and in permanent as opposed to rotating membership on committees, as with the UN Security Council. But the strains toward formal symmetry between members is very strong.

Yet the world economy is very asymmetric in its functioning. For technical reasons, it is both likely and desirable that one or a few currencies will emerge with special status in market transactions.[28] Even when this fact is fully known and acceptable, it cannot always be formally acknowledged and sanctified in treaties, in part for reasons of status touched on earlier in the essay. There thus emerges a discrepancy between what governments say in formal negotiations and what they do, or are willing happily to accept, in day-to-day operations—a discrepancy between their stated preferences and their revealed preferences. In the monetary arena this discrepancy can be observed in attitudes toward the US dollar, both as an

---

[27] Even without such bargaining across arenas, the attempt to achieve universalism may weaken an organization's effectiveness at task performance because its principles or procedures are diluted to accommodate the diverse circumstances of the enlarged membership. One of the factors weakening the General Agreement on Tariffs and Trade during the 1960s was the insistence by some new members that as less developed countries they were subject not only to different rules (which was generally agreed) but also were not bound by the GATT's procedures for settling disputes. No organization can maintain its function in the face of erosion of its internal procedures. The weakening of the GATT (which also has other sources) has redounded to the disadvantage of all countries, new as well as old members.

[28] See Richard N. Cooper, "Eurodollars, Reserve Dollars, and Asymmetries in the International Monetary System," *Journal of International Economics* 2 (September 1972): 325-44.

intervention currency and as a reserve currency, in attitudes toward the flexibility of exchange rates, and (within Europe) in attitudes toward European monetary unification.

Formal arrangements induce sovereign states to insist on formal symmetry in status, partly to cater to nationalist sentiment at home. Informal arrangements carry no such compulsion. To the extent that asymmetries of treatment are important for efficient functioning, informal arrangements are therefore likely to be superior to formal arrangements that emerge from a negotiating process. In the international monetary sphere, an English-style constitution, built up through a series of acceptable practices, may be both easier to attain and even superior in content to a fully negotiated American-style constitution. Indeed, precisely such informal arrangements seem to mark the current monetary regime of managed flexibility of exchange rates, which few (if any) countries are willing to accept formally but which most (if not all) fully accept in practice.

What should a renovated monetary system look like? I suggest that four major improvements must be made. First, we need greater flexibility of exchange rates than the Bretton Woods regime allowed but less than would obtain under a system of free floating. Sound economic policy calls for a greater brake on movements in exchange rates than private speculators can always be expected to provide. Thus, we need either a system of closely managed floating, with rules governing central bank intervention, or a system of exchange rate parities with strong presumptive rules for "gliding" the parities. In practice, these alternatives need not be very different, but a system of managed floating will perhaps be easier to achieve from the condition of general floating prevailing in 1974. Of course, not all countries need to float their currencies to the same degree; small, open economies may be well advised to link their currencies somewhat more rigidly to one of the major currencies.

Second, the SDR needs to be detached from gold and its characteristics need to be altered to strengthen its role, with a view to its becoming the major medium for international reserves in the future. This change will require formal negotiations between countries; charter building through practice will not achieve this aim. Gold should be downgraded as an international monetary medium by eliminating its formal role wherever practicable. Some gold will continue to be held by governments for some time, for precautionary reasons. But they stockpile other durable commodities as well; gold should have no special monetary role.

Third, the community of nations should establish an international lender of last resort that is able to extend large amounts of credit on short notice in order to forestall major economic collapse. At present, the lending capacity of the IMF is too limited in scale, too hedged about with restrictions, to play this role. With the SDR moving into a central role, this lending function could be performed through special issues of SDRs to be repaid as quickly as possible after each crisis has passed but not more quickly than is appropriate for sound economic policy.

Fourth, closer international surveillance is required over the Eurocurrency market to ascertain whether the pyramid of credit being built there is too great or too shaky. At this stage better information is mainly required; but at some point limits on Eurocurrency expansion may become necessary.

The changes outlined here could be accomplished by the leading countries in a variety of institutional frameworks, but because it exists and has performed reasonably well, and because it has a wide membership, the IMF offers a natural starting place for these changes. With suitable (and substantial) modification in its structure and in its mode of operation, it could oversee an adjustment process based on managed exchange rate flexibility, serve as a lender of last resort—a central bank for central banks—and track developments in the Eurocurrency market to make sure that they do not get out of hand. But as suggested above, the role of institutions should be derivative, not primary. If relying on the IMF requires too much compromise with proficiency in performing these tasks, other arrangements should be made.

In terms of table 1, I favor the regime designated IV.B.1. or a version of III.B.1. not very different: high but not complete exchange rate flexibility subject to collective management, SDRs, and freedom of capital movements. The last stipulation requires that national governments both can and do rely to a greater extent on fiscal policy and less on monetary policy for domestic economic stabilization. Monetary policy must be regarded increasingly from a global point of view. In the possibly long transition to this state, which will require substantial alteration in domestic economic policy in many countries, it will be necessary to maintain some limits on the freedom of international capital movements, especially short-term bank lending. Without such limits, national monetary policy will lose much of its leverage over domestic economic conditions, a loss that is not acceptable so long as governments are held responsible for macroeconomic stability (as they should be) yet are denied the flexible use of fiscal measures. This stricture applies especially to Germany, Japan, and the United States, where for different reasons fiscal policy is a clumsy instrument of stabilization policy.

International trade and international relations

Robert E. Baldwin and David A. Kay

Trade arrangements under existing international organizations

In the 21 years since the conclusion of the Second World War, a complicated, piecemeal framework of trading arrangements under various international organizations has been created. Now there is concern, internationally and domestically, as to whether this framework is a durable basis for expanded world trade.

Existing trading arrangements can be divided into four broad categories: (1) global trade arrangements that focus on multilateral trade expansion on a nondiscriminatory basis; (2) global trade arrangements with a principal objective of international income redistribution through the mechanism of international trade; (3) regional trade arrangements that focus on the economic relations of a particular political/geographic area; and (4) commodity-product trading arrangements that focus on the international terms of trade of a specific commodity or product. In 1971 about 70 percent of world trade moved under global arrangements and 30 percent under regional ones. The General Agreement on Tariffs and Trade and the Organization for Economic Cooperation and Development fall in the first category of global trade arrangements dealing with multilateral trade expansion on a nondiscriminatory basis.

The General Agreement on Tariffs and Trade (GATT)

The basic rules governing most international trade are laid down in the General Agreement on Tariffs and Trade. This agreement, drafted in 1947, has been signed by some 80 nations whose exports dominate world trade. As initially conceived, the GATT was to cover only the narrow commercial policy aspects of a

Robert E. Baldwin is a professor of economics at the University of Wisconsin-Madison, and David A. Kay is the director of the International Organizations Research Project at the American Society of International Law in Washington, D.C.

much more comprehensive agreement on trade. An expanded agreement, known as the Havana Charter (1948), with the International Trade Organization (ITO) as its administrative agency, was proposed to include detailed provisions on commodity agreements, restrictive business practices, economic development, employment, and an organizational structure. However, when ITO was not approved, the GATT became the main document and organization for international cooperation on trade matters. Since the various provisions of the GATT have been analyzed extensively by others,[1] only the main features of the agreement are mentioned here.

The two key objectives stated in the preamble to the document are a substantial reduction in tariffs and other barriers to trade by means of reciprocal trade agreements and the elimination of discriminatory treatment in international commerce. Thus far, in working toward the first objective, six multilateral trade negotiations have been conducted since 1947. The results of these tariff-cutting exercises have been impressive. The last negotiation, the so-called Kennedy Round (1963-67), brought tariffs on dutiable nonagricultural products to an average of only 9.9 percent in the United States, 8.6 percent in the European Community (excluding the UK, Ireland, and Denmark), 10.8 percent in the United Kingdom, and 10.7 percent in Japan. Through GATT negotiations and various bilateral agreements during the 1930s, the tariff level on all dutiable United States imports dropped from around 59 percent in 1932 and 25 percent in 1946 to less than 12 percent prior to the Kennedy Round and to 9.9 percent today. Although tariffs have been reduced, many other measures still distort international trade. The increased use of these measures in recent years has made the effort to reduce these so-called nontariff trade barriers a priority item in the current trade negotiations.[2]

The second objective of the GATT, achieving nondiscrimination, is the cornerstone of the agreement and most of its substantive articles deal directly or indirectly with this principle. The first article stipulates, for example, that tariffs and charges of any kind on imports or exports, as well as all rules and formalities involved in importing or exporting, must be administered so that all contracting parties are treated alike. The three main exceptions in the tariff field pertain to certain preferential arrangements existing prior to the GATT, to preferences granted to the developing countries by the developed countries, and to the formation of customs unions and free-trade areas.

Measures other than tariffs that artificially curtail or promote international trade are also to be administered in a nondiscriminatory manner under the GATT. These include quantitative restrictions (where allowed), marks of origin, sales and other indirect taxes, and the various governmental fees associated with trading. More generally, nontariff barriers (NTBs) to trade are regarded in the GATT as undesirable impediments that could thwart the expansion of world trade sought

---

[1] See, for example, Kenneth W. Dam, *The GATT—Law and International Organization* (Chicago: University of Chicago Press, 1970).

[2] See Robert E. Baldwin, *Non-Tariff Distortions of International Trade* (Washington, D.C.: Brookings Institution, 1970).

through reciprocal tariff reductions. Consequently, some NTBs are prohibited under the GATT. The two most important in this category are quantitative restrictions (except when imposed in connection with balance-of-payments difficulties, domestic price support programs in agriculture, and temporary domestic shortages of essential goods) and export subsidies.

The reduction of tariffs and the elimination of NTBs are provisions of the GATT aimed at increasing economic efficiency and growth rates in the world. The framers of the GATT believed these economic objectives contributed to greater political cooperation and improved the prospects for peace among all countries. In addition to global economic and political goals, however, there are articles in the GATT designed to deal with equity and growth considerations of particular interests within a country or of particular groups of contracting parties.

The more important of the provisions aimed at coping with economic difficulties faced by particular industries within a country are those relating to the escape clause, antidumping duties and countervailing duties, and "open-season" negotiations. The escape clause provision permits a country to withdraw a concession if domestic producers of an item are suffering from or threatened with serious injury as a result of that concession. (A country that uses this provision must grant equivalent concessions on other products or face the prospect of the withdrawal of equivalent concessions by other countries.) The antidumping article is based on the notion that if another country sells an article in a member country at a price less than the foreign country charges its own domestic users, the industry producing a similar product in the member's economy may be unfairly injured and, therefore, may be entitled to special protective assistance. The same rationale applies to domestic industries competing with foreign industries that are aided by government subsidies. Under "open-season" negotiations, which take place every three years, a contracting party may withdraw any concession it previously granted. In this event, the country may negotiate equivalent concessions with its trading partners or risk the loss of concessions that it was granted by others in the past.

The agreement concerning market disruption and the long-term arrangements on textiles, both of which were made within the GATT framework, are also directed at special groups within countries. The agreement on market disruption is aimed at finding solutions, consistent with the basic aims of the GATT, to the problem of a sharp and substantial increase in imports of a particular product that disrupt a market and may seriously damage domestic producers of the same good. The primary means that has developed to handle the problem is quantitative marketing agreements between major producing and consuming nations. One example is the series of agreements on textiles, which were first negotiated for cotton products in 1962 and then expanded in 1973 into a single agreement covering all textile products.

The GATT provisions on customs unions and free-trade areas, and on the special privileges of developing countries, recognize that a liberal, nondiscriminatory trade policy by all countries may cause an undesirable degree of industrial specialization and income inequality among nations. Customs unions and free-trade areas are excluded from the general GATT principle of nondiscrimination provided that they do not result in higher duties for nonmembers.

The GATT has always permitted developing countries to employ tariffs in order to encourage the establishment of a particular industry domestically and to use quantitative restrictions on trade in order to meet balance-of-payments problems associated with development programs. In 1965 an entirely new part devoted to the trade and development problems of less developed countries was added to the GATT. Under this part, the developed countries made commitments to accord high priority to reducing and eliminating trade barriers on products of current or potential export interest to the developing nations, to avoid increasing existing duties and NTBs, and to refrain from imposing new internal taxes on tropical products. In reducing these various trade impediments, the developed countries agreed not to expect reciprocal concessions from the developing countries. Still another important feature of the new section was an expression of willingness by the developed and developing economies to collaborate through international arrangements to provide improved access conditions and more stable markets for the primary products of the developing countries.

Given the number of important commitments that all signers of the GATT make, one would expect that a sizable apparatus would exist for the purpose of administering the agreement. An elaborate administrative structure was initially envisioned under the Havana Charter and proposed again in 1955. However, the refusal of the US Congress to approve ITO and the organizational changes suggested later have resulted in the GATT operating with a minimum of central direction. The contracting parties meet as a group only once or twice a year. However, the Council of Representatives, composed of all contracting parties "willing to accept the responsibility of membership therein," handles on a continuing basis the same range of problems covered in the general sessions. The latter sessions now mainly ratify decisions of the council and settle especially difficult issues. The council together with the secretariat form the essential administrative backbone of the GATT.

Organization for Economic Cooperation and Development (OECD)

OECD, along with the GATT, falls in the first category of trade arrangements that focus on multilateral trade expansion on a nondiscriminatory basis. OECD is the successor of the Organization for European Economic Cooperation, which was established in 1948 to administer Marshall Plan aid and to promote cooperative recovery efforts in Europe. The prime aim of OECD in the trade area is to contribute to the expansion of world trade on a multilateral, nondiscriminatory basis in accordance with international obligations. Its membership includes eighteen European countries plus Canada, the United States, Japan, Australia, and New Zealand.

Unlike the GATT or regional trade agreements, such as the European Community or the European Free Trade Association, the OECD Convention does not include detailed articles prohibiting certain types of trading practices. Instead, through various committees (e.g., the Trade Committee) the organization studies trade matters of current interest with the objective of harmonizing the practices of its members regarding the particular policy issue. Examples of issues where such harmonization has been pursued include government purchasing policies toward foreign suppliers and export credits. With respect to international transactions relating to the invisible items in the current account, a binding code of liberalization similar to the GATT's coverage of merchandise trade does exist. It specifically commits the members to eliminate (subject to various exceptions) restrictions on such current invisible transactions as transportation services, technical services, insurance, and income from capital.

One of OECD's primary aims in the trade field is to promote growth in the developing nations by expanding their export earnings. To achieve this the Trade Committee has worked out various means of honoring the broad commitment of the industrial countries to grant generalized tariff preferences to the developing countries.

United Nations Conference on Trade and Development (UNCTAD)

The United Nations Conference on Trade and Development falls into a second category of global trade arrangements which have the principal objective of international income redistribution through the mechanism of international trade. UNCTAD, consisting of all members of the United Nations, is primarily concerned with improving the relative income position of the developing countries by increasing the growth rates in these nations through better trading conditions. The first general conference on these matters, held in 1964, included a recommendation that resulted in making UNCTAD a permanent organization of the United Nations. Between periodic general conferences, the business of the organization is managed by the Trade and Development Board, whose membership is dominated by representatives from the developing countries.

There are four main committees of the board: on commodities, on manufactures, on shipping, and on invisibles and financing related to trade. The Committee on Commodities directs its efforts at stabilizing and raising the export earnings of the developing nations derived from exports of primary products. It has been particularly interested in the negotiation of international commodity agreements for tropical products, and it was instrumental in UNCTAD's sponsorship of such an agreement on cocoa. The Committee on Manufactures has been mainly concerned with obtaining tariff preferences from the developed countries on manufactures. One of the accomplishments of the second general UNCTAD conference in 1968-69 was a commitment by all the major industrial countries to grant such preferences. However, these commitments have not yet been fully implemented.

The Committees on Shipping and on Invisibles and Financing related to Trade deal with matters of vital importance to the developing countries that are not considered by the central organization on trade issues, namely, the GATT. Discriminatory freight rates, for example, are in some instances as significant barriers to exports by these countries as are the tariffs of the developed countries. Similarly, the securing of transportation insurance at nonmonopolistic rates can make an important contribution toward advancing export growth in the developing countries. Another issue reviewed by the Committee on Invisibles and Financing related to Trade is the granting of export credits by the developed countries.

The European Community

Our third category, regional trade arrangements, which focuses on the economic relations of a particular political/geographic area, includes the largest number of international organizations. As has been previously noted, the chief objective of the GATT has been to achieve multilateral trade liberalization on a nondiscriminatory basis. However, Article XXIV also stipulates that the provisions of the GATT shall not prevent the formation of customs unions or free-trade areas provided these regional arrangements do not lead to a net rise in external trade barriers. Since the late 1950s the increase in the number of regional trading arrangements under this provision has been as significant as the number of multilateral trade negotiations.

The European Community is by far the paramount regional trading group in the world economy. With the addition in 1973 of the United Kingdom,[3] Denmark, and Ireland to the original Six (France, West Germany, Italy, the Netherlands, Belgium, and Luxemburg), the volume of intra-Community trade now amounts to about 20 percent of total world exports. Although the main accomplishments of the Community have been in the economic field, broad political rather than narrow economic factors played the major role in its formation. It was thought that the formation of an economic community would not only contribute to the elimination of costly political and economic rivalries within Europe but also would form the basis of a cohesive political force that could deal effectively with the United States and the Soviet Union. The ultimate hope of the key founders was that economic union would eventually lead to political union within Europe.

Since the various provisions of the European Community have been analyzed in detail many times, the description presented here is brief and focuses on trading relationships between members and with nonmember countries. The general trading arrangement is one of free trade (including the movement of labor and capital) within the Community and the uniform treatment of all nonmembers. Among the members, freedom of trade involves not only the absence of tariffs but also efforts to eliminate or to harmonize the many nontariff devices that distort trade. Efforts to set up uniform government purchasing policies and common regional development policies are examples of activities in the nontariff field. Likewise, the establishment of a common agricultural policy, a common transport policy, and

---

[3]British entry to the EC led to the final termination of the British Commonwealth, which encompassed preferential tariffs between members, some developed and some less developed, and had been one of the major "regional" trading arrangements in the world since its formation in 1932.

mechanisms to reduce monopolistic practices by private firms represent part of the commitment to free or to harmonize trade conditions within the Community.

The uniform treatment of nonmembers assumes the form of a common external tariff and efforts to agree to similar treatment in the area of nontariff barriers. Furthermore, the objectives of establishing a fixed exchange rate relationship between the members' currencies, and ultimately a common currency, and of harmonizing monetary and fiscal policies are part of the aims of the Community.

Although the general policy of the Community is to treat all nonmembers in a nondiscriminatory manner, the Treaty of Rome does provide in Articles 131-36 for the extension of tariff preferences and other aids by the Community to the former colonies of France, Belgium, and Italy and for reverse preferences in favor of Community members by these "associated states."

Furthermore, Article 238 permits the Community to conclude agreements involving special trading relationships with any third country. The Yaounde Agreement, signed in 1963, provided for the association of eighteen former African colonies and dependencies of France, Belgium, and Italy with the Community. Certain tropical products produced by these countries, e.g., coffee, cocoa, tea, and pineapples, were immediately admitted free of duty into the Community, while arrangements for permitting the importation at preferred duty rates of products that compete with production within the Community are being worked out gradually. In addition to these benefits, the various African countries received nearly $1.5 billion in development aid from the Community. In return, the African states have gradually lowered their duties on imports from the Community. However, these states may reimpose tariffs if they regard them as necessary to the development process. In 1969 an agreement somewhat similar to the one signed at Yaounde took effect between the European Community and Kenya, Uganda, and Tanzania. Financial aid was not involved but reciprocal tariff preferences were granted.

A second group of nations that has concluded association or trade agreements with the Community are the developing countries bordering on the Mediterranean Sea. These include Greece, Spain, Turkey, Malta, Morocco, Algeria, Libya, Tunisia, Israel, and Yugoslavia. The agreements vary considerably in the extent of tariff preferences and in the time span for reducing duties. Moreover, some involve financial assistance from the Community while others do not.

A final group of countries that recently have concluded trade agreements with the European Community are the remaining members of the European Free Trade Association (EFTA). The agreement recently signed by Finland with the Community now means that all of these countries will eventually have a free-trade relationship with the European Community.

The European Free Trade Association (EFTA)

With the entrance of the United Kingdom into the European Community in 1973, the importance of the European Free Trade Association as a trading bloc decreased significantly, and its future status became uncertain. EFTA, whose membership initially comprised Austria, Denmark, Norway, Portugal, Sweden, Switzerland, and the United Kingdom, was organized in 1960 essentially in response to the formation of the European Economic Community in 1958. EFTA's members were unwilling to accept the degree of harmonization of economic and social policies involved in joining the Community. Instead, they wished to limit European cooperation to a mutual free-trade arrangement where each country would maintain its own external tariff. When the Community rejected this approach, the seven countries proceeded on this basis themselves. They hoped that the success of their organization would eventually lead to a free-trade agreement with the European Community.

The EFTA Stockholm Convention calls for cooperation of the members mainly on trade matters, with few obligations affecting internal social and economic policies. Even in the commercial area, the agricultural sector is excluded from any free-trade or harmonization requirement. However, the convention recognizes that means other than tariffs and quotas can effectively distort trade and, like the Treaty of Rome, attempts to eliminate or to harmonize these policies. Thus, the Stockholm Convention contains articles covering such matters as government aids, government purchasing policy, restrictive business practices, and the establishment of businesses within one member country by nationals of another member country.

Another similarity of the Stockholm Convention to the Treaty of Rome is the provision for the negotiation of association agreements. The language in Article 41 of the EFTA Convention is almost the same as in Article 238 of the Treaty of Rome. However, unlike the European Community, EFTA has not often used this provision. Only one association agreement—with Finland—was negotiated. Another development has been the addition of Iceland to the membership of EFTA.

Council of Mutual Economic Cooperation (COMECON)[4]

The international organization that coordinates trade and other forms of economic relations between the centrally planned economies of Eastern Europe (Bulgaria, Czechoslovakia, East Germany, Hungary, Poland, Romania, and the USSR) is the Council of Mutual Economic Cooperation. Formed in 1949, when the Eastern bloc countries resigned from the various economic committees of the United Nations that dealt with European problems, COMECON grew into an important organization only slowly and did not receive a formal charter until 1959.

Although some product specialization has been promoted by COMECON, the centrally planned countries of Eastern Europe fulfill more of their needs from domestic production than do most capitalist nations. A large share of foreign trade availabilities and needs are set only after decisions have been reached on the volume and composition of domestic output. Consequently, foreign trade has often been used to remedy unplanned shortages and to dispose of unplanned surpluses. Trade is also conducted mainly on the basis of bilateral agreements both between COMECON members and with nonmembers.

[4] For further details, see the essay in this volume by Holzman and Legvold.

In the centrally planned countries of Eastern Europe, trade decisions concerning a particular product are made by various state-trading organizations that have monopoly power over the buying and selling of the product. These organizations are quite separate from the state enterprises that produce or consume the product. Because of this monopoly power and the lack of any necessary link between prices and economic costs, it has been difficult to apply the trading rules of market-oriented organizations such as the GATT to bilateral agreements reached between COMECON countries and western market economies. The GATT article on state-trading enterprises stipulates that sales or purchases by such a firm should be consistent with the principle of nondiscrimination and be based solely on commercial considerations. However, in practice it is impossible to determine whether exports from a centrally planned economy are, for example, being subsidized or whether imports from nonmembers are undertaken on a nondiscriminatory basis.

Despite these difficulties, trade between the centrally planned economies of Eastern Europe and the rest of the world has expanded rapidly in recent years. Between 1960 and 1970, exports from these economies to the market-oriented industrial countries increased $4.9 billion, and exports to the developing areas rose by $3.2 billion. These increases were more rapid than the growth rate for intra-COMECON trade. The level of East-West trade is, nevertheless, far below what would have prevailed had these nations not become part of the communist bloc. The prospects for further trade expansion seem favorable, especially through coproduction agreements whereby companies in the market-oriented economies provide capital, technology, and certain managerial services to develop mineral industries and receive payment for these services in the form of the product that is developed.

Regional trading arrangements between developing countries[5]

One of the most significant developments in the trade field during the last fifteen years has been the establishment of numerous regional trading organizations in the developing countries. Within this period, ten major regional groupings, with membership accounting for over one-half of the total GNP of the developing countries, and three very loose trading arrangements have been established.[6] The ten major groups are as follows:

1. Latin American Free Trade Association (LAFTA), formed in 1960, comprising Argentina, Brazil, Chile, Mexico, Paraguay, Peru, Uruguay, Colombia, Ecuador, Venezuela, and Bolivia;
2. Andean Group, formed in 1969 as a subgrouping of LAFTA and comprising Bolivia, Chile, Colombia, Ecuador, Peru, and Venezuela;

---

[5] Centrally planned economies that are in the developing country category are excluded from the following description.
[6] In some cases, somewhat similar organizations preceded the ones established in this period.

3. Central American Common Market (CACM), established in 1960, composed of Costa Rica, El Salvador, Guatemala, Honduras, and Nicaragua;
4. Caribbean Free Trade Association (CARIFTA), formed in 1968, comprising Barbados, Guyana, Jamaica, Trinidad and Tobago, Antigua, Dominica, Grenada, Montserrat, St. Kitts–Nevis–Anguilla, St. Lucia, and St. Vincent;
5. East Caribbean Common Market (a subgrouping of CARIFTA), formed in 1968 and comprising Antigua, Dominica, Grenada, Montserrat, St. Kitts–Nevis–Anguilla, St. Lucia, and St. Vincent;
6. East African Community (EAC), formed in 1967 and composed of Kenya, Uganda, and the United Republic of Tanzania;
7. Central African Customs and Economic Union (UDEAC), established in 1964, composed of Cameroon, Central Africa Republic, Congo, and Gabon;
8. West African Economic Community (CEAC), established in 1972, composed of Dahomey, Ivory Coast, Mali, Mauritania, Niger, Senegal, and Upper Volta;
9. Arab Common Market (ACM), formed in 1964, comprising Egypt, Iraq, Jordan, and the Syrian Arab Republic; and
10. Regional Cooperation for Development (RCD), established in 1964 and composed of Iran, Pakistan, and Turkey.

The three loose regional organizations are: (1) the Council of the Entente (Dahomey, Ivory Coast, Niger, Upper Volta, and Togo) formed in 1959 in west Africa; (2) the Maghreb Group (Algeria, Morocco, and Tunisia) formed in 1964 in North Africa; and (3) the Association of South-East Asian Nations, or ASEAN (Malaysia, the Philippines, Thailand, Singapore, and Indonesia) formed in 1967.

The reasons for this burst of organizational activity are not difficult to perceive. Frustrated by their failure to penetrate the industrial markets of the developed countries because of high trade barriers on many simple manufactured products and by their inability to compete in high-technology products, and impressed by the success of the European Economic Community, these countries turned to each other to raise their levels of industrial development. They thought that the creation of regional groupings between themselves would yield benefits flowing from economies of scale in production and the more efficient use of resources due to greater competition. They hoped that these benefits would exceed any costs associated with trade diversion and that the net gains could be distributed equitably between the participants.

The more ambitious objectives of the various regional groupings involve not only trade liberalization between the members but also cooperation on industrial, agricultural, and infrastructure projects and the establishment of financial institutions for facilitating regional development. The provisions of the Central American Common Market (CACM), one of the earliest attempts at economic integration among the developing countries, illustrates these points. Trade on all but 21 items is completely free of import duties for the five members, and there is a unified external tariff on all but 37 commodities.[7] Intraregional exports, which amounted

---

[7] Honduras has suspended intraregional free trade and modified its external tariff on some goods.

to 27 percent of the members' total exports, grew at an annual rate of 30 percent per year since the formation of CACM, in contrast to 20 percent prior to the scheme.

Cooperative efforts in the industrial area include decisions to establish "integration industries" in each of the five countries and to permit free intraregional trade on the products of these industries. In order to facilitate an intercountry balance of these industries, no country with such an industry can acquire another until all other members have one. Thus far three projects have been established under this agreement: one each in textiles, glass, and chemicals. Joint infrastructure investments have been limited so far, but there are proposals for the establishment of a common telecommunications system. Cooperation in the agricultural field is typified by coordination of sugar export policies between the members and common policies to mitigate fluctuations in grain prices.

The Central American Bank for Economic Integration, formed in 1961, is the major financial institution funding cooperative ventures under CACM. Its resources, mostly from external sources, amount to about $300 million, and the value of the projects assisted in the 1962-71 period was $271 million.

Other regional schemes in which there is an associated development-financing institution are the East African Community and the Caribbean Free Trade Association. EAC also covers the other fields of cooperation included in CACM, but CARIFTA contains no provisions covering industrial cooperation. The Latin American Free Trade Association, which is the largest organization in terms of the GNP of its members, promotes cooperation in trade, industry, and infrastructure investments, but it has not accomplished much in the agricultural area and does not have a separate development-financing institution. Nor are there financing institutions in UDEAC, CEAC, and ACM, although they are in the formulation stage. Moreover, these groups have not achieved significant cooperative production efforts in industry, agriculture, and tertiary activities.

The last scheme listed at the outset of this section, RCD, differs from the others in that the joint planning of industrial projects rather than trade liberalization is the main goal of the organization. The expansion of trade is to follow the expansion of production through joint efforts. More specifically, each country agrees to purchase specified amounts of output produced in joint industries for a limited time period. In the agricultural area no formal programs exist, but some cooperative efforts are taking place regarding infrastructure investments. The establishment of a joint commercial bank to facilitate the financing of the various activities covered in the agreement is also under consideration.

International commodity agreements

International commodity-product agreements that focus on the international terms of trade of a specific commodity or product constitute our fourth category of trading arrangements. Some of these agreements include both exporting and importing countries, while some encompass only the exporters.

No single international organization is responsible for the negotiation of international commodity agreements. For example, the GATT was instrumental in concluding the several agreements on textiles and on wheat, whereas UNCTAD sponsored the conference resulting in an agreement on cocoa. Currently there are seven major multilateral commodity agreements which include both producing and consuming countries. They cover textiles, coffee, olive oil, sugar, tin, cocoa, and wheat.

The long-term cotton textile agreement was instigated in 1962 by developed countries that believed their domestic textile industries were threatened with market disruption as a result of rapid increases in imports from Japan and certain developing nations. Quotas are imposed to limit imports, though the consuming countries are pledged to provide growing market opportunities and progressively relax their import restrictions. The common objective of the commodity agreements on coffee, olive oil, sugar, tin, cocoa, and wheat is the prevention of excessive market price fluctuations. Also specifically mentioned is the goal of increasing the earnings of the nations producing coffee, cocoa, and sugar.

For two of the commodities, wheat and olive oil, exported mainly by developed countries, no controls over production or trade currently exist under the agreements. Exchange of information between the participating countries is the only mechanism employed to pursue the stabilization objective. However, export quotas are or have been employed to regulate price fluctuations for coffee, sugar, tin, and cocoa. A formal buffer-stock system is also used for this purpose in the cases of tin and cocoa. Two unique features of the coffee agreement, until their recent suspension, were the establishment of policies designed to control production and stocks and compulsory contributions to a diversification fund. Each country's contributions to this fund could be used for diversifying projects within its territory.

The most visible and successful of the international commodity-product organizations comprising only the producing countries is the Organization of Petroleum Exporting Countries (OPEC). Founded in 1960 by five of the oil-exporting developing countries, with the mandate to advance the interests of those states that have a heavy dependence on oil exports, OPEC now has eleven members whose exports accounted for over 85 percent of international oil trade in 1973.

Faced with an oligopolistic arrangement of petroleum companies, OPEC was organized, in effect, as a government cartel to raise the income derived from oil of the exporting states. Although by no means completely the result of OPEC, oil revenues have in fact risen dramatically for OPEC members. Zuhayr Mikdashi notes: "In 1961, the first full year after OPEC's establishment, oil revenues per barrel were 75.6¢ in the Middle East. In 1971, they were $1.255, and in 1972 they were $1.407 per barrel. Total oil revenues of OPEC countries rose over sixfold between 1962 and 1972, along with substantial increases in the volume of oil exports."[8] The more recent results are of course even more dramatic.

[8] Zuhayr Mikdashi, "Cooperation Among Oil Exporting Countries with Special Reference to Arab Countries: A Political Economy Analysis," *International Organization* 28 (Winter 1974): 20.

For our purposes, the major impact of OPEC is not its success in raising the income of oil-exporting states but the model it provides other developing states that export raw materials for pursuing their economic and political objectives. This model has already been adopted by the major copper-exporting states in establishing their Intergovernmental Council of Copper Exporting Countries (CIPEC) and by seven major bauxite-producing countries in establishing the International Bauxite Association. It seems very likely that in the next decade the developing country exporters of a number of scarce raw materials will attempt to emulate the success of OPEC. Although it is doubtful that they all will be as successful as OPEC, it is likely that the industrial world will have to adjust to the proliferation of this type of international trading arrangement.[9]

Alternative trading arrangements

The main alternative types of trading arrangements available to the international community for the pursuit of its economic and political goals can be discerned from the preceding description of existing international trading institutions. These institutions have already changed considerably from those of the early post–World War II years in response to altered political and economic conditions, and the trend of change seems clear enough to define the plausible trading approaches that may be followed.

Liberalization under nondiscriminatory conditions

One alternative is to proceed along the lines drawn at the end of World War II. The essence of this approach is long-range achievement of a substantial multilateral liberalization of world trade and elimination of all forms of international discrimination.

Seeking these goals does not mean that *no* restrictive or discriminatory trade policies are to be tolerated in the short run. The initial GATT agreement and ITO charter denote various conditions where such policies are permissible. Nor does it mean cessation of all further efforts at establishing or extending regional groupings. New uses of protective policies brought about by changed economic and political circumstances are also consistent with this approach. However, the basis of this alternative is that any deviations from trade liberalization and nondiscriminatory treatment must be only temporary. The trend of trade policy must be toward the long-range goals. Quantitative restrictions on products such as textiles must serve to ease the adjustment to long-run trade liberalization rather than become permanent

[9]For additional discussion of this point, see C. Fred Bergsten, "The Threat From the Third World," *Foreign Policy*, no. 11 (Summer 1973): 102-24; Zuhayr Mikdashi, "Collusion Could Work," *Foreign Policy*, no. 14 (Spring 1974): 57-67; Stephen D. Krasner, "Oil is the Exception," *Foreign Policy*, no. 14 (Spring 1974): 68-83; and C. Fred Bergsten, "The Threat Is Real," *Foreign Policy*, no. 14 (Spring 1974): 84-90.

instruments of trade policy. Similarly, the discriminatory treatment implicit in customs unions is permitted because the duty reductions involved in the formation of these unions is a step in the direction of world free-trade conditions.

A description of the nature of this trade alternative is, of course, not meaningful without some notion of what is meant by the short run and the long run. While one cannot be exact, those who set forth this approach in the immediate postwar period clearly believed substantial progress towards freer, nondiscriminatory trade was necessary for the developed countries every decade. For the less developed countries, the time horizon is less clear but would seem to be not much longer than a generation.

The country most responsible for instituting this liberalizing, nondiscriminatory approach in the postwar period was the United States. The political, economic, and military preeminence of the United States among the market economies (the Soviet Union was not interested at that time in trade with the West) was so significant that the world-trading framework it desired could hardly be effectively opposed. The promise of substantial aid from the United States and the right to continue to employ quantitative controls for balance-of-payments reasons were considerations that did much to weaken any opposition of other countries to the American vision of future trading relations.

The trading proposals set forth by the United States at the end of the war seem to have been formulated mainly within the government. An unusually talented group of individuals, who adopted a long-run view of political and economic problems, had been attracted into the trade field within the US government during the 1930s and World War II. Because the war had been over for only a relatively short period and the political power of the administration was great, these individuals were able to formulate a structure of postwar economic institutions and undertake international negotiations on these organizations without going through the usual long process of interaction between the public and private sectors that characterizes trade policy during a typical peacetime period. Their basic belief was that an expansion of world trade in a nondiscriminatory manner would significantly improve the prospects for world peace by promoting closer economic, social, and political ties. In their minds, the lesson of the 1930s was that when each country disregards the welfare of other nations in the pursuit of its economic interests, all countries eventually tend to suffer economically and the chances of political and military conflict are increased. Economists within key government circles also strongly supported the proposal for trade liberalization on the usual neoclassical grounds of greater efficiency in the use of world resources. Still, the political argument for trade liberalization was undoubtedly the dominant one in the minds of US planners.

The failure of the Congress to approve ITO and certain protective features tied to some of the trade bills of the late 1940s and 1950s indicate that the views of US government planners in the trade field were not uniformly shared within the country, even at that period of unchallenged US economic superiority. However, both political and economic factors operated to strengthen the position of those favoring continued trade liberalization. On the political level, the argument that the United States must take the initiative in liberalization efforts in order to forge closer political ties among noncommunist nations, and thus resist the political power of the communist nations more effectively, was used time and again with great success in securing trade-liberalizing legislation. Equally important, it became abundantly evident to most industrial, labor, and agricultural organizations that the competitive ability of American producers in foreign markets was very high. What was needed to take advantage of vast market expansions was the removal of import quotas and the easing of tariff and other nontariff barriers in other countries. In short, the opportunities for market expansion abroad far exceeded the dangers of domestic market penetration by foreign producers, and a policy of freer, multilateral trade appeared to be in the economic interests of most major economic groups.

Although United States economic domination of the market-oriented economic world has ended, the goal of global trade liberalization on a nondiscriminatory basis cannot be written off as an outmoded option. There are still many groups in the United States with considerable political power that believe, on political grounds, this is the best policy to follow. There are also indications that Japan and certain European countries are prepared to take over the advocacy of this position, which has so long been performed by the United States. Their position is similar to the earlier view of the United States: in open competition, they have the most to gain; in a world of restrictions, they have the most to lose. It may even not be too long before some of the more successful developing countries begin to see the advantages of free trade.

Another development that may favor continued emphasis on global trade liberalization is the internationalization of capital. Not only is American direct investment extensive in developing and in other developed countries, but European and Japanese capital is becoming increasingly international. The multinational corporation with its many-country interests supposedly adopts a global approach that favors the elimination of artificial trade constraints. Since some believe that the political power of the multinational corporations is already substantial and increasing, they see this as a powerful development favoring the liberal trade approach.

The regional approach

A second alternative course that may be followed in fashioning future trading relationships in the world involves placing greater emphasis on special regional relationships, coupled possibly with a move away from the unqualified use of the most-favored-nation (MFN) principle with respect to trade among regions. This approach represents a continuation of a trend that began shortly after the institutions facilitating the first approach were established. Again, the causes for the early regional agreements were mainly political.

The architects of the most important regional grouping, the European Community, wished to unify Western Europe politically in order to minimize intra-Western European disputes and to build a third political force between the United States and the Soviet Union. When movement toward direct political union was not successful, economic unification was attempted. Some thought the close ties established under a customs union would eventually lead to the desired degree of political cooperation. COMECON is another regional group formed mainly for political reasons. It was set up in reaction to the Marshall Plan and was used initially by the Soviet Union to strengthen its political hold over Eastern Europe. Even the formation of EFTA was more politically than economically motivated. The objective was to set up a countervailing force to the European Community with the hope that this would lead to a merging of the two groups.

The security factors dominated the decision-making process leading to the formation of the early regional grouping, economic considerations were also significant. In particular, many proponents of the European Community felt that the only way to establish certain industries essential for a modern industrial power and to reach an efficient size for others was to discriminate against United States imports. Free trade would merely lead to a greater concentration of industrial (and thus political) power in the United States. The creation of trading blocs among the developing countries has also been considerably influenced by economic (as well as political) factors. In this case, the belief has been that at least temporary discrimination is needed against imports of manufactured goods from all industrial countries in order to permit the growth of efficient productive units within a developing region.

The United States, though it had fashioned the MFN approach, encouraged the formation of the European Common Market. It did this not only politically but through economic aid and a trade policy that did not insist upon strict adherence to the customs union provision of the GATT and that provided liberal tariff concessions without demanding full reciprocity. The US position was, of course, that the economic strengthening of Western Europe (and Japan) would weaken the relative political power of the Soviet Union. Economists raised some questions about the trade diversion danger of customs unions, but their views did not carry much weight.

The central fact of the modern international political and economic community is that the power of both the United States and the Soviet Union has declined significantly in relative terms. Economically, the tremendous competitive advantage of the United States has been lost and now Western Europe and Japan are economic powers to be reckoned with. Moreover, certain developing countries are making substantial progress in improving their international competitive position. The disappearance of the traditional US trade surplus and the need to devalue the dollar are indicative of the competitive pressures placed on the United States. Of course, an important reaction to this pressure has been the spread of American direct foreign investment to areas of cheaper labor and/or lucrative markets. Thus, what started as a political and economic reaction to the dominance of the United States (and the Soviet Union), and which was encouraged by the United States, successfully led to a situation where the economic power of the United States is no longer sufficient to make its economic will effective. We now live in an international economic environment characterized by an oligopolistic relationship between the major nation states.

Given this system and its widespread use of preferential trading relationships, it could be argued that further developments along these lines are inevitable and perhaps desirable. These developments could proceed in three (non-mutually exclusive) directions: closer ties between developed countries, creation of new North-South blocs, and strengthening of regional relationships between developing countries.

The economic relations between the major Western powers as well as the relations of these countries with the socialist countries are far from stable. For the foreseeable future, each of the main competitors of the United States is likely to attempt to increase its economic power by a variety of neo-colonial and mercantilistic policies that are in opposition to the first trading alternative outlined. The United States and others may conclude that attempting to defend the multilateral, nondiscriminatory approach is no longer in their interests. In order to best maintain US economic power, a regional or at least a discriminatory trade stance may now be appropriate. For example, just as Western Europe has established special trading relationships with Africa, Japan might do so with southeast Asia and the United States could grant tariff preferences only to Latin America. The more manageable reaction in terms of increased imports from such a scheme is appealing to some domestic interests. Moreover, following the lead of EFTA members that have now either joined the European Community or have negotiated special trading relationships with this bloc, the United States might improve its economic position by establishing regional ties with other developed areas, such as Canada or countries around the Pacific Basin.

The recent oil crisis is another development that may favor the regional approach. Other groups of mineral or food producers are likely to band together in an effort to raise prices. In order to thwart such collusive action and to maintain the supplies needed for security and economic affluence, each of the major developed powers may seek to buy off particular mineral-supplying countries with major trade, investment, and aid concessions. To attempt to achieve a satisfactory sharing of world mineral supplies through global negotiations is likely to be far more difficult than this method and may not even be in the interests of particular industrial powers.

The prospects that East-West trade will expand may also favor the regional, non-MFN approach. It will be impossible to determine if centrally planned countries are following the nondiscriminatory principles of the GATT. Consequently, what is likely to emerge is various long-term bilateral agreements about supplies and market access that are more in the spirit of special regional trading relationships than the GATT approach. This will strengthen the position of those favoring the more general application of the discriminatory approach.

An extension of the regional approach—perhaps more in name than in substance—is the abandonment of the MFN principle. There is widespread support for this position in the United States, since it is argued that the burden of the regional relationships established by others falls heavily on this country. This weapon could be used to obtain more effectively equivalent concessions to compensate for the trade diversions associated with regional groupings. Perhaps a more important argument for permitting selective discrimination is to deal with a sudden and substantial flood of imports of particular goods from one or two countries that seriously disrupt the internal markets for these goods. To meet this inflow by raising tariffs or imposing quotas on imports of these goods from all sources is unfair to other suppliers, and could lead to substantial unravelling of previously granted concessions. Therefore, it is argued that selective discrimination should be permitted.

The regional approach differs from the first alternative outlined in that the main efforts are devoted to lowering trade barriers *within* regions, with little attention being devoted to liberalizing simultaneously *among* regions. In recent years the United States has consistently used its economic influence to tie intraregional liberalization to multilateral liberalization. Now the United States may decide that the regional-discriminatory approach is in its interests, and the continued push for interregional liberalization may no longer take place.

A retreat from trade policy

The last alternative trade approach to be discussed is one that involves a de-emphasis on trade liberalization either globally or within regions. The European Community, for example, may decide that with the special arrangements recently concluded with EFTA members, it is no longer desirable to expand regionally. Rather, the emphasis would be on consolidating the mutual benefits from its existing European and African ties. Similarly, the United States may not only abandon its pressure for global liberalization but decide to rely much more heavily on its own resources rather than to expand its regional trading relationships. In short, both the pattern of a broad multilateral trade negotiation every decade and the expansion of regional arrangements by developed countries would come to an end. As those involved in trade policy know, this retreat from global and regional liberalization would most likely be accompanied by the erection of new trade barriers.

Although the passage of a new trade bill in the United States makes this approach unlikely in the near future, it cannot be ruled out as a long-run possibility. If tariffs on dutiable manufactured products decline to 7 or 8 percent in the major industrial countries after the current negotiations, political leaders may decide it is not worthwhile to expend the needed political effort to achieve further cuts on such a low level of tariffs. The changed nature of the competitive ability of the major countries in the world economy together with a greater concern for equity consideration between groups within a country also favor this alternative.

While it was perhaps always the case, it is now clear that a liberal trade policy for the United States does not automatically bring balance-of-trade benefits. Moreover, the displacement impact of tariff cuts on American industry and labor is not only considerably more significant than in the immediate postwar period, but labor groups that are well organized and politically powerful are now being adversely affected by broad duty reductions. Consequently, the United States government may adopt the position that a vigorous pursuit of worldwide trade liberalization involves unacceptable adjustment costs within the country. The greater political and social concern for internal equity as contrasted with economic efficiency reinforces this view. There is widespread agreement in many countries that the income and employment problems of those who labor under the disadvantages of few skills and a poor education must receive more sympathetic attention. Since tariff cuts by industrial countries on items where duties are still important are likely to affect adversely precisely those who are already in economic difficulties, a consequence of the increased concern for internal equity may be a retreat from a liberal trade policy.

The minerals problem discussed under the previous trading alternative may also move some countries in an autarkical direction. For example, the United States may seek self-sufficiency in energy by the end of the decade. Additional minerals may soon be placed on this list. Many other countries, however, cannot obtain a self-sufficient position in key minerals. Presumably they will have to push either for a global or for a regional solution to their problem. But the lack of US pressures favoring either of these solutions could seriously weaken the chances for their success.

In considering this third option, the United States and other major trading states will face the choice of whether to create a minimum set of rules and arrangements to cover important areas of trade, e.g., trade in scarce raw materials, and to erect temporary import safeguards, or whether to face the retreat from liberalization without agreed rules of behavior for such significant areas. If, as now is apparent, states believe that the process of trade liberalization cannot guarantee security of access to supplies of critical materials markets, the political competition and economic uncertainty that will result from national autarkical efforts and unrestrained bilateral competition are likely to become a major source of international conflict.

The alternative is to refocus the trade liberalization efforts of the last 28 years on the more narrow goal of creating a minimum set of rules covering state conduct and responsibilities with regard to the major international trade flows that will continue to exist. This rule-making strategy would have both economic and political benefits. Economically, such rules might dissuade states from some of the more inefficient schemes of national autarky that are likely to subtract from net global welfare and may also have serious environmental side effects. Politically, such rules might prevent international conflict arising over market or supply disruptions or, at least, provide agreed mechanisms for resolving such disputes when they arise.

An evaluation of alternative trading arrangements

As the introductory article by Bergsten, Keohane, and Nye indicates, there are a variety of economic and political criteria that must be used to evaluate alternative world-trading systems. The economic criteria are efficiency, income distribution, full employment and price stability, growth, and quality of life, while the political criteria are security and domestic political effects. This part of the essay uses these criteria to appraise the relative merits and drawbacks of the various trading arrangements considered in the preceding section.

Efficiency

Efficiency in the allocation of given resource supplies among various productive uses is the criterion economists employ most frequently in judging alternative policies. It can be shown that some policies lead to economic positions from which it is possible to improve everyone's economic welfare. On the other hand, other policies result in economic solutions where no one can improve his position without reducing the welfare of some other individual. Economists consider the latter class of policies inefficient as compared with the first group.

It must be emphasized that under a given policy, e.g., free trade, there is not just one efficient position but many—depending upon the distribution of income. The efficiency criterion is a necessary rather than a sufficient condition for maximizing economic welfare. Judgments must be supplied concerning the most desirable distribution of income before a final, best position can be determined. Given these judgments, the economist then says that the best position can theoretically be reached with an efficient policy and appropriate lump-sum taxes and grants.

The traditional liberal trade position of economists rests on the fact that given certain economic conditions, free trade leads to an efficient allocation of world resources. Setting aside such aggregate conditions as full employment for later consideration, the two key relationships needed for this conclusion are the existence of perfect competition among producers and consumers and the absence of technological externalities in production or consumption. Both imperfect competition and real externalities can cause a divergence between social costs and benefits and market prices. Consequently, the free-market mechanism will not produce the appropriate signals needed to reach a socially efficient position. Economists have long known that the assumptions needed for favoring free trade are not fully met in the actual world, but they generally have minimized the practical significance of this fact. However, in recent years the appropriateness of this view has been increasingly questioned.

There are many types of market imperfections in factor and product markets that can thwart the achievement of an optimum allocation of world resources through free trade. They take such forms as domestic monopolistic actions by producers, monopsonistic practices by sellers of factor services, imperfect knowledge on the part of producers and consumers, government-imposed restraints on trade, and various barriers to the smooth adjustment of resources to new market conditions. In the presence of these domestic distortions, a move to free trade could reduce world welfare rather than increase it. Similarly, the imposition of a tariff could raise welfare under these circumstances.

A case in point where these circumstances apply is in judging the effects of customs unions and preferential trading arrangements. By liberalizing trade only within the region forming the arrangement, it is possible that world welfare can either increase or decrease. However, as has become familiar through discussions of the trade-creating versus the trade-diverting effects of customs unions, economists can specify circumstances that tend to result in an increase rather than in a decrease of world welfare when such arrangements are established. For example, the higher the initial duties on products exchanged by those forming the regional group and the larger the group relative to the rest of the world, the more likely it is that world welfare will increase. The empirical estimates that have been made of the net welfare effects of the major preferential arrangements, e.g., the European Community (EC) and EFTA, generally indicate that world welfare has increased on balance.

As Cooper has pointed out,[10] unfortunately little empirical work has been done on the significance of market imperfections on welfare (other than in the customs union field). One area where some work has recently been done, however, relates to the costs of adjusting to duty reductions. Free traders tend to assume that any unemployment associated with such reductions is of such a short duration that it can be ignored. Yet an analysis of data collected by the United States Department of Labor on the unemployment associated with displacement by imports indicates an average unemployment period of 36 weeks. The real income loss caused by such unemployment must be subtracted from the net consumer gains due to lower prices (all appropriately discounted) in determining whether welfare in a country rises as a result of tariff cuts. Such estimates have been calculated for selected US industries.[11] Although they clearly show net benefits for the economy as a whole,[12] for some industries positive gains from tariff reductions do not emerge when plausible estimates of the unemployment caused by these cuts are used.

It should not be concluded, however, that on static efficiency grounds tariff liberalization is unwarranted even in these industries. The unemployment costs associated with tariff costs can usually be substantially reduced by staging the

[10] Richard N. Cooper, "Economic Assumptions of the Case for Liberal Trade," in C. Fred Bergsten, ed., *Toward a New World Trade Policy: The Maidenhead Papers* (Lexington, Mass.: D.C. Heath and Co., 1975).

[11] Robert E. Baldwin and John H. Mutti, "Policy Issues in Adjustment Assistance: The United States," in Helen Hughes, ed., *Prospects for Partnership* (Baltimore, Md.: The Johns Hopkins Press, 1973).

[12] See also Stephen P. Magee, "The Welfare Effects of Restrictions on U.S. Trade," in *Brookings Papers on Economic Activity, 3:1972* (Washington, D.C.: The Brookings Institution, 1973).

reductions over time as well as by providing workers better facilities for retraining and for finding new jobs. In addition, the real income losses referred to above do not take into account the increase in employment in export industries caused by the reciprocal tariff cuts of trading partners. Many manufacturing firms produce both import-competing and export products, and they are thereby easily able to shift workers made redundant by greater imports to export production.

Casual empiricism tentatively suggests that most other domestic market imperfections in the industrial countries are not sufficiently serious to overturn the traditional, free-trade view of economics. Moreover, it is usually possible to attack these distortions directly by an appropriate policy measure and thus eliminate the problem. In developing countries the situation is much less clear. Market imperfections are more significant in these countries, and feasible policy options for dealing with them are more limited.

Some of the arguments for infant industry protection are based on these facts. For example, the existence of monopolistic capital markets may make it impossible for individual producers to obtain sufficient funds to exploit fully economies of scale. The first-best policy of eliminating the monopoly may not be politically feasible. Consequently, a second-best policy such as a temporary tariff may raise the profits of these producers sufficiently to enable them to finance the socially desirable expansion from internal funds. Although many economists think that some developing countries have carried protection beyond the point of their own self-interest, most nevertheless regard the selective use of protective measures as appropriate.

Another type of market imperfection that can result in a nonoptimal allocation of world resources arises when a country is sufficiently large in an international market to improve its terms of trade by imposing tariffs or export taxes. Under these conditions, the best policy for the country to pursue from its own viewpoint does not result in an optimum allocation of world resources. A policy of free trade requires such countries to sacrifice part of their own static welfare for the good of the entire world community. In the immediate postwar period, the United States clearly could have exploited its monopoly power to improve its short-run income position but did not follow this course. Even now the large trading nations could act collusively in the manufacturing area to improve their positions relative to the developing nations, just as the developing countries may do in the minerals field. The world as a whole would suffer as a result.

As mentioned at the outset of this section, the existence of technological externalities can also cause free trade to lead to a nonoptimal position. For example, unencumbered trade could result in the creation of pollution-intensive industries that cause significant welfare losses in other sectors. The spillover effects related to knowledge acquisition are another example of the problem. The fact that some producers may obtain at no cost to themselves the benefits of the efforts of others in acquiring knowledge may cause the latter group to fail to undertake the socially optimal amount of effort to acquire knowledge. This is another aspect of the infant industry argument, but its applicability seems fairly limited. Moreover, although tariffs and industry subsidies may improve upon free-market policy under these circumstances, they usually are too blunt to be counted upon to correct fully the underlying difficulty.

Another problem associated with the free-market mechanism, which seems appropriate to mention in view of the growing concern for adequate mineral supplies, is the weight given to the welfare of future generations in reaching current decisions. Setting aside market imperfections and externalities, the free-trade solution maximizes the welfare of the present generation. It is those who are living who decide, through setting the discount rate and the time horizon for their decisions, just how much future generations are weighed. However, it is frequently argued that current generations are too myopic and understate the welfare interests of future generations. Therefore, the state must intervene as a representative of these generations. In the case of minerals, the argument takes the form that supplies are exploited too rapidly under free trade, and that taxes on the use of these supplies are, therefore, socially desirable.[13] This is likely to be an argument that carries increasing weight as the degree of world interdependence increases.

Income distribution

A central problem faced by economists in trying to persuade governments to adopt such policies as free trade is that the policy may result in unfavorable redistributive effects. As previously noted, the free-trade case is based on the auxiliary condition that income can be redistributed by other means in any way desired. In practice, however, this is often not feasible. Internationally, there is no regular mechanism for offsetting any undesirable redistributive effects, and even within most countries such mechanisms are very imperfect. Thus, a particular step toward liberalizing trade must often be judged at least partly on its own redistributive implications.

In theory the domestic redistributive effects of various trade policies are fairly straightforward. Measures that expand trade along the lines of a country's comparative advantage tend to increase the income received by its relatively abundant factors and to decrease that of its scarce productive factors. This relationship helps to explain some of the increased opposition to liberal trade policies in certain industrial countries. In these countries, unskilled labor tends to be relatively scarce and, therefore, to suffer from a liberal trade policy. Since there is now greater concern for improving the income position of the unskilled, the policy of freer trade is not supported with its traditional vigor by many politically important groups.

An attempt to test the initial redistributive impact of tariff cuts was made using US trade data. Actual United States duty levels before and after the Kennedy

---

[13] Another pro—free trade implication of giving greater weight to future generations than the free market does is that the short-run adjustment costs of tariff cuts become less important in assessing net welfare changes.

Round were calculated for some 60 manufacturing sectors in the 79-sector United States input-output table. In order to estimate the duty barriers faced by US exports, a weighted average of pre–Kennedy Round and post–Kennedy Round duties for the EC, Japan, and the UK were determined for these same sectors. Next, appropriate import-demand elasticities were assigned to each of the industrial sectors.[14] On the basis of these elasticities, of the change in duties resulting from the Kennedy Round cuts, and of the distribution of exports and imports by the various sectors (1969 was used as the base year), it was possible to estimate for each industry the change in exports and imports caused by the tariff reductions. Both the 1969 composition of exports and imports as well as the new trade composition that would have emerged from Kennedy Round cuts on this base were normalized on a per million dollar basis in order to abstract from balance-of-trade effects. The last step was to calculate for six categories of labor the changes in the direct and indirect demand for labor brought about by the industrial shifts in the pattern of US imports and exports.[15]

The results are not entirely what may be expected. Considering the compositional effects on the import side first, there is the expected net increase in the total amount of labor that would be needed to produce the new per million dollar import bundle domestically. This means that the shift in the pattern of imports acted to reduce employment and that the United States shifted to more labor-intensive imports. What is surprising is that the numbers of engineers and scientists, other professional, technical, and managerial employees, clerical and sales personnel, craftsmen and foremen, and operatives that would be required to produce the new per million dollar bundle of imports domestically all increased whereas the demand for nonfarm unskilled labor decreased. Consequently, the compositional effects of the duty cuts acted to displace labor in the first five skill groups but reduced the displacement of unskilled labor caused by imports.

The compositional effects on the export side are an increase in the total labor demand but one that is less than the amount of the decline in labor demand caused by the change in imports. Thus, even if the change in exports was balanced in value terms by the change in imports, cuts similar to those of the Kennedy Round cause some net decline in labor demand. The net decline is about 1 percent of the labor involved in export production. On the export side there is a rise in the required number of man-years of labor for engineers and scientists, other professionals, and clerical and sales personnel, no change in the demand for craftsmen and operatives, and a decline in the need for unskilled labor. These results are not surprising, since

---

[14] Using an import-demand study by R. Ball and K. Marwah ("The U.S. Demand for Imports: 1948-58," *Review of Economics and Statistics,* November 1962: 395-401), the industries were divided into semimanufactures and manufactures and assigned elasticities of −1.64 and −4.04, respectively, for both the import and export side.

[15] Direct and indirect labor coefficients by industry for each of the six skill groups were based on the Bureau of Census, *1/1000 Sample of the Population of the United States, 1960,* and 1958 employment data by industry furnished by the US Department of Labor.

exports could be expected to shift toward items requiring relatively abundant factors in the US, namely, highly skilled categories of labor. When both exports and imports are taken into account, the demand for all types of labor decreases as a result of the compositional changes.

A crude attempt was also made to assess the short-run effects of the Kennedy Round tariff cuts on the trade balances of the major participants and nonparticipants. For this purpose the 1964 dutiable imports of nonagricultural goods for the United States, the European Community, the United Kingdom, other European Free Trade Association countries, Japan, and Canada were divided into five categories, according to whether the import demand for each three-digit Standard International Trade Classification (SITC) group was considered to be inelastic, relatively inelastic, relatively elastic, elastic, or highly elastic.[16] In addition, the import shares for 1964 of the six groupings from each other and from the developing countries as well as from an all-other group (mainly Australia, New Zealand, and South Africa) were determined for each of the five commodity categories. On the basis of these data and the initial tariff-cutting offers made in the Kennedy Round by the six groupings, it is possible to estimate the change in the balance of trade for these countries as well as for the developing countries and the all-other group.[17]

The estimates obtained indicate that the balance-of-trade effects varied considerably between the six groupings. These effects were (in millions of dollars): United States, −179; European Community, 225; United Kingdom, −229; other EFTA, −392; Japan, 125; and Canada, −9. Other than the European Community, the major trade gainers are the developing countries (228) and the all-other group (231).[18] Although the participants often talk about a balance of trade concessions and apparently mean by this that a rough balance of changes in exports and imports should be achieved, there are no carefully prepared and seriously considered economic investigations of the overall trade effects of various negotiating rules. Noneconomic factors and pressures from selected economic interests dominate the determination of the package a country finally accepts. Consequently, except for the "free-ride" benefits likely to accrue to the developing countries, the distributive

---

[16] The elasticities assumed for the five groups are, respectively, −1.0, −1.5, −2.0, −3.0, −4.0. An alternative set of elasticities were also used that varied between the countries involved in the manner suggested by Bela Balassa, *Trade Liberalization Among Industrial Countries* (New York: McGraw-Hill, 1967), p. 190. The highly elastic and elastic groups were assigned the elasticities for finished manufactures used by Belassa; the relatively elastic and relatively inelastic, his semimanufactures elasticity figure; and the inelastic group, his crude materials elasticity coefficient.

[17] It should be noted that the final offers were modified somewhat from the initial offers. Besides the direct price effects of the tariff cuts, the trade repercussions include estimates of the reduction in the trade diversion impact of the EC and EFTA.

[18] The estimates calculated by using the other set of elasticities are: US, −358; EC, 50; UK, −122; other EFTA, −155; Japan, 182; Canada, 36; developing countries, 169; and all other, 197.

trade effects of liberalizing exercises are not likely to appeal to one's concept of global equity.[19]

Although the developing countries have benefited from the trade-creating spillover effects of recent trade-liberalizing negotiations, this does not mean that in the long run free trade operates to equalize income levels between countries. Free trade tends to yield the highest benefits to the most efficient, and this can lead to an increase in the degree of intercountry income inequality. The popularity of regional groupings has partly been a response to this possibility. However, as many countries have found, these arrangements are no panacea for unfavorable redistributive effects of free trade. The same centralization that occurs under global free trade can occur within a customs union, especially if there are appreciable differences in development levels. However, it does seem easier to establish income-redistributing mechanisms within reasonably small economic unions than between many nations linked by free trade.

Full employment and price stability

One of the outstanding accomplishments of modern liberal traders has been to link the major trading countries together in common tariff-reducing exercises. When one country alone cuts its duties, it benefits from the consumer surplus gains that form the basis of the case for free trade, but, if the cuts are widespread, a significant increase in aggregate unemployment could occur. When others also cut, the stimulus to export reduces unemployment in other sectors (or sometimes in the sectors adversely affected by greater imports) and tends to at least maintain the aggregate level of employment—a highly sensitive variable politically.

There is no reason, of course, why there should not be a net effect of reciprocal tariff reductions on aggregate employment, even if there is no net balance-of-trade effect. The labor-intensiveness of exports versus imports determines the outcome under these conditions. Although a representative bundle of US exports is more labor-intensive than a representative bundle of competitive US imports, the Kennedy Round cuts apparently did not tend to increase aggregate employment, as the study cited in the last section indicates. US duty-reduction effects were concentrated on more labor-intensive products than were the export concessions obtained by the US.

The unemployment in particular industries brought about by tariff concessions is another aspect of the problem that has been inadequately handled under existing institutions. As the investigation cited in the section on efficiency shows, this unemployment can sometime be serious enough to offset the consumer benefits of tariff cuts.

---

[19] The trade effects of tariff reductions are, of course, relevant to a discussion of intercountry income shifts only because they are likely to be correlated with short-run employment changes in the countries. A longer run measure of the real income effects caused by the duty reductions would be the increase in consumer surplus in each country. For the variable elasticities model, estimates of such gains as a result of the Kennedy Round, expressed as a percentage of dutiable imports, are as follows: United States, 2.4 percent; EC, 1.7 percent; UK, 3.5 percent; other EFTA, 2.1 percent; Japan, 1.7 percent; Canada, .04 percent.

Both the regional and the inward-looking approaches to trade policy have certain advantages over the liberal trade approach in coping with the employment problem. The free movement of labor and capital within customs unions coupled with the special funds usually set up under such schemes to assist unemployed workers enable those adversely affected by intraregional free trade to adjust more easily than is the case under the global free-trade approach. Likewise, if a country's competive position is such that reciprocal tariff cuts are likely to increase imports more than exports and if its import-competing production is labor-intensive, the inward-looking policy of not attempting to liberalize trade eliminates a potentially damaging shock on the labor force.

Within recent years it has come to be appreciated once again that a liberal trade policy is an effective anti-inflationary weapon.[20] Political pressures now make it extremely difficult for governments to pursue the type of harsh monetary and fiscal policies needed to control effectively an inflationary episode. However, to the extent that domestic consumers can turn to imports as inflationary pressures spread, the economy possesses a built-in device to break the cost-price spiral that can so easily develop in the modern industrial economy. Of course, for this to be effective the exchange rate must not be completely flexible (or else the country's currency will merely depreciate as imports rise) nor must inflation abroad be as bad as it is domestically.

Growth

The classical and neoclassical case for a liberal trade policy rests not only on static efficiency grounds but also on growth considerations. According to this theory, trade is an engine of growth because of its effects in raising the level of capital accumulation and in widening markets (thus enabling the world economy to benefit more fully from economies of scale, from a greater interchange of technological knowledge, and from the stimulative effects of increased competition). However, as with the efficiency arguments for a liberal policy, the case for free trade on growth grounds relates to world income rather than to the income of each member of the international community. It is actually possible for free trade to lead to immiserization for a particular country.

In addition to such well-known development arguments for imposing trade restraints as the existence of market imperfections, technological spillovers, and positive incentive effects from a do-it-yourself approach, the long-run impact of free trade in structuring production in an economy may serve as an argument for state intervention in the trade field. Free trade may maximize each generation's welfare, given its resources, but in so doing may affect the nature of factor growth and production, so that growth is not maximized if a time preference pattern is introduced that weighs the interests of future generations more heavily than current

---

[20] See Herbert Giersch, "Freer Trade for Higher Employment and Price Level Stability," in Bergsten, ed., *Toward a New World Trade Policy: The Maidenhead Papers.*

generations do. For example, the creation in some developing countries of economies dominated by exports of labor-intensive tropical products that are produced under the plantation system probably maximized the growth rate of income for the generations involved. But the resulting distribution of income and the stimulus given to the demand for unskilled labor may have brought these economies to a development plateau from which a high rate of industrial growth is very hard to initiate. If a different, less growth-oriented productive structure had been initially established, more rapid industrial growth may now be taking place.

The problem with arguments such as the above is that they benefit greatly from hindsight and are very difficult to apply to the future. The developing countries, for example, have generally believed that forced industrialization would yield them higher growth rates in the long run than liberal trading policies. However, it now appears that a number of these countries have carried their industrialization policies to the point where long-run growth will be less than if no state intervention had occurred. Liberal economic policies may not trace the optimal growth path precisely, but their probabilities of being closest to this path may be higher than what can be realistically expected from extensive state intervention in the market place.

Quality of life

Points quite similar to the ones used above in stating the case against free trade on growth grounds can be made in evaluating the effects of free trade on the quality of life. The freedom of choice associated with the set of liberal policies of which free trade is a part gives individuals the maximum right to select goods or jobs according to their own tastes. However, the choices available are limited by the previous economic decisions of others, and the free-price mechanism may unfavorably restrict these choices. The current social environment created by a competitive system may itself be regarded as undesirable. John Stuart Mill, for example, remarked:

> I confess I am not charmed with the ideal of life held out by those who think that the normal state of human beings is that of struggling to get on; that the trampling, crushing, elbowing, and treading on each other's heels, which form the existing type of social life, are the most desirable lot of human kind, or anything but the disagreeable symptoms of one of the phases of industrial progress.[21]

Even considering the effects of trade policy on the quality of life from a narrower viewpoint, there are reasons for a growing dissatisfaction with the results of uncontrolled trade. The increasing interdependence of nations and groups within these nations brought about by modern technology and economic growth means

---

[21] J. S. Mill, *Principles of Political Economy*, vol. 2 (London: J. W. Parker, 1888) p. 308.

that technological externalities related to a country's production for trade affect more people within the country as well as in other countries. For example, increases in offshore fishing activities by one country now significantly curtail the fishing yields of other countries. Similarly, pollution is no longer mostly an intracountry problem; the health and comfort of those living in other countries can be adversely affected by a country's industrial expansion.

Multilateral organizations such as the GATT have difficulties in dealing with problems of these sorts because any one spillover problem is likely to affect only a few members. Consequently, interest in the problem is not sufficiently widespread to generate action. The regional trade approach, on the other hand, has a better chance of successfully solving such issues, since the usual proximity of the regional members increases the likelihood that more externality problems will be shared in common. A serious drawback of the retreat-from-trade approach is that it tends to ignore the ever increasing economic interdependence of nations.

Security

Free trade is not only theoretically neutral in its income distribution implications but, as viewed by some economists, it is also apolitical. Yet the nation state is the basic institution of international relations, and the maximization of its welfare is a major goal of international relations. As is evident from all but a narrow economic perspective, free trade in fact is not neutral in its political effects. It is no surprise that countries achieving a dominant competitive position internationally, e.g., Great Britain in the latter part of the last century and the United States from the 1930s to the 1960s, favored free trade. Increased trade enables such countries to strengthen their security position not only by accelerating their rate of income growth but also by creating dependency relationships on the part of other countries through trade and investment ties. Reverse ties on such items as raw materials and foodstuffs are, of course, also established, but when a country is politically powerful and the raw material exporters are numerous and weak, these ties are not likely to cause any serious security problems. It is only when the country's export ability declines without a similar decline in its dependence on others for security-intensive imports that the disadvantages of free trade for such countries become apparent.

Since the market-oriented international community is characterized by three major powers (the United States, the European Community, and Japan) and the centrally planned economies by two dominant members (the Soviet Union and China), there seems little chance in the foreseeable future that any one nation will be able to impose a liberal trade policy in the way the United States did after World War II. This does not necessarily mean, however, an end to liberal trade. As previously mentioned, it might be that the power of multinational corporations will become sufficient to achieve this goal.

But the recent history of national controls on these organizations does not make one very confident of such an outcome. A more plausible basis for a liberal trade policy would be a belief by each of the major trading powers that it has a chance of improving its market position, and perhaps even becoming the dominant economic power, through a world in which trade can expand readily. The present system of political and economic power can be compared to an unstable oligopolistic market situation. The participants are still testing their competitive strengths. Moreover, the changes in their underlying power foundations brought about largely by technological developments in the last quarter of a century have not been fully worked out. Another factor keeping the liberal trade approach in the forefront is the belief by many that in the present type of oligopolistic environment, efforts to solve economic problems with international implications must be undertaken on a global basis in order to minimize the possibility of future military conflicts. On the other hand, the escalation of the scale of military power and its consequent lethal impact, as well as the de-emphasis during the last decade of ideological conflict between most major political antagonists, is eroding this factor as a strong basis for a liberal trade approach.

Though none of the major Western economies seems ready to rule out the possibility that freer trade may enhance its economic and political power under certain circumstances, all seem prepared to consider alternative approaches in the trade field to further their political goals. The regional approach, in particular, can have security advantages. If the economic benefits and costs are distributed fairly evenly between the participants, the arrangement cannot only give the members greater economic power in the international community but can generate actions within the group that improve the collective security status of the members. In the jockeying for position that characterizes an unstable oligopolistic situation, it seems likely that new regional ties will be established either by the major or the lesser economic powers.

The liberal free-trade model rests on a fundamental assumption that the industrial goods and raw materials needed to sustain a modern economy can be obtained by the price mechanism through trade. This assumption is reasonable in a world where raw material exporters are motivated only by a desire for maximum economic return and are politically weak and disorganized. For an increasing range of scarce raw materials, this assumption of ready availability through the price mechanism may no longer be accurate. Although oil is the currently fashionable example of the raw material dependence of the industrial world upon a few nonindustrial suppliers and of the economic and political disruption that can be caused by an interruption of supply, it is not the only example and, in terms of comparative global reserves, may not even be the best example.

The exponential growth in demand by the industrial world for raw materials and the location of several of these critical materials in a small number of developing states raise the fear that these countries will be able to withhold the raw materials to gain international political and economic objectives. In addition to oil, the raw materials most often mentioned are copper, bauxite, tin, and molybdenum. While it may turn out that of all the raw materials only petroleum meets all of the classical conditions for effective collusion between suppliers, the political effect of the Arab oil boycott has been to embolden other suppliers to consider similar moves and to almost traumatize the industrial world with the prospect of raw material shortages.

Most of our attention in the last three decades has been upon the terms under which exports may enter a country and how closely these terms approach MFN. United States trade legislation prior to the 1974 trade bill and the relevant international law of trading arrangements assume the availability of exports and have almost nothing to say concerning the terms of access to scarce raw materials. This is understandable in terms of the economic issues that have dominated the last 50 years. However, with regard to raw materials we appear to be in a transition from a concern with the terms of trade and the conditions governing access to markets to a concern with the security of supplies and their very availability. The temptation will be great for industrial states to attempt to penetrate, economically and politically, raw material-supplying states to control the production and availability of raw materials. In the wake of the Arab oil boycott, the prospect has been raised that strategic dominance in raw materials can be used to extract benefits other than wealth and to effect the relative economic fortunes of "friends" and "enemies" in the industrial world.

If the fear of raw material scarcity is to become a characteristic of industrial production for the next 30 years, then we are likely to see develop bilateral and unilateral trading arrangements primarily directed toward the issue of security of supply and availability of raw materials. Bilaterally, such arrangements could be directed toward ensuring more favorable or secure access to raw materials for one region or state than would be available to other states. Or, alternatively, multilateral arrangements could be directed toward ensuring equal access to raw materials, the functional equivalent to MFN except that it would apply to exports instead of imports.[22]

Domestic political effects

As the Bergsten-Keohane-Nye article notes, the structure of international relations influences the ability of political leaders to achieve and maintain power through the effects of the particular policies chosen on the domestic political situation. The shift in the position of the politically powerful American Federation of Labor–Congress of Industrial Organizations (AFL-CIO) against the policy of liberal trade is perhaps the most significant recent development in the United States relating to this point. However, the growing willingness throughout the world of groups that feel injured by certain economic policies to assert their interests in a disruptive manner suggests that outward-looking trade policies face serious internal political obstacles everywhere—unless more satisfactory adjustment and compensation policies can be put into operation. The expansion of trade through regional

[22] For proposals to this end, see C. Fred Bergsten, *Completing the GATT: Toward New International Rules to Govern Export Controls* (Washington, D.C.: British-North American Committee, November 1974).

arrangements can also face this problem, as has been discovered by several countries.

In large economies, domestic political considerations based on short-run economic interests appear to favor an inward-looking trade policy. Particular economic groups that are relatively depressed for some reason see the curtailment of competing imports as an obvious solution to their problem. Because of their plight, they pursue this objective vigorously. Exporters who benefit from expanded trade usually are already doing well, and consumers' benefits are quite small for each consumer. Thus these groups do not push for freer trade as hard as the opponents push against it. The fear that they themselves sometime will be in a weak position internationally weakens their opposition to protectionists. Consequently, the more significant becomes the number of economically depressed groups, the more difficult it becomes for political leaders to work for liberal trade policies. Long-run economic interests, such as the need to secure adequately supplies of raw materials and to maintain efficiency in domestic industries through international competition, may provide political reasons for a liberal trade policy, but the time horizon of domestic leaders is often too short and the short-run decisional bias of many political structures is too great for these factors to be politically decisive.

Some conclusions

International trading relationships are in flux. Moreover, the chances are not favorable for the emergence in the short run of a set of economic and political power relationships that will produce a stable trade environment. Actions that run counter to the liberal trade approach undoubtedly will be taken by large and small countries, both for international and domestic political reasons and for certain economic purposes. The self-interests of the nation state in an uncertain world justify such actions. But there are also strong political and economic reasons for liberalizing trade on a global basis, and many of these also serve the self-interests of nation states. Thus, future trade policy is likely to be a combination of all three approaches outlined.

There is need of support for adopting a long-run view of the potential for international economic development and political cooperation. The inward-looking approach, though it probably will eventually break down anyway because of interdependence realities, will—if vigorously pursued—increase the long-run chances of international conflict and impose serious obstacles to achieving the world's economic potential. The long-run price for pursuing short-run economic and political goals through this approach thus may be very high. The regional approach is likely to prove more successful in terms of the self-interest of its members and also involves fewer obstacles to eventual global cooperation. It can even be argued that the achievement of global economic and political goals is hastened by this apparent detour. The push for a liberal trade policy that will continue to occur even for short-run economic and political reasons needs to be encouraged as a major means of furthering the long-run objectives of world peace and prosperity. A sufficiently stable set of political and economic relationships may be established among nations in the intermediate run to permit trade liberalization that does not upset these relationships and that yields substantial mutual economic benefits.

Changes in international trading institutions are clearly needed to facilitate this possibility. In the GATT, these include improved negotiation mechanisms, better means of settling disputes, new articles covering nontariff means of distorting trade and access to supplies, and a stronger secretariat. The trade concerns of the developing countries as expressed in UNCTAD, and some of the problems dealt with in OECD need more explicit attention in the GATT. A more fully integrated consideration of financial, international investment, and trade issues is also required. A new organization replacing the GATT may be appropriate for these purposes but the possibilities of obtaining such an organization are not favorable. The essence of the approach in either the GATT or in a new organization should be a flexible set of rules that recognizes the unstable set of political and economic relations now existing in the international community and that facilitates the achievement of the potential world benefits from an efficient use of world resources.

Foreign aid: its speckled past and future prospects

Charles R. Frank, Jr., and Mary Baird

At the present time, the political popularity of foreign assistance, both bilateral and multilateral, has reached a low point in the United States. The lack of enthusiasm is epitomized by the vote of the House of Representatives in January 1974 against the United States's pledge of $550 million to support the International Development Association (IDA), the soft-loan subsidiary of the World Bank (even though that vote was subsequently reversed). Total US commitments of official development assistance have declined from 0.59 percent of GNP in 1963 to 0.29 percent in 1972.[1]

The malaise is not confined to the United States. Official development assistance of all members of the Development Assistance Committee of the Organization for Economic Cooperation and Development (OECD) declined from 0.51 percent to 0.34 percent of GNP between 1963 and 1972.[2] Aid from France suffered an absolute decline, while that from Germany and the United Kingdom, although increasing absolutely, also declined with respect to GNP.

The disenchantment with aid is not confined to the donor countries. Until fairly recently, nearly all less developed countries clamored for more aid. Through United Nations channels, particularly the United Nations Conference on Trade and Development, and in their relations with developed countries and with multilateral institutions, the less developed countries attempted to use a wide range of hortatory devices to draw attention to their need for more aid. The alleged long-run tendency for the terms of trade to turn against the poorer nations and threats of

Charles R. Frank, Jr., is with the United States Department of State, and Mary Baird is with the First National Bank of Chicago. The authors wish to thank C. Fred Bergsten and Larry Krause for their extensive comments on this essay, Gerald Epstein who served as a research assistant, and Ann Ziegler who typed a couple of drafts in her usual competent fashion.

[1] Organization for Economic Cooperation and Development, *Development Cooperation: Efforts and Policies of the Members of the Development Assistance Committee* (Paris: Organization for Economic Cooperation and Development, 1973), p. 189.
[2] Ibid.

the dire consequences of a "widening gap" between incomes in the developed and the developing worlds were a consistent part of the rhetoric.

In more recent times, however, a number of less developed countries have begun to doubt the efficacy of foreign assistance. For example, Tanzania's policies of self-reliance, developed in the late sixties, were based on the belief that it was a mistake to rely too heavily on foreign aid, which could be terminated at any time, was not always efficiently used, and required political commitments by Tanzania as a quid pro quo.[3] Until recently, India also moved increasingly toward less dependence on foreign aid.[4] The trend toward less reliance on aid has its greatest support among Latin American intellectuals who write of the evils of political and economic *dependencia.*[5]

Another reason for a decline in interest in foreign aid has been the successful performance of a number of countries in terms of rapid growth of GNP and exports. This performance has reduced the need for aid as a supplement to internally generated savings or foreign exchange availability. Thus, there are a number of countries, such as Brazil, Colombia, Korea, Mexico, and Taiwan, that are graduating to a semideveloped state and are becoming more self-reliant in economic terms.

Although aid giving has become very unpopular in the United States and in the major European countries, in some donor countries it has become increasingly important. In the late sixties and early seventies, Australia, Austria, Canada, Japan, and the Scandinavian countries have experienced striking increases in their aid programs. Likewise, not all the recipient countries spurn dependence on foreign aid. Many African and Asian countries, in particular, would welcome increased aid flows. The oil crisis and sharply rising food prices have significantly reduced resistance in the poorest countries to further aid dependence. The most notable example is the recent Indian desire to resuscitate an aid relationship with the United States.[6]

The main purposes of this essay are to analyze the reasons for differences in attitudes toward aid in donor and recipient countries, to analyze the changing role over time that development assistance has played in relations between rich and poor countries (or in the language of this volume, between the North and the South), and to suggest a framework for the role of foreign aid in the future.

In the first section we discuss the historical development of modern foreign-assistance institutions. In the second section we analyze the multiple purposes that foreign aid has served. Within most countries, motivations for supporting foreign aid are mixed and different groups have different conceptions of the goals of

---

[3] See "The Policy of Self-Reliance—Excerpts from Part III of the Arusha Declaration of February 5, 1967," *Africa Report* 12 (March 1967): 11-13; and Henry Bienen, "An Ideology for Africa," *Foreign Affairs* 47 (April 1969): 545-59.

[4] See "India Seeking Renewal of U.S. Economic Aid," *Washington Post,* 5 April 1974.

[5] See Osvaldo Sunkel, "Big Business and 'Dependencia': A Latin American View," *Foreign Affairs* 50 (April 1972): 517-31.

[6] See "India Seeking Renewal of U.S. Economic Aid," *Washington Post,* 5 April 1974.

foreign aid. Motivations differ between donor countries, between recipient countries, and between donor and recipient countries. They change over time and are reflected in the various forms foreign aid may take.

We argue in the third section that much of the disillusionment with foreign aid stems from the enormous gap that exists between expectations and actual performance. We speculate about the reasons for these gaps and ways of closing them. In the fourth section we suggest a framework for foreign assistance that could make aid programs more productive and responsive to both donor and recipient country needs. The basic requirements for a more effective aid program are: (1) integration of foreign aid more carefully into the overall set of relationships between rich and poor countries; (2) clear separation, whenever possible, of different forms of aid that serve very different purposes; and (3) realistic expectations as to what aid can do.

In the fifth section we discuss the multilateralization of humanitarian and development-oriented foreign aid. We focus in the next two sections on aid programs designed to achieve clear national economic or security goals. Finally, we synthesize our analysis and reach some general conclusions.

A brief history of development assistance

The flow of capital from the developed countries of Europe and the United States to less developed areas has a number of historical precedents. During the colonial period in Africa and Asia in the nineteenth and first half of the twentieth centuries, large amounts of capital were transferred from the colonial powers to their overseas territories. Before World War I, much of the capital that flowed into the colonial territories was private capital encouraged by the colonial governments in various ways, including the granting of monopoly rights of exploitation. Special projects such as new railroads were financed by the colonial governments. The general philosophy, however, was that the overseas territories should be self-financing. Gradually, and particularly after World War I, colonial governments began to assume greater responsibility not only for financing development expenditures but, in quite a number of cases, for general administrative costs as well.

Another precedent to modern capital flows is the substantial bond purchases by the developed countries in the late nineteenth century to finance a wide variety of projects in Latin America. However, the use of public funds on subsidized terms to assist in the development and growth of sovereign nations has no significant precedent before the Marshall Plan, following World War II. Marshall Plan aid took place on a massive scale, amounting to about 2 percent of United States GNP in 1949.[7]

Since the height of the Marshall Plan, US foreign aid has flowed on a much smaller scale, but it has become increasingly institutionalized. In 1949 President

---

[7] Goran Ohlin, *Foreign Aid Policies Reconsidered* (Paris: Organization for Economic Cooperation and Development, 1966), pp. 9, 15.

Truman announced his Point Four Program, which signaled the beginning of development assistance as a national policy. The Korean War diverted attention away from economic aid toward military aid, although a modest expansion of ad hoc technical and capital assistance programs took place. Sales of surplus agricultural commodities under public law 480 (PL480) began in the early fifties. After the Korean War, economic aid efforts were increased. Foreign economic aid reached its zenith in the early part of President Kennedy's administration, when the Agency for International Development took over a wide range of technical and capital assistance functions and the Alliance for Progress was begun. Since the middle sixties, United States foreign economic assistance has become a less important policy tool, although the administrative and bureaucratic structure has remained largely the same.

The colonial powers—France, England, Belgium, Holland, and Portugal—financed large portions of government capital formation and, in some cases, substantial amounts of current budgets in their overseas territories before independence. In the late fifties and early sixties, when independence was achieved in most of these territories, financial assistance continued. The aid programs of the former colonial powers are still oriented largely toward their former colonies.[8]

Particular bilateral aid programs

Other developed countries have initiated important aid programs in the last decade or so. West Germany began making appropriations for technical assistance in 1953. Its program of capital and technical assistance grew quite rapidly in the sixties. The Scandinavian countries began making substantial aid commitments in the early sixties. The rate of growth in Scandinavian bilateral assistance has been most spectacular since 1966. Official development assistance of Denmark, Norway, and Sweden[9] rose from $92.1 million in 1966 to $356.6 million in 1972.[10] In Japan foreign aid has been part of official policy since the mid-fifties. Japanese aid flows are quite large, but grants tend to be tied strictly to purchases in Japan and loans are on fairly hard terms.[11] Canada has participated in the foreign aid process since the fifties through the Colombo Plan, a multilateral aid scheme designed to promote regional cooperation in south and southeast Asia. About 80 percent of Canada's total aid went through the Colombo Plan until the sixties when Canada

[8] See Francis X. Colaço, *Economic and Political Considerations and the Flow of Official Resources to Developing Countries* (Paris: Organization for Economic Cooperation and Development, 1973).

[9] As defined by the Development Assistance Committee of the OECD in *Development Assistance: Efforts and Policies of the Development Assistance Committee* (Paris: Organization for Economic Cooperation and Development, 1969), pp. 241-43.

[10] OECD, *Development Cooperation: Efforts and Policies of the Members of the Development Assistance Committee*, 1973, p. 181.

[11] For a much more extended discussion of Japanese aid programs, see Alexander Caldwell, "The Evolution of Japanese Economic Cooperation, 1950-1970," in Harald B. Malmgren, ed., *Pacific Basin Development: The American Interests* (Lexington, Mass: D.C. Heath & Co. for the Overseas Development Council, 1972), pp. 23-60.

began to develop an independent aid program. Canada's development loan terms have been particularly generous and its technical assistance program has been greatly expanded. In the sixties, Israel mounted a substantial program of technical assistance directed largely toward Africa.[12]

The Soviets and Chinese also entered the aid scene in a substantial way in the early sixties. The biggest projects have been the Aswan dam in Egypt, financed by the Soviets, and the Tanzam railway between Tanzania and Zambia, built by the Chinese. The Soviet Union has also provided assistance to Ghana, Algeria, Mali, and Guinea in Africa, to India, Afghanistan, Iran, and Indonesia in Asia, and to Cuba and Chile following socialist take-overs in those latter two countries. Soviet aid in recent years has become much less important. The demise of Sukarno in Indonesia, Allende in Chile, and Nkrumah in Ghana ended programs in those countries. The Soviet aid program in Guinea was terminated in the early sixties.[13]

Multilateral institutions

In addition to the proliferation of bilateral aid programs in the last few decades, multilateral assistance institutions have grown increasingly important. The 1944 conference at Bretton Woods resulted not only in a new international monetary framework with the International Monetary Fund as its capstone, but also in a companion organization, the International Bank for Reconstruction and Development (IBRD, or the World Bank), a development-lending institution designed to tap private financial markets. The World Bank group includes a soft-loan subsidiary, the International Development Association (IDA), established in 1960, and an equity-financing affiliate, the International Finance Corporation, which began in 1956.[14] The IBRD and IDA were responsible for two-thirds of all multilateral aid commitments over the period from 1961 to 1972 (see table 1).

The Inter-American Development Bank, established in 1961, increased its commitments rapidly between 1961 and 1972. Its commitments, however, are still less than one quarter of that of the IBRD/IDA. The Asian Development Bank first began making commitments in 1968 and has expanded rapidly. The African Development Bank has remained relatively small since its inception in the middle sixties.[15]

Although the World Bank group and the Inter-American and Asian regional banks are the most important multilateral institutions from a development-lending point of view, there is a large and proliferating number of multilateral institutions

---

[12] For a detailed analysis of the Israeli aid programs, see Leopold Laufer, *Israel and the Developing Countries: New Approaches to Cooperation* (New York: The Twentieth Century Fund, 1967).

[13] A good discussion of the Soviet aid program is contained in Marshall I. Goldman, *Soviet Foreign Aid* (New York: Praeger, 1967).

[14] For an historical account of the World Bank group, see Edward S. Mason and Robert E. Asher, *The World Bank Since Bretton Woods* (Washington, D.C.: Brookings Institution, 1973).

[15] For a discussion of regional development banks, see John White, *Regional Development Banks* (New York: Praeger, 1972).

Table 1. Commitments of multilateral and bilateral aid institutions (in millions of dollars and in percent)

	Multilateral commitments		Bilateral commitments of DAC countries		Total multilateral and bilateral commitments
YEAR	MILLIONS OF DOLLARS	PERCENT OF TOTAL	MILLIONS OF DOLLARS	PERCENT OF TOTAL	MILLIONS OF DOLLARS
1961	1,170	14.25	7,042	85.75	8,212
1962	1,515	16.43	7,708	83.57	9,223
1963	1,202	14.87	6,884	85.13	8,086
1964	1,602	15.29	8,875	84.71	10,477
1965	2,110	21.81	7,566	78.19	9,679
1966	1,939	18.68	8,446	64.56	10,382
1967	2,036	17.34	9,709	82.66	11,745
1968	1,915	17.19	9,222	82.81	11,137
1969	2,999	24.55	9,215	75.45	12,214
1970	3,577	25.08	10,687	74.92	14,264
1971	4,201	25.01	12,882*	76.71	16,794
1972	4,972	24.82	15,525*	77.51	20,029
Total	29,238	20.42	113,761	79.55	142,999

SOURCE: Annual issues of OECD-DAC *Review*.
*estimated
NOTE: Multilateral commitments include the World Bank group, the three major regional development banks, UN agencies, and European regional funds. DAC countries are the members of the Development Assistance Committee of the Organization for Economic Cooperation and Development.

that are significant in providing technical assistance to developing nations or in supplementing the capital sources of the big banks. The most important of these is the United Nations system,[16] a vast and complicated web of more than 30 administrative units. There are three basic types of United Nations organizations that play a role in development assistance: (1) the special funds, (2) the executing or specialized agencies, and (3) the regional commissions. The special funds include the United Nations Development Program (UNDP), the United Nations Fund for Population Activities (UNFPA), the United Nations Children's Fund (UNICEF), and the United Nations Environmental Program (UNEP). The special funds conduct some of their own technical assistance operations, but most of the resources available to the funds are channeled through executing agencies, such as the Food

[16] Formally, the World Bank group is part of the UN system, but in practice it is quite autonomous. For a comprehensive analysis of the economic and social functions of the UN system, see Mahdi Elmandjra, *The United Nations System: An Analysis* (Hamden, Conn: Archon Books, 1973).

and Agricultural Organization (FAO), the International Labor Organization (ILO), the World Health Organization (WHO), the United Nations Educational, Scientific and Cultural Organization (UNESCO), the United Nations Industrial Development Organization (UNIDO), and the United Nations Conference on Trade and Development (UNCTAD). The regional Economic Commissions for Asia and the Far East (ECAFE), for Latin America (ECLA), and for Africa (ECA) undertake research, coordinate efforts among their member countries, and provide advice and technical expertise in the scientific, educational, and economic fields.

There are a host of smaller, regionally oriented, development banks which have expanded their operations over the last decade. These include the aid institutions of the European Economic Community—the European Investment Bank (EIB) and the European Development Fund (EDF)—the Caribbean Development Bank (CDB), the Central American Bank for Economic Integration (CABEI), the East African Development Bank (EADB), and the Andean Development Corporation.[17]

A major development during the sixties was the growth in importance of consortia, consultative groups, and other forms of bilateral and multilateral aid coordination. The term *aid consortium* is usually applied to groups of aid donors that meet and make formal pledges or commitments to provide assistance for a particular recipient country. Consultative groups of aid donors ordinarily do not involve formal pledges of assistance.

The World Bank has become a leader in helping establish consortia and consultative groups. The Bank sponsors two consortia, for India and Pakistan, and sixteen consultative groups.[18] The OECD heads a consortium for Turkey, and the Netherlands sponsors what is called the Intergovernmental Group for Indonesia, a consortium-type institution. The Organization of American States (OAS) has its own system for reviewing recipient country requirements for external assistance through its Inter-American Committee on the Alliance for Progress (CIAP). The country reviews undertaken by CIAP provide a means for each country to detail how far it has advanced and how much more external assistance it needs to attain certain objectives.[19] Finally, the Development Assistance Committee (DAC) of the OECD has provided a continuing impetus and forum for rationalizing and coordi-

---

[17] For further analysis of these banking institutions and funds, see White, *Regional Development Banks;* and John White, *Promotion of Economic Integration Through Development Finance Institutions: Three Cases,* forthcoming; also see David Jones, *Europe's Chosen Few: Policy and Practice of the EEC Aid Programme* (London: Overseas Development Institute, 1973).

[18] Countries or subregions are: Colombia, East Africa, Ethiopia, Ghana, Guyana, Indonesia, Korea, Malaysia, Morocco, Nigeria, Peru, the Philippines, Sri Lanka, Sudan, Tunisia, and Zaire. Formal meetings for ten of these were conducted in fiscal 1973.

[19] For further discussion of consortia and consortialike institutions, see John White, *Pledged to Development: A Study of International Consortia and the Strategy of Aid* (London: Overseas Development Institute, 1967); OECD, *Development Assistance: Efforts and Policies of the Development Assistance Committee* (Paris: Organization for Economic Cooperation and Development, 1971), pp. 131-36; and OECD, *Development Cooperation: Efforts and Policies of the Members of the Development Assistance Committee,* 1973, pp. 60-61.

nating the world aid system. It is active in setting criteria for burden-sharing between donor countries.[20]

In recent years, multilateral aid has increased in relative importance compared to bilateral assistance. Total commitments of the major multilateral institutions rose from $1.2 billion in 1961 to almost $5.0 billion in 1972, an increase averaging about 14 percent per year (see table 1). As a percentage of total foreign aid commitments, the multilateral institutions have risen from 14.5 percent in 1961 to 25.0 percent in 1972.

Total bilateral commitments of official development assistance increased much less rapidly, from $6.6 billion in 1961 to $11.7 billion in 1972. In particular, United States official development assistance hardly grew at all from an average of $3.7 billion in 1961-63 to $3.9 billion in 1970-72. Its share of total bilateral commitments declined from 59.8 percent to 41.0 percent. If one corrects for inflation, United States official development assistance actually declined from $3.7 billion in 1961-63 to $3.1 billion in 1970-72 in constant 1961 prices.[21]

Aid from the World Bank group has begun to play a predominant role in many countries compared to aid from the United States. In 1965, bilateral commitments by the United States were larger than IBRD/IDA commitments in 40 out of 47 countries. By 1972, World Bank commitments exceeded US commitments in 21 out of 46 countries, or in countries with a population of almost 1.0 billion out of a total population of about 1.7 billion.[22]

Motivations in donor countries

The differences in attitudes among donor and recipient countries and the changing role of aid over time prompt a number of basic questions. An aid relationship between donor and recipient is a two-way transaction. Policymakers in donor countries who support foreign aid expect to receive some benefits by providing assistance. Similarly, decision makers in the recipient country expect to gain something by receiving aid. What, then, are the motives and goals of those connected with the aid process?

From the donor point of view, four motivations have seemed to predominate: (1) achievement of greater national security, (2) fulfillment of humanitarian obligations to provide assistance to less fortunate nations and peoples, (3) economic gains

---

[20] The development activities of the OECD are described in Milton J. Esman and Daniel S. Cheever, *The Common Aid Effort; the Development Assistance Activities of the Organization for Economic Cooperation and Development* (Columbus: Ohio State University Press, 1967).

[21] For the deflators used to perform these calculations, see OECD, *Development Assistance: Efforts and Policies of the Development Assistance Committee* (Paris: Organization for Economic Cooperation and Development, 1973), p. 176.

[22] See William R. Cline, "The Role of Multilateral Lending Institutions in Development Finance," paper presented to the Society of Government Economists, New York, 28 December 1973, pp. 3-4.

brought about either through opening and maintaining access to less developed country markets on favorable terms or through ensuring access to raw material supplies in less developed countries at favorable prices, and (4) diplomatic gains achieved through the expansion of national prestige and power.

In debates over foreign aid in the United States during the fifties and early sixties, the security rationale predominated. In the fifties, a rather crude set of cold-war dominated, anticommunist arguments were used to justify much economic and military aid to such strategically located countries as Turkey, Greece, Iran, Pakistan, and Taiwan.[23]

The reasoning as applied in the sixties became rather more involved—perhaps tortuous. Foreign economic aid was not justified to Congress or to the public on the grounds that payments of foreign aid could result in an immediate and clear quid pro quo in the form of loyalty to US leadership in the security field. Rather, it was generally argued that foreign aid would lead to economic development that, in turn, would be accompanied by the emergence of stable, democratic governments, and that the existence of stable, democratic governments would help ensure peace and cooperation among countries.

This complicated reasoning was used not only to justify a substantial aid program but was supposed to guide the manner in which foreign aid was administered. Emphasis was to be placed on satisfying economic efficiency criteria, and the greatest rewards were to be given to those governments that most assiduously followed efficient, self-help policies. Aid was not to be allocated on the basis of short-run political criteria, for example, to influence negotiations on an air base or to win a United Nations vote.[24]

These technocratic criteria for economic aid allocation were adhered to only in part. Large amounts of assistance (particularly those funds labeled supporting assistance) went to United States military allies and were often used to supplement military aid.

The humanitarian basis for aid giving plays a role in nearly every economic aid program. In the United States, however, humanitarian arguments have been subsidiary. In some countries, such as in Scandinavia, the humanitarian rationale predominates. In others, such as Canada, Germany, and the Netherlands, it plays an important role. In those countries in which humanitarian assistance plays a substantial role, aid programs emphasize loans on very soft terms, multilateral contributions, and technical assistance projects, particularly in the areas of health, education, cooperatives, and community and rural development.

The economic gains that foreign aid can bring are emphasized in Japan and Italy. The organization of their aid programs reflects the importance of economic considerations: trade credits on fairly hard terms are substantial; soft loans are

---

[23] United States Department of State, "The Scope and Distribution of United States Military and Economic Assistance Programs," report to the President of the US from the Committee to Strengthen the Security of the Free World (Clay Report), 20 March 1963.
[24] For a full development of these arguments, see Max F. Millikan and Walter W. Rostow, *A Proposal; Key to an Effective Foreign Policy* (New York: Harper & Brothers, 1957).

carefully tied to procurement in the donor country; and aid agreements and trade agreements are closely entwined.

Germany and Canada mix economic types of aid with liberal doses of humanitarian assistance. The economic aid largely takes the form of trade credits.

United States PL480 assistance was largely motivated by economic considerations. In the early days of the program, PL480 shipments were seen mainly as a convenient way to reduce the large US food surpluses that were exceedingly costly to carry and tended to exert a depressing influence on US commodity markets. Since the PL480 loans were repayable in local currency, they were tantamount to grants in some countries. In the sixties, as balance-of-payments considerations came to the fore, PL480 loans were converted from a local-currency to a hard-currency basis.

Considerations of national power and prestige are part of nearly all aid programs, just as humanitarian concerns seem to be pervasive. All development assistance is given with mixed motivations, some supporters in a donor country emphasizing one aspect and others another. In the French aid program, national prestige is particularly important and explicit. This type of motivation was made clear in the Jenneney report of 1963, of which Ohlin says: "Among the genuine reasons for a French assistance policy, the first was said to be the simple duty imposed by human solidarity, and the second, France's need of 'rayonnement'—the diffusion of a civilization claiming universal validity and the legitimate desire of a nation to implant its culture peacefully."[25]

The importance of Commonwealth ties to England also has strong elements of wanting to maintain English traditions and culture abroad. Much of the United States aid program, particularly its technical assistance aspects, is geared toward spreading the American way of doing things or the American approach to problems. Soviet aid has been, at least in part, an attempt to maintain or increase influence in areas where American power and prestige were on the ascendency.

The spread of a national culture and the publicity or public relations aspects of foreign aid can enhance a country's diplomatic leverage. It is undoubtedly true that if the elites in many less developed countries have been trained in America, France, or England, then diplomatic relations with the United States, France, or England may be very much facilitated. Furthermore, if most developed countries have programs of financial assistance to less developed countries and if such programs are regarded as part of a moral responsibility of the developed nations, a country that balks at providing foreign aid cannot expect to exercise a leadership role. To the extent that diplomacy relies on moral suasion or faith in the integrity and sincerity of national leaders and policymakers, a country without a responsible foreign assistance program is handicapped in pursuing its international interests.

Foreign aid is also useful in providing a set of important issues to discuss between diplomatic representatives in a country and the country's leaders. The communication channels established and the mutual respect and trust generated in

---

[25] Ohlin, *Foreign Aid Policies Reconsidered*, p. 29.

these discussions can be very useful assets in diplomatic exchanges or negotiations on matters not directly related to aid.

Finally, foreign assistance may be used as leverage to obtain concrete diplomatic goals. Aid has been promised in return for military bases or for support on specific issues.

Attitudes in recipient countries

From the developed country point of view, the major benefits of foreign assistance relate to national security, economic gains, humanitarian concerns, national prestige, and diplomatic leverage. What, then, are the motives of the less developed countries in accepting aid?

There are economic benefits to less developed countries to be derived from foreign aid. If capital and skilled manpower are very scarce and returns on these scarce inputs are high, then the return on capital and technical assistance may exceed its subsidized cost. The returns on foreign capital, however, may be limited by absorptive capacity. The identification of projects with a high rate of return or of other profitable uses of foreign aid funds is not an easy task. Furthermore, it takes time to identify these uses. Thus, the amount of financial and technical aid a country can usefully absorb in any given period of time may be limited.

Another reason for accepting aid, or continuing to receive aid for whatever reason aid was initially accepted, is the heavy cost of a disruption in the flow of aid funds. The most instructive example is the case of Guinea. Upon obtaining independence, most of the French territories continued their close ties with France. The former colonies' monetary systems were tied into the French system; there were preferential trading arrangements and a considerable flow of capital and technical assistance. But Guinea chose to dissolve ties with France, and the French retaliated. According to Goldman: "In 1958, after Guinea voted to leave the French family of nations, the French, in anger, ripped out the phones and tossed most of the country's machinery into the sea. Simultaneously, France induced the rest of the Western world to boycott Guinea in the hope that the country would be forced to turn again to the French for assistance. Instead, Guinea turned to the members of the Communist bloc for economic and political help."[26] The experience with Soviet aid, however, was extremely unsatisfactory. Inexperience on the part of the Soviets and poor planning by everyone concerned soon resulted in such a degree of disillusionment that, in 1963, construction on all Soviet aid projects was halted.

The Guinea case is an extreme example, but it is true that whenever there is heavy and long reliance on a set of external sources of capital, it is difficult and costly to substitute other resources, either from other countries or from domestic sources. Projects must be terminated, and in all likelihood private and government expenditures have to be reduced. Taxes have to be raised, and both consumption

[26] Marshall I. Goldman, *Soviet Foreign Aid* (New York: Praeger, 1967), p. 168.

and investment suffer. Thus, there is a certain amount of historical inertia that maintains aid relationships between particular donors and recipients.

Although economic gains are stressed in their rhetoric, policymakers in less developed countries see other advantages in foreign aid. They may see foreign aid as a means of providing for their own national security. If a less developed country can achieve closer ties with a powerful aid donor, the donor country may be made to feel an increased obligation to help and support the less developed country in a time of diplomatic or military crisis with third parties.

Leaders in less developed countries often welcome aid not so much because of the national security or economic gains that are possible but because of the increased availability of resources that can be used to consolidate political control. Aid programs generate jobs that can be used for patronage purposes. They provide financial resources that are often allocated on political grounds and are sometimes diverted into covering election costs.

In some cases, foreign aid funds are used for the personal financial gain of political leaders in the recipient country. The use of foreign aid funds to enhance the political power of those in office or to finance corruption creates tensions between donor and recipient countries, particularly if practices are especially abusive or create a public scandal.

The gap between expectations and performance

The recent disillusionment with foreign aid on the part of a number of donor and recipient countries is due in large part to the very wide gap between the expectations and goals set for foreign assistance in donor and recipient countries and actual performance over the last two decades or so. If the use of foreign aid had been confined to achieving well-defined and immediate national security goals of both partners, there would have been successes and failures and individual aid programs could have been debated on their merits. The expectation that assistance to less developed nations could advance United States long-run security interests through economic development, however, was certain to be disappointed. The security arguments advanced by Millikan and Rostow were attacked by Morgenthau and by Banfield as fallacious in each link of the logical chain.[27]

Foreign aid and economic growth

The weakest link, however, is that between foreign aid and economic development. There is little evidence that foreign capital has made a large contribution to economic growth. For example, Raymond Mikesell points out: "Historically some countries have developed without significant capital imports and in some cases, the

---

[27] Millikan and Rostow, *A Proposal; Key to an Effective Foreign Policy;* Hans Morganthau, "A Political Theory of Foreign Aid," *American Political Science Review* 56 (June 1962): 301-9; Edward C. Banfield, *American Foreign Aid Doctrine* (Washington, D.C.: American Enterprise Institute for Public Policy Research, 1963).

achievement of sustained growth preceded a substantial capital inflow. On the other hand, large capital inflows have frequently made little contribution to development. As a general proposition external capital or aid is neither a necessary nor a sufficient condition for development."[28]

Given that large foreign capital inflows have not necessarily been associated with rapid growth, it is even less likely that foreign aid, which tends to be much smaller than the total influx of foreign capital, is likely to be associated with rapid growth. A major problem is that for most aid-receiving countries, foreign aid is much too small to make much of a difference either in terms of supplementing domestic savings or foreign exchange availability. In some of the few countries that did receive large amounts of aid, economic policies were followed that did not make efficient use of the resources obtained. In only a very few countries have aid flows been large enough and have policies been shaped to utilize that aid efficiently.[29]

A number of critics argue that foreign assistance has not been effective in promoting growth because it reduces domestic savings. Griffin, Rahman, and Weisskopf assert that the governments of poor nations have savings targets and their own savings efforts are reduced by an equivalent amount when foreign funds are made available. Both Griffin and Houthakker suggest that there are limited investment opportunities in the recipient country, and that foreign capital inflows preempt these opportunities and induce a compensating decline in domestic savings. Griffin also argues that the availability of imported consumer goods financed by foreign capital reduces savings incentives. In fact, Rahman, Griffin and Enos, and Weisskopf, using data on countries receiving aid, demonstrate through regression analysis the negative correlation between foreign aid and domestic savings.[30]

Weisskopf and Bauer both suggest that foreign assistance is ineffective since it is often linked to the imposition of policies such as high taxation and extensive

---

[28] Raymond F. Mikesell, *The Economics of Foreign Aid* (Chicago: Aldine Publishing Co., 1968).

[29] Charles R. Frank, Jr., estimates that without foreign savings between 1960 and 1970, Korean GNP in 1971 would have been about one-third less. Foreign savings constituted about 10 percent of Korean GNP during the decade of the sixties. In the early sixties, the bulk of the foreign savings was due to aid but commercial capital began to predominate in the late sixties. See Frank, *Foreign Trade Regimes and Economic Development: South Korea* (New York: National Bureau of Economic Research, 1975 [forthcoming]), chapter 7. Neil H. Jacoby estimates that US aid to Taiwan probably doubled the rate of growth of GNP between 1951 and 1965. See Jacoby, *U.S. Aid to Taiwan* (New York: Praeger, 1966), pp. 150-73.

[30] See: Keith B. Griffin, "Foreign Capital, Domestic Savings and Economic Development," *Bulletin; Oxford University, Institute of Economics and Statistics* 32 (May 1970): 99-112; Anisur Rahman, "The Welfare Economics of Foreign Aid," *Pakistan Development Review* 7 (Summer 1967): 141-59; Thomas E. Weisskopf, "The Impact of Foreign Capital Inflow on Domestic Savings in Underdeveloped Countries," *Journal of International Economics* 2 (February 1972): 25-38; Hendrik S. Houthakker, "On Some Determinants of Saving in Developed and Underdeveloped Countries," in E. A. G. Robinson, ed., *Problems in Economic Development*, proceedings of a conference held by the International Economic Association, London (New York: St. Martin's Press, 1965), pp. 212-24; and Keith B. Griffin and John L. Enos, "Foreign Assistance: Objectives and Consequences," *Economic Development and Cultural Change* 18 (April 1970): 313-27.

controls that encourage capital flight and provide a breeding ground for corruption. In addition, foreign aid may have a deleterious effect on people's attitudes and motivations and on their political and social institutions. Bauer argues that continuous and large amounts of foreign assistance pauperize recipients by encouraging the idea that unearned doles are the primary ingredient in the livelihood of countries. The valuable process of generating resources internally is foregone and the status and prestige of self-reliance are undermined. Hirschman argues that inflows of foreign capital reduce incentives to local entrepreneurs and preempt investment opportunities that local private entrepreneurs may otherwise take up.[31]

It is also argued that the efficacy of aid in promoting development is reduced since the terms and conditions under which it is offered are often very harsh. Relatively high interest rates, short maturities, and the tying of aid to purchases in the donor country or with contractors in the donor country greatly reduce the value of aid to the recipient country.[32] If the inflow of capital fails to raise productivity sufficiently to yield an increase in real income greater than the interest and amortization charges on the loan, then net real national income is reduced; or if a sufficient export surplus is not generated, the debt-servicing charges may exacerbate any balance-of-payments difficulties.

Supporters of foreign aid counter many of these arguments. Papanek argues that the data are poor and not sufficiently disaggregated to perform the regression analysis attempted by the critics. He also points out that although there may be a *correlation* between increases in foreign aid and reductions in domestic savings, this correlation does not necessarily indicate *causality*. In a number of countries, he states, such factors as wars, civil strife, poor harvests, and falls in commodity prices can provide a causal explanation of both reduced domestic savings and increased foreign aid.[33] Chenery and Carter purport that even if foreign aid reduces domestic

[31] See Weisskopf; Peter T. Bauer, *Dissent on Development; Studies and Debates in Development Economics* (Cambridge, Mass.: Harvard University Press, 1972), pp. 95-135; and Albert O. Hirschman, *How to Divest in Latin America and Why*, Essays in International Finance, no. 76 (Princeton, N.J.: Princeton University, November 1969). pp. 4-6.

[32] On the costs of tied aid, see: Jagdish Bhagwati, "The Tying of Aid," UNCTAD Secretariat, New York, 1966, reprinted in UNCTAD Conference Proceedings (New Delhi), *Problems and Policies of Financing*, vol. 4 (New York: United Nations, 1968), pp. 45-71; Thomas L. Hutcheson, *The Cost of Tying Aid: A Method and Some Colombian Estimates*, Essays in International Finance, no. 30 (Princeton, N.J.: Princeton University, March 1972); Mahbub ul Haq, "Tied Credits—A Quantitative Analysis," in John H. Adler, ed., *Capital Movements and Economic Development* (London: Macmillan & Co., 1967; New York: St. Martin's Press, 1967), pp. 326-59; Eprime Eshaq, "Study of Excess Cost of Tied Economic Aid Given to Iran in 1966/67," UNCTAD (UN Document TD/7/Supp. 8/Add., 2 December 1967), and "Study of Tied Economic Aid Given to Tunisia in 1965," UNCTAD (UN Document TD/7/Suppl. 8/Add., 8 November 1967). On loan terms and their effect, see Charles R. Frank, Jr., *Debt and Terms of Aid* (Washington, D.C.: Overseas Development Council, 1970), reprinted in Frank, Jagdish N. Bhagwati, Robert d'A Shaw, and Harald B. Malmgren, *Assisting Developing Countries, Problems of Debts; Burden Sharing, Jobs and Trade*, Overseas Development Council Studies, I (New York: Praeger 1972).

[33] Gustav F. Papanek, "The Effect of Aid and Other Resource Transfers on Savings and Growth in Less Developed Countries," *Economic Journal* 82 (September 1972): 934-50; and Papanek, "Aid, Foreign Private Investment, and Growth in Less Developed Countries," *Journal of Political Economy* 81 (January/February 1973): 120-30.

savings somewhat, the relationship is not dollar for dollar and foreign aid provides foreign exchange resources that are not equivalent to domestic resources saved through domestic savings. Foreign exchange resources will be more valuable if the so-called foreign exchange constraint is binding.[34] Chenery and Carter's statistical analysis, as well as that of Papanek, indicates substantial net contributions of foreign aid to growth. Also, it is quite clear from individual country studies that foreign aid helped promote economic growth, not only because it provided extra resources, but because the donor country played a role in helping the recipient country policymakers pursue policies appropriate for growth.[35]

Aid and national security

Yet even the supporters of aid do not argue that aid is nearly always effective in promoting growth, but rather that in some countries and at some times, aid may facilitate growth. The lack of a clear and strong link between aid and growth, however, greatly undermines the long-run national security argument for aid. Many critics of US aid argue that aid programs have the opposite long-run effect on US security. It involves the United States in countries in which it initially has little real interests. Foreign aid is the "slippery slope" that leads eventually to an overextension of commitments and to a greater likelihood of military involvement.[36]

The way in which aid is administered may have deleterious effects on donor relationship with poor nations and thereby affect both economic returns and security interests. For example, the organization and operating methods of the United States Agency for International Development (AID) were designed in the sixties to help ensure that foreign aid would serve a useful economic purpose. A key technique used was *performance conditioning*. Aid was made conditional by various means on the adoption of preferred policies and on successful economic performance in a number of key economic areas.

Performance conditioning never worked very well. First, it was never clear that developed country economic experts had better answers to the economic policy questions faced by less developed countries than did the experts in the recipient countries. The attempt to force recipient countries to act on the advice of developed country experts was demeaning to the recipient country policymakers and was a source of resentment. Secondly, many of the economic policies advocated by AID officials, if adopted, would have had profound political effects. Devaluation and economic stabilization policies generate large shifts in income, wealth, and power, thus changing the political status quo. AID officials could not be expected to be as sensitive to these issues as political leaders in recipient countries. Thus, many times policy suggestions would be resisted or undermined by political leaders whose interests were at stake. Considerable hostility and resent-

---

[34] Hollis B. Chenery and N. G. Carter, "Internal and External Aspects of Development Performance," World Bank Discussion Paper No. 141, December 1972.

[35] Frank, *Foreign Trade Regimes and Economic Development: South Korea.*

[36] J. William Fulbright, *The Arrogance of Power* (New York: Random House, 1966).

ment were generated because of the interference in setting policies that had such great internal political consequences. Thus, aid programs not only were often unsuccessful in generating more rapid growth and development, but they sometimes exacerbated political relations because of the way they were administered.[37]

Equally misguided was the US attempt to incorporate criteria for internal political participation into the aid process. Title IX of the United States Foreign Assistance Act of 1966, and its subsequent amendments in 1967 and 1968, made political participation an explicit goal of the United States aid program. One of the reasons for introducing political criteria into the program was the fear that a participatory form of government did not necessarily immediately follow economic development. Since the development of democratic-minded government was one of the links in the long-run national security justification for aid, it was felt that performance conditioning was required to ensure the most rapid growth of political participation. In practice, implementation of the criteria of Title IX was difficult and was subject to many of the same criticisms applied to economic performance conditioning.

The disappointment caused by the lack of a clear relationship between foreign assistance and growth had deleterious effects on recipient country attitudes toward donor countries for other reasons. Recipient country leaders needed tangible economic gains to compensate for the increased vulnerability, dependence, and loss of sovereignty felt by many in recipient countries. Furthermore, as debt service payments mounted up, many recipient countries found themselves in a financial and economic squeeze since exports and national output were not growing rapidly. A recipient country would become evermore dependent on continuation of foreign aid flows, a large part of which simply covered service payments on debt contracted under foreign aid programs. One way out of this dilemma for the recipient country is to repudiate all its debts,[38] but most countries are reluctant to take such a drastic step. The more likely result is continuation of a slow buildup of tension and resentment toward the donor country.

Given the gap between economic performance and expectations, and the way in which aid was administered, political and diplomatic problems were exacerbated rather than ameliorated. The scandals and corruption associated with aid programs also did little to enhance donor country prestige and weakened support for aid within donor countries.

It may still be argued that foreign aid is an instrument that can be used to extract specific strategic goals or to force immediate diplomatic concessions. The record in this regard is mixed. Although, for example, it might be argued that denial of foreign assistance was a factor in Allende's downfall and that this was clearly a goal of United States foreign policymakers, Chile had in the past received vast

[37] For a thorough analysis of the way United States aid officials have tried to influence policies in less developed countries, see Joan M. Nelson, *Aid, Influence and Foreign Policy* (New York: Macmillan Co., 1968).

[38] Wilson Schmidt, "Default of International Public Debts," *The National Banking Review* 2 (March 1965): 403-8.

amounts of aid but this did not prevent the demise of the Christian Democrats, which was something US policymakers fervently sought to avoid.

Aid and economic goals

Aid has received reasonable support in those donor countries in which donor country economic gains are made an explicit goal. Using aid to foster increased trade and investment opportunities is a well-understood and accepted practice in international relations.

Often, however, the tie between aid and economic advantage is not made explicit. Rather, it is expected that foreign assistance will enhance growth in less developed countries and increase the size of the market. A problem arises, however, when a less developed country increases restrictions on trade or makes the climate unfavorable for foreign investment through investment controls, high rates of taxation, or nationalization, threatened or actual. Many of the gains that were expected to result from increased market size are vitiated by these kinds of policy measures in less developed countries.

Also, unless there are specific agreements concerning access to raw material supplies, foreign aid provides no guarantee that access will always be available. The oil crisis of 1973/74 demonstrated this forcefully, but export of other commodities can be controlled as well.[39]

Aid and income distribution

The humanitarian argument for aid has been weakened not only by the lack of correlation between aid and development but also by the fact that in many countries that were able to develop rapidly, relatively few jobs were created, unemployment and underdevelopment remained high, and, worst of all, most of the benefits of development went to the wealthier classes. Donor agencies began to realize that a major rationale for foreign aid was imperiled unless assistance could be reoriented toward: (1) increasing employment opportunities, (2) helping the poorest groups in developing countries, and (3) among developing countries, helping the poorest countries.[40] The World Bank group in particular has taken a strong public stance in favor of employment and income distribution objectives in devel-

---

[39] In July 1974, for example, Brazil placed controls on soybean exports and many African and Asian countries control their exports of primary products through government-run marketing boards.

[40] See, for example, *Renewing the Development Priority, Implementation of the International Development Strategy: First Overall Review and Appraisal of Progress During the Second United Nations Development Decade,* comments and recommendations of the Committee for Development Planning, Department of Economics and Social Affairs (New York: United Nations, 1973); and OECD, *Development Cooperation: Efforts and Policies of the Members of the Development Assistance Committee* (Paris: Organization for Economic Cooperation and Development, 1972), pp. 31-37.

opment programs.[41] The use of income distribution criteria has also become more prominent in bilateral donor agencies.[42]

Within the World Bank group, the IDA has always concentrated its lending activities in the poorest countries. World Bank loans are on relatively hard terms and are usually given to richer, more credit-worthy countries while IDA soft loans are reserved for countries with a per capita income of less than $375. In recent years IDA has moved further in the direction of helping the least developed countries (see table 2). In 1973, IDA channeled 70 percent of its resources to the poorest countries (per capita income of $120 or less). The share received by countries with a per capita income of greater than $250 was less than 10 percent.[43] Within the range of countries in the low to middle categories of income per capita, the IBRD has shifted its activities toward the less wealthy countries (see table 2).

The trend toward lending to the poorest countries is also evident in the Inter-American Development Bank in recent years. In 1972, 30 percent of ordinary capital lending (compared to 21.4 percent in 1970) and 50 percent of the lending from the Fund for Special Operations (compared to 24.7 percent over the period 1961-71) was extended to countries classified as least developed.[44]

The emphasis on income distribution *within* recipient countries is manifested in part by the expansion of lending activities in the agriculture, education, and population sectors (see table 3). In the period 1969-73, the World Bank quadrupled its lending to agriculture. At the same time, it tripled its lending to education, paying increased attention to the financing of educational software (i.e., improving curriculum and teaching tools and systematically planning types of education to be offered) whereas in the past its primary concern was with the construction and furnishing of school buildings. Despite numerous pronouncements on the importance of family planning by World Bank officials, population projects accounted for less than 1 percent of its activity.[45]

Although there has been considerable concern and attention paid to the goal of income distribution in and among less developed countries, established administrative procedures often dictate that the income distribution effect of foreign assistance is negligible. For example, most donor agencies use the project approach to capital transfers rather than the so-called programming approach. Major lending agencies can process only a few hundred project loan applications each year.

---

[41] See Robert S. McNamara, Address to the Third UN Conference on Trade and Development, Santiago, Chile, 1972; McNamara, Address to the Board of Governors, International Bank for Reconstruction and Development, Nairobi, Kenya, 24 September 1973; and McNamara, *One Hundred Countries, Two Billion People* (New York: Praeger, 1973).

[42] Francis X. Colaço, however, shows that at least as concerns distribution of bilateral aid among less developed countries, political considerations are the most important. See Colaço, *Economic and Political Considerations and the Flow of Official Resources to Developing Countries.*

[43] World Bank/IDA, *Annual Report* 1973, p. 5.

[44] Inter-American Development Bank, *Annual Report* 1972, p. 27; US Congress, House, Committee on Foreign Affairs, *The United States and the Multilateral Development Banks* (Washington, D.C.: US Government Printing Office, March 1974), p. 68.

[45] McNamara, *One Hundred Countries, Two Billion People.*

Table 2. IBRD and IDA lending by income category of borrower (in millions of dollars and in percent of total)

1970 GNP PER CAPITA	NUMBER OF COUNTRIES	Through 1963				1964 to 1968				1969 to 1973			
		IBRD		IDA		IBRD		IDA		IBRD		IDA	
		$	%	$	%	$	%	$	%	$	%	$	%
Up to $120	28	1,259	18	335	68	501	12	886	66	842	9	2,785	71
$121 to $250	22	713	10	48	10	471	11	346	26	1,582	18	841	21
$251 to $375	17	745	11	69	14	343	8	104	8	1,500	17	286	7
$376 to $500	7	744	10	18	4	864	20	—	—	2,274	26	20	1
$501 to $800	9	794	11	25	5	722	17	—	—	1,466	16	—	—
Above $800	14	2,867	40	—	—	1,395	32	—	—	1,254	14	—	—
TOTAL		7,122		495		4,296		1,336		8,918		3,932	

SOURCE: World Bank/IDA *Annual Report 1973*, p. 15.

Table 3. IBRD and IDA lending to developing countries (in millions of dollars and in percent)

SECTOR	Through 1963		1964 to 1968		1969 to 1973		1963 to 1973	
	MILLIONS OF DOLLARS	PERCENT	MILLIONS OF DOLLARS	PERCENT	MILLIONS OF DOLLARS	PERCENT	MILLIONS OF DOLLARS	PERCENT
Agriculture	456	8.6	621	12.3	2,589	20.2	3,666	15.8
Education	5	0.1	157	3.1	726	5.7	888	3.8
Development finance companies	206	3.9	483	9.6	1,224	9.5	1,913	8.2
Industry	550	10.3	118	2.3	598	4.7	1,266	5.5
Nonproject	173	3.3	455	9.0	715	5.7	1,343	5.8
Population	—	—	—	—	66	0.5	66	0.3
Power	1,834	34.5	1,461	29.0	2,245	17.5	5,540	23.9
Telecommunications	47	0.9	152	3.0	695	5.4	894	3.9
Tourism	—	—	—	—	80	0.6	80	0.3
Transportation	2,038	38.3	1,466	29.1	3,257	25.4	6,761	29.1
Urbanization	—	—	—	—	52	0.4	52	0.2
Water supply	11	0.2	119	2.4	589	4.6	719	3.1
Technical assistance	—	—	—	—	14	0.1	14	0.1
TOTAL	5,320		5,032		12,850		23,202	

SOURCE: World Bank/IDA Annual Report 1973, p. 17.
NOTE: Percentages may not add to 100 due to rounding.

Emphasis on large-scale projects minimizes the administrative efforts and maximizes the amount of project aid received. Thus, the project approach provides incentives to both donor agencies and recipient countries to select large-scale projects at the expense of smaller-scale projects. Large projects, such as main roads, dams, and irrigation systems, have a dubious long-run impact on the poor. In addition, the least developed countries tend to be penalized by their inability to present adequate project proposals.

Another problem is local cost financing. Most donors follow the principle of financing only the foreign exchange component of projects, leaving local costs to the borrower. Although such a policy may be useful in inducing the recipient country to improve its efforts to raise local capital, it may have perverse income distribution implications. It encourages capital-intensive projects with large foreign exchange components at the expense of smaller-scale, labor-intensive projects with high local cost components. Projects such as small farmer credit extension, labor-intensive construction of feeder roads, and integrated rural development programs, which typically have large local cost components, are discriminated against.

Employment objectives have received specific focus in the ILO's World Employment Program, which provides technical assistance to developing countries in devising projects and plans that emphasize employment generation. Donor agencies have tried to stress employment objectives in their lending programs. Employment and income distribution objectives, however, are closely related. One of the major reasons for income inequality in less developed countries is the fact that so many members of the labor force have low-paying, unproductive jobs or are chronically underemployed or unemployed.

Aid style

The failure of foreign assistance to achieve all the goals that have been expected of it in both donor and recipient countries has led to a diminution in the importance of foreign aid flows, certainly in real terms and relative to the growth of world GNP. Many observers have lost hope that the mechanisms for foreign assistance can be reformed. Many of the problems and frictions between the developed and less developed world might be mitigated if a hands-off approach were adopted, as advocated by Carlos Diaz-Alejandro in his essay in this volume. This would require considerably less emphasis on aid and much more focus on commodity and trade arrangements between developed and developing countries.

There are two issues at stake in a determination that relations between developed and less developed countries should be more standoffish. First, there is the moral issue—whether it is justifiable for developed countries to impose their standards on less developed countries and whether developed countries should become involved in this internal decision-making process in less developed countries. There is a tendency among aid advocates to find better moral justification for imposing income distribution standards rather than economic growth criteria in allocating aid. However, if any interference is unjustified, then certainly the recent stress on income distribution is no more desirable than any other criteria, such as control of inflation, liberalization of imports, greater tax effort, more investment incentives, or greater political participation.

Unfortunately, the moral issue cannot be avoided. As long as foreign aid funds are limited, their allocation involves at least an implicit choice of values. The only way to avoid value judgments would be to allocate funds on a random basis. As long as moral choices are made, therefore, the real issue is whether the choices are good ones. If income redistribution is a desirable goal, there should be no reason, in principle, why countries that make sincere efforts to redistribute income should not be rewarded.

The second issue is one of practicality. What kinds of goals and criteria does it make sense to impose? A major problem is that social scientists, development administrators, and aid officials often have little idea about how to solve a wide range of social problems either in their own country or in less developed countries. In imposing detailed performance criteria, there is often an implicit assumption that the donor country officials know the solution to a wide set of problems while the recipient country professionals do not. There is often considerable presumptuousness on the part of the donor that exacerbates the already fragile aid partnership.

Another problem of imposing detailed specifications and criteria is that the process of planning solutions to problems is taken out of the hands of officials in less developed countries. A better approach may be to allow officials of less developed countries to take greater responsibility for whatever mistakes are incurred and for whatever successes are achieved. If aid officials or technical experts from donor countries try to orchestrate the decision-making process, a parasitic relationship can develop, which frustrates the goal of increasing the expertise and responsibility of officials in the recipient country.

A future framework for foreign aid

In the next few sections we argue that foreign aid can be made to serve a specific set of well-defined goals for both donor and recipient country officials. Although the role of foreign aid may be limited and may give way to increased emphasis on other forms of interaction between rich and poor countries, we expect foreign aid programs to be more than vestigial for quite some time in the future.

In our analysis of a desirable future framework for foreign aid, we would like to stress the variety of circumstances and the diversity of prevailing problems and opportunities in different donor and recipient countries at different points of time. For example, African countries are poorer, more rural, less characterized by extremes in the distribution of land and wealth than most Latin American countries. India is vastly different from Korea, and the problems of Bangladesh are often dissimilar from those of Thailand.

In the same way, donor countries may vary. In some countries economic and political circumstances allow a transfer of aid resources to take place smoothly, and the aid provides mutual benefits to policymakers and the general public in both donor and recipient countries. In a donor country with severe balance-of-payments problems in which the political mood favors a cautious foreign policy, aid commitments are not part of a viable or desirable strategy for interacting with poor countries.

More importantly, the needs of the less developed countries change over time. For example, in the late fifties and early sixties, South Korea was sorely dependent on United States military help for survival, and policymakers realistically recognized this dependence. The country lacked technical expertise in its bureaucracy, was very poor in terms of per capita income and natural resources, and had survived two devastating wars. It was clearly a good candidate for foreign assistance at that time. Korea has undergone more than a decade of exceedingly rapid export growth and more moderate but substantial increases in income per capita and in employment and wage rates. It is not and should not be a prime candidate for foreign aid at the present time.

On the other hand, the countries of Indochina, devastated by war over a long period, may someday soon find themselves in a position in which foreign assistance would be very useful. Many African states are desperately in need of assistance, ranging from famine relief to help in building rural infrastructure.

Conditions in the developed world also change over time in ways that alter the feasibility and desirability of aid or the mechanism through which aid is given. For example, when the United States had large farm surpluses, the farm bloc encouraged PL480 food aid and made substantial contributions to many less developed countries. As Japan became a major world-trading power, it found it useful to expand its economic cooperation with those less developed countries that played an important role in its trading relationships.[46]

Because of the varying purposes and roles that foreign aid plays, both over time and among countries, the institutions used to administer capital transfers should be as diverse as possible and the institutions themselves should be flexible. There should be a variety of both bilateral and multilateral aid programs, funded in different ways, operated differently, and meeting a wide range of possible needs and circumstances.

In a future foreign aid framework, we see three basic and distinct forms of assistance: (1) humanitarian and development-oriented assistance, (2) aid to encourage economic cooperation between rich and poor countries, and (3) strategic aid designed to achieve specific national security goals. These basic forms are outlined in table 4.

Humanitarian and development-oriented aid would be designed largely to help the poorest countries and the poorest segments of the population within poor countries. Such assistance might take a number of different forms: (1) relief from floods, famines, epidemics, and other natural disasters; (2) general budgetary support for the very poorest countries, especially those burdened by serious natural or economic calamities, war, or civil strife; (3) capital lending for infrastructure

---

[46] See Caldwell, "The Evolution of Japanese Economic Cooperation."

Table 4. Proposed basic forms of foreign assistance

Aid type	Basic forms	Primary administering agencies	Recipients
Humanitarian assistance and development oriented	Relief	UN system	Poorest countries and poorest segments of the population
	Budgetary support	World Bank and regional development banks	Poorest countries and poorest segments of the population
	Capital financing	World Bank and regional development banks	Poorest countries and poorest segments of the population
	Technical assistance and research	UN system	Poorest countries and poorest segments of the population
Economic cooperation assistance	Short-term balance-of-payments support	IMF	All countries
	Medium-term balance-of-payments supports	IMF	Poorest countries and countries in most severe balance-of-payments difficulties
	Liberalization support of balance of payments	IMF	All poor countries
	Export credits on hard terms	Bilateral agency	All countries
	Export credits on soft terms	Bilateral agency	Poorest countries and poor countries at the limit of debt-servicing capacity
Strategic aid	Military aid	Bilateral agency	All poor countries
	Budgetary support	Bilateral agency	All poor countries
	General fund for loans and grants	Bilateral agency	All poor countries

development or for directly productive capital assets; and (4) technical assistance and research, particularly in the fields of agriculture, education, health, population control, economic planning and analysis, and project preparation and appraisal. We envision that most humanitarian and development assistance would be channeled through multilateral institutions, particularly the World Bank group, the UN system, and the regional development banks.

Economic cooperation assistance would include short-term balance-of-payments support to assist in compensating for short-run fluctuations in export earnings, import requirements and debt-servicing capacity, as well as medium-term balance-of-payments support to assist in the adjustment of a trade deficit caused by imbalances in the structure of production or by sudden but permanent changes in the terms of trade (such as that caused by the recent sudden and substantial increase in petroleum prices). The short-term and medium-term balance-of-payments support would be administered largely through the International Monetary Fund as it is now. In addition, however, the IMF would sponsor a special fund for balance-of-payments support to facilitate the introduction of measures to liberalize trade policy in developing countries, such as eliminating import and export controls and increasing incentives to export. Other forms of economic assistance include export credits on normal terms as well as export credits on softer terms for the poorest of the less developed countries and those countries with the most severe debt-servicing problems. Export credits would be administered by donor country agencies rather than by multilateral institutions.

Finally, strategic aid would encompass military aid programs and general budgetary support for close allies that a donor country wishes to reward. Strategic aid might also take the form of special loans and grants that might supplement export credits for particularly favored countries. For example, production loans may be made in conjunction with export credits, which would be used to finance purchases of imported capital equipment, or loans may take the form of a grant to subsidize interest payments on trade credits.

Multilateralization of development and humanitarian assistance

The framework for foreign assistance proposed here calls for a multilateralization of those forms of assistance that are designed primarily to stimulate economic development and to redress inequities in the distribution of income among poor countries and within poor countries. Relief assistance would also be primarily a multilateral responsibility. The arguments for multilateralization of aid are many and have been made often.[47] We summarize briefly some of the main arguments here:

[47] See, for example: "U.S. Foreign Assistance in the 1970's: A New Approach," report by the Task Force on International Development to the President of the US (Peterson Report), 4 March 1970; Robert E. Asher, *Development Assistance in the Seventies; Alternatives for the United States* (Washington, D.C.: Brookings Institution, 1970); Ohlin; and Fulbright.

1. Multilateral aid programs avoid the political antagonisms and conflicts that come about in bilateral programs when the donor attempts to impose performance criteria in giving aid.
2. Multilateral donor agencies are more efficient in stimulating development because they make decisions based on more technical and objective criteria.
3. Less developed countries are likely to be more receptive to the advice of policy experts when that advice emanates from multilateral institutions, since they will be less suspicious that the advice is politically motivated.
4. With the use of multilateral institutions, less developed countries can feel a sense of greater participation in the aid process and are, therefore, more likely to cooperate with donor countries.
5. Channeling aid through multilateral institutions promotes a feeling of cooperation rather than competition among major aid donors and reinforces the humanitarian as opposed to the strategic objectives of foreign aid.

Our main contention is that the arguments for multilateral aid apply most forcefully to those forms of aid that are development oriented, are inspired largely on humanitarian grounds, and clearly do not involve the national interests, narrowly defined, of the donor. Other kinds of assistance, such as export credits, military assistance, and loans and grants made with strategic purposes in mind, clearly involve tangible national, economic, and security interests. Administration of assistance of this kind properly is the national responsibility of the donor country.

Aid based on humanitarian considerations should not be mixed with assistance given to achieve national economic and security goals. The two different types are incompatible in the long run since assistance designed to stimulate development and better distribution of income should have a stable existence. In order for such assistance to be of most use, aid commitments should be made over long periods, and the recipient country should be able to make a sustained effort to develop without being made vulnerable by the threat of a cutoff in the flow of foreign aid. By way of contrast, aid designed to achieve economic and security goals should be administered very flexibly. There may be periods when large amounts of such aid can be justified. At other times such assistance may be either unnecessary or improperly used by executive agencies so that legislatures can and should substantially reduce funds for such aid programs. If the two different forms of aid are mixed, as they often are in bilateral aid programs, basic development assistance is subject to the vicissitudes of aid designed to accomplish clear national objectives.

In administering the humanitarian forms of assistance, two goals should be primary: economic development and equitable distribution of income. Recent studies by Cline, and Reynolds, and others have shown that there need not be any basic conflict between these two objectives.[48] Savings rates tend not to be ad-

---

[48] William R. Cline, *Potential Effects of Income Redistribution on Economic Growth: Latin American Cases* (New York: Praeger, 1972); Clark W. Reynolds, "The Recent Evolution of Savings and the Financial System in Mexico in Relation to the Distribution of Income and Wealth," paper prepared for the Workshop on Income Distribution and Its Role in Development, Rice University, the Program of Development Studies, 25 April 1974.

versely affected by the distribution of income. Nevertheless, the distribution goal should be paramount since a failure to achieve more equity in less developed countries would seriously undermine the humanitarian rationale for such aid and would ultimately diminish the flow of funds from donor countries.

The goals of growth and distribution can be achieved most efficiently if some effort is made at performance conditioning. No doubt recipient countries will resist efforts to make them conform to performance standards as a criterion for receipt of capital assistance, but some degree of pressure, provided it is practically and tactfully applied, is necessary to maintain the integrity of humanitarian assistance programs. The World Bank is in a particularly favorable position to exert its influence in less developed countries. Although there is considerable suspicion in recipient countries that Bank policies are dictated by the major Western powers,[49] the Bank has earned a good deal of respect and the competence and integrity of its technical staff is generally recognized. Certainly, efforts by the Bank to insist on performance standards are less likely to meet with resistance and hostility than the same efforts exerted by a bilateral aid agency.

The World Bank has historically tended to operate on a project basis. The kinds of standards on which it has insisted relate to project design and implementation. In fact, the World Bank group has only recently become much more interested in general economic performance criteria. In the past, Bank/IDA allocations have not generally correlated with overall economic performance.[50] The regional development banks also have not had a particularly impressive record of allocating on a performance basis.[51]

If the Bank is to become the preeminent foreign aid institution, it has to be very flexible in its approach to capital transfers. More experimentation with program aid, greater implementation of income distribution objectives, use of overall economic performance criteria rather than project criteria, loans to social and economic overhead projects, even more emphasis on agriculture, education, and population, and a willingness to participate meaningfully in debt-restructuring exercises—all these are prerequisites if the Bank is to assume and maintain a leading role. To date, however, the World Bank has moved rather cautiously in these directions.

Part of the reason for this caution lies in the way that the Bank's operations are funded. The World Bank as well as the Inter-American and Asian Development

---

[49] A particularly strident proponent of this view is Teresa Hayter, *Aid as Imperialism* (London: Penguin Books, 1971).

[50] Statistical studies indicate that actual aid disbursements are not significantly correlated with performance or self-help efforts. The studies regressed aid flows against variables thought to be indicative of good performance. The independent variables used included: tax effort, savings effort, growth in the country's export earnings, inflation policy, the efficiency of resource use as measured by the incremental output/capital ratio, and the growth rate of GNP per capita. See William R. Cline and Nicholas P. Sargen, "Performance Criteria and Multilateral Aid Allocation," Washington, D.C., 1973 (mimeographed); and Mary Baird, William Perkins, and Christopher Zook, "The International Development Association: A Critical Analysis," Williams College, Williamstown, Mass., 1973 (mimeographed).

[51] US Congress, House, Committee on Foreign Affairs, *The United States and the Multilateral Development Banks*, p. 68.

Banks finance a large part of their capital transfers by selling bonds in private markets. They pay a market rate on these bonds and then lend to developing countries on near-market terms. For example, the World Bank makes loans with 7¼ percent interest rates, four-to-ten-year grace periods, and fifteen-to-thirty-year maturities. Ordinary capital from the Inter-American Development Bank is loaned at 8 percent with repayment made in fifteen to twenty years after project completion. The Asian Development Bank makes loans at 7½ percent interest, with four-year grace periods and maturities ranging from ten to twenty-seven years.

The manner in which the World Bank finances a large part of its operations requires that Bank officials be sensitive to opinions in private money markets. A broad-ranging approach to development would evoke suspicion among the banking and money market community and could have the effect of making Bank financing more costly and difficult. In reality, the Bank's capital is guaranteed by the subscribing government and there is little risk in lending to the Bank. The effect is largely psychological, but nonetheless real.[52]

Another, perhaps more important consequence of the main source of World Bank finance is that regular Bank lending terms are too severe for many less developed countries, particularly for the poorest countries, and for countries with wide fluctuations in the demand and supply of foreign exchange. The only way these countries can be helped is through the soft-loan windows of the multilateral development banks which provide aid on much more favorable terms.[53] For example, IDA credits are available at a 3/4 percent interest charge, a ten-year grace period, and forty-year maturities. Concessionary loans from the Fund for Special Operations of the Inter-American Development Bank range from 1 percent interest during a ten-year grace period with 2 percent charge thereafter for up to a forty-year maturity (offered to the poorest Latin American countries) to 4 percent interest with five-year grace periods and repayments spread over twenty-seven years (for the more developed countries). Soft-loan rates on Asian Development Bank funds range from 1½ percent to 3 percent, grace periods may be as long as ten years, and loans mature in fifteen to thirty years.

If the World Bank is to play a significant role in financing the capital needs of the less developed world, then it must expand its soft-lending operations through IDA. The regional banks must also expand their lending from their soft-loan windows. There are two reasons why there is a need to expand multilateral soft lending. First, the total amount of bilateral and multilateral soft lending available is inadequate in relation to the needs of the poorest countries. (In contrast, the supply of funds on standard World Bank terms seems virtually unlimited.) Second,

---

[52] For an elaboration of these points, see Charles R. Frank, Jr., "Comment: Debt Adjustment; the Tyranny of Bankers, Brokers and Bondholders," in John P. Lewis and Ishan Kapur, eds., *The World Bank Group: Multilateral Aid and the 1970's* (Lexington, Mass: D.C. Heath & Co., 1973).

[53] On the desirability of soft-term lending, see Frank, *Debt and Terms of Aid;* and Charles R. Frank, Jr., "Optimal Terms of Foreign Assistance," *Journal of Political Economy* 78 (September/October 1970): 1106-14.

increased availability of soft funds will enable multilateral institutions to operate more flexibly. The World Bank can afford to be much more experimental with IDA funds, if only because it is not answerable to private investors with respect to IDA subscriptions.

Unfortunately, it is precisely in the area of soft-loan finance that the funding problem is most acute. The World Bank has shown, for example, that it can raise large amounts of finance through bond sales. It has also demonstrated that IDA funding is a thorny problem. But without sufficient IDA funding, the World Bank will find it difficult and should not attempt to expand the volume of its lending very rapidly and will be forced to behave not as a foreign aid institution but rather continue to function as a development bank.[54]

Within our framework, although the World Bank would be the prime institution for capital transfers, we envision the United Nations as playing the major role in relief operations and in supplying technical assistance. The reduction in United States surplus food stocks and the gradual demise of the PL480 food programs have greatly increased the cost and difficulty of providing relief.

This suggests the need for a world food stock program. One may argue that the responsibility for providing enough stocks to suffice during periods of poor harvests should be an individual country responsibility. Yet there are significant economies to be gained by the pooling of stocks of major grains. Furthermore, the poorest countries, on the verge of subsistence, will have a difficult time financing a food stock program and face even more difficult political obstacles when even in the best of times many people go hungry. The Food and Agricultural Organization of the United Nations can and should play a major coordinating role. Contributions to the cost of a stock program should be borne by all participating countries and graduated on the basis of ability to pay.[55] Thus, a world food program should contain elements of aid to the poorer nations.

The United Nations Development Program (UNDP) is the best vehicle for coordinating multilateral technical assistance efforts. The Jackson report recommended a substantial strengthening of the UNDP, and some of its suggestions are being implemented.[56]

The major question regarding multilateralization of humanitarian and development-oriented assistance relates to obtaining sufficient funds. In part, the prob-

---

[54] For further discussion of the role of the World Bank as a development institution, see Mason and Asher, *The World Bank Since Bretton Woods;* Lewis and Kapur, *The World Bank Group, Multilateral Aid and the 1970's;* Escott Reid, "McNamara's World Bank," *Foreign Affairs* 5 (July 1973): 794-810; and Escott Reid, *Strengthening the World Bank* (Chicago, Ill.: Adlai Stevenson Institute, 1973).

[55] For a discussion of a world food stock program and the costs of maintaining reasonable stock levels, see Lyle P. Schertz, "World Food: Prices and the Poor," *Foreign Affairs* 52 (April 1974): 511-37; and US Congress, Senate, Select Committee on Nutrition and Human Needs, "National Nutrition Policy: Report and Recommendations—VI," prepared for the Panel on Nutrition and the International Situation, which argues for a food stock reserve program for the benefit of less developed countries only, but with costs borne by the developed countries.

[56] Sir Robert G. A. Jackson, *A Study of the Capacity of the United Nations Development System,* 2 vols. (Geneva: United Nations, 1969).

lem is general: there is considerable reluctance to fund any aid program when there are substantial poverty problems within the donor countries. Aid funds compete with many other priority uses of government funds. Some of the flavor of the arguments made is captured in the words of a member of the United States House of Representatives in the debate over IDA replenishment: "I am not going to vote to increase our commitments at a time when we cannot take care of the folks back home, when the dollar has been under heavy pressure, when the national debt has increased by about 1/5 in the last four years, and when we are going into debt this year by another $15 billion."[57]

Although there is certain to be opposition of this kind, there is still substantial public support in most countries, even in the United States, for a continued strong role in development assistance. Paul Laudicina reports that in a survey of American opinion, 68 percent of the American public supported foreign aid and that 53 percent strongly supported it. Furthermore, the same survey indicated: "The U.S. public does not understand development assistance as a *quid pro quo* for securing new supplies of energy or strategic materials, or for gaining markets in poor countries. Rather, Americans tend to perceive U.S. foreign aid as an act of national generosity. Such largess (in the public's mind) is granted not for political favors, but because it is 'right' for the rich to help the poor."[58]

Thus, public support for humanitarian-oriented development programs does exist. This support is likely to be better mobilized if development-oriented aid programs are multilateralized, the humanitarian basis for these programs is made clear, and emphasis is placed on the poorest segments of the population. Such assistance has a better chance of surviving if it is not mixed with aid oriented to other objectives as well.

There is, however, significant opposition to the funding of multilateral programs as against bilateral aid programs. The opposition to funding of multilateral aid is severe in the United States and stems largely from two sources.

First, vested interests in the Congress and the executive departments have made special efforts to preserve the bilateral aid program and view multilateral aid as a threat or substitute. In the framework proposed here, we have a very definite and clear role for bilateral assistance, which would be oriented toward national economic and security interests and would be less directly competitive with the more development-oriented multilateral programs.

Secondly, there is the fear that the donor countries will lose control of multilateral aid programs and that allocation of multilateral aid will degenerate into international pork-barreling operations. In fact, however, donor countries have significant control over the basic directions of policy of multilateral institutions,

[57] *Congressional Quarterly* 32, no. 4 (Washington, D.C.: US Government Printing Office, 26 January 1974), p. 154.
[58] Paul A. Laudicina, *World Poverty and Development: A Survey of American Opinion*, monograph no. 8 (Washington, D.C.: Overseas Development Council, October 1973), pp. 34-35.

although perhaps not over policy details. This is evidenced, first of all, in the voting structure. The World Bank and the Asian Development Bank are clearly donor dominated in terms of votes, and major donors have substantial voting power in the Inter-American Development Bank.

Voting power is only a reflection of a more fundamental relationship between power and source of finance. The African Development Bank lacks financial resources precisely because of the lack of developed country participation. Regardless of the distribution of voting power, the World Bank and the regional banks cannot follow policies grossly inconsistent with the desires of major donors. They cannot jeopardize their main sources of finance.

The United Nations system is less obviously subject to donor control. Voting power is more diffuse. UN assessments are regularized and are less subject to changing political winds in individual developed countries. It is not widely recognized, however, that major donors have significant influence on the allocation of voluntary contributions to special funds in the UN system.

The successful multilateralization of humanitarian and development-oriented forms of assistance requires sources of funding that will be fairly regular and automatically renewed. Multilateral aid cannot play its proper role if it is subject to extreme variations from year to year due to changing political circumstances. Recipients very rationally may not want to subject themselves to the vagaries and risks of the appropriations process but prefer to confine themselves to more reliable sources of finance for their investments. Not all funding for multilateral aid programs needs to be on a regularized basis, but at least a substantial part should be to preserve continuity, reduce risks, and allow for longer-term planning and programming of financial flows to less developed countries.

For example, the main virtue of the special drawing rights link or of proposals to share returns on development of ocean resources is not that they would provide a costless form of funding for the IDA but that they would provide a regular source of funding not subject to the prevailing political winds in the major donor nations at the time of an IDA replenishment exercise. The failure of the United States House of Representatives to vote for IDA replenishment in early 1974 was the result, in part, of the lack of strong executive branch support in a time of political crisis and the oil embargo. Later, when oil difficulties seemed less troublesome, passage was achieved.

The pressures for multilateralization of development and humanitarian aid are likely to continue to grow. Nearly every major report on aid recommends a multilateralization of aid.[59] The multilateral agencies can improve and refine their operations and the vested interests in bilateral aid programs will gradually lose strength.

---

[59] William L. Thorp, "Foreign Aid: A Report on the Reports," in Robert Hunter and John E. Rielly, eds., *Development Today: A New Look at U.S. Relations with Poor Countries* (New York: Praeger, 1972).

Aid to foster economic cooperation

Capital transfers to foster economic cooperation between rich and poor countries should be a joint bilateral and multilateral responsibility. The major multilateral agency in the area of aid for economic cooperation should be the International Monetary Fund (IMF). Although the IMF has not traditionally been regarded as an aid institution, it can play an important role in fostering certain kinds of capital transfer to poor nations.

Balance-of-payments support by the IMF

Short-term support to ease adjustments in the balance of payments has been a traditional function of the IMF. Medium-term support (three to five years) for shortfalls in export earnings is available through the IMF's compensatory finance program. Longer-term support and assistance in adjusting to other kinds of shortfalls, such as those caused by the sharp change in oil prices, have not been available until recently. When the oil crisis hit a number of developing countries very badly, there were few sources for the kind of financial assistance needed to help these countries adjust to the new set of circumstances that was expected to result in a permanent change in their terms of trade.

The World Bank could provide little help since its project approach involves long delays and is not geared to payments support, but rather to project appraisal and implementation. Bilateral program lending might have been appropriate, but this kind of support has been gradually phased out by the United States, the major supplier of program aid. The International Monetary Fund stepped into the breach with loans to a number of less developed countries that had particular difficulties. These loans, however, were either standard compensatory finance loans, which are supposed to be related to export shortfalls, or purchase agreements. The availability of such loans in the future is limited, and the conditions under which they are offered tend to be very strict. There is a future need, therefore, to provide medium-term and long-term adjustment support on a reasonable scale at subsidized interest rates for the poorest countries or those with already significant debt-servicing difficulties. The IMF would be an appropriate institution to provide such support since this would be a simple extension of existing activities.

The IMF has just instituted a special oil facility as well as approved in principle a special fund for extended loans to less developed countries. The special oil facility provides loans at between $6^7/_8$ and $7^1/_8$ percent for seven years for countries experiencing large increases in oil costs. The details of the extended fund facility have not been worked out as to sources of funds and terms of lending. It is expected, however, that loans from this facility will be for longer terms than other IMF loans and will be designed to help countries in changing their basic economic structure over a fairly long period of years.

Another desirable IMF function is support for trade liberalization efforts on the part of less developed countries. Liberalization can help both the developed and the less developed countries. Developed countries would gain from greater access to markets and raw material supplies; less developed countries would achieve more rapid growth. The latter conclusion stems from our belief that much of the stagnation in less developed economies results from monetary and exchange rate policies that have caused substantial overvaluation of local currencies. This overvaluation has led to ad hoc measures to alleviate the resulting balance-of-payments pressures, including prohibitive tariffs, quantitative restrictions on imports, capital controls, exchange controls, and the like. These measures have encouraged the establishment of very inefficient import substitution industries and have drastically cut incentives to export. The increasing inefficiency of import substitution industries, the slow growth of exports, and continued inflation result in a continually increasing overvaluation of the local currency, more ad hoc measures aimed at the balance of payments, and more inefficiency—until the growth process is choked off. By adjusting their exchange rates frequently to prevent overvaluation and to permit liberalization of the trade and payment regime, fewer less developed countries will fall into the stagnation trap caused by increasing overvaluation of their currency.

IMF credits can greatly ease the adjustment to a more liberal trade payments regime.[60] Less developed countries often have such large distortions induced by trade and payments policy that the short-run adjustment costs of a quick change to a very liberal regime would be very great. A balance-of-payments support loan could speed the process of liberalization, which would benefit both the donor country and the less developed country.

Export credits

Export credits are a recognized means of facilitating trade, and they have been increasingly liberalized. The volume of export credits to less developed countries expanded greatly between 1967 and 1971, from $1.4 billion to $3.3 billion, but has declined in recent years, apparently due to the great increase in Eurocurrency lending to less developed countries, which has tended to substitute for export finance.[61] United States official and officially guaranteed export credits (mostly by the United States Export-Import Bank), however, showed a sustained rise from $211 million in 1970 to $529 million in 1972.

Export credits are on relatively hard terms and are not the most appropriate form of capital transfer to the poorest countries and to countries with debt-servicing problems. A proposal to institute an export credit development fund to

---

[60] Ronald I. McKinnon has argued against heavy reliance on support of this kind on the grounds that such support provides an incentive to delay necessary adjustments in the structure of production and demand. Obviously, if the financial support is excessive, none of the necessary changes in production and demand will take place, but a carefully designed support program can permit less costly, smoother, and more efficient adjustment to occur in the poor countries. See McKinnon, *Money and Capital in Economic Development* (Washington, D.C.: Brookings Institution, 1973), pp. 170-72.

[61] See OECD, *Development Assistance: Efforts and Policies of the Development Assistance Committee,* 1971, pp. 100-102; and OECD, *Development Cooperation: Efforts and Policies of the Members of the Development Assistance Committee,* 1973, pp. 54-151.

provide finance on soft terms to the poorest of the less developed countries was reported out by the Foreign Affairs Committee of the United States House of Representatives and the US Senate Foreign Relations Committee in 1973, but was killed on the floor of the House and in the US Senate Finance Committee. The proposal involved the use of repayments to the United States on past debt incurred by less developed countries to subsidize the interest on regular export credit. The bill did not specify the administering agency, but the Export-Import Bank seems to be the most appropriate one.

Soft-loan windows in bilateral export credit institutions would provide clear benefits to developing countries in the form of subsidized credit and greater flexibility in foreign debt management. In the donor countries such credits could be expected to stimulate employment and production for export, especially in periods of slack capacity.

Strategic aid

Finally, there would be two basic sorts of strategic aid: (1) military aid and budget support for close military allies, and (2) loans and grants for economic purposes to favored countries. In this essay we do not intend to discuss in detail the former category and have only a few observations with regard to the latter. We would envision a flexible loan and grant fund that would be administered in close connection with the conduct of foreign policy. These loans and grants, for example, might be offered to provide extra subsidy on regular export credits or balance-of-payments loans to close allies. They might be offered as part of a quid pro quo in an economic agreement guaranteeing access to markets with a country that has a large supply of a particularly crucial raw material. The fund for strategic loans and grants would be the source of financial assistance for reconstruction in war-torn areas, such as Indochina and the Middle East. Political considerations, which would vary from year to year, would govern the circumstances and conditions under which these loans and grants would be given. The use of the funds would be justified in terms of explicit foreign policy objectives in the donor country.

Conclusions

The proposed framework for foreign aid developed in this essay stresses the differentiation of donor goals and purposes for foreign aid and the assignment of aid tasks to a fairly wide range of different agencies, each of which has a reasonably well-defined major goal or task in contrast to the current foreign aid network where tasks and goals are confused. The advantages of this approach are best described in the words of Huntington:

> An activity that has a multiplicity of goals should command support, one would think, from a multiplicity of sources, Multiple support is, however, rarely given to bureaucratic programs and governmental agencies. Best off are those in which there is a clear identification of one major purpose with one

particular program and that particular program with one distinctive agency. When an agency serves a large number of purposes, no one constituency feels that it has any great stake in its program, and the general public lacks a clear perception of the public needs met by the agency. Most important of all, the agency's personnel tend to become demoralized as they find themselves having to serve a variety of often conflicting purposes. They also feel vulnerable to criticism by Congress and the public, because they can always be attacked for not making sufficient effort to achieve one goal when they have been preoccupied in trying to achieve several others. An agency asked to serve many different purposes tends to lose its sense of commitment to any one of them.[62]

In specific terms, the key provisions of our proposed framework are the following:

1. Humanitarian and development-oriented aid would be multilateralized. Technical assistance and disaster relief would be a basic United Nations responsibility while general development assistance would be undertaken by the World Bank and the regional development banks. Development aid would be employed mainly to achieve goals of equity. Economic growth would not be expected to result automatically from development aid. Rather, it should be recognized that the effort to achieve both more rapid economic development and more equitable distribution of income in poor countries is a worthwhile human endeavor to support but is subject to many risks and uncertainties of both a political and economic nature.

2. Aid programs to foster economic cooperation would play a subsidiary, but supportive, role in attempting to improve economic relationships with poor countries. Poor countries would be encouraged to liberalize their trade and payments regimes and to allow access to both their markets and their supplies of basic commodities. The rich countries have most to offer in terms of liberal access to their own markets and supplies, but they can also furnish assistance in various forms to provide additional incentives to the poor countries. The major forms of assistance would be export credits on both hard and soft terms and balance-of-payments support for trade liberalization efforts.

3. Strategic aid would be either direct military assistance and general budgetary support to assist a military effort indirectly or general economic aid with clear political strings attached.

A foreign aid framework of the sort outlined here would be more efficient in terms of meeting needs in both donor and recipient countries. It would require considerable institutional change in both multilateral organizations and bilateral agencies. It would be more suited for the kinds of economic issues and relationships between rich and poor countries that have emerged in the seventies.

---

[62] Samuel P. Huntington, "Foreign Aid: For What and for Whom?," in Hunter and Rielly, eds., *Development Today; A New Look at U.S. Relations with Poor Countries.*

The multinational firm
and international regulation

Robert O. Keohane and Van Doorn Ooms

Writing about alternative international regimes to deal with direct foreign invest-ment (DFI) may seem to be somewhat like discussing a perpetual motion machine: most people would like one for their own purposes; no one has ever built one; and discussions about their construction often take on a certain air of unreality. In contrast to the issue areas of money, trade, and aid, there is no important set of international institutions concentrating primarily on DFI. Numerous bilateral agree-ments and multilateral arrangements regulate or facilitate, in one way or another, the activities of private investors, but these have not been systematized into a coherent structure. Negotiations for new agreements do not take place within a large and semiformal international arrangement, such as the General Agreement on Tariffs and Trade (GATT), and no large international institution, such as the World Bank in the aid field, exists primarily to give direction to activities in this area.

This institutional confusion is compounded by lack of agreement on the value of DFI itself. The desirability, indeed necessity, of world trade, and of appropriate monetary relationships, is seldom questioned by writers on those subjects, although the distribution of benefits from existing arrangements is often debated. Yet the desirability of direct investment per se is often questioned in precisely this way. Critics of multinational firms—the dominant organizational vehicles for direct investment—argue that with reference to less developed countries at least, "poverty is the product."[1] Defenders of the enterprises counter with claims about the contributions of the firms to global welfare.

Robert O. Keohane is an associate professor of political science at Stanford University. Van Doorn Ooms is an associate professor of economics at Swarthmore College. A number of colleagues and friends have read this essay in manuscript and offered constructive criticism. Valuable discussions of earlier drafts were held by Professor Ooms with the Swarthmore College social science faculty, and by Professor Keohane with participants in a Stanford conference on multinational enterprises and international regulation, supported by the National Endowment for the Humanities. The authors particularly appreciate the perceptive comments and sug-gestions of Jonathan Aronson, James Kurth, Joseph S. Nye, Jr., Raymond Vernon, and the editors of this special issue.

[1] Ronald Müller, "Poverty is the Product," *Foreign Policy,* no. 13 (Winter 1973-74): 71-102.

Although this debate is by no means irrelevant, it does miss the key policy question faced by governments confronting multinational enterprises. This is rarely the simple query, Should there be direct foreign investment?, or even Should multinational firms be allowed to operate in our country? Rather, the critical question focuses on the *conditions* under which various *types* of direct foreign investment should be allowed. Almost every government in the world, including Communist regimes in the Soviet Union and Eastern Europe, attempts to entice foreign capital. Yet no major government allows unrestricted, unregulated foreign direct investment, and some establish very stiff conditions. Thus governments agree that foreign investment can, under some conditions, be beneficial, but that the effects cannot be optimized without developing explicit policies.

Governments, in contrast to academic "scribblers," must take the world as it is, and must therefore consider alternatives. They are not allowed the luxury of making policy on the basis of judgments, such as that of Richard Barnet that "the performances of the global corporation and its claims must be judged not against the failures of alternative institutions but against the needs of mankind."[2] At some extreme point of disillusion and dismay, the government can displace the corporation, but only if the government is willing to bear the economic and, in some cases, the political costs and risks of so doing. Intellectuals often urge displacement of the corporation, and militantly nationalistic or revolutionary regimes are sometimes willing to follow their advice. But, in general, when an important value seems threatened by actions of the multinationals, the policy question is not Should we throw the rascals out? but a rather more prosaic one: What further constraints can we devise to minimize the costs imposed on us by these firms and to maximize our rewards from their activities?

In such a situation attitudes are likely to be ambivalent. Thoughtful observers will recognize that the ideal and the real are far apart; they will see clearly the severity of the constraints imposed by contemporary political and economic institutions, as well as by the moral limitations of the species. In countries with little economic importance in the world, or whose governmental institutions are not highly effective, a pervasive sense of dissatisfaction is likely to ensue.

Even where the government is strong and effective, ambiguity abounds. Proper policy construction requires not only a set of decisions about trade-offs between governmental values (for instance, political autonomy and economic welfare may be in conflict at the margin) but also a set of estimates about the likely consequences of governmental action. Yet the behavior of one or a few oligopolistic, strategically minded firms is not as easily predictable as the aggregate activities of many atomistically competitive economic actors, and it is therefore more difficult to calculate the probable results of particular policies toward them than to devise policies to affect the behavior of units in a competitive market. Economic analysis offers some guidance but no definitive guidelines. It is therefore not surprising that national elites are often frustrated when facing the apparently

---

[2] Richard J. Barnet, "Comment," *Foreign Policy,* no. 13 (Winter 1973-74): 121.

self-confident foreign firm, or that governments are frequently inconsistent in their behavior.

Recent discussions on international arrangements to govern direct foreign investment should be viewed within this context of normative dissatisfaction and conceptual uncertainty, which is particularly acute where less developed countries are concerned. Largely on the initiative of countries and groups that perceive themselves at a disadvantage vis-à-vis the firms, the United Nations Conference on Trade and Development (UNCTAD) and the International Labor Organization (ILO) have held extensive discussions on various aspects of direct foreign investment.[3] The UN Economic and Social Council has commissioned a report on the subject.[4] The Organization for Economic Cooperation and Development (OECD) has been seeking to develop new norms for DFI among the industrial countries. The International Chamber of Commerce has offered a set of suggestions for an international code of conduct for multinationals, and a number of trade unions have campaigned for restrictions on their activities. The minister of finance of the Federal Republic of Germany has recently called for "an international code of conduct for the multinationals which would ensure that they will not shirk their obligations to the countries of residence," mentioning specifically the usefulness of "greater transparency of international trade and capital movements."[5] Only minor steps have been taken thus far by international agencies, but the interest shown in this topic during the past few years suggests that now may be an appropriate time to evaluate various alternatives for international action.

In the first part of this essay, we discuss various economic and political effects of direct investment. This section defines and defends one attitude toward DFI upon which an analysis of international regulation must be based. It also allows us to note the complexity of the phenomenon and the tensions it produces in relation to specific groups, both of which give rise to the sharply divergent attitudes toward it that we have noted. The second part of the essay contains a brief discussion of international measures to promote direct investment. In the third part we turn our attention to international strategies for dealing with the activities of multinational firms, examining first measures of policy coordination and then strategies designed to alter the relative bargaining power of governments in their dealings with multinational firms. We conclude, in the fourth part, with some speculation about prospects for future international action in relation to the problem.

[3] See, for instance, the Report of the Secretary-General of UNCTAD to the Secretary-General of the United Nations on measures adopted by UNCTAD III (UN Document TD/179, p. 10); and International Labour Organization, *Multinational Enterprises and Social Policy,* Studies and Reports, New Series, no. 79 (Geneva: International Labour Organization, 1973).
[4] United Nations, Department of Economic and Social Affairs, *Multinational Corporations in World Development* (UN Document ST/ECA/190).
[5] Speech of Helmut Schmidt, minister of finance for the Federal Republic of Germany, before the opening plenary session of the International Industrial Conference, San Francisco, California, 17 September 1973. (Mimeographed.) Available from the Stanford Research Institute in Menlo Park, California.

Effects of direct foreign investment

Economic effects

Any consideration of the economic effects of direct investment must ultimately focus upon the economic gains or losses of particular elites and interest groups in the source and host countries. These gains and losses, however, will depend upon the product and income resulting from the investment, that is, upon global efficiency and growth effects, and upon the distribution of that income. Since the distributional question has both international and intranational dimensions, we must consider three levels of economic effects: global efficiency and growth, international equity, and national equity.

Global efficiency and growth

Until relatively recently, direct foreign investment was viewed largely in the context of the neoclassical theory of factor movements, in which the verdict for improved economic efficiency was unequivocal. Capital and technology move abroad because their productivity, and hence returns, will be higher there. Firms, in their quests for profits, raise world efficiency by acting as "perfectors of markets," mobilizing and organizing a complex bundle of productive factors in combinations, at scales, and in locations that minimize real costs of production.[6] The mobilization of capital and technology by large firms in mineral and petroleum extraction provides the most striking historical example, but illustrations from manufacturing industries can also be found. Electronics firms move continually—first Texas, then Mexico, now Singapore—to source component production in areas possessing abundant and cheap manual dexterity. The Swedish firm SKF exploits scale economies by allocating European export orders among its plants in different countries in accordance with short-term capacity availabilities.[7] Arguments have also been made with respect to the efficiency gains resulting from the financial intermediation by large international firms, which provide an efficient mechanism for hedging against exchange risk and whose size allows the organization of large and efficient equity markets, such as those in New York and London.[8]

Direct investment may have positive effects upon the global rate of economic growth as well as on global efficiency. An increase in the *rate* of diffusion of technology, such as we are experiencing during the present period of rapid DFI expansion, will temporarily raise the rate of growth. Over the longer run (and more problematically) the rate of growth may rise as a result of an increase in the rate of

---

[6] Charles P. Kindleberger, *American Business Abroad: Six Lectures on Direct Investment* (New Haven, Conn.: Yale University Press, 1969), pp. 187-92.

[7] Christopher Tugendhat, *The Multinationals* (London: Eyre & Spottiswoode, 1971), chapter 8.

[8] For an interesting recent discussion, see Giorgio Ragazzi, "Theories of the Determinants of Direct Foreign Investment," *International Monetary Fund Staff Papers* 20 (July 1973): 471 ff.

return to investment in the production of technology, where an extension of the domain of the firm increases the total rents from such investments.

It would be foolish to deny the existence of these positive effects, especially where the competitive assumptions of neoclassical economics are reasonably approximated; there are simply too many instances in which foreign investment has paid off handsomely from a global point of view. However, economists have recently become increasingly aware of certain inadequacies of the neoclassical theory of factor movements in explaining direct investment, and they have turned instead to the theory of industrial organization, and to explicit consideration of the imperfections in the competitive environment in which the multinational firm operates.[9] Viewed from the perspective of the theory of firm expansion, direct investment may appear less benign in its effects.

Multinational enterprises "happen" to be extremely large firms in oligopolistic industries—in manufacturing, normally differentiated oligopoly where behavior is likely to have substantial efficiency costs.[10] Natural resource industries such as oil and aluminum have provided some of the most dramatic examples of oligopolistic behavior by multinational firms, but oligopoly structures in manufacturing, the other sector in which they predominate, will also impose significant efficiency costs. There are two basic variants of the oligopoly model of direct investment. In one, the firm moves aggressively into foreign production to exploit a monopoly of superior "knowledge" (products, processes, organizational or financial skills), or to improve its position vis-à-vis large competitors or to forestall entry.[11] In the second variant, the firm reacts defensively, moving production abroad to protect an export market that it would otherwise lose to competitors due to lower costs or tariff protection.[12] In practice the two cases are extremely difficult to distinguish. The competitive characteristics of the defensive variant are often stressed as an argument for the efficiency of such investment. But in the case where defensive investment must be undertaken to prevent the loss of markets to *local* firms, it must be asked whether such investment does not *displace* investment

[9] This theoretical approach derives from the innovative work of Stephen H. Hymer, "The International Operations of National Firms: A Study of Direct Investment" (Ph.D. dissertation, Massachusetts Institute of Technology, 1960). For a summary, see Kindleberger, Lecture 1. See also Richard E. Caves, "International Corporations: The Industrial Economics of Foreign Investment," *Economica* 38 (February 1971): 1-27.

[10] Caves, pp. 1-27. See also the statement of Stephen H. Hymer in US Congress, Senate, Committee on the Judiciary, Subcommittee on Antitrust and Monopoly, *International Aspects of Antitrust: Hearings before the Subcommittee on Antitrust and Monopoly of the Committee on the Judiciary*, 89th Cong., 2d sess., 20 April 1966, pp. 19-32.

[11] Stephen Hymer and Robert Rowthorn, "Multinational Corporations and International Oligopoly: The Non-American Challenge," in *The International Corporation*, ed. Charles P. Kindleberger (Cambridge, Mass.: M.I.T. Press, 1970), pp. 57-91.

[12] See the extensive discussion of this product-cycle model of direct foreign investment in Raymond Vernon, *Sovereignty at Bay: The Multinational Spread of U.S. Enterprises* (New York: Basic Books, 1971), chapter 3. For case studies of the same phenomenon, see Robert B. Stobaugh, et al., "U.S. Multinational Enterprises and the U.S. Economy," in US Department of Commerce, Bureau of International Commerce, *The Multinational Corporation: Studies on U.S. Foreign Investment*, vol. 1 (Washington, D.C.: Government Printing Office, 1972), section II.

abroad rather than supplement it. In such a case, if domestic investment has been foregone in the source country, global efficiency and growth may fall; whatever the "institutional necessity" of expansion to the firm, its growth can be seen as a *socially* unnecessary extension of market power.[13]

The issue is a complicated one since the initial impact of foreign corporate penetration may well be to disrupt local restrictive arrangements; and the reaction by governments and regional organizations in attempting to encourage mergers to strengthen national (or "European") firms, while allegedly discouraging restrictive practices, may produce a period of changes in market structure, and in interfirm power relationships, that are uncongenial to the stabilization of market-sharing or price-fixing arrangements, and hence are relatively competitive. But the question for the long run is whether relatively stable oligopoly structures will emerge after the competitive dust has cleared, much as the extensive cartelization of international business in the interwar period was a response to the disruptive penetration of European markets by American firms, largely through exports, prior to World War I.[14] Bhagwati and Hymer have recently called attention to the model of cartelization through equity interpenetration—the "internationalization of capital" by a group of firms of different nationalities—as an important means for the division of markets and avoidance of competition.[15] In most less developed countries (LDCs), of course, the problem of restrictive business practices is especially prevalent, since the power of the large firm to extract concessions as a condition of entry is large and countervailing competitive forces are weak.

Quite apart from the efficiency costs of the profit-maximizing behavior of large firms, questions arise with respect to the efficiency of their investment behavior. Multinational firms generate large internal cash flow, and the use of such savings, in the presence of capital market imperfections due in part to US tax legislation, is highly sector specific. Managers may primarily seek expansion rather than profitability, and considerations of antitrust and market strategy often preclude domestic expansion; the firm is then faced with a choice of domestic "conglomeratization" or of expansion abroad. Under such circumstances, there is no presumption that returns from investment abroad will exceed the opportunity cost of capital in the source country, and investment will be inefficiently allocated internationally.[16]

---

[13] For an argument relating to the "institutional necessity" of direct investment, see Theodore H. Moran, "Foreign Expansion as an 'Institutional Necessity' for U.S. Corporate Capitalism: The Search for a Radical Model," *World Politics* 25 (April 1973): 369-86.

[14] Vernon, pp. 81-86.

[15] Jagdish N. Bhagwati, review of *Sovereignty at Bay*, by Ramond Vernon, in *Journal of International Economics* 2 (September 1972): 457; Stephen Hymer, "The Internationalization of Capital," *Journal of Economic Issues*, March 1972.

[16] See Grant L. Reuber, *Private Foreign Investment in Development* (London: Oxford University Press for the Development Centre of the Organization for Economic Co-operation and Development, 1973), p. 103; and Peggy Musgrave, "Tax Preferences to Foreign Investment," in US Congress, Joint Economic Comittee, *The Economics of Federal Subsidy Programs, Part 2—International Subsidies* (Washington, D.C.: Government Printing Office, 1972), p. 204.

Finally, and of special importance, especially in relation to direct investment in LDCs, is the situation where direct investment is a response to policy measures, such as protection from imports and tax incentives, which raise private returns above social returns. The costs here are probably quite high. The response of direct investment to foreign tariffs has been extensively documented,[17] and while the efficiency losses in developed countries may be moderate, there is persuasive evidence to show that highly protected investment oriented toward domestic markets in LDCs results in extensive efficiency costs, especially since the supply of foreign capital is likely to be highly elastic.[18] The rather dramatic decline in tax haven investment in Switzerland following 1962 changes in the tax law suggests that significant distortions result from tax effects;[19] and it is certainly not implausible that, as Cooper has argued, the overvaluation of the dollar, in a monetary regime where significant adjustment was regarded as unlikely, and perhaps even unnecessary, made an important contribution to the growth of United States direct foreign investment during the 1960s.[20]

There is a basic difficulty here, of course, since the first-best policy response *may* be to change the policy, in which case one may be tempted to regard the efficiency costs of direct foreign investment as a pseudoproblem.[21] However, it is not particularly useful to draw a sharp distinction between the distorting policies made by the governments in question and the distorting investment responses made by the multinational corporations; very often the policies themselves are induced by enterprise behavior, whether explicit or implicit, which makes protection or favorable tax treatment a condition of the investment. Generalization of this phenomenon, of course, leads to competitive policies that erode the tax base and escalate protection.

We thus have a lengthy set of credit and debit entries for multinational firms on the efficiency-growth criteria, and no very satisfactory way of drawing a balance. Careful case studies have found substantial efficiency gains for developed

---

[17] See the references cited in John H. Dunning, "Introduction," in *International Investment: Selected Readings*, ed. John H. Dunning (Middlesex, England: Penguin Books, 1972), p. 16.

[18] Reuber, p. 179.

[19] Richard N. Cooper, *The Economics of Interdependence: Economic Policy in the Atlantic Community*, The Atlantic Policy Studies (New York: McGraw-Hill for the Council on Foreign Relations, 1968), pp. 101-2.

[20] See Richard N. Cooper, "The Nexes among Foreign Trade, Investment, and Balance-of-Payments Adjustment," in *United States International Economic Policy in an Interdependent World, Papers submitted to the Commission on International Trade and Investment Policy and published in conjunction with the Commission's Report to the President, Volume II* (Washington, D.C.: Government Printing Office, 1971), p. 529.

[21] See, for instance, Harry G. Johnson, "The Efficiency and Welfare Implications of the International Corporation," in Kindleberger, ed., *The International Corporation*, p. 47; and Ronald I. McKinnon's discussion of Stephen Hymer's article, "The Efficiency (Contradictions) of Multinational Corporations," in *The American Economic Review, Papers and Proceedings* 60 (May 1970): 452-53.

host countries and for export-oriented investment in developing countries,[22] and since distortions are small in these cases, the global effects are likely to be positive. For market-oriented investment in LDCs, the results are less clear, but even radical critics of direct investment often admit efficiency gains and direct their attack at distributional effects.[23] We are inclined to believe that direct investment normally produces increased global product. When costs are assessed by governments, however, criteria other than global efficiency come to the fore.[24]

Two final caveats about effects on economic efficiency should be entered. First, given consumer sovereignty, the concept of efficiency itself is contingent upon the distribution of income. There are many efficient solutions, and the one chosen will depend upon income distribution within the society. In the face of existing extreme income disparities both nationally and internationally, those who do not find efficiency and growth arguments by themselves compelling—particularly with respect to underdeveloped countries—may perhaps be forgiven. Second, and related to the first, the preference-diffusing effects of transnational business raise the question of consumer sovereignty itself more urgently than at the national level. The tastes induced by corporate advertising among well-to-do elites in poor countries may be inappropriate to the countries' resources. If the thirst for "knowledge" is to be quenched by Coca Cola, planners in poor countries may well wonder about paying the rent.

International equity

The neoclassical theory of international capital transfer noted both national and international distributive effects: private returns to foreign investment exceeded social returns at the margin, so that income was transferred from source to host country; and the shift in relative resource endowments transferred income from labor to capital in the lending country, and the reverse was true in the borrowing country.[25] More recently, it has been emphasized that such transfers imply a change in relative growth rates in the two countries, that this may affect

---

[22] See John H. Dunning, *American Investment in British Manufacturing Industry* (London: George Allen & Unwin, 1958); Donald T. Brash, *American Investment in Australian Industry* (Cambridge, Mass.: Harvard University Press, 1966); A. E. Safarian, *Foreign Ownership of Canadian Industry* (Toronto: McGraw-Hill Book Company of Canada, 1966); Helen Hughes and You Poh Seng, eds., *Foreign Investment and Industrialization in Singapore* (Madison, Wis.: University of Wisconsin Press, 1969); Reuber, chapters 5, 6.

[23] Hymer, "The Efficiency (Contradictions) of Multinational Corporations," p. 448. Hymer notes elsewhere: "It is little wonder, then, that those at the top stress growth rather than equality as the welfare criterion for human relations." See his discussion, "The Multinational Corporation and the Law of Uneven Development," in Jagdish N. Bhagwati, ed., *Economics and World Order from the 1970s to the 1990s* (New York: Macmillan Co., 1972), p. 125.

[24] See the discussion in Jack N. Behrman, *National Interests and the Multinational Enterprise: Tensions Among the North Atlantic Countries* (Englewood Cliffs, N.J.: Prentice-Hall, 1970), part I.

[25] G. D. A. MacDougall, "The Benefits and Costs of Private Investment from Abroad: A Theoretical Approach," *Economic Record* 36 (March 1960): 13-35.

the terms of trade, and that, in the presence of nontraded goods, no general conclusions about the change in income distribution can be deduced.[26] So much for the likelihood of deriving formally satisfying conclusions. Nonetheless, we will risk some observations in this section on effects of direct investment on *relative* levels of economic welfare between countries—international equity—and in the next section on effects on national equity, both with respect to factor returns and the burden of adjustment costs.

The complexity of the phenomenon of direct investment is well illustrated by the wide divergence of views of critics of the multinational enterprise. Some argue that the multinational enterprise transfers income from source to host countries,[27] while others argue, especially with respect to LDCs, that firms extract exploitative rents that transfer income to the source countries from the hosts.[28] From a purely economic point of view, the former view is surely more plausible. Corporations will tend to compare after-tax earnings at home and abroad in allocating investment, but the appropriate comparison from the standpoint of source country welfare is *net* returns from abroad versus *gross* (pretax) returns at home. Given present international tax arrangements, which offer the host country the first cut of the pie, "the rate of return on foreign investment net of foreign tax is likely to be substantially below the domestic return gross of tax,"[29] and data for the United States tend to support this view. Were all countries able to deal equally effectively with multinational firms, therefore, host countries and their tax collectors would tend to start with substantial gains.

The problem with this analysis, of course, is political: countries are not equally able to deal effectively with large corporations. As Ronald Müller has pointed out, "Third World countries are characterized by an absence of the 'countervailing' power of government and organized labor for setting limits on the power of the modern corporation."[30] In the absence of effective regulation, it is not difficult to imagine ways in which multinational firms could impose significant losses on poor countries. A combination of the extraction of large rents through monopolistic control of technology, distortions introduced through capital-intensive techniques, and the displacement of local entrepreneurship and capital could more than offset the potential tax gains. Those potential tax gains may themselves be eroded or entirely eliminated, furthermore, by corporate profit shifting through

---

[26] Ivor F. Pearce and David C. Fowan, "A Framework for Research into the Real Effects of International Capital Movements," in John H. Dunning, ed., *International Investment: Selected Readings,* chapter 7.

[27] Robert Gilpin, *The Multinational Corporation and the National Interest,* report submitted to the US Congress, Senate, Committee on Labor and Public Welfare, 93d Cong., 1st sess. (Washington, D.C.: Government Printing Office, 1973). For an analysis of how increasing capabilities of host countries, both developed and developing, are increasingly enabling them to foster this outcome, see C. Fred Bergsten, "Coming Investment Wars?" *Foreign Affairs* (October 1974): 135-52.

[28] Müller.

[29] Musgrave, p. 208.

[30] Müller, passim.

the manipulation of transfer prices. Insofar as governmental institutions in less developed countries are *systematically* less effective than those in more developed states, one can expect a general political bias against LDCs that must be set against the economic arguments indicating that they will tend to benefit disproportionately from the activities of multinational firms.

The evidence about the effects of direct investment on international equity seem inconclusive. Hymer has argued that in the absence of more substantial national intervention, international growth will take the form of rapid *output* growth in the periphery, with disproportionate *income* gains accruing to the technology-exporting center.[31] Reuber's study of the effects of direct investment on development, however, tends to be far more optimistic.[32] Yet since so much depends on the governmental capabilities of the host country, general economic conclusions are probably less significant than the major political implication: increasing the capabilities of LDC governments is likely to increase international equity. As we will see in the third section of this essay, strategies for international action to alter bargaining power often take this proposition as an assumption.

It should be remembered, finally, that the issue of international equity is not restricted to a comparison of the shares of source and host countries, or of developed and less developed countries. The firm itself may benefit at the expense of both countries primarily concerned, particularly if it is aided by the government of a "tax haven" state. Where large efficiency losses occur, furthermore, whether due to host country policies or to monopolistic practices by the firm, it is perfectly possible that firm profits will increase but that both source and host countries will have lower incomes than they would have had if the firm had invested domestically rather than abroad.

National equity

Critics of multinational enterprises have launched some of their most vigorous attacks on the effects of these firms on employment and income distribution in host countries, particularly in the underdeveloped world. It is observed that unemployment has grown sharply, and that this has been accompanied by increasing maldistribution of income in many countries, especially in Latin America, whose industrialization has involved heavy foreign participation.[33]

The problem here is how to assess responsibility for these problems. To what extent do they result from the existence or practices of multinational enterprises? The latter can hardly be held accountable for the demographic factors behind the labor force explosion. Nor is it evident that *foreign* investment is primarily at fault,

---

[31] Stephen H. Hymer and Stephen A. Resnick, "International Trade and Uneven Development," in Jagdish N. Bhagwati, et al., eds., *Trade, Balance of Payments and Growth: Papers in International Economics in Honor of Charles P. Kindleberger* (Amsterdam: North Holland, 1971), pp. 473-94.

[32] Reuber, chapters 5, 6.

[33] Müller, pp. 78-83.

since capitalist industrialization per se, in its early stages, appears to skew the distribution of income. Finally, host country policies themselves may have had pernicious employment effects, both for foreign and domestic firms. There is insufficient evidence at the moment to gauge the relative importance of such factors, but it is wise to keep them in mind when evaluating effects of multinational firms in order to guard against spurious attributions of causality.

From an economic point of view, the effect of direct investment on factor prices and income shares within countries will depend critically upon which factors are transferred and upon the effects of the ensuing income changes on capital accumulation. The impact on the demand for labor relative to capital will be very sensitive to (1) the factor-saving bias of the technology, (2) the factor intensity of the sector to which it is directed, and (3) factor price distortions resulting from market imperfections or government policy. Concern has been widely expressed that as a result of the labor-saving, capital-intensive nature of most direct foreign investment, DFI will characteristically generate disproportionately little employment in less developed economies. However, other authors have found very extensive adaptation by foreign firms to factor endowments, especially where labor-intensive activities within a vertically integrated firm could be sourced separately abroad.[34]

The problem we encounter here is similar to the one dealt with in our discussion of international equity: government policy becomes a critical variable in any realistic analysis of the economic effects of direct foreign investment. *If* a fair degree of labor mobility existed in less developed host countries, *if* government policies did not subsidize capital and maintain high wages for urban labor elites, and *if* enterprises did not practice capital-intensive "good citizenship" by buying off the government and a small work force with high wages and "fair" labor standards, direct investment might do its job of closing income gaps nationally and internationally. But as Paul Streeten has noted, "It is precisely in the area where host government and foreign firm seem to pursue common interests, where the profit

---

[34] The adaptation by international firms to factor endowments by sourcing labor-intensive activities in low-wage areas is described in G. K. Helleiner, "Manufactured Exports from Less Developed Countries and Multinational Firms," *Economic Journal* 83 (March 1973): 21-47. With respect to the adaptation of techniques to factor endowments for a given country, it has been argued that opportunities for economical substitution are very limited; see Walter A. Chudson, *The International Transfer of Commercial Technology to Developing Countries,* UNITAR Research Report No. 13 (New York: United Nations Institute for Training and Research, 1971). However, some authors have found evidence of considerable adaptation, at least in the sense that foreign firms do not use techniques that are significantly more capital intensive than local firms. See R. Hal Mason, "Some Observations on the Choice of Technology by Multinational Firms in Developing Countries," *Review of Economics and Statistics* 60 (August 1973): 349-55; W. Paul Strassmann, *Technological Change and Economic Development: The Manufacturing Experience of Mexico and Puerto Rico* (Ithaca, N.Y.: Cornell University Press, 1968), chapters 4, 5; Howard Pack, "The Substitution of Labor for Capital in Kenyan Manufacturing," Department of Economics, Swarthmore College, Swarthmore, Pa., 1973 (mimeographed). Reuber (pp. 194-97) finds that adaptations of techniques to smaller scale for market-orientation investment were common, but that those to low labor costs were much less so.

motive and national aspirations seem to coincide, that most damage is done."[35] The great danger from an equity point of view is that a symbiotic functional relationship between enterprises, governments, and labor elites will reinforce at the national level the international inequities noted above: "The rich of the world would be integrated transnationally, while the poor remain marginal, . . . cluster about the centers of industry, providing some supplies and services, but not participating in the decisions or benefits of development."[36]

From a short-term political point of view, it seems ironic that the most damage could be done by enterprises cooperating closely with governments. After all, such cooperation, even with inefficient and inequitable effects, is generally considered politically responsible. Further, it is difficult to argue that enterprises will oppose governments on grounds of equity among citizens of the host countries, or even that they should. Governments are expected to represent the interests of their citizens, and from one point of view, if they fail to do so, it seems bizarre to blame the corporation.

On the other hand, corporations influence governments, as well as vice versa. They do so indirectly, by the opportunities their presence provides for symbiotic elitist strategies, as well as directly. Foreign investment may, under some conditions, bolster the position of a government, strengthening its support among key elites and reducing the necessity to satisfy nonelite demands. It is, furthermore, a potential political resource that is more readily available to right-wing than to left-wing regimes.[37] A world in which DFI is significant is thus a more favorable environment for right-wing regimes in less developed countries than a world without DFI would be. In that sense, DFI contains a political bias, quite independent of whether any particular enterprise attempts to influence an individual government's policy. Insofar as inequitable distributional effects result from the policies of right-wing governments, the phenomenon of direct foreign investment may partially be held accountable, even if no particular firm can be justly blamed.

On the source country side, one effect of direct foreign investment could be to retard or to accelerate capital accumulation, thus lowering or raising labor's share, though it must be noted that the former result is more likely the greater the propensity to reinvest earnings abroad, which makes US labor's opposition to tax deferral of unrepatriated foreign income hardly surprising. Adjustment costs, however, may raise more serious problems of equity if they fall disproportionately on

---

[35] "Costs and Benefits of Multinational Enterprises in Less-Developed Countries," in John H. Dunning, ed., *The Multinational Enterprise* (New York: Praeger, 1971), p. 244.

[36] Robert W. Cox, "Labor and Transnational Relations," in Robert O. Keohane and Joseph S. Nye, eds., *Transnational Relations and World Politics* (Cambridge, Mass.: Harvard University Press, 1972), p. 233.

[37] For some interesting data on US investment to five countries experiencing regime changes (right to left, or left to right) in the 1960s, see Steven Rosen, "The Open Door Imperative and U.S. Foreign Policy," in Steven Rosen and James Kurth, eds., *Testing Theories of Economic Imperialism* (Lexington, Mass : D.C. Heath Lexington Books, 1974).

one sector or another. With appropriate government policies, it makes little sense to talk about a long-run tendency for direct investment to create or destroy jobs, or to improve or worsen the balance of payments; the joint selection of expenditure-controlling variables and the exchange rate should provide for internal and external balance, whatever the propensities for capital and technology to flow between regions. The appropriate long-run question concerns the effects on comparative advantage, and thence on the structure of output and employment.

In the short run, however, the employment picture cannot be so easily swept aside, since, given imperfect labor markets and short-run fixed stocks of human and physical capital, serious factor adjustment problems may remain even with appropriate exchange rate and expenditures policies and are likely to be much more acute in their absence. We therefore pose what seems to us the important short-run question: Assuming appropriate exchange rate and expenditures policies, what is the impact of DFI upon adjustment costs, and upon whom are these costs likely to fall?

Since DFI is a flow of technology and capital from relatively well-endowed to relatively poorly endowed regions, its primary effect will be to narrow factor endowment differences among countries, and thereby both to change the structure of comparative advantage and to make that structure more sensitive to other changes in the international economy.[38] This, of course, has the effect both of destroying *existing* jobs and capital values and of potentially (given appropriate adjustment policies) creating *new* jobs and investment opportunities in different activities and in different areas.

These adjustment costs, however, will be very unequally distributed. The dynamic process of changing comparative advantage will continually shift demand in favor of the owners of new technology and high-level labor skills; their prices and incomes may be expected to increase. At the same time, the demand for blue-collar unskilled labor in import-competing industries, and in export industries that have lost their comparative advantage, will decline. Where owners of capital have no monopoly of complementary inputs that can be profitably transferred abroad, they will bear substantial adjustment costs along with labor in the absence of protective policy intervention, as capitalists owning steel, textile, and shoe-producing facilities in the United States have discovered.

But where monopolistic advantage makes foreign investment profitable, the situation is very different. The multinational firm provides an efficient mechanism for owners of capital to transfer it abroad through depreciation allowances, to earn foreign rents on complementary inputs to defray the loss of capital values at home, and to borrow abroad to finance the cost of the new investment. Unskilled labor does not, of course, have available such a mechanism for easing the burden of adjustment, and the American Federation of Labor—Congress of Industrial Organi-

---

[38] Cooper, *The Economics of Interdependence,* chapter 4.

zations (AFL-CIO) hardly displays an "ideological fixation"[39] in the strong stand it has recently taken against the export of capital and technology. The crucial point is that direct investment can both increase adjustment costs and allow (some) capitalists to avoid (or at least finance) those costs, which fall heavily on labor. The creation of new high-skill jobs in high technology industries is precisely what one would expect from a "product cycle" model; but new jobs are not old jobs, and upgraded skills are not existing skills. "Higher skills are associated with higher income and a higher standard of living. But the adjustment process is costly and its burden falls hardest on those who can least afford it. A society that has reaped the benefits of freer trade and greater choice should be willing to share the cost."[40]

Political effects

To a considerable extent, the responses of public and private agents to forces unleashed by the multinational enterprise will reflect the considerations noted above—conventionally denominated *economic*, although, as we have pointed out, politics is often critically important in their determination. But overtly political considerations are also important. Most obviously, governments seek the capacity to respond effectively to an uncertain and often hostile world, and to shape their environments, at least to some extent, according to their wishes. This inclination to maintain their effectiveness reflects not megalomania, necessarily, but a prudent willingness to be prepared for the unexpected. As the petroleum crisis of 1973-74 illustrated, governments that neglect these considerations in the single-minded pursuit of economic growth do so at their peril.

Governmental effectiveness, however, is not the only relevant kind of political concern. Some of the most trenchant criticisms of direct foreign investment, as we point out below, rest essentially on concerns not about effectiveness but about status. Status, which is closely related to self-esteem, is from one point of view a more basic value than political effectiveness, which is largely instrumental.[41]

Governmental effectiveness

It is host countries that most often raise objections to multinational firms on grounds that they threaten governments' political effectiveness. The size, self-confidence, and mobility of multinational manufacturing firms, at any rate, are all too

---

[39] Phrase used in testimony by N. R. Danielian, president of the International Economic Policy Association, in US Congress, Joint Economic Committee, *A Foreign Economic Policy for the 1970s, Hearings before the Subcommittee on Foreign Economic Policy of the Joint Economic Committee, Congress of the United States,* 91st Cong., 2d sess., part 4—*The Multinational Corporation and International Investment,* p. 888.

[40] José de la Torre, Jr., Robert B. Stobaugh, and Piero Telesio, "U.S. Multinational Enterprises and Changes in the Skill Composition of U.S. Employment," in Duane Kujawa, ed., *American Labor and the Multinational Corporation,* Praeger Special Studies in International Economics and Development (New York: Praeger, 1973), p. 137.

[41] The importance of status was brought clearly to our attention by Professor Joseph S. Nye.

obvious to government leaders. It is clear that these enterprises have the potential for removing certain key decisions from the government. They can effect involuntary transfers between state treasuries by shifting the location of profits, move regulated activities beyond the law's arm, obtain additional banking reserves by borrowing Eurodollars from abroad, and (at least jointly) force a floating of the exchange rate by buying foreign exchange. The potential of the multinational firm for eroding governmental autonomy is a familiar theme, reinforced by spectacular examples of deliberate political inteference, such as International Telephone and Telegraph's behavior in Chile. Economists may well conclude that "two companies, one foreign, one Canadian, operating in the same circumstances . . . will operate in the same way"[42] —but don't try it as a campaign slogan!

Yet too much is sometimes made of the threat posed by enterprises as independent actors to the effectiveness of governments. It is true that some governmental elites may have been "captured" by corporations, and may do their bidding. Governments of small states may find the costs of effectively regulating huge corporations beyond their means. Yet governments in more developed countries have significant means at their disposal to cope with multinational firms. Governments continue to command the primary loyalties of most citizens (even those who are employed by multinational firms), and governments control the means of violence. In a crunch they can prevail, if opposed only by the firm and not by its parent government as well, although the cost may be great.

For cases in which the multinational firm faces a government as an independent actor, and in which the firm provides economic benefits, Samuel P. Huntington has put the issue of political conflict well. Huntington makes a distinction between *duplicative conflict,* involving similar entities in direct confrontation with one another, and *complementary conflict,* which is non-zero-sum and involves entities performing different functions. Huntington argues:

> The conflict between national governments and transnational organizations is clearly complementary rather than duplicative. It is conflict not between likes but between unlikes, each of which has its own primary set of functions to perform. It is, consequently, conflict which, like labor-management conflict, involves the structuring of relations and the distribution of benefits to entities which need each other even as they conflict with each other. The balance of influence may shift back and forth from one to the other, but neither can displace the other.[43]

Multinational firms, of course, affect power relations among states, as well as between themselves and governments. They may be instruments of governmental policy or "transmission belts" between societies. In some ways, the changes

---

[42] Irving Brecher and S. S. Reisman, *Canadian–United States Economic Relations* (Ottawa: Queen's Printer, 1957), cited in Kindleberger, *American Business Abroad,* p. 4.
[43] Samuel P. Huntington, "Transnational Organizations in World Politics," *World Politics* 25 (April 1973): 366.

induced by the enterprises seem to increase source country as against host country power. On a few highly publicized occasions, the United States has exercised its control over US-based enterprises for explicitly political reasons, such as to bar the sale of sophisticated computers to France or of ordinary trucks to China. On other occasions, the American government has used its power as the largest capital exporter to pursue balance-of-payments adjustment policies, as with the capital controls of 1965 and 1968. Some US senators have recently suggested that American-based multinational firms *ought* to give preference to United States consumers when an oil shortage arises, although no formal action was taken by the United States government to require this during the Arab oil boycott of 1973-74.

Yet source and host countries trade hostages with each other, as well as with fortune, and even incompetent governments can play with hostages. To the extent that source countries become dependent on integrated operations of multinational firms for their welfare, perhaps in the future in manufacturing as currently in certain raw materials, any government that controls one link in the chain gains considerable potential power from that position. In some cases, furthermore, host country governments can improve their power by manipulating the enterprise rather than by dealing directly with its home state. Thus Canada improved its outcomes from several important issues in the 1960s (auto trade, Arctic pollution) by extracting concessions from US-based enterprises that it could not get from the American government.[44]

Thus the net effects of multinational firms on governmental effectiveness are mixed. Nevertheless, a few observations relevant to questions of international regulation can be made. In the first place, the presence of large and organizationally sophisticated firms introduces a new element of uncertainty into the states' environments. Even if net effects on governmental effectiveness turn out to be neutral or even positive, the government is likely to have found it necessary to devote considerable attention to the question. Secondly, insofar as enterprises seem able to avoid the controls placed on them by any one government—either because they can escape its jurisdiction or because they are powerful enough to deter it from effective regulation—governments will have incentives to coordinate their actions. (We discuss some examples of, and prospects for, such coordination in the third part of this article.) Finally, however, insofar as the most important issues among a set of governments reflect conflicts between the policies and interests of the various governments, with firms either being instruments of government policy or actors that increase policy interdependence, international policy coordination is hardly likely to be an effective solution to the problem. We can only expect extensive international regulation on a global scale where the principal issues pit the state against the enterprise, rather than state against state with the enterprise only as a willing or unwilling intermediary.

---

[44] Joseph S. Nye, "Transnational Relations and Interstate Conflicts: An Empirical Analysis," *International Organization* 28 (Autumn 1974): 961-96.

Status

As we noted above, fears about effectiveness and concern about status are difficult to disentangle. One area in which this is particularly true involves the concern of many developed country governments about controlling high-technology sectors in their economies. Some arguments about the necessity of independent technological capabilities for national power are relevant, although Prime Minister Wilson's famous remark about Britain becoming a "hewer of wood and drawer of water" bespeaks a deep concern about status. A recent study of German, French, and British policies toward direct foreign investment "failed to uncover any [solidly based] official economic rationale" for the mix of policies adopted, and concluded that the most satisfactory explanation was concern over the "technology gap" and the high technological demand made by great power status in the age of the scientific state.[45] Many of the Canadian critiques of American direct investment are best interpreted in terms of status rather than in terms of welfare or governmental effectiveness.[46] Nevertheless, this concern for domestic technological capability may have an economic rationale as well, since under conditions of private ownership, the location of knowledge-producing activities is determined by total rents, and therefore market size, rather than by relative efficiency.[47] Other nations can hardly be expected to accept American economic size as a persuasive argument for disbanding efficient research and development activities.

Critics of multinational enterprises have argued that extensive multinational business activity will create a hierarchical structure of economic activity on a global scale. As Stephen Hymer puts it, that structure would involve

> a hierarchical division of labor between geographical regions corresponding to the vertical division of labor within the firm. It would tend to centralize high-level decision-making occupations in the advanced countries, surrounded by a number of regional sub-capitals, and confine the rest of the world to lower levels of activity and income. . . .[48]

Even if income gains were more equitably distributed, one would not expect states toward the bottom of this hierarchy permanently to accept their low status, particularly if they had sufficient size and resources to aspire to a higher place. The frustrations of being at a relatively low point on the hierarchy could very well outweigh even significant gains in absolute levels of economic welfare.[49]

---

[45] Robert W. Gillespie, "The Policies of England, France, and Germany as Recipients of Foreign Direct Investment," in *International Mobility and Movement of Capital,* eds. Fritz Machlup, Walter S. Salant, and Lorie Tarshis (New York: National Bureau of Economic Research, 1972), p. 430.

[46] For example, see Karl Levitt, *Silent Surrender: The Multinational Corporation in Canada* (Toronto: Macmillan of Canada, 1970).

[47] Johnson, p. 38.

[48] Hymer, "The Multinational Corporation and the Law of Uneven Development," p. 125.

[49] This is likely to be particularly true for elites, who are not hungry for food but who thirst for status. See Robert Gilpin, "Integration and Disintegration on the North American Continent," *International Organization* 28 (Autumn 1974): 851-74.

From the point of view of conflict, this problem is more intractable than questions of welfare or jurisdictional issues between state and enterprise. The latter tend to be non-zero-sum; potential arrangements generally exist that will make both partners better ɔff, in absolute terms, than they would be without the interaction. Thinking in neoclassical terms about welfare gains from trade and investment, economists can thus be quite complacent about the results, when all are to benefit to some extent. Status concerns, on the other hand, are inherently zero-sum or close to zero-sum, as long as the criteria for high status are uniform. Were it considered better in some societies to be poor and close to the land, rather than to dominate international economic arrangements, status conflict between those societies and the dominant ones would be relatively small. But in a world in which aspirations to control high technology are virtually universal, the effects on one's status of failing to do so are likely to be severe. The frustrations of being doomed to low status roles would be likely to lead to conflicts over direct foreign investment even if all issues of economic welfare and political effectiveness were resolved.

This concludes our discussion of the economic and political effects of direct foreign investment. The results, especially as regards the economic effects, are dramatically inconclusive. There is an argument to suit almost every interest or prejudice. It is hardly surprising, then, that policy prescriptions regarding the multinational corporation will diverge widely. International business, which stands to profit handsomely from global efficiency gains, will argue that direct investment should be promoted, and support for this position will come from international bureaucrats, liberal intellectuals, and others who profess a cosmopolitan interest. National groups, which fear unfavorable distributive effects, such as unskilled labor in source countries or capitalists in host countries, will press for regulation of the international firm, normally at the national level. Bureaucratic elites, acutely conscious of the limitations and dangers of national regulation in an interdependent world, will seek means of coordinated action through international regulation.

While the dominant trend to date has been a movement toward increasing national regulation, our interest centers upon strategies for international action. We therefore proceed to a brief discussion of international measures to promote direct investment, before considering strategies of international regulation.

International measures to promote direct foreign investment

It has long been recognized that consistent and predictable legal infrastructure promotes the development of business activity, and arrangements that simply extend such consistency and predictability across national boundaries should therefore promote DFI and reinforce the impact of the multinational firm, indeterminate though that may be. The existing international legal environment, to the extent that it has an impact on direct investment, was generally designed to provide such consistency and predictability.[50] Schemes to accomplish this purpose more systematically have also been proposed from time to time.

Existing arrangements

The most common existing arrangements are bilateral, such as United States treaties of friendship, commerce, and navigation (of which over 130 have been signed since the eighteenth century) and bilateral tax treaties dealing especially with double taxation. Of growing importance in recent years have been bilateral agreements on investment protection negotiated between source and host countries in conjunction with the development of investment-guarantee programs in the former.[51] Such bilateral arrangements have in some cases been facilitated by multilateral action: the Organization for Economic Cooperation and Development (OECD) has drawn up a Draft Convention on Double Taxation (1963) and a Draft Convention on Protection of Foreign Property (1967). There are also, of course, multilateral arrangements for the protection of industrial property rights, some of them long standing, such as the Convention of Paris (1883) and the Inter-American Convention on Inventions, Patents, Designs and Models (1910), and others more recent, such as the European Patent Convention (1972). Of multilateral agreements directed specifically at direct investment, however, two are particularly noteworthy.

On 12 December 1961, OECD adopted the Code of Liberalization of Capital Movements, which has been revised several times since then but is still in force, with various reservations. Canada does not adhere to the code, and its liberalization obligations do not apply to Greece, Iceland, Turkey, or to Portuguese overseas provinces. But for the other states of OECD, the code represents an attempt to induce members, in the language of the code, to "progressively abolish between one another . . . restrictions on movements of capital to the extent necessary for effective economic cooperation." Related to this code is the OECD Code of Liberalization of Current Invisible Operations, also adopted in 1961 and more recently amended.[52]

These OECD arrangements are not focused specifically on direct foreign investment, although they serve to facilitate that as well as other types of transnational economic activities. The International Bank for Reconstruction and Development (IBRD), however, took the initiative in the middle 1960s of sponsoring the

---

[50] For a brief summary, see Stefan H. Robock and Kenneth Simmonds, *International Business and Multinational Enterprises* (Homewood, Ill.: Richard D. Irwin, 1973), chapter 14, "The Legal Environment."

[51] OECD, *Investing in Developing Countries: Facilities for the Promotion of Foreign Private Investment in Developing Countires* (Paris: OECD, 1972), describes different national arrangements in some detail, with a chapter on each OECD country.

[52] The basic sources are OECD, *Code of Liberalization of Capital Movements* (Paris, January 1969) and *Amendments* thereto (Paris, April 1972); and *OECD Code of Liberalization of Current Invisible Operations* (Paris, March 1973). *The OECD Observer* 55 (December 1971) provides a useful summary.

Convention on the Settlement of Investment Disputes between States and Nationals of Other States, which came into force on 14 October 1966. A new international organization, the International Centre for Settlement of Investment Disputes (ICSID), located at the headquarters of the IBRD, was created in that year for the purpose of facilitating the flow of funds from developed to less developed countries by providing arbitration facilities equipped to deal with disputes between states and nationals of other states, particularly multinational firms. Previously, parties to a dispute would have had to have recourse to local courts or to private arbitration facilities, such as those provided by the International Chamber of Commerce, unless they wished to take the dispute to the Permanent Court of Arbitration at the Hague. Few less developed countries belong to that court, and in any case its rulings are not binding on the parties involved.[53]

As of 30 June 1973, the Convention on the Settlement of Investment Disputes between States and Nationals of Other States had 68 signatories. Most Latin American governments refused to sign, on the grounds that the convention would give preference to foreign over domestic investors and that both sets of investors should be equally subject to domestic law and domestic courts.[54] With the exception of Yugoslavia, socialist states have also not signed the convention, nor has Australia, Canada, India, Iran, or Saudi Arabia. Apart from the major capital-exporting states, most members are small and economically unimportant. Most major capital importers, for which the convention was apparently designed, have decided that they would rather retain sole domestic jurisdiction over investment activities within their borders.

Under the best circumstances, the arbitration and conciliation procedures of ICSID would be better suited to handling relatively minor disputes, such as disagreements over the interpretation of contracts, than to dealing with politically explosive questions of nationalization and expropriation.[55] Yet the efficacy of ICSID in handling even those secondary matters is called into question not only by its limited membership but by the fact that it can consider only certain disputes between the members. The convention does not provide for automatic ICSID jurisdiction in the event of a dispute; on the contrary, consent to ICSID jurisdiction must be specified in writing by the parties before arbitration can begin. This consent, however, may be given before disputes arise, after which consent cannot be unilaterally withdrawn by either party. Arbitration rulings are legally binding once given.

Until 1974, only one case had come to arbitration, and it seemed hard to disagree with the conclusion of one observer that "the lack of use of the convention

---

[53] Paul C. Szasz, "Using the New International Centre for Settlement of Investment Disputes," *East African Law Journal* 7 (June 1971).

[54] For a list of signatories, see the *Seventh Annual Report* of the International Centre for Settlement of Investment Disputes (Washington, D.C., 1973). For some early discussions on the project, see *International Legal Materials* 3: 1174-76; 4: 524-44; 5: 820.

[55] P. K. O'Hare, "The Convention on the Settlement of Investment Disputes," *Stanford Journal of International Studies* 6 (1971).

to date further attests to the lack of enthusiasm of the less developed countries for this approach to private investment problems."[56] During the first half of 1974, however, four more disputes were registered, three of which involved requests for arbitration by US-based aluminum companies operating in Jamaica.[57] The government of Jamaica, like other governments, can hardly be expected to be enthusiastic about having its discretion limited by an international tribunal, even one to which it once agreed to refer certain types of disputes. The efficacy of the ICSID procedures and the extent to which governments can be expected to abide by ICSID rulings are likely to be severely tested during the next few years.

Proposals for international action

The United States has had bilateral investment guarantee programs with selected countries since the Marshall Plan period, and other major countries followed suit in the 1950s and 1960s. Around 1960, a number of proposals were made to supplement these arrangements with schemes for multilateral investment insurance. This was formally taken up by the World Bank at the request of the Development Assistance Group (later, the Development Assistance Committee) of OECD. In July 1961, in conjunction with the International Chamber of Commerce, the Bank undertook a survey and made some suggestions about arranging a multilateral insurance program in a staff report.[58] In 1965, an OECD group of experts transmitted to the IBRD, with the approval of the OECD Council, the "Report on the Establishment of a Multilateral Investment Guarantee Corporation," which was used by the IBRD staff and executive directors to prepare a draft set of "Articles of Agreement of the International Investment Insurance Agency" (IIIA) in 1966, a second draft set of articles in 1968, and still a third set in 1972.[59]

From an economic point of view, the effect of successful investment guarantee schemes is to narrow the differential between private and social risk.[60] To the extent that such a differential exists, there is an efficiency argument for reducing political risk to the same degree for different lenders through multinational arrangements, which would also be able to effect guarantees for multinational consortia, which are presently ineligible for national guarantees. Administrative simplification could also result from multilateralization.

The rub comes on the political side. Source country governments tend to gain in a double sense. On the one hand, multilateralization provides a vehicle for coordinating policy, to avoid mutually costly competition to maintain the positions

[56] Stanley D. Metzger, "American Foreign Trade and Investment Policy for the 1970's: The Williams Commission Report," *American Journal of International Law* 66, no. 3 (1972): 548.

[57] See ICSID, press releases of 13 March 1974 and 24 June 1974. See also ICSID Document AC/73/5 (15 January 1974), which contains summary proceedings of the Seventh Annual Meeting, held on 27 September 1973, in Nairobi, Kenya.

[58] IBRD, *Multilateral Investment Insurance*, a staff report (Washington, D.C., March 1962).

[59] OECD, *Investing in Developing Countries*, pp. 101-2.

[60] Marina von Neumann Whitman, *Government Risk-Sharing in Foreign Investment* (Princeton, N.J.: Princeton University Press, 1965), chapter 2.

of their national firms. On the other hand, such an arrangement will tend to weaken host country positions, since multilateral threats of coercion may be more effective than bilateral ones. As the IBRD staff report commented, with reference to the insurance scheme: "Whereas under a bilateral program the action of one party could offend only the other party, in the context of a multilateral program the act of a capital-importing participant could bring that country into disfavor with the community of industrialized nations as well as with the other capital-importing nations."[61] In the light of the political bias of this sort of proposal, it is not surprising that it has not been accepted by the executive directors of the World Bank. All indications are that the proposal is, if not quite dead, certainly dormant.[62]

Following a French initiative in 1969, the European Commission, in July 1971, suggested a number of steps "to further an active, coherent private investment policy in developing countries," including instituting a community system of guarantees for private investment. However, a subsequent "initial action program" for development cooperation, released in February 1972, included no reference to this proposal. Thus, although the sixth general report of the European Commission lists this proposal as pending, little has apparently been done about it.[63]

In view of the difficulties states have had in agreeing on multilateral investment guarantees or insurance schemes, it is hardly necessary to comment on the political feasibility of proposals such as that by George Ball, for the creation of an international companies law, administered by a supranational regulatory body, facilitating the development of stateless corporations, or Cosmocorps. Even Ball agrees that it "may seem utopian and idealistic." The mixture of motivations for direct foreign investment, however, and the variety of effects that such investment may have throw doubt also on Ball's notion that such an arrangement would tend to assure "the most economical and efficient use of the world's resources."[64] In any case, such a proposal neglects a primary political requirement for any international scheme—providing for accountability. When perceived interests diverge widely, they can be reconciled only through mechanisms that are accountable to those interests and that are therefore perceived as legitimate, and the Cosmocorps and their regulators will hardly meet the test.

International facilitation of direct foreign investment is not where the action is. Governments see little incentive in the present environment to commit them-

---

[61] IBRD, *Multilateral Investment Insurance*, p. 21.

[62] IBRD, *Annual Report*, 1971, p. 35. The 1972 *Annual Report* of the IBRD does not mention the issue; a letter of 29 June 1973 from a member of the Information and Public Affairs Department of the Bank, received by one of the authors, indicates that the proposed International Investment Insurance Agency was not at that time under active consideration by the Bank's executive directors.

[63] See *Commission Memorandum on a Community Policy for Development Co-Operation, Summary* (27 July 1971), Supplement 5/71, Annex to *Bulletin of the European Communities* 9/10 (1971); see also Supplement 2/72 to the *Bulletin*, and the *Bulletin*, 5-4 (1972), p. 95, and 5-10 (1972).

[64] George W. Ball, "Cosmocorp: The Importance of Being Stateless," *Columbia Journal of World Business*, November-December 1967, p. 27.

selves further to protection of multinational firms, particularly when this could mean sacrificing powers to outside authority. The multinational firm is unlikely soon to be the beneficiary of an international rescue operation.

International regulation of direct foreign investment

The primary subject of this article is international regulation of direct foreign investment, yet our discussion so far has focused primarily on national concerns. Governmental attention to these issues is clearly a necessary condition for international action, and the effects of DFI that are perceived as important by national policymakers will influence heavily the nature of any international regulation that may appear. This explains our decision to emphasize the national perspective so strongly. Nevertheless, national concern is by no means a sufficient condition for international action. Governments must perceive common interests with one another, and must be able to communicate. Their interests in collaborating must be great enough to overcome the barriers of organizational inertia and reluctance to become constrained in their own policies by the policies and practices of others.

In a period of rising national regulation of multinational firms, the relative underdevelopment of international measures is striking. This may suggest that national regulation is generally effective, or that much of what is often seen as conflict between firms and governments in fact reflects deeper conflicts between governments or the societies that they represent.[65] Both of these explanations may contain some truth. But it is also possible that international regulation has lagged for other reasons, such as the difficulty in getting cumbersome governments to develop coherent positions and to act on issues that are not urgent at the moment. In that case, further international regulation may be desirable, whether or not it is politically feasible.

For analytic purposes, we make a distinction between two kinds of international arrangements designed to regulate direct investment. We refer to *policy coordination,* discussed in the following section, where the governments involved are from highly developed capitalist countries and have favorable orientations toward multinational firms in general. Here there is characteristically considerable overlap between governmental and business elites, and a general sense of common interest between them. Yet to some extent the governments may find their attempts to regulate multinational enterprises thwarted by the firms' abilities to evade governmental jurisdiction by operating abroad. An extension of governmental jurisdiction through international measures—to encompass as wide an area as the decision domain of the firm—seems the natural course of action. Nevertheless, as we will see, policy conflicts between governments may complicate the issue.

[65] For an interesting argument that problems in the area of private international financial flows fundamentally reflect conflicts of governments with one another rather than with multinational enterprises, see Robert W. Russell, "Public Policies Toward Private International Financial Flows," paper prepared for the Fifteenth Annual Meeting of the International Studies Association, St. Louis, Mo., March 1974.

Policy coordination is distinguished from *alteration of bargaining power* as a motive for international action. In the latter case, governments of less developed countries or groups (such as labor organizations) that consider themselves disadvantaged by DFI use international measures—through regional groupings, producers' cartels, or international organizations—to increase their bargaining power vis-à-vis multinational firms. Here there is generally much less sense of common interest between the regulators and those they hope to regulate. Furthermore, situations such as these frequently involve conflicts between host governments, banded together to increase their political leverage, and source country governments, as well as between host governments and multinational firms.

Policy coordination as an international strategy

It is within common markets that the mobility of multinational firms often poses the most severe problems for advanced-country governments, since traditional national means for coping with such problems, particularly the erection of trade barriers, are proscribed. Thus, in the 1960s France found itself quite disadvantaged in its attempt to regulate American firms, which could, if displeased by French policies, simply locate across the borders in Belgium or Germany and export freely to France. The fact that the firms in question were American is significant: it has often been remarked that the most "European" firms, in the sense of having a continent-wide outlook, during the 1960s were based in the United States.

It was therefore natural that some attempts would be made to use the institutions of the European Community in developing regional policies to strengthen European enterprises, primarily through transnational mergers. The policies to be involved in the effort are fiscal harmonization, unification of capital markets, public sector support for research and development activities, and the creation of a European company law.[66] Yet, to date, progress in these areas has been very slow. Although the European Commission has prepared proposals on tax standardization, harmonization of capital market structures, industrial development contracts, and a European company law,[67] political agreement in the European Economic Community (EEC) Council has not been forthcoming.[68] Not altogether surprisingly, it has been precisely in those key sectors involving high technology, where the need for regional cooperation is argued to be strongest, that national resistance to the surrender of any control has been most adamant. As the European Commission remarks rather ruefully with respect to one of these areas:

> although in the case of standard supplies the liberalization of public contracts in the Community shows some progress . . . the same cannot be said of certain capital goods and advanced technological items such as computers,

[66] Behrman, *National Interests and the Multinational Enterprise*, pp. 161-72.
[67] Commission of the European Communities, *Sixth General Report on the Activities of the Communities*, 1972 (Brussels-Luxembourg, February 1973), pp. 65, 204, 78-79.
[68] Ibid., p. 302.

aircraft, conventional and nuclear power plant equipment, railway and tele-communications equipment.[69]

It would appear to remain the case that "European governments have *not* decided that the loss of sovereignty to other Europeans is better than a loss to U.S. enterprises."[70]

Indeed, the feeling of the EEC Council seems to be that regulating multi-national enterprises is properly a problem for all developed countries, rather than for Europe alone:

> The phenomenon of the multinational corporation must be viewed in a wider context than the Community, even the enlarged community. It should really be viewed in a world context. This is why the Commission is participating in the work of certain international organizations, such as the OECD in Paris, which are trying to establish a code of good conduct for these companies and possibly to find a more efficient method of control.[71]

Thus the issues have primarily been Atlantic ones. And as David Leyton-Brown has recently shown, interstate conflicts arising from activities of multina-tional firms in Britain, Canada, and France since World War II have arisen primarily from extraterritoriality problems.[72] Although a number of notorious cases are repeatedly cited in the literature, the number of severe intergovernmental policy conflicts has been small.

Among the OECD countries, there have been significant efforts to coordinate various policies affecting multinational firms, in areas such as antitrust policy, export controls, and securities regulation, where extraterritorial application of United States law has given rise to issues. OECD has a working party of experts within its Industry Committee to study on a continuing basis problems related to multinational enterprises.[73] OECD has also attempted to coordinate antitrust policy through a committee of experts on restrictive business practices, which periodically issues descriptive reports as well as recommendations to member governments to take measures against practices found to be harmful.[74] Issues revolving around the American Trading with the Enemy Act, which produced twelve of the sixteen conflicts cited by Jack N. Behrman as arising from activities of

[69] Ibid., pp. 204-5.
[70] Behrman, *National Interests and the Multinational Enterprise*, p. 169.
[71] Statement by Mr. Albert Borschette, member of the Commission, to the European Parlia-ment, 12 February 1973, in *Bulletin of the European Communities*, 2-73, p. 35.
[72] David Leyton-Brown, "Governments of Developed Countries as Hosts to Multinational Enterprise: The Canadian, British and French Policy Experience" (Ph.D. dissertation, Harvard University, 1973), p. 423, cited in Joseph S. Nye, "Multinational Corporations in World Politics," prepared statement before the Group of Eminent Persons to Study the Multinational Corporation, Geneva, 5 November 1973.
[73] Cited in Jack N. Behrman, "Sharing International Production Through the Multinational Enterprise and Sectoral Integration," *Law and Policy in International Business* 4, no. 1 (1972): 1-36.
[74] See, for instance, *Market Power and the Law*, a report of the Committee of Experts on restrictive business practices (OECD, Paris, 1970).

US corporations in the Atlantic area during the 1960s, were dealt with in special committees established for that purpose.[75] Except for these export control issues (which now seem to focus on mighty Cuba due to changes in American trade policy toward the Soviet Union and China), the most striking fact about questions of extraterritoriality is the apparent success of quiet negotiation and intergovernmental coordination. This leads us to agree with a close observer of the legal-economic scene, Seymour Rubin, who has argued with respect to problems of extraterritoriality that "governments having a reasonably similar polity are increasingly desirous of avoiding conflicts and increasingly accustomed to the consultative procedures that can accomplish that purpose."[76]

Taxation and capital controls raise more difficult issues. Here the macroeconomic effects of policy can be considerable. What is at stake for policymakers is not merely the existence of a firm or the legitimacy of some of its practices but the flows of taxes across borders and into government coffers, and the inexorable imperatives of the balance of payments. Robbins and Stobaugh have argued that enterprises do a suboptimal job of managing their financial assets, both in realizing returns on liquid assets and in avoiding excessive taxation.[77] As these firms move toward optimal financial policies, effects on government tax revenue will be substantial, and there will be greater yearly variation in tax receipts.

At a conference held in 1973 on international regulation of the multinational firm, a number of speakers, including Fernand Braun from the EEC and Nicholas deB. Katzenbach of International Business Machines (IBM), focused on taxes as an area in which further international harmonization of government policy could take place. With respect to questions of tax havens, Charles Kindleberger was quite explicit:

> From the viewpoint of economic efficiency, taxes should be neutral. In the real world, without harmonization of tax systems, they are distortionary. Tax havens continue to distort resource allocations despite the limitations on them in the 1962 Revenue act in the United States and the Swiss-German double taxation agreement. In the long run, the Netherlands Antilles, Lichtenstein, Luxembourg, Andorra, San Marino, Zub, and Appenzell are going to have to stop trying to entice tax evaders. It is not attractive for the big countries to push around the little entities, but it is strongly dysfunctional to continue them. Like Delaware and Hoboken in the United States, in the long run they will have to give up exploiting gaps in the system.[78]

[75] The computation is from Nye, "Multinational Corporations in World Politics," and from Behrman, *National Interests and the Multinational Enterprise.* For discussions of the US embargo policy and the activities of the relevant committees, see Gunnar Adler-Karlsson, *Western Economic Warfare, 1947-1967* (Stockholm: Almquist and Wiksell, 1968).

[76] Seymour J. Rubin, "The Multinational Enterprise and National Sovereignty: A Skeptic's Analysis," *Law and Policy in International Business* 3, no. 1 (1971): 14.

[77] Sidney M. Robbins and Robert B. Stobaugh, *Money in the Multinational Enterprise: A Study in Financial Policy* (New York: Basic Books, 1973).

[78] Charles P. Kindleberger, "Comment," in *International Control of Investment: The Dusseldorf Conference on Multinational Corporations,* ed. Don Wallace, Jr., assisted by Helga Ruof-Koch (New York: Praeger, 1974), p. 64.

Since the benefits could be significant and the entities to be regulated are weak, tax neutrality would appear to be a suitable subject for international policy coordination.

The situation with regard to capital movements has recently been more pressing. Particularly in the years before 1971, transfers of funds by multinational enterprises became a source of great concern to governments wrestling (for the most part unsuccessfully) with the contradictions between freedom of short-term capital flows and the requirements of fixed exchange rates. It has been estimated that in 1971 as much as $268 billion in short-term assets were held by principal institutions in the international money markets, that a "dominant share" ($190 billion) of this was held by multinational corporations, and that a 1 percent flow would therefore be "quite sufficient to produce a first-class international financial crisis."[79] Robbins and Stobaugh estimate that approximately 100 multinational firms control about $25 billion in cash and marketable assets, overshadowing the reserves of any single country except Germany. They point out that financial decisions by multinational managers can collectively have drastic effects on international reserve positions: if all debts to United States parents by foreign affiliates were paid immediately, the US official reserves could triple.[80] In the Schydlowsky simulation model which the authors employ, balance-of-payments swings produced by short-term capital transfers under optimal multinational enterprise policies are very substantial.

Clearly, the potential for disruption represented by these funds poses an important policy problem. Governments will probably be under pressure to regulate and restrict capital transfers further. Robbins and Stobaugh go so far as to argue:

> Sooner or later government action will severely limit the multinational enterprise's use of credit tools in shuttling funds throughout its system; thus the enterprises will be shackled in their ability to protect against currency changes. As a result, multinational enterprises may come to accept losses and gains from devaluations and revaluations as a routine element in operating internationally. As long as all multinational enterprises are faced with the same rules, no one enterprise will suffer unduly. In fact, such rules will remove a major tension between firms and national governments and thereby make multinational enterprises more welcome than they might otherwise be.[81]

Clearly, national regulation of short-term capital movements may involve heavy costs to individual governments, as testified by recent events in Germany and Japan. Such controls would fall disproportionately on a country's own firms, putting them at a competitive disadvantage, at the same time that it diverted direct invest-

[79] US Congress, Senate, Committee on Finance, *Implications of Multinational Firms for World Trade and Investment and for US Trade and Labor, Report to the Committee on Finance by the US Tariff Commission,* 93d Cong. 1st sess. (Washington, D.C.: Government Printing Office, 1973), p. 539.
[80] Robbins and Stobaugh, pp. 178-83.
[81] Ibid., p. 186.

ment away from the country in question to other host countries. The argument for international agreement on control policies therefore becomes persuasive.

The importance of achieving such agreement is reinforced by the dangers of intergovernmental conflict in this area. As Cooper indicates in his contribution to this volume, the international monetary situation carries continual dangers of destructively competitive national action. National attempts to impose controls on capital movements for balance-of-payments or exchange-rate purposes may well collide. This is widely recognized: the *First Annual Report of the U.S. Council on International Economic Policy,* for instance, stressed capital controls as an area of international investment policy needing review by OECD.

The political problems in this area, however, are immensely complicated by the fact that conflicts over capital movements and exchange rates frequently pit major governments against one another, as well as against mini-jurisdictions, banks, or corporations. The behavior of firms may stimulate or compound intergovernmental conflict, but this does not make the national conflicts of interest any less real. From governments' point of view, the game is non-zero-sum; great losses are possible and the stakes are therefore very high. Indeed, the question is so complex that we cannot discuss it adequately here. The reader is referred to Cooper's analysis in this volume.

When a case for the desirability of international policy coordination has been made, the question immediately arises: How institutionalized should the regulation be? In a well-known article, Paul Goldberg and Charles Kindleberger have called for a "General Agreement for the International Corporation" (GAIC), modeled after the GATT, which would establish an international agency to deal with five important problems involving foreign investment: taxation, antitrust policy, foreign exchange controls, export controls, and securities regulation.[82] Their goal is the "creation of an international agreement based on a limited set of universally accepted principles. This agreement would be structurally similar to GATT." The agency's role would be to investigate facts and issues and to make recommendations, which would not be binding but would be accepted voluntarily if the agency "succeeded in acquiring a reputation for thorough analysis and impartiality. . . . As its status in the world community improved, the agency could act as an ombudsman for corporations and countries seeking relief from oppressive policies."[83]

The agency's findings would be based on a set of legal agreements:

> A contractual arrangement could be developed from agreement on a few fundamental concepts of substance and procedure. Then, as a seminal body of accepted principles emerge, broader and deeper agreement as to foreign investment practices would be generated. Perhaps after a guarded and gradual start gathered momentum, an international treaty of substantial coverage could be accepted by the nations of the world.[84]

---

[82] Paul M. Goldberg and Charles P. Kindleberger, "Toward a GATT for Investment: A Proposal for Supervision of the International Corporation," *Law and Policy in International Business* 2 (Summer 1970): 295-323.

[83] Ibid., p. 323.

[84] Ibid., p. 322.

In considering the GATT as a model for the proposed GAIC, it is useful to recall that the GATT operates in two rather different ways. It is primarily a contractual agreement in which members (or those countries that accede to it) are governed by rules that set out specific rights and obligations. It also "creates in a flexible and pragmatic way committees, working parties, and informal discussion groups to explore new problems and to settle conflicts in relation to the rules and obligations set out in the GATT agreement."[85] It is clearly the former, legalistic structure that Goldberg and Kindleberger have primarily in mind in calling for a *new* multilateral organization, with the massive political task of negotiation and institution building that this implies. The proposal raises rather sharply, then, the relative merits of such a legalistic model and the more informal consultative framework that, while applied in a limited way by the GATT, is employed by OECD. The key question is whether formal codification would have more advantages than liabilities.

Assuming a high degree of consensus on substantive principles, the codified rights and obligations of the proposed GAIC might, like those of the GATT, have the advantage of legally committing governments to the common interest of capitalist countries by providing for liberal, equitable arrangements for direct investment. This commitment would then serve the purpose of protecting such arrangements, and the general interests they serve, from the erosion to which less public and formal arrangements are subject due to the pressures of special interests or the temptation to use ad hoc measures in one area to avoid adjustment costs in another, as in the use of investment controls to improve the balance of payments. Such arrangements, if feasible, have the related advantage of adding an element of stability and predictability to policy.

But all this begs the question of whether such consensus exists. While the OECD countries cannot be said to be in fundamental disagreement on these questions, problems in Canada, Japan, and France notwithstanding, it seems unlikely that consensus is wide enough to negotiate an agreement or use one successfully. Nor is there much enthusiasm for making the effort. A 1973 conference of academics, businessmen, and officials of governments and international organizations, held on this subject, resulted in "a considerable unanimity of opinion as to result: that a GATT for investment, much less a disinvestment agency, would be neither feasible nor desirable at present."[86]

In such a situation, attempts to negotiate a GAIC would probably come to nought. If negotiations became serious, however, there could be negative effects. A major negotiation would tend to politicize the direct investment issue further,

---

[85] Harald B. Malmgren, "The International Organizations in the Field of Trade and Investment," in *United States International Economic Policy in an Interdependent World,* vol. 2, p. 429.

[86] Seymour Rubin, "Report on the Conference," in *International Control of Investment,* p. 9. Even Kindleberger seemed to agree: "I am a little embarrassed by the occasional reference to the fact that I have suggested that we need international rules for the international corporation, a sort of GATT. I do not feel very strongly about this: I just threw out the suggestion" (ibid., p. 249).

through the increased involvement of legislatures and high officialdom, and through subsequent attention from the press and general public. The politics of direct investment would become increasingly nationalistic and symbolic. This would particularly be the case if Third World countries were involved, although, in view of the experience of the International Investment Insurance Agency noted above, and as Goldberg and Kindleberger admit, this seems most unlikely. Because negotiators at relatively high levels would need to adopt coherent positions and maximize bargaining leverage, more linkages would be drawn between issues in the direct investment area, and further linkages with other economic or political issues would become likely. For all of these reasons, it would probably become more difficult to reach workable agreements, even on narrowly defined issues on which some degree of consensus now exists.

There are situations where wide-sweeping negotiations and a high degree of politicization are desirable, and even necessary—Bretton Woods, the Treaty of Rome, and the Kennedy Round come to mind. But at the moment, as Katzenbach has argued, "governments are unsure of what their positions are. . . . There are just too many problems. There is too much dispute, too much dissension, too much uncertainty."[87] Until direct investment issues become much more politically salient in OECD countries, and until positions become clearer, an attempt to negotiate a comprehensive agreement seems premature.

Thus those international arrangements among OECD countries that develop over the next few years will probably be relatively informal and issue specific. Since OECD is not a powerful organization, and since the difficulties of coordinating policies are extensive, there can be no guarantee that the informal measures that evolve will be sufficient to cope effectively with the problems. At a minimum, OECD policy coordination represents a holding action, until the point at which pressure for more far-reaching agreements becomes sufficient to produce action by governments.

Yet it may be possible to be more optimistic. As we pointed out above, OECD has developed a number of special committees for policy coordination in areas related to direct investment, and on issues of extraterritoriality these have had some success. Other issues have also been considered; in particular, the Fiscal Committee has concentrated some attention on transfer pricing and tax revenues. Over the past two decades, in a variety of issue areas, OECD governments have developed a remarkable number of relatively informal methods of intergovernmental policy coordination, which are feasible because of the highly specialized nature of those governments and the close communication among them at working levels, and which are rendered necessary by the inability of high-level decision makers, in highly complex and bureaucratized governments, to oversee detailed decisions and to coordinate policies effectively among many branches of govern-

---

[87]Nicholas deB. Katzenbach, "The Realistic Prospects for Greater Political Integration and Organization of Developed Countries Related to Investment," ibid., p. 69.

ment. Where political agreement exists, these informal procedures may be quite effective.

Having considered the feasibility of international policy coordination, we turn now to its likely effects. It is important to note that not all international policy coordination will restrict enterprise behavior. Agreements to observe national self-restraint in matters of antitrust, exchange controls, and export prohibitions would increase the freedom of action of firms, while agreements on the necessity, ends, and means of regulation in these areas would tend to narrow it. But even if the direction of coordination were clear in these terms, the economic effects would remain obscure, and it is partly this obscurity that makes a rapid or comprehensive convergence of views on these matters unlikely. Where firm behavior presently reduces efficiency or intended distributional arrangements, as in the use of transfer pricing to bar entry or avoid taxation, coordinated regulation would be beneficial. Where the same practice is presently used to avoid exchange controls, regulations might have efficiency costs, at least in this partial sphere.

In other areas, regulatory activity would have to face squarely the efficiency and distributional conflicts generated by multinational corporation activity, as in the imposition of short-term adjustment costs in securing (presumably) efficient location of the firm. The regulatory effects of certain policies may appear relatively clear, such as the use of standard disclosure requirements for security issues to lower information costs and improve markets. But there are others, such as antitrust policies to limit market concentration, where different states are in fundamental disagreement on the presumptive effects of current practice and the appropriate degree of regulation. It is therefore difficult to reach any settled conclusions in this area. Since progress, in whatever end, is likely to be gradual in the best of circumstances, one should at least hope that these problems are put in proper perspective by removing them from the arena of balance-of-payments conflict through reform of the monetary adjustment mechanism.

Altering bargaining power

Problems, plans, and prospects

When one set of actors in a relationship believes itself to be at a fundamental and systematic disadvantage, it is unrealistic to believe that measures to institutionalize the relationship or to coordinate policy more closely with the more powerful actors are likely to alleviate the situation for the actors that perceive themselves to be disadvantaged. On the contrary, these actors are likely to be inclined either to seek assistance from outside organizations or to concert policy more closely with one another in order to increase their joint bargaining power with the outsider. With respect to the modern multinational enterprise, both international trade unions and less developed countries find themselves in this general position.

International trade unions have attempted, in some instances, to coordinate their behavior vis-à-vis particular firms, although with indifferent success.[88] They have also turned to their most familiar and friendly international organization, the International Labour Organization (ILO), among others, for help. Here the emphasis has been on securing a code of conduct that would ensure the firms' respect for trade union rights. The International Confederation of Free Trade Unions (ICFTU) has adopted resolutions specifying that multinational enterprises should follow relevant ILO conventions, and both the International Metalworkers' Federation and the Miners' International Federation have called for a code of conduct whose provisions would include the requirement that companies abide by such conventions.[89]

A number of proposals emanating from the less developed countries or from individuals and groups sympathetic to their interests have stressed the need for concerted international action to alter economic power relationships. This is one of the major themes of a recent United Nations report, *The Impact of Multinational Corporations on the Development Process and on International Relations,* by a Group of Eminent Persons working under the authority of Economic and Social Council (ECOSOC) Resolution 1721 (LIII). This report makes three major institutional proposals: (1) the establishment of an information and research center on multinational corporations within the United Nations Secretariat; (2) the formation of a commission on multinational corporations, composed of individuals rather than government representatives, which would "act as the focal point within the United Nations system for the comprehensive consideration of issues relating to multinational corporations," and which would direct the activities of the information and research center; and (3) regular arrangements for at least annual meetings of ECOSOC on issues related to multinational firms, at which reports by the commission on multinational corporations would be considered.[90]

It seems clear that United Nations agencies are moving toward serving, not only as sources of support for governments dealing with particular enterprises, but as catalysts for policy harmonization among less developed countries seeking to strengthen their general position and to avoid competitive actions that benefit none of them in the long run.[91] This does not mean that a grandiose new UN operating agency to deal with multinational firms is likely to arise: due to opposition to such a development by existing agencies, as well as the efficiency costs, it is more likely

---

[88] David H. Blake, "Trade Unions and the Challenge of the Multinational Corporation," *Annals of American Academy of Political and Social Science,* no. 403 (September 1972): 34-45.

[89] ILO, *Multinational Enterprises and Social Policy.*

[90] The report is listed as UN Document E/5500/Add.1 (Part I), 24 May 1974. Part II consists of dissents and other comments by members of the group. The discussion of "institutional machinery and action" appears on pp. 34-41; the quoted phrase can be found on p. 40. The fact that the report appeared after this article had been completed and sent to the editors accounts for the relatively brief attention given to it here.

[91] See the discussion of this question in United Nations, Department of Social and Economic Affairs, *Multinational Corporations in World Development* (UN Document ST/ECA/190), New York, 1973, p. 90.

that an attempt will be made to coordinate various actions taken by a variety of UN bodies that bear on the direct investment problem.[92]

The information-sharing approach may be particularly relevant in helping governments decide on what terms to permit the transfer of technology from industrialized to less developed countries through multinational firms. Both UNCTAD and the Andean Common Market (ANCOM) have been concerned with rather stringent controls usually placed by parent companies upon the use of technology acquired under collaborative arrangements. Studies commissioned by UNCTAD on India, the Philippines, and the Andean countries indicate that export restrictions on goods produced with foreign-controlled technology are very widespread. A study by the Junta del Acuerdo de Cartagena, for instance, found that 81 percent of the technology transfer contracts for Bolivia, Columbia, Peru, and Ecuador prohibited exports entirely, and that 86 percent had some export restrictions.[93] An UNCTAD-sponsored study of the Philippines indicated that 65 percent of technical collaboration agreements involving local enterprises between 1965 and 1970 contained export restrictive clauses; a similar study of the Indian experience showed that approximately 40 percent of such agreements had export restrictions.[94]

These formal restrictions upon exports do not, of course, provide an adequate measure of the barriers to export. Joint ventures or licensees may find themselves restrained from exporting, in the absence of any formal prohibitions, by the areas specified in licensing agreements, by considerations of market structure, and ultimately by the necessity of remaining on good terms with the licensor. Thus the problem of restrictive practices goes far deeper than formal export restrictions. Yet such restrictions, with their implication of economic and political dependence, have emerged as a highly visible symbol of the use of economic power by the monopolists of technology.

The fundamental problem here, as the reports point out, is that sellers of technology have great bargaining strength. Not only do purchasers not know

[92] This sentence was written before the publication of the report by the Group of Eminent Persons, but its conclusion seems to be supported by that report. The group did suggest that as a "longer term objective," a "general agreement on multinational corporations" should be negotiated, but it argued that serious steps in this direction were premature at this time.

For a previous elaboration of the argument that vested interests of established international organizations would create pressures for coordination machinery rather than a powerful new operating agency to deal with multinational firms, see Robert W. Walters, "International Organizations and the Multinational Corporation: An Overview and Observations," *Annals of American Academy of Political and Social Science,* no. 403 (September 1972): 127-38.

[93] See the UNCTAD study by the Junta del Acuerdo de Cartagena, *Politics Relating to the Technology of the Countries of the Andean Pact: Their Foundations* (UN Document TC/107).

[94] UNCTAD, *Restrictions on Exports in Foreign Collaboration Agreements in India* (New York: United Nations, 1972), pp. 1-18; and UNCTAD, *Restrictions on Exports in Foreign Collaboration Agreements in the Philippines* (New York: United Nations, 1972), pp. 1-13. See also a discussion of these in the context of African countries' bargaining problems in Robert L. Curry, Jr., and Donald Rothchild, "On Economic Bargaining Between African Governments and Multinational Companies," paper presented at the Sixteenth Annual Meeting of the African Studies Association, Syracuse, New York, November 1973.

exactly what they are buying until they have done so (since it is information that is for sale), they also do not know what the terms of sales were elsewhere. Furthermore, the transfer of technology commonly takes place between the subsidiary of a multinational firm and its parent, where the transfer price is a matter of internal firm policy. The manipulation of transfer prices may be used to transfer profits out of the country, escaping the local tax collector as well as exchange controls. The study of the experience of the Andean countries referred to above found, in support of this suspicion, that foreign subsidiaries of multinational firms pay much more for technology than do national firms.

It is thus not surprising that UNCTAD is moving toward providing "action-oriented research, training, and advisory services and the formulation of appropriate policies in the context of UNCTAD's activities."[95] In its report, the Junta del Acuerdo de Cartagena proposes, as a remedy, regional cooperation in the technology-bargaining process. The Junta's report looks toward the day when exchanges of information are effective enough among countries that a most-favored-nation principle in technology would take effect: discriminatory pricing or restrictions on the basis of variations in bargaining power would be outlawed. Information may not be a sufficient weapon for the weak, but it is surely a necessary condition for effective bargaining by small countries or groups of countries attempting to deal with large multinational firms.

The Andean Common Market itself has moved further than the recommendations of the Junta, its technical secretariat, to UNCTAD. If fully implemented, the ANCOM foreign investment rules, drafted in 1970, would fundamentally change the nature of foreign direct investment, particularly in the industrial sector, by making majority ownership by foreigners a temporary, rather than a permanent, result of successful direct investment. After fifteen years (twenty in Bolivia and Ecuador), a majority of the stock of any new firm or of any preexisting firm that wishes to enjoy the benefits of trade liberalization within the Andean Group must be owned by local investors. Stricter provisions have been developed for banks, which must sell 80 percent of their capital to Andean sources within three years, and which, along with the mass media, internal transportation, and domestic marketing, may not receive new direct foreign investments. Restrictions are also placed on the transfer of profits outside of the region, but it is the divestment provisions of the code that are the most innovative and structurally far-reaching.[96] If the Andean arrangements work as the group's membership hopes (despite grumblings of opposition from foreign investors), one of the most disturbing aspects of direct foreign investment—the permanence of foreign control—will have been eliminated. But the economic risks will be substantial, as we note below.

[95] *Report of Secretary-General of UNCTAD to Secretary-General of United Nations* (UN Document TC/179), 30 June 1972, p. 10, paragraph 35.

[96] See William P. Avery and James D. Cochrane, "Innovation in Latin American Regionalism: The Andean Common Market," *International Organization* 27 (Spring 1973): 181-224. See also the UN Secretariat study, *Multinational Corporations in World Development*, p. 77; and Ralph A. Diaz, "The Andean Common Market: Challenge to Foreign Investors," *Columbia Journal of World Business*, July-August 1971, pp. 22-28.

Even more decisive action directed at changing bargaining positions has come from the Organization of Petroleum Exporting Countries (OPEC), a producer's cartel, which at the time of writing had succeeded in increasing the price of crude oil about fivefold over the last three years. Little that is intelligent can be said in a short space about the many issues involved here, or about the future of producers' cartels in such commodities as copper, cocoa, or coffee. In view of the unique importance of petroleum to industrialized economies and of the political affinity of many of its suppliers, it would seem unwise to generalize OPEC's experience too readily. The failures of international cartelization are legendary, and very much the stock-in-trade of liberal economists. Such cartels may, as one Third World proponent has described it, "give us some equity in a world of wolves," but they are unlikely suddenly to effect drastic changes in bargaining relationships on a larger number of important commodities.[97]

As governments attempt increasingly to use international organizations to alter bargaining power in their favor, we should expect to see two types of organizational action. Specific, programmatic action is most likely from organizations, such as OPEC or ANCOM, that are partisan and either regional in scope or product or sector specific. Even with respect to a commodity as critical as oil, concentrated action is difficult in an organization as large and diffuse as OECD. Nevertheless, OECD countries have enough common interest that cooperation on some issues, although not on all, may be expected. At another level, rhetorically oriented organizations, such as UNCTAD, ECOSOC, and perhaps the UN General Assembly, will examine developments, but strongly coherent and concerted positions are unlikely to emerge, given the wide diversity of interests. (Within UNCTAD, for instance, the conflict between oil-importing LDCs and the oil exporters will be sharply drawn.) Both the rhetoric from the incoherent organizations and the action from the coherent ones will generate and exacerbate, rather than ameliorate, conflict. For international politics, and particularly North-South politics, these organizations will constitute a continuous irritant rather than a soothing balm.

Economic effects of measures to alter bargaining power

Several types of action to alter bargaining power would seem to imply rather high efficiency costs. The development of producer (or consumer) cartels raises the issue in sharpest form, as well as creating severe distributional problems, as reflected in the difficulties of poor, oil-importing countries such as India. Yet the issue is also raised in the international labor area. Union goals of "wage parity and harmonization of conditions of work," and of preventing the "exploitation of wage differen-

---

[97] The quotation is from the *New York Times,* 31 December 1973, p. 2. For an opposing view, see C. Fred Bergsten, "The New Era in World Commodity Markets," *Challenge,* Sept./Oct. 1974, pp. 32-39. A symposium on this subject, with contributions by C. Fred Bergsten, Stephen Krasner, and Zuhayr Mikdashi, can be found in *Foreign Policy,* no. 14 (Spring 1974).

tials,"[98] imply restrictions on efficiency as well as distributional effects favoring the interest of labor in developed countries and of skilled unionized labor in less developed countries over those of the unemployed or other workers in poor lands.

In some cases, international regulation could increase efficiency as well as serve other goals. One example is provided by the attempts made by less developed countries to obtain information through international organizations in order to bargain more effectively with enterprises on questions such as technology transfer. Lower information costs should help to improve efficiency as well as have desirable distributional effects. Another case in point might be the exercise of restrictions by less developed host countries on the granting of patents and copyrights to foreigners, since the social cost to them of such monopoly power is large, and the contribution to innovative activity in the industrial countries is probably negligible.

The most interesting case on which to speculate, however, is that of the Andean Common Market. *If* implemented collectively and enforced stringently, the 1970 ANCOM foreign investment rules are likely to have far-reaching economic implications for the development of the countries involved. These provisos must be entered, since even countries with highly organized bureaucracies have been known to modify well-established restrictive policies under the pressure of circumstances, and such flexibility might have a strong tendency to become nationally competitive among the Andean countries.[99] As of late 1973, the Andean countries had by no means consistently implemented the ANCOM code; this was particularly true for Bolivia, Ecuador, and Colombia.[100]

It seems very likely that the restrictions placed on profit transfer and reinvestment in the manufacturing sector, the more stringent regulations and prohibitions in other sectors, and in particular the divestment requirements will have substantial costs in terms of investment foregone, but the size of the costs is difficult to estimate. There have been protestations of alarm from organs of international business, and individual executives have also voiced pessimism about the reactions of foreign investors. There was also, in 1972 and 1973, a falloff in foreign investment in the ANCOM countries.[101] ANCOM is not an inconsiderable market, with GNP roughly equal to that of Brazil. The long-term attractions of an

---

[98] See ILO, *Multinational Enterprises and Social Policy*, p. 65. Also see the statement of Herbert Maier, director of the Economic, Social and Political Department of the International Confederation of Free Trade Unions, in US Congress, Joint Economic Committee, *A Foreign Economic Policy for the 1970's*, p. 824.

[99] John M. Stopford and Louis T. Wells, Jr., *Managing the Multinational Enterprise* (New York: Basic Books, 1972), chapter 11. One senior executive of a US manufacturing concern noted of Decision 24 of the Andean Pact: "I won't be surprised if it passes, but then I won't be surprised if it stretches like an accordian with all the clauses." See "How Will Multinational Firms React to the Andean Pact's Decision 24?," *Inter-American Economic Affairs* 25 (Autumn 1971): 57.

[100] Council of the Americas, *Andean Pact: Definition, Design, and Analysis* (New York: Council of the Americas, no date, but contextually set in late 1973 or early 1974); particularly, "Implementing Legislation and Juridical Trends of ANCOM Members," by Dr. Mary Mercedes Martix. Her conclusion is that the ANCOM code "will be much milder than it looks on the books" (part 3, p. 39).

[101] John R. Pate, Jr., "Activities of Non-U.S. Companies and Governments in Peru," in ibid., part 4, p. 4.

integrated and protected market offer something of a counterweight to restrictions on behavior and ownership, and existing companies may well "adopt a strategy of divestiture in order to maintain a foothold in the area."[102] This will, however, depend to some extent on ANCOM's apparent prospects: the better its chances seem of holding together, the more incentive firms will have to cooperate.

New investment, however, is far more problematical. Stopford and Wells note a tendency for firms with a strong preference for wholly owned subsidiaries to avoid countries with "insistent" policies on local equity participation, but the effect is hardly dramatic.[103] If firms really maximized present net worth, one might not expect divestment requirements at some distance in the future to have large effects; but since firm growth and long-term market strategy are undoubtedly extremely important, one must be less sanguine about the prospects.

The *type* of investment that would be discouraged is perhaps a more important concern than the overall total. Stopford and Wells have found that firms that emphasize marketing techniques, the international rationalization of production, control of raw material sources, and product innovation tend to avoid local equity participation.[104] The loss of new investment in the first three areas may not be viewed as especially costly, and in some cases may be welcome; but the loss of technology transfer by firms in the last category is a matter for greater concern: even countries of the size of India and Japan have discovered that IBM comes in on its own terms or not at all.[105] As Vernon has pointed out, there is a fundamental difference between firms that do not continuously innovate (for which divestment may be well suited as nationals acquire capabilities over the standardized products and processes involved) and those that maintain a stream of innovations.[106] The latter are likely to make a significant contribution to efficiency and growth, where innovations are not the results of trivial product differentiation or of a demand structure based on highly unequal income distribution, and they will be especially costly to lose.

A further source of concern is possible changes in the behavior of existing firms. There will be greater incentives to take short-term profits instead of concentrating on long-term growth objectives, and one may also expect the use of transfer pricing and other accounting techniques to repatriate capital in anticipation of divestment.[107] Effective control over such behavior will present severe challenges to the limited administrative capabilities of the countries involved.

---

[102] "How Will Multinational Firms React to the Andean Pact's Decision 24?," p. 62.
[103] Stopford and Wells, pp. 152-53.
[104] Ibid., chapter 8.
[105] Ibid., p. 154.
[106] Vernon, *Sovereignty At Bay,* pp. 266 ff.
[107] Reuber discusses two cases in which firms were forced into a minority ownership position at the insistence of the host country. "Agreements were finally signed allowing managerial fees, royalties for technology, and guaranteed dividends which, in combination, far exceeded anything that . . . the firms had repatriated from these projects up to that time or hoped to repatriate later; . . . they were no longer prepared to reinvest earnings on the basis of future growth potentials. Lack of control over the direction of growth and the distribution of potential profits changed the fundamental purpose of the companies' involvement." Reuber, pp. 86-87.

Given some of these probable costs, the net economic effects, over the long run, are likely to depend very much on whether this attempt at integration will have significant effects on the mobilization of domestic resources, and in particular entrepreneurship, as argued by Hirschman.[108] But on that critical question not much can be usefully said. There may also be some positive effects generated by the pressures for regional planning which result from the restriction of DFI; resource scarcity can be a severe taskmaster, and it could lead either to a higher regional "rationality" in investment planning or to competitive nationalistic retreats into small markets. The Andean Agreement contains provisions for sectorial planning of industry which go well beyond the complementarity agreements of the Latin American Free Trade Association (LAFTA) and the integrated industry provision of the Central American Common Market (CACM), and these, in conjunction with a flexible application of DFI regulation, could lead to more efficient investment allocation. But the aborted development of the other two Latin American attempts to integrate industrial planning does not provide the basis for much optimism, despite the fact that such failures may have been due more to external than to internal causes.[109]

Prospects for the future

Likely trends

The future of the multinational firm within the international system is sometimes posed in highly dramatic terms, usually based upon crude extrapolations from recent experience: either the uncontrolled growth of multinationals will lead to their domination of a global industrial system, or comprehensive international control mechanisms will be developed. We find both outcomes rather unlikely. While we do expect strong forces for the control of multinationals to develop at various levels, it seems clear that no general international institution to handle questions of direct foreign investment is likely to emerge in the foreseeable future. On the contrary, various more or less informal arrangements are developing, each with a different international organization, responding to a different constituency, as the focus of activity.

OECD is emerging as the central institution for policy coordination among developed countries on questions involving multinational firms. The arrangements for policy coordination are rather informal, and, although arrangements are likely to become more extensive, it seems unlikely that a formalized structure modeled on the GATT will be consciously constructed. The interests of most top government

---

[108] Albert O. Hirschman, *How to Divest in Latin America, and Why*, Princeton Essays in International Finance, no. 76 (Princeton, N.J.: Princeton University Press, 1969), pp. 4-9.

[109] See Miguel S. Wionczek, "The Rise and the Decline of Latin American Economic Integration," *Journal of Common Market Studies* 9 (September 1970): 49-66; Gary W. Wynia, *Politics and Planners: Economic Development Policy in Central America* (Madison, Wis.: University of Wisconsin Press, 1972).

leaders and of almost all working level officials seem to run in the opposite direction. The EEC, meanwhile, is very slowly struggling toward a policy on direct foreign investment, but in view of the importance of trans-Atlantic investment, and of the rapid emergence of Japan as both source and host country, a wider framework for consultation, coordination, and perhaps eventually negotiation will be required even if European progress accelerates. But such developments are, of course, in no sense exclusive: the evolution of a GATT-like bipolar or tripolar structure is quite likely to be the outcome of a gradual process beginning with less formal arrangements.

The developed countries would like to use the World Bank as the key international institution for dealing with less developed economies on direct investment questions. Yet as the difficulties with ICSID and the multilateral insurance scheme indicate, the poorer countries are not likely to accept this approach. They will turn, we expect, increasingly to UNCTAD or other elements of the UN system for a monitoring and communications system to provide them with information, technical assistance, and an aura of collective legitimacy to assist with national, regional, and sectoral attempts to increase their bargaining power relative to multinational firms. UNCTAD and other UN organs dominated by poor countries are likely to be used increasingly as forums to publicize adverse aspects of enterprise relationships with less developed countries, to criticize the behavior of firms, and to discuss the effectiveness of any international regulatory measures or agencies that may be developed. Whereas OECD's natural constituencies are government bureaucracies in developed countries, the UN's are the governments of less developed countries. These are likely to be the two international groupings with the broadest scope and membership, although the most important developments may take place either at the national regulatory level or at the level of regional groups or producers' (and eventually perhaps consumers') organizations. Certain functionally specific organizations such as the ILO and international trade unions are also likely to play a role, if only to remind us of the extreme difficulties in organizing transnationally nongovernmental groups such as labor.

We are likely to see an expansion of national and regional regulation and control measures, as in Canada and ANCOM, as we are seeing OPEC's measures imitated. The consequence could be pressure toward generalizing ANCOM's divestment practices, as large states and regional organizations apply similar principles. In this event, large firms would tend to change from being foreign owners of capital in less developed countries to being suppliers of technological and managerial services.[110] The hallmark of the modern multinational firm, even now, is the transfer of technology and management skills rather than capital, which can often be transferred equally well or better through markets, and much of which is raised locally in any case. Less developed countries can be expected increasingly to insist, either individually or collectively, that the transfer-of-funds-and-ownership aspect

---

[110] For an interesting discussion of this possibility, see Peter H. Gabriel, "MNCs in the Third World: Is Conflict Unavoidable?," *Harvard Business Review* 50 (July-August 1972): 93-102.

of the multinational firm is obsolete, and that the package of tied resources should be unbundled.[111]

It is possible, therefore, that as a result of national measures as well as international, particularly regional, ones, there will be a shift toward the use of contractual arrangements between governments and multinational enterprises and away from traditional direct investment. The experience of Fiat with the Soviet Union may become more general than that of either Anaconda or Kennecott in Chile. Enterprises would take lesser risks of expropriation, while governments would be assured that in attracting valued foreign technology and management skills, they were not also inviting a permanent liability to foreign capitalists.

It should be recognized that divestment of foreign ownership will tend to take place independently of national or international regulatory action in cases where the monopolistic advantage of the foreign firm erodes through the diffusion of technology and the acquisition of managerial capabilities and other complementary factors of production by host country firms. If direct investment is indeed defensive, the same competitive forces that promote it will contain the seeds of its destruction. Where monopoly positions are weak enough for those forces to emerge, we may witness a "renationalization of capital" rather than its progressive internationalization. But where foreign firms possess great market power, regulatory assistance and countervailing power will be required; divestment in the international petroleum industry is guided by OPEC, not the invisible hand.

Careful discrimination will be required if divestment regulations are to be appropriately devised and applied. If they can be confined to situations where future infusions of technology or other scarce factors by the foreign firm are unlikely, and where domestic capabilities are strong, they will promote efficiency and increase the domestic share of remaining monopoly rents. But if divestment regulations are indiscriminately applied, or investors fear that they will be so applied, valuable inflows of scarce factors will be lost. In any case, whether promoted by market forces or nationalistic fervor, divestment of foreign ownership in many sectors is likely. It seems difficult to escape the recent pungent conclusion that "the Mesozoic Era of direct foreign ownership investment has ended. A more limited notion of 'property' will evolve for this purpose. The future belongs to the adaptable and their lawyers."[112]

A summary evaluation

It should be clear that the policy problems associated with direct foreign investment are essentially *design* problems: How can governments construct the proper systems of incentives and constraints to achieve their purposes? Since the

---

[111] See the related discussion by Carlos Diaz-Alejandro in this volume.

[112] Covey T. Oliver, "The Andean Foreign Investment Code: A New Phase in the Quest for Normative Order as to Direct Foreign Investment," *American Journal of International Law* 66 (October 1972): 784.

effects of direct investment on efficiency and equity will depend upon the circumstances of each case, we are generally sympathetic with the inclination of governments to experiment with regulation. Very frequently, however, national regulation will be ineffective due either to problems of limited national decision domains (when policy coordination is called for) or of inadequate national bargaining power (when concerted action to change bargaining power is required). International regulation should then be considered. It should not be seen, however, as a device to subvert national autonomy (as in some of the schemes to promote DFI) but rather as a way of making national regulation more effective and less likely to contribute to international conflict or mutual harm through competitive policy intervention.

This orientation leads us to a problem-specific rather than a grandiose structural approach. Various types of states have varying needs. Each issue raises different problems. Industries have different structures and patterns of behavior that cannot be dealt with according to a single model. Furthermore, the divergencies of interests between relevant actors—enterprises, trade unions, governments—make it unfeasible to construct a single system with a new and powerful international organization at its center.

Marx once remarked: "Men make their own history, but they do not make it just as they please: they do not make it under circumstances chosen by themselves, but under circumstances directly encountered, given, and transmitted from the past." [113] This is certainly as true for attempts to reshape international economic arrangements as for efforts to change domestic societies; it is a reality faced by government planners as well as by revolutionaries. We have focused on proposals and possibilities for dealing on an international basis with direct foreign investment that are relatively consistent with the circumstances "directly encountered, given, and transmitted from the past." That is, we have assumed a continuation of capitalism in major countries, great inequalities of wealth and power internationally, and no sharp shift toward altruism in the motivations of leading actors. One could relax those assumptions and write about direct investment (if any) "after the revolution." But that would be a subject for another article—and perhaps for other authors as well.

---

[113] Karl Marx, *The 18th Brumaire of Louis Napoleon*, in Lewis Feuer, ed., *Basic Writings on Politics and Philosophy: Karl Marx and Friedrich Engels* (New York: Doubleday & Co., 1959), p. 320.

Section III

North-South relations:
the economic component

Carlos F. Díaz-Alejandro

This essay presents a framework for viewing North-South economic relations which, it is hoped, will facilitate positive analysis and will contribute toward normative prescriptions regarding the desirable trend of North-South economic relations in the future. The primary point of departure is the viewpoint of the South as it faces the whole range of its relationships with the North.

Possible social and economic typologies of Southern nations, or less developed countries (LDCs), are explored first, as international economic links differ in importance among groups of states. Key features of the political economy of the Northern nations, or developed countries (DCs), are also examined. The arena of interaction between North and South is then discussed, focusing on fundamental asymmetries in the working of the international economic system. This is followed by more detailed analysis of international commodity and factor markets. The implications of such analysis for international aid and monetary reform are discussed toward the end of this essay.

The economist will quickly recognize the basic approach of this essay: the analysis of different types of international markets, viewed as more or less desirable mechanisms for handling economic interdependence among nations. The desirability of such mechanisms will be judged not only on the basis of their purely economic efficiency but also on whether they help or hinder the achievement of other national goals as developed in the first essay in this volume. The point is to search for mechanisms to handle international interdependence that are compatible with the pursuit of a variety of purely national goals. The search is motivated by the assumption that two apparently contradictory forces will continue to dominate

Carlos Díaz-Alejandro is a professor of economics at Yale University in New Haven, Connecticut. An earlier draft of this essay benefited greatly from criticisms received during a conference held at the Brookings Institution on 10-12 January 1974. Detailed comments from C. Fred Bergsten, Benjamin I. Cohen, Richard N. Cooper, William Diebold, Jr., Gerald K. Helleiner, Albert O. Hirschman, Lawrence B. Krause, Charles P. Kindleberger, Vahid Nowshirvani, and Gustav Ranis are also gratefully acknowledged. Many of the ideas in this essay were either picked up from the work of Stephen Hymer or were developed as a reaction to his stimulating thought. This essay is dedicated to his memory.

international economics in this century: a technology that makes the international division of labor economically attractive, and a desire for political and cultural self-determination of states and/or ethnic groups.

The essay views markets as creatures of social and political systems, not as mechanisms arising spontaneously and inevitably out of economic necessity. Which markets are allowed to operate and how, which are encouraged and which are repressed—these are political decisions, both nationally and internationally. On the other hand, there are in some cases technical difficulties that even a firm political will to create an international market may be unable to overcome at reasonable social costs. Other mechanisms may then be called upon to handle international interdependence.

The South: types and strategies

LDC economic and political heterogeneity, more so than that of DCs, presents a difficult barrier to generalizations about North-South relations. But postwar research on LDCs has yielded some laws of development, which can be helpful in sorting out a manageable number of LDC types, at least in the economic sphere.

The work of Kuznets and Chenery, in particular, has isolated certain impressive regularities in the path toward higher per capita income.[1] Much of the observed variation in the productive structure and export pattern of LDCs can be econometrically explained by per capita income and by population. A third important variable is the endowment of natural resources in a given country. In other words, if one knows the per capita income, the population, and the resource endowment (somehow quantified) for a given LDC, one can make a very good guess about the structure of production and foreign trade in that country, which, in turn, as we will see, plays a central if not necessarily determinative role in the formulation of its foreign economic policy.

One can thus differentiate between large and small LDCs, and between those that are relatively rich in natural resources and those that are not. As each type of country moves up the per capita income ladder, its productive and international trade structures will change in a fairly predictable way, given contemporary technology. A large, resource-poor country with a low per capita income, such as India, will have different priorities for its economic interactions with DCs than a smaller, relatively resource-rich LDC, already well along the per capita income ladder, such as Chile. The Kuznets-Chenery empirical patterns of growth also suggest that once the three major objective facts (per capita income, population, resource endowment) are taken into account, the key variable influencing changes in productive

---

[1] See, for example, Simon Kuznets, *Modern Economic Growth* (New Haven, Conn.: Yale University Press, 1966); and Hollis B. Chenery, "Alternative Strategies for Development," paper presented to the Rehovot Conference on Economic Growth and Developing Countries, September 1973.

and trade structures is the growth rate of per capita income. Domestic policies, this line of thought would argue, will affect those structures mainly via their impact on per capita income growth. Indeed, domestic policies that try to change those structures directly, in contradiction with the three objective facts, will simply decrease the growth rate without changing the productive and trade structures of the country very much (e.g., the case of Uruguay, which defied its "fate" as a small, resource-rich country).

The above has a deterministic flavor leaving little room, apparently, for policy innovation, except insofar as it can accelerate growth. It could be countered, inter alia, that such generalizations are based on observations of more or less market-oriented LDCs, leaving aside the experience of socialist countries. Yet some evidence suggests that the invariance of productive structures, except to the three objective variables, also extends to socialist countries. It could be that the major difference between a socialist and a capitalist LDC of the same per capita income, population, and natural resource endowment will not be in productive and foreign trade structure but in the structure and distribution of public and private consumption and investment. The striking originality most observers find in the Cuban economy, for example, certainly does not lie in its production and trade structure, which probably fits well in the Kuznets-Chenery patterns. But more evidence is certainly needed in the comparison of socialist and nonsocialist trade, production, and expenditure structures. The experiences of the People's Republic of China, in particular, are only beginning to be incorporated systematically into development studies. It remains to be seen whether and when such incorporation will yield another Indian-type observation, or something qualitatively different.

Therefore, some of the deterministic flavor arising from the descriptive laws of development disappears when one considers the political and economic possibility that a given structure of production and trade, broadly defined, will be compatible with more than one pattern of expenditures and income distribution. Such patterns may differ in the balance of consumption of private and public goods, in the level of other social services, in the equity of income distribution, etc. A priori, one could argue that such differences will be reflected in the pattern of production and trade. The hypothesis is that the link is weak, and that it is overshadowed by the three variables discussed earlier.

This hypothesis receives some support from recent simulation exercises, which show that even radical redistribution experiments affect the sectorial composition of gross output only modestly, and that resulting indirect effects on importation and on capital and labor use are correspondingly modest. Moreover, equally concentrated income distributions seem feasible under a variety of basic development strategies.[2]

---

[2] This paragraph paraphrases William R. Cline, "Income Distribution and Economic Development: A Survey and Tests for Selected Latin American Cities," paper prepared for Estudios Conjuntos de Integración Económica de América Latina, International Conference on Consumption, Income and Prices, Hamburg, October 1973, p. 50.

From the above, it follows that in today's world the manner in which the international economic links of a given LDC will influence its domestic economy, its expenditure structure, and its internal political balance cannot be assumed mechanically from a knowledge of its trade pattern. Exports of sugar may strengthen the oligarchical power of landlords and finance luxury consumption or they may sustain the building of socialism.

Regardless of which groups are leading and controlling the process of capital accumulation, are determining the distribution of its fruits, and are carrying the burdens of adjusting to change, a given LDC will have an interest in international economic relations that will vary depending on its income, population, and natural resources, but that in almost all cases is likely to be strong and viewed as a potential source of economic gains. The gains will be mainly those usually associated with the division of labor, whether in commodities or technology. During transitional or revolutionary periods, rejections of the international link may occur, but such withdrawal will typically end with the establishment of a new political order.

The international link, of course, can be manipulated by the ruling groups or classes not only to achieve broad socioeconomic goals but also to strengthen their own narrow economic or political interests. Ruling LDC groups, for example, may be eager to welcome direct foreign investment from a hegemonic country, not for the sake of obtaining capital or technology, but with the expectation that by thus tying the fortunes of those investors to the political survival of the allied LDC groups, their power will be strengthened by the acquisition of lobbyists within the councils of the rich and powerful.

To avoid misunderstanding, it should be stressed that the laws of development obtained using data generated by postwar history and technology will not necessarily apply to nineteenth or twenty-first century circumstances. But at the very least they offer a compact and manageable summary of the heterogeneity of the LDCs.

The North: what matters most for the South

From the viewpoint of the South, the following interrelated questions are the most crucial regarding Northern economic characteristics: Is the Northern demand for Southern goods and services expanding fast? Are the Northern countries competitors vis-à-vis the South, or do they tend to present a common, cartelized front in most economic transactions? Are there groups within the DCs that have specific and quantitatively strong economic interests in LDCs, and are they many or few? If there are such groups, are they politically powerful within the DCs, so that they exert an important influence on DC public policy toward LDCs?

Historically, for a given LDC, the typical answers to these questions were not encouraging. LDCs dealt with the DC economic groups that were few and concentrated, that had the ear of their respective governments, and whose well-being was perceived to depend heavily on profits from LDC operations. Rivalries between DC economic interests were kept down by formal or informal divisions of the Third World, assuring each DC hegemonic power over its own preserve. DC demand for the LDC products, quite dynamic before the First World War, turned sluggish between then and the 1950s, except for petroleum.

The picture for the 1960s reveals some improvement for the LDCs, reflecting slow-working historical forces. The full presence of the USSR in the world scene has introduced not only one new major competitor among the great industrialized powers but one with an ideology making it less likely to play by the old rules of the capitalistic game. Furthermore, with the passing of cold-war confrontation, the presence of the USSR need not reduce competition *within* the capitalist camp, opening up a potentially more fluid world scene for at least some LDCs. While the presence of the USSR has essentially provided a security umbrella for some LDCs, under which economic and political decisions have been taken that in the old days would have led to overt or covert military intervention by capitalistic LDCs, the postwar economic expansion of Japan has brought back onto the world stage an actor missing since around the First World War: a rapidly growing, resource-poor, industrial archipelago with a high propensity to import primary products.

The improved and still expanding economic and political expertise of LDC policymakers has allowed many of these countries to take advantage of the more favorable world circumstances, to achieve not only economic goals but also a more effective degree of national autonomy.[3] Yet the interplay between forces tending toward cartelization and those for rivalry and competition is far from settled in the North. Evidence could be produced for the argument that either one or the other is likely to prevail, say, during the next ten years. On the cartelization side, consider, for example, trends toward Western European unity, US-USSR cooperation, concentration of capitalistic trade and production in multinational corporations, and increasing cross investments in the securities markets. But my own guess is that the presence of a socialist camp that does not threaten Western Europe and Japan militarily tips the scale in favor of a scenario of at least oligopolistic rivalry among DC economic interests, permanently at the verge of warfare.[4]

Such warfare, even assuming it remains purely economic, is not without some dangers for LDCs. It could lead to a breakdown of prosperous, multilateral world

[3] For a strong statement of this view, see C. Fred Bergsten, "The Threat from the Third World," *Foreign Policy*, no. 11 (Summer 1973) and "The Response to the Third World," *Foreign Policy*, no. 17 (Winter 1974-75).

[4] As put by Premier Chou En lai, in his report to the 10th National Congress of the Chinese Communist Party: "They contend as well as collude with each other. Their collusion serves to the purpose of more intensified contention. Contention is absolute and protracted, whereas collusion is relative and temporary" (*New York Times*, 1 September 1973, p. 6).

As an example of what the cartelized world would look like, consider the following remarks of Mr. Harold Geneen, president of ITT: "What these countries [the LDCs] need most are long-term investments. If our government is not going to support us, there is going to be less investment. The answer may be a multinational approach. By this I mean the Germans, the Swiss, the World Bank, and others share in the investment. Then six countries are involved, not one. If something goes wrong, the countries can get tough and do things. You don't go to war, but maybe everybody refuses to give the offending country credits" (*Business Week*, 3 November 1973, p. 44).

trade, thereby reducing world demand for LDC products and rekindling pressures for reviving neo-colonial "special relationships" between subsets of DCs and LDCs. Under these circumstances, LDCs could suffer not only from concentrated DC economic groups using their political power but also from an increase in populist DC pressures, such as those arising from beet farmers and textile producers in those countries.

The choice of arenas of North-South economic interaction

It is tempting to separate North-South interactions into political and economic spheres, the former being direct and the latter indirect, operating via different markets. The distinction, of course, cannot be that clear-cut. In particular, market rules of the game, and the determination of which markets are allowed to operate, are essentially political decisions. Power, whether military or corporate, abhors an uncontrolled and truly competitive market. It would be an extraordinary world in which asymmetries in military and political power were not reflected in asymmetries in economic relations.[5]

This seems quite straightforward, and it has been at the root of center-periphery, or *dependencia*, theories for a long time. Yet by a curious psychological mechanism, similar to the one that leads some to blame the victim for a crime, even informed liberal opinion in DCs often views LDC emphasis on such asymmetry with ill-disguised impatience, or with a curious eagerness to show up minor inconsistencies in LDC arguments.

Take, as an illustration, the goal of world economic efficiency. A pure technocrat would know that there are several possible ways of approaching that target: freer trade in commodities, freer international capital movements, or freer labor migration. It may not be necessary, in fact, to follow all of those policies, as trade and factor movements are substitutes for each other, at least in the type of models on which efficiency policy advice is often based.[6] The obvious questions are: Why not seek world efficiency via labor movements instead of capital movements? Or why seek it via some type of capital movements (direct foreign investment, or DFI) rather than others (portfolio investment)? Why world efficiency is sought via one combination of policies (capital having the option of going to immobile labor) rather than with other possible packages is explained less by references to Malthusian specters than by looking at who makes the rules regarding which markets are to operate and how.

---

[5] However, as noted in the introductory essay, important asymmetries have now developed between the military *and economic* power of nations: both those that are economically strong but militarily weak, such as the smaller oil producers, and those that are militarily strong (at least in regional terms) but economically weak, such as India.

[6] "To achieve efficiency in world production it is unnecessary that both commodities and factors move freely. . . . If it were not for the problem of transporting interest payments . . . one mobile factor will be sufficient to ensure price equalization." Robert A. Mundell, *International Economics* (New York: Macmillan Co., 1968), p. 95. In this barter model, interest is paid in the form of commodities.

It is instructive to compare actual Western European treatment of immigrant labor with the treatment some LDCs have tried to impose on immigrant capital, and which has incurred the disfavor of many economists worried about the inefficiency and "irrationality" of those rules. A related comparison could have been made between United States treatment of Mexican labor and Mexican treatment of US capital. Consider the following aspects:

1. The Calvo doctrine. It is taken for granted that Turks working in Germany will be subject to German laws, and that the Turkish government will act at most as a friend in court if one of its nationals gets in trouble while in Germany. The Calvo doctrine applies fully in such a case, and no one has proposed, as far as I know, special international arbitration tribunals to settle disputes between guest workers and host nations, as has been proposed in the case of guest capital.

2. Fade-out rules. Most Western European countries appear to encourage guest workers to go back home after a few years. Few incoming workers are led to believe they can stay forever. Rotation has been a key word.

3. Discrimination between nationals and foreigners. A few European liberals have proposed the principle of nondiscrimination between nationals and foreigners (a principle expected in the case of capital) in such things as social and job security, access to housing, etc. But in practice, when not in law, the treatment is discriminatory. While during recessions in LDCs foreign investors are more likely than domestic entrepreneurs to have access to credit, guest workers are typically the first to feel the burden of slack demand in Europe.[7]

4. Discrimination between foreigners according to nationality. This is a practice frowned upon when LDCs use it in the case of guest capitalists. Both de facto and de jure, European countries discriminate not only between workers from inside and outside the European Economic Community but also between those from outside countries.

5. Consultation regarding the framing and the changing of regulations. Guest capitalists, and often their source country government, will howl if new rules

---

[7]Some have argued that this statement exaggerates the adjustment burden borne by migrant workers already residing in Western Europe, claiming that changes in the demand for labor are mainly reflected in the gross inflow rate of fresh guest workers. Nevertheless, a real burden remains. The *Economist* (London) reported, in its issue for 26 January 1974, p. 43, in a story entitlted "Holiday at Your Peril," reluctance among Turkish workers in the Federal Republic of Germany of returning home for the new year holidays, for fear of being fired while they were away. The report added:

> ... how do the foreign workers, who make up a tenth of the German labour force, feel? Very frightened indeed. . . .
> The way to protect German workers, and at the same time avoid paying out millions of marks in unemployment benefits, would seem to be to encourage a million or so foreigners to go home. The problem is how.
> One idea that has been kicked around . . . is that the foreign workers should be given a departing financial handshake. . . . Other, cruder, methods are rather more effective. At local level, a wink from an employer to a local authority can result in the non-renewal of work and residence permits. Or accommodations that used to be considered acceptable can suddenly become "uninhabitable."

are sprung on them by host governments without previous discussions. The European Community Commission recently held a conference on migrant workers attended by close to 300 experts, administrators, and union leaders. "Perhaps symptomatically, there were almost no representatives there from the migrant workers' organizations themselves."[8]

Even the limited European effort at removing imperfections in the world labor market seems to be running into serious difficulties. Sociological reasons are being brought forth to explain why too high a presence of guest workers leads to difficulties. Thresholds of tolerance, beyond which the presence of foreigners becomes unacceptable to the local population, are increasingly being referred to. Ugly incidents such as the rash of murders of Algerians in Marseilles (or perhaps the murders of US executives in Argentina) are part of the price of going beyond the thresholds.

The point of the previous discussion is obviously *not* to suggest that free international migration is the optimal path to worldwide factor price equalization. The purpose has been to highlight the fact that the selection of which markets are allowed to operate more or less freely, and/or which imperfections receive most attention by both journalists and mainstream social scientists in the rich countries, is neither random nor based on purely technocratic criteria. In a similar vein, the asymmetrical handling by DCs of different types of capital outflow could be explored; while most subsidize their DFI via insurance schemes and tax policies, they hamper free foreign access to their capital markets. In a very imperfect world, the choice of imperfections to decry and tackle is a matter of subjective judgment, often justified on grounds of common sense or "realism." But let us try to be clear as to what usually determines realism and whose common sense we are talking about.[9]

Furthermore, the point of the previous discussion is *not* to argue that the asymmetries in the international economic order will inevitably lead to losses for LDCs. The argument implies that whether or not they gain, or how much they gain, and how much of the burdens of adjustment they are likely to bear, has been of secondary importance to those responsible for setting or changing the rules of the game.

---

[8]*Economist* (London), 9 February 1974, p. 48. The same article reports that Germany plans an outright ban on further hiring of guest workers in cities with an immigrant population of more than a quarter of the total. A kind of crude rule-of-thumb restriction much lamented when imposed by LDCs on DFI.

[9] In an article informing readers on the editorial page of the *Wall Street Journal*, 13 December 1972, p. 22, that "the relations among nations are governed by a few fragile covenants which we call international law, by some vague consensus of world opinion which we call international morality and, above all by common sense," the Henry Luce Professor of Urban Values at New York University, Dr. Irving Kristol, goes on to say: "Gunboats are as necessary for international order as police cars are for domestic order. Smaller nations are not really worried about American atom bombs any more than the Mafia is. And smaller nations are not going to behave reasonably—with a decent respect for the interests of others, including the great powers—unless it is costly to them to behave unreasonably."

The path toward one world: a digression

Before taking a closer look at markets for commodities and at factors of production, some discussion is necessary on the different perceptions by North and South of concepts of *nationalism* and *internationalism* (or *cosmopolitanism*). Those perceptions influence attitudes toward which mechanisms of interdependence should be used between states and toward which markets should be emphasized as areas of interaction between North and South. Those attitudes are also manipulated by vested interests to obtain their own private ends.

Put briefly, in the North nationalism evokes Hitler, Mussolini, pre-1959 Franco, Enoch Powell, and George Wallace. At best, it evokes Gaullist France, although judging from the often outrageous US and UK press treatment of General de Gaulle and his successors, the difference between French nationalism and the others may be perceived as slight. In the South, cosmopolitanism evokes memories of distant foreign kings or queens or company presidents with different skin colors, different tongues (or at least different accents), and different cultures. In the North, nationalism was misused not long ago to suppress human dignity, rights of self-determination, and cultural heterogeneity. The flag of cosmopolitanism has been used in the South for the same purposes. If patriotism is the last refuge of the scoundrel, cosmopolitanism is the favorite fig leaf of the imperialist.

Before going further, it should be borne in mind that, as in the case of economic conditions, Southern nationalisms are quite heterogeneous. Most LDCs (and DCs) are multiethnic or multiculture states.[10] In some areas, such as Latin America, loyalty to the state overlaps fairly closely with loyalty to the national culture or ethnic group, broadly defined or perceived. In others, such as many new African states, strong tensions are likely to remain between different ethnic "nations" or cultural groups brought together under the same state. Without denying the importance of those tensions, and related language problems, such as those in India, in this essay I am concerned primarily with the type of LDC nationalism that rallies loyalty to the state as a mechanism to defend the culture(s) and self-respect of LDC peoples against witting or unwitting encroachments originating in DCs.

Its primarily *defensive* nature is the key characteristic of this type of LDC nationalism. It is not a matter of promoting loyalty to one's state to suppress other countries, or to brag about being "number one." It is a matter of promoting cultural survival and self-respect. While aggressive nationalism, historically found mainly in DCs, finds a need to create myths about the intrinsic inferiority of other states and nations that it seeks to dominate, defensive nationalism may at worst promote a general mistrust of foreigners, a feeling likely to remain vague and pacific so long as the foreigners do not come into one's own turf and try to dominate.

---

[10] See the stimulating article by Walker Connor, "Nation-Building or Nation-Destroying?," *World Politics* 24 (April 1972): 319-55. He charges that theoreticians of LDC nationalism and of nation building have slighted problems associated with ethnic diversity. One could speculate that in the same fashion that economists have sought to define optimal currency areas, political scientists could attempt to define optimal nation states, bearing in mind ethnic diversity, which plays the role of factor immobility in limiting larger optimal areas.

Hegemonic powers will tend to cloak their nationalism with claims of promoting internationalism. In Orwellian fashion they argue that promoting their independence, say of imported oil, will really lead to world interdependence, or they say that proletarian internationalism calls for putting down proletarians with foreign tanks. They will often justify their own nationalistic actions as being taken only after the rest of the world has selfishly and foolishly rejected benevolent hegemonic leaderships; this is the Noble Siegfried syndrome. The rhetorical excesses of LDC defensive nationalism typically do not include these mental contortions.

Clearly, neither nationalism nor internationalism can be judged as good or bad independently of historical circumstances. Few defenders of LDC nationalism will justify it as an end in itself. Humanity, one hopes, moves toward becoming one nation, but premature cosmopolitanism imposed by hegemonic powers can be as negative for the march toward that goal as anachronistic tribalism. My hypothesis is that the optimal path for the South, en route to true internationalism, should take it through national self-assertion and defensive nationalism. Even under extremely favorable circumstances, such as the case of Puerto Rico, jumping stages (particularly by passive choice) yields ambiguous social and psychological results. Ideologists for multinational empires of all times have sung the benefits to peace and to the economy of suppressing national particularisms, excepting of course those of the hegemonic power. The long-run results of such Augustean ages and the shortcuts to one world have been so far most unimpressive.

Even within the South, of course, the mystique surrounding the state can be misused. A dominant class, ethnic group, or cultural group within an LDC can turn that potentially powerful engine of growth and integration toward buttressing its own power or suppressing weaker ethnic or cultural groups. But it would be a mistake to think that nationalism is *just* the creation of a dominant class or an elite to maintain its power; it goes deeper than that, particularly in states fairly homogenous culturally or ethnically. Another possible retrogressive use of nationalism in the Third World involves opposition to regional integration schemes that are potentially favorable for both economic and political reasons in areas without deep ethnic or cultural cleavages. Under those circumstances, some LDC nationalisms can also become anachronistic and a barrier in the path toward a more efficient defensive nationalism, structured around a larger political unit. But it is not inconceivable that large LDCs may try imposing regional hegemonies mostly for their own profit, provoking defensive (and healthy) nationalistic reactions from other LDCs against such "premature" regionalism. Finally, LDC nationalisms could be manipulated by the North to decrease Third World solidarity.

The subject matter is ambiguous and cannot be settled a priori and, in general, independently of specific circumstances. Put simply, the above discussion suggests that nationalisms should be judged by their promised or realized fruits. In the South, they have enormous potential for raising living standards as well as human dignity and self-respect. That such an instrument can be misused is no argument for throwing it away—particularly while those historically in the position of leading the way toward the fading away of nationalisms, the DCs, show no sign of doing so.

The ambiguities surrounding the issue of nationalism may explain the wildly different responses evoked, even among scholars, by different historical attempts at nation building. Contrast, for example, attitudes toward the struggles led by Attaturk and those led by Isabel and Ferdinand. The same observers who are appalled by language riots in India, or tribal clashes in Africa, will often sympathize with the actions of separatist Basques, Ukranians, and Puerto Ricans. And more than one nationalistic intellectual has been taught the value of transnational alliances by a tyrant in his homeland.

One last word on this messy subject. History, especially colonial history, has left us with a crazy quilt of states and arbitrary boundaries (just look at a political map of the Caribbean). But one must be suspicious of possible uses of ad hoc arguments pointing to the irrationality of having a few thousand citizens of country X or Y control high percentages of this or that world resource. The suspicion is strengthened by the realization that the DCs, where one often hears that argument, in the past often deliberately helped to create such small or sparsely populated countries, with the excuse of promoting national self-expression. Examples include US involvement in the creation of the Republic of Panama and British policy in the Persian Gulf. Note that even today the British claim to defend the rights of self-expression of the handful of people on Gibraltar, placed there by the British in the first place, against Spanish claims. Furthermore, having a small percentage of the world's population control a huge share of the *production* of a given resource does not appear, prima facie, more shocking than similar calculations for *consumption* of the same resources. Eventually the world community may handle both matters more equitably and rationally; right now the discovery by some in the DCs of the irrationality of existing LDC states and boundaries must be regarded with skepticism and concern.

If the primacy and persistence of desires for national self-determination are granted, we should seek arenas of North-South economic interaction compatible both with LDC goals of greater autonomy and with economic advantage for all participants. Economists have traditionally viewed competitive markets as being theoretically capable of reconciling individual freedom with an efficient and inter-dependent social division of labor. I now turn to examine whether this vision is relevant for contemporary North-South economic relations. In particular, in addition to the traditional questions about their efficiency and competitiveness, we will want to ask the following questions of actual or potential international markets:

1. Can transactions be carried out at arm's length? How much will those international economic links intrude into the national social and political life of participants? In short, can arenas for standoffish arrangements be created?
2. Can international markets provide the goods and services desired by LDCs in separate compartments, or in packages that can be decomposed if the buyer wants one part of them but not other parts? Can the LDCs abstain from participating in some international markets without impairing their chances of becoming effective buyers or sellers in other international markets?

3. Can international markets provide contracts that have clear termination dates or that have built-in renegotiating provisions?

In general, of course, the unintrusiveness, decomposibility, and reversibility of commercial arrangements will be interrelated. On the whole, the more competitive an international market, the more likely it is that it will have these desirable characteristics.

Commodity (silent?) trade

Surveying the world trade scene in 1974, it appears that both LDCs and DCs have much to gain from the maintenance and expansion of commodity trade. It also seems that such trade could be carried out in the future in a manner that allows each community a plentiful amount of control over its own economy and society. It can have some of the quality of unintrusiveness anthropologists find in the "silent trade" undertaken between primitive tribes.

That LDCs, particularly the smaller LDCs, *may* gain a good deal by active participation in international commodity trade would seem to be another obvious proposition, to be taken for granted. Yet it still meets with considerable resistance, perhaps because the proposition in the past was framed in terms of the inevitability of gains from trade to everybody. There was also, and there still is, a good deal of misplaced concreteness attributed to the intrinsically desirable or undesirable qualities of commodities, e.g., sugar and coffee are bad, butter and steel are good. While such views have some use in understanding the economic history of countries with weak central governments, they are far less useful for many contemporary LDCs, which have a respectable array of policy tools usable to correct distortions and deformations that could arise from staple exports. Note that a recent slogan of the Cuban revolutionary government is: "Sugar for Growth." The historical link between exports of primary products and open economies and landlord-dominated regressive governments can still be seen in several LDCs, and in some countries it may have been strengthened by the 1972-73 commodity boom, but there are now enough counterexamples to show that such link is no iron law.

LDC export pessimists, and those in DCs who delight in convincing poor countries of their alleged economic impotence, not long ago used to argue that imports from LDCs were of marginal importance to the rich, and their purchase was presented almost as an act of DC altruism. This altruism, of course, could be terminated if LDCs were naughty; witness the elimination of imports of Cuban sugar into the United States during the early 1960s and the boycott of Iranian oil in the 1950s. Hypotheses regarding the importance of cheap raw materials and primary products from the South for the prosperity of the North were brushed aside during the late 1950s and 1960s by pointing to the small percentages of those imports in gross national products. Arguments about supply reliability were also deemed mistaken or naive: it was all a matter of price, it was noted. Only frantic radicals or Third World types could be expected to take seriously the notion that

Northern foreign policies had anything at all to do with assuring those countries with cheap and reliable supplies of primary products from the South. Events in commodity markets during 1972 and 1973, particularly the oil situation, have shaken those DC perceptions.[11] Indeed, among some DC observers, attitudes on these matters have gone from indifference or contempt to a somewhat paranoid hysteria.

The discussion of commodity trade so far has a decidedly old-fashioned flavor; nothing has been said of trade in manufactured goods, billed often as the new breakthrough in LDC exports. For some LDCs, mainly those with a poor natural resource endowment, those exports no doubt offer hope to break out of severe foreign exchange limitations. But it seems far from inevitable or desirable that successful development for all LDCs must be characterized by a sharp increase in the share of manufactures in their export bill. Many can expect to follow a path similar to that of Australia, Denmark, or New Zealand, a path in which growing industrialization of productive structure need not be accompanied by a corresponding change in the export bill structure.[12]

From several viewpoints, those LDCs may be regarded as the lucky ones. The luck, in the first place, is in their endowment of natural resources, producing export values that typically include large pure rents, i.e., those exports have low domestic resource costs. One could, of course, have too much of a good thing, if in the very long run excessive rents lead to a flabby society that is unable to adapt to new circumstances when the rent-yielding resources become exhausted. Secondly, and regardless of what happened in earlier historical periods, international markets in 1973 for primary products are often more standoffish than those for the new manufactured exports. Placing soybeans, cotton, or copper in international markets will involve less dependent relationships with foreigners than trying to sell internationally Ford engines, parts of Olivetti typewriters, or bits and pieces of electronic equipment. The difference is negligible when the comparison is made with steel, cement, or flat glass, but, except for textiles, not much of the celebrated increase in LDC manufactured exports seems to be in the category of standardized finished industrial goods, sold in open competitive markets. The comparative disadvantage of LDCs in international marketing is less of a problem with primary products than with many manufactured exports.

Finally, there has been a remarkable trend, which may be deemed basically irreversible, toward LDC control over the exploitation and marketing of those natural resources. Such control, incidentally, may result in more competitive world markets in commodities using those resources as inputs, as LDC nationalizations have diminished the oligopolistic power of several vertically integrated companies.

---

[11] C. Fred Bergsten, "The Threat is Real," *Foreign Policy*, no. 14 (Spring 1974): 84-90; and Bergsten, "The New Era in World Commodity Markets," *Challenge*, September-October 1974: 32-39.

[12] Carlos Díaz-Alejandro, "Some Characteristics of Recent Export Expansion in Latin America," and C. Fred Bergsten, "The Future of World Trade and a Resume of the Conference," both in Herbert Giersch, ed., *The International Division of Labour Problems and Perspectives* (Tubingen: J. C. B. Mohr, 1974), pp. 215-36, and pp. 543-54, respectively.

For many LDCs, participation of private and public national entrepreneurs is greater in primary product exports than in those of manufactures.

The dependence associated with exports of many types of manufactured goods would naturally increase if exports were to occur only thanks to tariff preferences granted by DCs to favorite LDCs. Under those circumstances, it is not difficult to foresee that the major LDC exports benefiting from such schemes will be those produced by firms owned by citizens of those Northern countries granting special trade preferences. A case can still be made for generalized and unconditional DC preferences granted to all LDCs, but the likely benefits to LDCs from politically feasible schemes of that sort appear out of proportion to the attention they have received during the last ten years.

From all that has been said so far, it should be clear that commodity trade under steady multilateral rules of the game, and in open and competitive markets, is a possible arena of economic interaction between LDCs and DCs offering arrangements that are economically efficient while maintaining desirable characteristics of unintrusiveness, reversibility, and decomposibility. Historically, such an arena has not existed. Northern countries first developed their LDC sources of primary products under colonial or neo-colonial circumstances, and throughout have manipulated rules of the game in international commodity markets mostly to suit their own ends, not hesitating to change them as their own convenience dictated. Protection to Northern farmers has taken precedence during peacetime over commitments to trade liberalization.

The most recent example of asymmetrical DC attitudes toward international commodity markets is the outcry regarding freedom of access to raw materials and alleged cartelization by LDCs. During 1953-70, when commodity prices were low or tending to fall, DCs argued that international commodity markets worked best when left alone, including those that even then gave evidence of being either fragmented or far from competitive (diamonds and oil under the *ancien régime* of the seven sisters). On the other hand, since at least the Second World War, LDCs have argued the case for commodity agreements that would avoid price instability. At first sight, it would appear that this is the right time to resurrect plans for generalized stabilization of commodity markets, giving DCs security about "access on equal terms to the trade and to the raw materials of the world," as put by the Atlantic Charter, in exchange for assuring LDCs of reliable markets at predictable prices.[13]

[13] The Keynes plan for commodities, recently unearthed from British archives by Dr. Lal Jayawardena and published in the *Journal of International Economics* 4, no. 3 (August 1974): 299-315, deserves at least a fresh look in discussions about a new international monetary and economic order. The second draft, dated December 1942, opens by referring to the fourth point of the Atlantic Charter, quoted above. Note that the Keynes plan coupled freedom of access for DCs to freedom of sales at predictable prices for LDCs, a point ignored by most DC observers and officials. In his original draft, Keynes starts by calling for the internationalization of Vice-President Wallace's "ever-normal granary." I recently heard a brilliant mainstream US political economist justify US bans on its wheat exports. He went on to argue that wheat sales should be permitted only to foreign countries willing to sign long-term purchase agreements. He was clearly surprised by, and failed to answer, a question as to whether he also advocated

The case for a worldwide "ever-normal granary" has been strengthened by the 1973 inflationary pressures, which have baffled the most learned macroeconomists of the industrialized world. In retrospect, and on the basis of a neo-structuralist view of inflation, it can be argued that one of the benefits obtained by the industrialized countries from low or falling LDC export prices during 1953-70, coupled to the reserves generated by US agriculture, was a relatively stable price level. More than a few DC observers are putting their hope for an end of the present inflationary burst on a collapse of primary product prices from their 1972-73 levels. It should not be beyond the wits of a rational world community to devise generalized commodity agreements that, without interfering with long-run price trends, smooth out violent price fluctuations, which can trigger inflationary spirals, and provide stocks against natural calamities. Failures of past sporadic commodity agreements could be blamed on lack of political will among participants as much as on intrinsic failings of such arrangements.

It should be noted that even at the purely technical level, it is not clear that a competitive market will generate efficient results for the case of exhaustible natural resources. In an uncertain world, lacking a full set of futures and insurance markets, the market mechanism can become an unreliable means of pricing and allocating those resources, generating myopic decisions and considerable price instability. [14]

Therefore, which mechanism is more desirable in the commodity area: imperfect markets or imperfect commodity agreements? Given the medium-term outlook of demand for LDC commodities, which is reasonably good even when the excesses of the 1972-73 commodity boom are discounted, I end up leaning toward the former. Unequal LDC bargaining power and interests would make *generalized* commodity agreements difficult to negotiate, and would present Northern countries with rich opportunities to "divide and rule." Outside a few possible special cases, such as oil, LDC bargaining power could best be employed in broadening and improving existing international markets; DC commitments regarding freedom of access to their markets and a gradual end of their protectionism must be the necessary price for their gaining freedom of access to LDC supplies. In some commodity markets, greater use can be made of long-term contracts as substitutes for missing futures markets. More thought could also be given to improving the latter. Fear of losing access to raw materials has led some DC observers to dream of reviving special relationships with selected LDCs; on balance, LDCs have much to gain from multilateral markets free of neo-colonial overtones.

---

long-term contracts for US purchases of primary products. It is not without certain irony that the same officials who not long ago turned down Venezuelan requests for greater access to the US oil market now complain of unreliability of foreign oil supplies. It is also ironic that as late as 13 September 1973, the *New York Times*, p. 71, reported attempts by US diplomats to organize a boycott of Libyan oil.

[14] See William D. Nordhaus, "The Allocation of Energy Resources," *Brookings Papers on Economic Activity, 3:1973*: 529-71. Using energy as an example of exhaustible resources, and noting that besides the basic economic problems (lack of future markets, uncertainty about future technology, etc.), political interference is also present, Nordhaus remarks: "It takes an act of faith to believe that the market can somehow see the proper allocation through this tangle of complexity, uncertainty, and politics" (p. 538).

Physical control over a good share of the earth's land surface and subsoil remains the big LDC asset. Notable improvements in LDC political and economic management, plus favorable world market conditions, put many of these countries in circumstances unmatched in their contemporary history, particularly for taking advantage of export growth for local development.[15]

Service transactions

International service markets and transactions, and the characteristics of participants in them, are more heterogeneous than those for commodities. Some are quite standardized, and involve many buyers and sellers dealing at arm's length. Shipping services not controlled by "conferences" approach such description. Other service markets may be quite competitive, but their geographical domain may be such as to produce interactions between DC and LDC citizens that are not always satisfactory, such as tourism.[16]

A third type of service market, that of technology, or more generally nonacademic knowledge, has recently received a considerable amount of attention.[17] The characteristics of the generation of technology or commercial knowledge, and of the product itself, are typically such as to make these markets, particularly those involving DCs and LDCs, far from purely competitive ones.

The market power of DC sellers of technology is buttressed institutionally by the Paris Convention on Patents, and by packaging practices of multinational

[15] The improvement of LDC foreign trade policies by itself cannot be expected to provide automatically in all countries substantial help in achieving development targets, except for faster growth, not related directly to the foreign trade sector. For example, export promotion policies may hurt equity in income distribution (by much or little) in some countries while helping equity in others (by much or little). Neither qualitative nor quantitative generalizations appear warranted regarding the link between trade policies and income distribution. The problem, relevant also for DCs, is that different positive theories of trade have different implications for income distribution and, therefore, for political attitudes toward freer trade. If one believes, for example, that the key source of comparative advantage for a given country is a large endowment of capital to labor, one will expect *all* capitalists to be protrade biased as compared with *all* laborers. But if the key source of comparative advantage is best explained by research and development in new products, industries leading in that field will be the main champions of freer trade.

[16] In passing, it may be noted that tourism is made more palatable to host countries by the application of the Calvo doctrine to foreign guests. The occasional injustices suffered by DC tourists at the hands of unscrupulous LDC officials abusing the Calvo doctrine have not led to many calls for international arbitration tribunals, as far as I know, but have led to some passable popular songs, such as "Tijuana Jail." Nevertheless, it should be noted that alleged fears for the lives of DC nationals happening to be visiting a given LDC going through acute political turmoil have been used as an excuse to land DC "guest troops" (without visas or tourist cards) in LDCs.

[17] See, for example, Constantine V. Vaitsos, *Intercountry Income Distribution and Transnational Enterprises* (Oxford University Press, forthcoming); Jorge M. Katz, *Patents, the Paris Convention and Less Developed Countries,* Yale Economic Growth Center Discussion Paper No. 190 (New Haven, Conn.: Yale University, November 1973); and Edith Penrose, "International Patenting and the Less Developed Countries," *The Economic Journal* 83 (September 1973): 768-86.

corporations (MNCs), on which more will be said below. The recent upsurge of interest in the economics and politics of technology markets has not yet offset accumulated dismal ignorance regarding their mechanisms. Nevertheless, LDC interest in this area appears fully justified. It is not obvious, for example, that LDCs benefit from the Paris Convention, and a plausible case can be made for the withdrawal of those LDCs that are now signatories. The difficult balance between incentives to generate new knowledge and the efficient dissemination of existing knowledge appears at present overly tilted in favor of the former.

However, national rather than international action should take clear priority in this area. The knowledge needed to buy knowledge must be built up by the LDCs as a first step, perhaps in regional associations. Regional development banks, and the International Bank for Reconstruction and Development (IBRD), could help much more than in the past (the record here is quite bad). In contrast with the commodity area, and similar to the field of finance, there is a danger here that expansion of international markets and channels of intermediation may weaken indispensable local markets and institutions.

The cruel asymmetry in knowledge about knowledge between LDC buyers and DC sellers must be corrected by first building up LDC-controlled expertise *and* institutions in this area. By now the pool of LDC experts in various fields is most impressive, but due to a lack of indigenous institutions, their work within LDCs is often channeled via foreign or international organizations. It is not unusual, for example, to have a DC consultant firm obtain a contract in an LDC to be carried out to a large extent by experts hired by that firm within the same (or in another) LDC.

Once emphasis is given to developing local expertise and institutions, LDCs would be in a better position to press for reform of international markets in technology, in some cases using their increased bargaining power in commodity markets for that purpose, as some oil-exporting LDCs have attempted recently.

Finally, it could be noted that public enterprises of socialist countries, at least in some fields, could play an important role in increasing the flexibility of international technological markets, as presumably they are not as bound by the fears of competition that are used to justify the technological secrecy of developed capitalistic firms. But so far their participation has been timid.

International markets for labor and capital

Unplanned international markets for unskilled labor are typically characterized by a sharp division between those who in the host country reap the fruits from a labor inflow and those who bear the adjustment costs to such an inflow. The gains are often quickly reaped, while the adjustment costs are drawn out and may carry to future generations. This explains mass resistance in most DCs to large labor inflows from LDCs. The ugly racism in which such resistance often expresses itself should not obscure the fact that unplanned international labor flows, such as those in Europe, even when benefiting LDC nationals and DC capitalists, are also an example of premature cosmopolitanism, difficult to generalize massively in today's world. Note that within the South such flows also generate friction; witness the status of Colombian workers in Venezuela and that of Paraguayans in Argentina.

While international markets for unskilled labor are limited and imperfect, the market for skilled labor of human capital has undergone considerable international-ization since World War II. Two-way flows have been established between North and South, often via the intermediation of international organizations. Leaving aside those flows from DCs to LDCs that are explicitly subsidized, the question has been raised as to whether the counterflow from LDCs to DCs, which occurs overwhelmingly as an ostensibly commercial transaction, does not contain a per-verse subsidization and resource transfer from the South to the North. A high degree of competitiveness in that market is not in doubt; the issue centers on whether the returns on public investment in education are appropriable, on the possible externalities of human capital in LDCs, and on the manipulation of markets by DCs using asymmetrical treatment for different types of labor inflows.

Optimal national and international policies in this area, on both economic and political grounds, are likely to exclude both laissez-faire and absolute bans on migration. The numbers involved in these flows are small relative to total popula-tions, and they should not generate the frictions associated with mass migrations of unskilled labor to already settled areas. Tax schemes, involving both host and home countries, and known *ex ante* to all concerned, could reconcile the legitimate claims of home countries for returns on their public investment in education and individ-ual desire for mobility. Whether such taxes are levied at the time of exit or are spread out through time is a matter that could be settled on practical grounds, with the latter possibility gaining appeal from imperfections of capital markets in an uncertain world. If international taxation treaties have been worked out for physical capital, similar ones should not be too difficult to establish for human capital.[18]

The reader should not be surprised that uncontrolled direct foreign invest-ment carried out by large MNCs owned by DC nationals, particularly those from hegemonic powers, is regarded in this essay as the major example of premature and misguided cosmopolitanism, having most of the undesirable characteristics dis-cussed for arenas of LDC-DC economic transaction. This is not the place to summarize the vast literature on MNCs; a few remarks on the subject should be sufficient.

The relationships between large MNCs and host LDC governments and ruling groups, unless closely controlled and watched, are unlikely to be standoffish in the sense of keeping economic decisions at a reasonable and decent distance from political decisions. It can be plausibly argued that the same can be said regarding

---

[18] Jagdish Bhagwati and William Dallalfar have advanced a concrete proposal along these lines in their paper, "The Brain Drain and Income Taxation: A Proposal," Working Paper No. 92, Massachusetts Institute of Technology Department of Economics, September 1972.

the relationships between MNCs and DC governments and ruling groups. But given the greater frailty of LDC governments and societies, an even greater concern is warranted. Compare, for example, the opportunities for mischief by International Telephone and Telegraph (ITT) when dealing with the US versus the Chilean or Ecuadorean governments.

It is well known that MNCs provide a package of services, which is difficult to untangle and cost separately. The package often can be said to include particular links to the international community, such as participation in the Paris Convention on Patents, when a host country is too weak to reject this fashion of signaling its commitment to a favorable investment climate. Local production of some commodities by MNCs can also limit a host country's export potential and even its foreign policy. During 1973 and early 1974, for example, General Motors Argentina, Ford Argentina, and Goodyear Argentina had to wait for US permission regarding industrial exports to Cuba, even though the sales were to be financed by supplier credits from the Argentine government.[19]

Unless a host country makes a special and often jerky effort, involvements with MNCs are difficult to reverse. Note the difficulties that even well-behaved Canada has had to go through to *buy back* (at rather handsome prices) an interest in Texasgulf, Inc. Clearly, a marriage so difficult and painful to break up should be entered into only with the greatest of circumspection. The Romanian publication in its official gazette of its detailed "marriage" contract with Control Data, said to include 29 appendices, is an example that LDCs should consider following.[20] Whenever possible, of course, such LDC actions should be adopted under common rules, to expand their bargaining leverage, in the spirit of the Andean Group.

The tendency of MNCs to interact negatively with LDC market imperfections and to replace both national and international markets for internal corporate planning explains why some market-oriented economists express serious reservations about the role of MNCs in LDCs. Consider the following two statements, the first by Hla Myint and the second by Ronald McKinnon:

> But it may be wondered whether, instead of their current policies of protection and selective admittance of foreign manufacturing industry, they [the LDCs] might not find a more promising 'second-best' policy in combining restrictions on all foreign enterprises with free trade.[21]

---

[19] See *Business Latin America*, 12 December 1973, pp. 393-94. Canadian subsidiaries of US-owned firms have also been plagued by this issue. Recently, a Canadian political leader asked: "On what basis is it necessary for the Canadian Government to request the intercession of a foreign government in an export deal between a Canadian company and some other company?" (*New York Times* 6 March 1974, p. 47). Some hope exists that the US will finally decide to end its extraterritorial claims on foreign subsidiaries of US-owned firms during 1974.

[20] See report "A Warm Hand for US Business," in *Business Week*, 8 December 1974, pp. 24, 27. The *Wall Street Journal* reported on 30 August 1973, p. 8, that Senator Lloyd Bentsen of Texas had personally appeared in court to express his reservations about the Canadian attempts to purchase Texasgulf, Inc.

[21] Hla Myint, "International Trade and the Developing Countries," in P. A. Samuelson, ed., *International Economic Relations* (London: Macmillan, 1969), p. 35.

Correspondingly, the bootstrap theory here implies that reliance on foreign direct investment—with its package of finance, modern technology, and managerial skills—should be curtailed by LDCs themselves in order to promote balanced indigenous development.[22]

The fact that DFI carried out by large MNCs, particularly those with headquarters in hegemonic powers, often tends to replace markets and has a number of undesirable political and social effects does not rule out the possibility that such MNCs frequently will turn out to be economically more efficient than the uncontrolled markets they replace. Centralized planning, either public or corporate, may improve on uncontrolled market performance, both theoretically and in practice. Indeed, some popular criticisms of MNCs in the North relate not to their monopolizing tendencies but to the burdens of adjusting to MNC actions that essentially reproduce what competitive markets would yield but do so more brusquely and perhaps faster, as in the case of transferring labor-intensive production from high-wage to low-wage areas.

It should also be noted that even if the DFI package could be totally untangled, many LDCs will still prefer at least some amount of packaging, preferably in the form of joint ventures, as a way of insuring continuous access to the ongoing technological research of foreign companies. Such deals will be healthier, however, when chosen over other options, especially the one of total unpackaging, as contrasted with their reluctant acceptance as the only possible way to obtain technology and capital.

There is, of course, no economic reason why international capital movements should occur solely or primarily via MNCs. Before the Great Depression of the 1930s, large sums were transferred from DCs to LDCs using debt instruments, via capital markets, that were no models of perfect competition but that allowed greater flexibility, in many respects, than direct foreign investment. Technology, on the other hand, was transferred massively and largely independently of those capital flows. Influenced by the unfortunate experience of the 1930s, Anglo-Saxon planners sought to replace those markets in the post–World War II new order partly by institutions such as IBRD, for long-term capital, and the International Monetary Fund (IMF), for short-term capital. The MNCs also stepped into the void, becoming not only investors of their own funds, but also acting as financial intermediaries, borrowing in DCs and in LDCs to invest within LDCs.

Many DCs emerged from the 1930s and the Second World War with formal and informal regulations limiting foreign access to their national capital markets. Not surprisingly, and until very recently, international capital markets worthy of that name remained thin and lethargic, shackled by restrictions and dominated by the competition from MNCs, the IBRD, and the IMF.

---

[22] Ronald I. McKinnon, *Money and Capital* (Washington, D.C.: The Brookings Institution, 1973), p. 172. Both Myint and McKinnon refer favorably to the Japanese experience during the Meiji period.

The remarkable upsurge during 1972-73 of LDC medium-term borrowing in the unregulated Eurodollar market, so far mostly in the form of bank loans, could signal a revival of the use of international markets to transfer capital from DCs to LDCs, as well as their use of intermediaries for capital flows *within* the LDC group. Without underestimating the danger that international capital markets could be subject to increasing cartelization, nor that their expansion could jeopardize the development of such markets within LDCs, it nevertheless appears that transactions in the Eurodollar market between DC private institutions and LDC borrowers show characteristics of unintrusiveness, decomposibility, and reversibility to a much greater extent than those involving MNCs. The list of borrowers includes countries such as Algeria, Cuba, Hungary, Peru, and Yugoslavia, which have not been favorites of MNCs. The Peruvian example may be particularly significant, since much of that country's borrowing took place while the World Bank, the Inter-American Development Bank, and of course the US Agency for International Development (AID) engaged in an informal financial blockade following Peruvian nationalization of some direct foreign investments.

It is noteworthy that this trend has not met with universal acclaim. This partly reflects a legitimate concern for the fragility of the Eurodollar market and for the dangers of excessive borrowing by LDCs. But one also detects in some of the worried commentary a touch of the fear of the intermediary who is being cut out, and of the bureaucrat who is losing control and power. Others actually prefer a tied package to markets providing each component separately. Some of these attitudes may be reflected in the following quotations from a recent speech by William S. Gaud, executive vice-president of the International Finance Corporation:

> Nevertheless, I see very real risks for the developing countries in borrowing so heavily in a market with no established lending standards and no overall surveillance to prevent unsound practices. . . . There is another feature of these Euro-currency loans which should not be overlooked. Foreign private investment is important to the developing countries not only because it contributes capital for their development but because it brings with it technology, management, training and access to foreign markets—items which are all in short supply in the Third World. Euro-currency loans bring with them none of these. Indeed, they are often made even without any appraisal of the soundness of the projects they are intended to finance.[23]

Suitably extended and reinforced (on which I say more below), a reasonably competitive international (private) market for LDC debt can provide a useful arena for economic interaction between DCs and many LDCs. This is the path of

[23] William S. Gaud, "Private Investment and Local Partnership," speech at a Financial Times conference on "The European Community and the Third World," London, 7-8 November 1973, pp. 2-4 (distributed by the International Finance Corporation). The same speech notes the sensitivity of the Eurocurrency market to speculative waves, and the difficulty of planning investments under the Eurodollar regime of floating interest rates. It should be noted that Mr. Gaud recognizes positive features in LDC Eurodollar market borrowing.

independence and a minimum of controls, as put by Charles P. Kindleberger in his pioneering advocacy of this thesis.[24] But the LDCs committed to a market economy would do well to expand also their own internal capital markets. The richest and more sophisticated LDCs can also increasingly take a bigger share of the profits from intermediation by developing their own financial institutions, capable of operating at the international level, particularly for flows among LDCs (and a fortiori for flows among nationals of the same LDC).

Concessional finance

The two arenas singled out as particularly favorable for DC-LDC interaction, i.e., commodity and debt markets, even if working well, may leave the population of the *least* developed countries, which are devoid of much of a natural resource base and therefore are not credit-worthy by current commercial standards, in extreme poverty for the foreseeable future. These countries provide the strongest argument for the continuation of international concessional financial flows, which otherwise share with direct foreign investment low grades in standoffishness, although doing somewhat better in decomposibility,[25] and much better in reversibility or ability to terminate the arrangement relatively smoothly.

It may be possible that international concessional finance going to the least developed countries will include, in the future, the participation of other, more prosperous LDCs, particularly in regions with a strong sense of cultural solidarity, such as Latin America and the Moslem nations. Be that as it may, aid to the least developed countries will be more successful when targeted to a clearly defined charitable purpose, such as avoiding a famine, than when seeking more general goals, e.g., promoting development. This, of course, will not surprise those who have followed the aid story during the last twenty years.

The orders of magnitude for concessional finance that realistically can be expected during the foreseeable future do not warrant much discussion of this form of DC-LDC interaction. Looking back, it is clear that the attention given by

---

[24] See Charles P. Kindleberger, "Less Developed Countries and the International Capital Market," in *Industrial Organization and Economic Development, In Honor of E. S. Mason,* edited by Jesse W. Markham and Gustav V. Papanek (Boston: Houghton Mifflin, 1970), pp. 337-49. See also Richard N. Cooper and Edwin M. Truman, "An Analysis of the Role of International Capital Markets in Providing Funds to Developing Countries," *Weltwirtschaftliches Archiv,* no. 2 (June 1971): 153-82. It should be clear that international bankers must not be credited with extraordinary angelic virtues, and LDCs must be on guard to prevent 1920s-type abuses arising from high-pressure salesmanship, more recently associated with suppliers' credits.

[25] Aid, particularly bilateral aid, is likely to be tied not only to commodities from the donor country but also to accepting the donor country's direct foreign investment. As expressed by the US secretary of the treasury, Dr. George P. Shultz: "Every sovereign nation has, of course, the right to regulate the terms and conditions under which private investment is admitted or to reject it entirely. When such capital is rejected, we find it difficult to understand that official donors should be asked to fill the gap" (*New York Times,* 26 September 1973, p. 5).

academics and others to this area was out of proportion to its actual or potential importance for development in most LDCs.

The soft windows of existing multilateral institutions, such as IBRD/International Development Association (IDA) and the regional development banks, are likely to continue limping along undramatically, except in the unlikely case that they were to receive large and steady funds from special drawing right (SDR) link schemes, from oil-rich states, or from controlling seabeds. These institutions will have to rely mainly on their usefulness as intermediaries between world capital markets and LDCs that find direct access to those markets too expensive, or that prefer, for a variety of reasons, to place part of their debt with multilateral institutions. The greater variety of possible sources of finance open to the more advanced LDCs will no doubt put some competitive pressure on the World Bank group and on regional development banks. Such pressures may lead to difficult dilemmas for those institutions: viewed as organizations wishing to survive and expand or desiring to influence domestic LDC policies, they will want to woo their best customers, such as Mexico, Nigeria, Brazil, and Thailand; but from a development viewpoint, they should consider charging higher rates of interest to their best customers (who may then stop borrowing from them), while passing on to the poorest countries via lower interest rates all of the gains obtained by public multilateral borrowing.

The influence that bilateral or multilateral aid agencies will be able to exert on the domestic priorities of borrowing countries will continue to wane for those LDCs with alternative borrowing possibilities. Regardless of the good intentions of those attempting to guide LDC priorities, or of the wisdom of whichever happens to be the fashionable top priority at a given time among world development executives, the experience of the last ten years suggests that such waning is mostly to the good. Whatever the levels of concessional bilateral or multilateral aid that remain to be granted in the future are, they would best be disbursed quietly and routinely, with a greater sense of automaticity and without too much involvement in other countries' domestic affairs.[26]

International monetary reform

One major LDC interest in international monetary reform, narrowly defined, is to obtain the scheme most favorable to smoothly expanding world trade in a multilateral framework. On this point all LDCs, large and small, as well as DCs, appear to agree. One can go further and suggest that as most LDCs are (and are likely to remain for a long time) net debtors, they will benefit from a system

---

[26] This viewpoint is eloquently presented by I. G. Patel, "Aid Relationship for the Seventies," in Barbara Ward et al., eds., *The Widening Gap; Development in the 1970's* (New York: Columbia University Press, 1971), pp. 295-334. See also Albert O. Hirschman and Richard M. Bird, *Foreign Aid—A Critique and A Proposal*, Princeton Essays in International Finance, no. 69 (Princeton, N.J.: Princeton University Press, July 1968).

yielding a world aggregate demand that induces a mild inflationary trend in the world price level, a trend that will hopefully not be fully anticipated by lenders. A rising world price level resulting from cost-push forces in the industrialized world, particularly if accompanied by slack capacity utilization in those countries, however, is unlikely to be accompanied by external circumstances that are on balance favorable for LDCs.

A relatively flexible exchange rate system, with rules for crawling or wiggling, among industrialized countries and large and/or inflationary LDCs seems most suitable to the maintenance of full capacity use and expanding world trade. It is at first sight somewhat surprising that LDCs as a group, a group within which *small* LDCs have the most votes, have supported fixed rates for the DCs. The explanation, however, seems straightforward. Economically small and open LDCs, small and open with respect to both trade and finance, will usually want to maintain fixed parities vis-à-vis a major industrial power for optimum currency area reasons, whatever the world exchange rate system is. Thus, Guatemala will want to keep its currency pegged to the US dollar, Chad will wish to peg to the French franc, etc. Note that even large Mexico wishes to remain pegged to the US dollar. Given such a starting point, it is not surprising that those LDCs will prefer the major currency to which they peg to remain in turn pegged to the rest of the world, particularly when their trade, although oriented toward one industrial power, has a reasonable degree of geographic diversification. This will not only maximize the economic benefits derived from optimum currency area considerations, but it will also cloak the unpleasant neo-colonial flavor of being in a dollar area, a franc area, etc. A world without an obvious single international money also presents a number of minor headaches for managers of LDC external asset and debt portfolios. Finally, it can be argued that as LDCs wish to expand the amount of SDRs issued, even under present rules, they will naturally oppose exchange regimes that would reduce the need for international reserves.[27]

The gross loss to small (and not so small) LDCs of having the industrialized countries move to more flexible exchange rates, however, may in fact be turned into a net gain when one compares that scenario, not with the pre-1971 world, but with realistic alternative monetary arrangements for the future. A future system of pegged rates among industrial countries is unlikely to work without severe controls over trade and capital flows, or without a close and cozy degree of policy coordination among DCs. Neither prospect should be particularly attractive to LDCs, which may not escape the dangers of hegemonic currency areas and preferential zones even under a formally fixed exchange rate system. In spite of the image projected by official declarations, this is in fact recognized by many LDC policymakers.

---

[27] See Gerald Helleiner, "The Less Developed Countries and the International Monetary System," *Journal of Development Studies,* forthcoming. Some LDCs, confident in their resources and macroeconomic management, may consider that disturbances are more likely to arise outside rather than inside their economies, and therefore will use changes in their exchange rates to shield themselves from inflation coming from the industrialized world.

Contrary to some panicked commentary, the LDC experience in the post-1971 world has been, so far and on balance, quite good, and many an LDC central bank has learned that it is not so difficult to keep tabs on cross rates or to calculate reasonable portfolio combinations in different currencies. While granting that the extraordinary 1972-73 commodity boom has helped adjustment to the new order a good deal, it must also be pointed out that forces fueling that boom, including fiscal and monetary policies in the North, were encouraged by the new floating policies. It may also be noted that while flexible rates in major industrial centers are supposed to discourage, *ceteris paribus*, international capital flows, the post-1971 world has witnessed a large expansion of LDC activity in those markets.

In short, a world trading community with low and decreasing DC controls over commodity and capital flows, with expanding trade, and with loose policy coordination among DCs is difficult to visualize without the adoption by those countries of reasonably flexible exchange rates. Such a system, while providing LDCs a potentially favorable external environment, will impose some minor adjustment costs on many of them. A weak case could be made for compensating them for such costs via more favorable allocations of SDRs.

On the assumption that major industrial countries will consolidate a system of floating exchange rates while most noninflationary and small LDCs will keep fixed rates in terms of one of the key currencies, it can be argued that the reserve needs of the latter will be greater than those of the former, relative to their shares in world trade.[28] Participation in SDR allocations, and perhaps IMF quotas, could be expected to adjust to this new situation. It could also be expected that the rules for crawling that may emerge from international monetary reform will make allowances for the different characteristics of LDC balance-of-payments situations, rather than rigidly trying to apply the same rules to all, regardless of serious structural differences. For example, a net debtor can be expected to keep a level of gross international liquid reserves different from that of a net creditor. LDCs exporting exhaustible natural resources may, in their optimization plans through time, accumulate large liquid reserves in the near future, to be drawn down at a later date. Rigid rules built around reserve levels, or even changes in levels, would neglect those special circumstances.

Some alternative Southern strategies

A tactical decision for LDCs as a group has been whether to seek to broaden negotiations for a new international monetary order into a more general discussion

---

[28] Inflationary LDCs, i.e., those whose price levels rise chronically at a faster rate than the world price level or than that of the major industrial country to which they would otherwise peg, may also have a legitimate claim to larger reserves if all their crawling pegs achieve is the elimination of the difference in inflationary trends, without seriously smoothing out other sources of balance-of-payments disturbances, which may remain virulent in those countries.

of international economic reform, in the spirit of 1944, and if so, on which related issues to concentrate their bargaining power. So far, the LDCs have chosen to emphasize plans for a link between SDR creation and a favorable allocation to LDCs. Such proposals have run into serious opposition. The main problem is that the nonacademic opponents are unwilling to yield DC political control over the grant element that would be involved in link schemes. At the same time, however, and mainly for technical reasons, the idea that SDRs should bear an interest rate not too far below those ruling in the world markets for prime short-term paper has gained ground. This implies that net users of SDRs would gain less net real resources even from favorable allocations. The use of SDRs would then still be an attractive form of borrowing for LDCs, particularly to those with weak international credit standing, but not *that* different from other forms of borrowing.

It may well be that a reallocation of IMF quotas and SDR allocations, justified primarily by generalized floating by industrial countries plus widespread pegging by LDCs, and the recognition of special LDC balance-of-payments problems, with greater quotas and SDR allocations going to the LDCs, are all that can be expected at the moment. This, of course, could be made to yield some net gains to LDCs as a group.

There are other issues of international economic reform where LDC bargaining power could be fruitfully applied under present circumstances. Reduction of DC protection for commodities of special LDC export interest and the removal of DC practices restricting the diffusion of technological knowledge have been already mentioned as candidates for discussion.

An important area that has been neglected so far in international monetary discussions is the establishment of liberal and clear rules guaranteeing LDC access to the national capital markets of industrialized nations. This may be partly explained by the boom in LDC borrowing in the international Eurodollar market. But the lesson from that experience is then not being correctly learned. Such a boom *does* show that very large sums, estimated at around $8 billion in 1972 and more in 1973, can be mobilized by LDCs, with a minimum of strings, via international capital markets. There is, however, some truth to the criticism that the Eurodollar market is still a fragile and limited capital market. For example, LDC borrowing has been heavily in the form of bank loans with maturities of not much more than ten years and with floating interest rates; the market for long-term LDC bonds has not expanded very much yet. The continuity of these flows is far from assured.

It is time to consolidate LDC advances in the Eurodollar market by extending them to the national capital markets of DCs. Restrictive rules on DC imports of LDC debt paper, inherited often from the 1930s, have survived almost intact, even as the corresponding rules for commodity imports were gradually liberalized during the postwar period. Those restrictive rules may sometimes appear not to be binding simply because the discouragement they signal precludes the actual testing of the limits they impose. Frequently, the rules on debt imports are not just restrictive, formally or informally, but also discriminatory. Thus, in some DC national capital markets, only favored LDCs, usually ex-colonies, are allowed to place their debt paper.

At a time when international monetary reform is being discussed, certainly these are matters that deserve a close review by DCs and LDCs. The payoff could be substantial, not only in increased capital availability to LDCs and lower borrowing costs, but also in decreasing the political frictions associated with other forms of capital transfer between DCs and LDCs. Possible large financial surpluses of some oil-exporting states support the need to develop and strengthen world financial markets.

It could be argued that easier access to external capital markets will only benefit large, resource-rich LDCs with a diversified or very lucrative export bill. However, even small, undiversified LDCs have been borrowing in the Eurodollar market. Furthermore, smaller LDCs could band together to enter international capital markets, as the relatively poor Central American countries have done. In some cases, more prosperous LDCs could guarantee the debt instruments of less fortunate LDCs. Regional and subregional development banks could be used as instruments in these activities, in the same fashion that similar institutions could be used by small and medium size LDCs to handle their joint search for, and purchase of, foreign technology. Organizations would thus be created or strengthened to improve the conditions of access to world markets by the smaller LDCs, institutions that could be turned around to accelerate commercial integration *within* the group if world market circumstances turned adverse. Had Latin America developed such institutions during the 1930s, its crash industrialization programs during the 1930-45 period would have been probably more ambitious and rational.

LDCs committed to a mixed domestic economy and to active links with world commodity and financial markets will find a growing need for sophisticated management in their fiscal, monetary, and exchange rate policies. While those world markets during the 1970s have opened up new options for LDCs, they also limit freedom of action regarding the use of domestic policy instruments. The freewheeling experimentation with domestic policy tools, which many mixed-economy LDCs underwent during the 1950s, has now become riskier and potentially costlier.

A few final remarks

This essay has been written around two basic working hypotheses, one political and one economic. The former assumes a multipolar world, with several major centers of political and military power, all limited in their hegemonic pretensions by the nuclear stalemate. Out of such political underpinnings, relatively free international markets could provide a plausible mechanism for interdependence between the citizens of different states. The basic economic hypothesis, which has a somewhat neo-Leninist flavor, is that for the foreseeable future the North will have a substantial and growing excess demand for Southern commodities, mainly but not exclusively for primary products, plus an excess supply of finance capital, a supply that could be enlarged by the surplus funds of some oil-rich LDCs. The North can also be expected to maintain an excess supply of new technology and capital goods. Handled via relatively open international markets, those circumstances can yield gains for all participants.

Much of this, of course, is already happening. But those markets are still quite imperfect, and will always be at the mercy of political decisions regarding whether and how they will be allowed to operate. Those in LDCs and DCs interested in obtaining both economic efficiency and national autonomy would do well to use whatever bargaining power they have to strengthen those markets. The Southern countries are not without bargaining strengths, and can be expected to use them with increasing sophistication to achieve less asymmetrical international economic relations. Their potential bargaining strength arises not only from conflicts among the Northern countries but also from clashes of interest between different groups within industrialized states.[29]

Besides concessional aid to the poorest LDCs, there will remain some areas of economic interaction between DCs and LDCs where it may be difficult to even imagine the operations of decentralized markets, and where political decisions will have to be quite open and explicit, often involving the creation of supranational authorities to regulate economic activity. An obvious example involves the economic use of the commons of mankind, particularly the seas and the seabed assets for which nobody has ownership titles. The only alternative to an explicit political settlement in this area, where potentially large pure rents are up for grabs, is a de facto or de jure enclosure movement using technological, political, and military power.[30]

Leaving aside difficulties associated with nonappropriated resources, it is perhaps worth emphasizing that one should not exaggerate the ease of obtaining efficient, stable, and competitive world commodity markets, particularly for exhaustible natural resources. Notions of discount rates, intergenerational equity, conservation, and inevitable uncertainties about future technologies greatly complicate the picture, heating up the scramble for control of large rents. If, as in the case of oil, sellers of those commodities generate surpluses for which investments with small risk and reasonable returns are difficult to find without the cooperation of commodity buyers, the tangle becomes monumental, even if producers and buyers are many and competitive. Some politicization of these markets may thus be

---

[29] On this point, see the outstanding document presented by Tanzania to the Lusaka conference of nonaligned states, *Cooperation Against Poverty*, Dar es Salaam, Government Printer, United Republic of Tanzania, 1970.

[30] Those confident of their technological and military muscle are calling for just that. The *Wall Street Journal*, 17 December 1973, p. 14, has editorially suggested, in the following terms, that the US should withdraw from the UN Law of the Sea Conference: "Enough is enough. For the sake of form, the United States may as well send its negotiators to Venezuela and Vienna, though there is much to recommend a clean break. But the important thing is that the US government should free the petroleum and mining industries of any caveats linked to some future treaty, and let them go to work adding to the world's store of available resources."

inevitable, except perhaps in a world where natural resources were evenly divided between 350 countries having ten million inhabitants each.

More generally, it is difficult to visualize any future international community with even minimum claims to legitimacy and fairness that would exclude LDCs from negotiations settling worldwide economic matters either directly or by establishing market rules of the game. Full LDC participation in international trade and monetary reform discussions, even if it spoils past clubby atmospheres,[31] should thus be regarded not as an absent-minded concession by DCs but as a first step toward full LDC participation in world economic planning.

---

[31] On 21 September 1973, the *Wall Street Journal,* p. 12, reported from Nairobi that: "For all their old complaints, though, officials of industrial countries now find it difficult to suppress their longing for the days when they could meet without having to share every secret with, or explain every technicality to, the Tanzanians and Chileans."

South-South relations: the economic and political content of interactions among developing countries

H. Jon Rosenbaum and William G. Tyler

Traditionally, examinations of the international relations of the less developed countries (LDCs) have focused on influences that can be attributed generally as originating in the developed countries (DCs). In fact, relatively few scholarly analyses of inter-LDC relations have been undertaken.[1] Since South-South relations have grown appreciably in recent years, however, it is important that a framework for studying these relations be developed, and this framework must include an awareness of the significance of the international economic system.

At present the existing international economic system is under pressure on many fronts—monetary, trade, investment, and aid—and recent years have witnessed the deterioration of existing arrangements to the point where reform appears imperative. However, any form of change will involve many issues that are of paramount importance to the economic welfare of the LDCs. Trade, for example, is proportionally more important, in general, to the economic growth of the LDCs than it is for the developed countries. Yet the role of the LDCs, with the possible exception of the oil-producing states, in moderating or affecting the outcome of existing reform efforts is extremely limited. While the nature of North-South

H. Jon Rosenbaum is an associate professor in the Ph.D. program in political science of the Graduate School and the Department of Political Science, The City College, The City University of New York. William G. Tyler is a senior fellow in the Institute for World Economics at Kiel University and an assistant professor in the Department of Economics at the University of Florida.

[1] Among the exceptions are the following studies: Michael Brecher, "The Subordinate State System of Southern Asia," *World Politics* 15 (January 1963): 213-35; Leonard Binder, "The Middle East as a Subordinate International System," *World Politics* 10 (April 1958): 316-33; Weston H. Agor and Andres Suarez, "The Emerging Latin American Political Subsystem," in Douglas A. Chalmers, ed., "Changing Latin America: New Interpretations of its Politics and Society," *Proceedings of the Academy of Political Science* 30 (August 1972): 153-66; H. Jon Rosenbaum, "Argentine-Brazil Relations: A Critical Juncture," *The World Today* 29 (December 1973): 537-42; and David F. Ronfeldt and Luigi R. Einaudi, "Conflict and Cooperation among Latin American States," in Luigi R. Einaudi, ed., *Beyond Cuba: Latin America Takes Charge of Its Future* (New York: Crane, Russak & Co., 1974), pp. 185-200.

relations accounts, in part, for this relative lack of influence, it would seem reasonable to expect that a more extensive use of the existing mechanisms available to the LDCs could provide them with greater leverage when seeking to promote their common interests. Nevertheless, attempts to establish a common economic front vis-à-vis the industrialized nations, with a few exceptions such as the Special Economic Coordinating Commission for Latin America (CECLA), have been timid and restricted largely to the articulation of common interests.

The continued failure of the LDCs to advance their common economic interests effectively will surely mean a forfeiture of an opportunity to affect any new international system that may emerge. While traditional bilateral South-South interstate relations have been and continue to be rather weak, the proliferation of international and regional organizations since World War II affords the LDCs a new environment in which to conduct relations, settle differences, aggregate collective interests, and influence the direction and extent of change in the international economic system.

A central dimension of South-South relations, as we have said, is that they are normally shaped by North-South relations. The international economic system's four functional areas—monetary, trade, investment, and aid—provide a constellation of issues capable of stimulating consensual and conflictual relations among the LDCs, but these relations generally are also conditioned by North-South relations.

This article provides a description and analysis of South-South relations that pertain to questions raised by changes in international economic arrangements and institutions. We are concerned with: (1) the environment within which South-South relations occur, (2) the nature and growth of these relations, (3) domestic and international policy priorities for selected developing countries, (4) the implications of the major international economic issues for South-South relations, and (5) the value international organizations will have in the future in assisting the LDCs to affect, and benefit from, changes in the international economic system.

While much of the ensuing discussion is general in nature, an attempt has been made to focus on certain key developing countries. Examples, therefore, are drawn mainly from the experiences of Argentina, Brazil, Egypt, and, to a lesser extent, India. No claim is made that these countries are entirely representative of the developing nations; the examples cited are merely illustrative. In addition, the increase in the quantity and visibility of South-South relations, resulting from a decline in great-power capabilities and reinterpretations of their interests and policies, is a comparatively new phenomenon. While trends are emerging, it is too early to identify them with great specificity.

Finally, a definitional note is in order before proceeding with an examination of the primary concerns of this article. When considering South-South relations, there is the dilemma of determining exactly which nations are participants. This boundary problem is created by the lack of homogeneity among the LDCs. Moreover, any decision about which countries to label as LDCs can provide only a static view; growth occurs at varying rates, and the underdeveloped and dependent status of some of today's LDCs may be terminated.

A related question involves the proper placement of the People's Republic of China. Although still underdeveloped economically by most conventional criteria, China is clearly a world power. Therefore, in terms of the paradigm we have accepted, devoted exclusively to South-South relations, we must exclude China.

On the other hand, the Latin American nations are included in the following discussion, although it could be argued that they differ substantially from the other LDCs. After all, most of the Latin American nations obtained their independence at least 125 years before the African and Asian states, and, as a group, the Latin American nations enjoy a higher per capita income than the African and Asian LDCs. Nevertheless, the Latin Americans also have been subjected to a dependency relationship at least as long as the Asians and Africans.

For purposes of this article, South-South relations are essentially those interactions between actors representing economically weak and relatively powerless countries. This operating definition is susceptible to the charge that it results in an inaccurate perception of the world; indeed, the dichotomy that it suggests, a globe divided between developed and developing nations, is fallacious. In reality, a continuum provides a far more satisfactory representation of the status of nations. For instance, even among the LDCs some nations belong to a Fourth World of least developed countries while others are quickly attaining the role of subregional powers. Nevertheless, our simplistic definition hopefully will suffice for the following analysis.

The environment

The psychocultural setting

Third World spokesmen during the past 25 years have claimed repeatedly that their countries share a common culture, one derived from poverty and exploitation. Moreover, numerous attempts have been made by LDC leaders since the completion of the independence struggle to transform this culture into an economic asset.[2] In short, these attempts have been based on the notion that unified action by the LDCs would allow them to surmount their individual weaknesses and, in particular, deal more effectively with the developed nations.

This proposition probably was advanced initially in the post–World War II period by Argentina's Juan Perón, when he espoused what came to be known at the "Third Position." The LDCs, Perón argued, could best serve their own interests if they practiced nonalignment and embraced neither capitalism nor communism.[3] In the 1950s and 1960s this view was advanced by such Third World leaders as India's Nehru, Indonesia's Sukarno, and Ghana's Nkrumah.

---

[2] While it is recognized that the old colonial epoch has not been closed completely, the vast majority of LDCs have obtained at least formal political sovereignty and are distracted by other matters.

[3] For a discussion of Perón's "Third Position," see chapter 6 of Albert Conil Paz and Gustavo Ferrari's *Politica exterior Argentina 1930-1962* (Buenos Aires: Editorial Huemul, S. A., 1964), pp. 163-212.

Nevertheless, the policy succeeded in attracting only a limited number of adherents. A variety of impediments, including traditional rivalries, preoccupation with internal integration, and conflicting ideologies, prevented the developing nations from acting in concert. However, probably the greatest obstacle preventing the adoption of a viable common policy was the inability of Third World leaders to agree on the appropriate methods to be used when dealing with the developed countries or with each other. Nonalignment was not sufficient as a determinant of policy since it called for abstention but suggested little in the way of positive action, and, in fact, there were even disputes about the exact meaning of the concept itself.

National culture is derived from a country's total experience, and while the LDCs, with a few exceptions, have experienced colonization, the development of a Third World culture has been more of an aspiration than a reality.[4] To date, the common anticolonial attitude of the LDCs has not been sufficient to stimulate a great deal of commitment to cooperative economic policies.

Appeals to Third World cultural consciousness have abated in recent years, and the notable successes in developing common economic policies at the regional level by the Arabs, the Andean countries, and the East Africans, among others, during the 1960s and early 1970s have been the result of pragmatic rather than emotional considerations. Nonetheless, a new, less ambitious regional and cross-regional employment of cultural identity for economic purposes appears to be gaining momentum. Brazil, for example, currently is trying to promote trade relations with black Africa, and the Brazilian foreign minister has frequently stressed the ethnic origins of his country's extensive black and mulatto population in foreign policy proclamations dealing with Africa.[5] Likewise, the Arab states have been soliciting political support for their confrontation with Israel from certain African and Asian nations that share their Islamic heritage.

The invocation of common culture for relatively modest purposes, both political and economic, is likely to prove more successful than the previous vague and undefined, but overly ambitious, efforts. Yet even here optimism must be tempered by the realization that the value of invoking cultural identity, particularly as an economic instrument, is circumscribed by many factors, some of which are unique to the developing nations. For instance, the Brazilians have found that the African masses know little more about Brazil than that their country produces outstanding soccer teams. Because of illiteracy, poor communications, and disinterest, they are unaware that some Brazilians share a partial cultural legacy with them. Moreover, national interest, rather than cultural sentimentality, will probably continue to be a more important factor in South-South economic relations. Afri-

---

[4] A good summary of Third World politics during the 1950s and 1960s is contained in J. D. B. Miller, *The Politics of the Third World* (London: Oxford University Press, 1967).

[5] There is a substantial literature on Brazilian-African relations. Among the most comprehensive works is José Honório Rodrigues, *Brazil and Africa* (Berkeley: University of California Press, 1965).

cans are unlikely to purchase Brazilian products merely because a tenuous cultural identification has been established.

Cultural solidarity among the LDCs may not increase significantly in the near future, but it is likely that cultural curiosity will spread as education improves and incomes rise, and this may stimulate an expansion in inter-LDC tourism and other cultural exchange. This will represent a new element in South-South economic relations. Of course, it is also quite possible that tourism and other forms of cultural exchange will contribute to political friction and reduce the possibility of economic cooperation in other areas. Tourism, as well as other forms of international intercourse, can contribute to animosity, under certain circumstances, as well as to greater understanding.

The increasing number of Brazilians visiting Argentina is instructive in this regard.[6] Although contact between most Argentines and Brazilians has been amicable, taciturn Argentines have been offended occasionally by the relaxed manner of Brazilian tourists frequenting their resorts and entertainment attractions. Due to exchange rate differences, Brazilian visitors have become avid travelers and consumers of Argentine products, and, while Argentine per capita income remains much higher than that of Brazil, this has appalled some Argentines who, having experienced years of economic stagnation, fear that Brazil's new prosperity will permit it to dominate Latin America economically and perhaps also politically. Brazilians, for their part, at times have been subjected to racial slurs while touring Argentina and have returned home with bitter memories. Tourism thus has had the effect of exacerbating the renewed rivalry between the two countries which has been produced by other factors.

Shared culture also may affect South-South economic relations by facilitating technological transfers and labor mobility. Technicians and scientists able to speak the same language find it easier to participate in joint projects, and laborers are likely to seek employment in countries that are not culturally alien, provided opportunities are greater than in their own country.

In conclusion, however, while the LDCs will no doubt gain knowledge and, in some cases, perhaps even come to appreciate each other's culture in coming years, in the near future, at least, nationalism probably will continue to be the dominant culture of individual LDCs. With the exception of nations having somewhat homogeneous cultures, reserve is likely to be the response to cultural courtship, and South-South economic relations will be affected only marginally.

As for ideology, it too seems to be an inconsequential variable in South-South relations at present. Either the LDCs are not particularly cognizant of one another's ideological biases or are willing to consider them, in general, a matter solely of domestic concern. For instance, even the staunchly anticommunist Brazilian government was willing to cooperate with Allende's Marxist regime in Chile, and the

---

[6] While 17,000 Brazilian visitors entered Argentina in 1960, in the first three months of 1972 alone 20,000 Brazilians traveled to Argentina. See "Brasileiros invadem a Argentina," *Visão*, 1 August 1972, pp. 18-20. In great part, such tourism is a result of Brazilian policy to maintain an overvalued exchange rate.

Bank of Brazil was one of the few foreign banks not nationalized during the Allende years. More recently, the Brazilians, who formally subscribe to the principle of ideological containment, were reported to have had discrete discussions with the Castro government in an effort to develop a common sugar exportation policy.[7]

This is not to suggest that there are no ideological hatreds among the LDCs; the ideological enmity among the Arab states clearly demonstrates that this is not the case. There is little ideological solidarity among the LDCs. In Latin America, for instance, christian democracy, corporativism, liberalism, and Marxism all have failed to serve as a regional unifying force. Nevertheless, if the relative indifference to each other's ideological preferences can be maintained, economic cooperation among the LDCs may develop more smoothly and be more lasting. Cooperation based on ideological affinity is fragile since nonconformity can breed hostility. The development of additional cartels for the marketing of raw materials will be simplified, for example, if ideology is not a consideration.

Psychologically, the South continues to feel a sense of unity when it comes to economic relations with the North. However, in the future there is likely to be a decline of interest in what is happening in the developed countries as the LDCs become more preoccupied with their own development. Yet, on certain questions, an identification with the East or West is likely to endure despite the current relaxation of international tensions, and, even within particular regions, some elites may remain psychologically attached to certain Northern nations. Many Argentines, for example, continue to associate psychologically more with Europe than with neighboring countries.

The strategic-political setting

The terms *development* and *security* are closely related in the lexicon of the LDCs. It is widely recognized that a semblance of security and stability is a prerequisite for successful economic development. Yet a regime threatened, or perceiving that it is endangered, by overt attack, domestic subversion, or more subtle perils must divert valuable resources to defense. It is also generally understood within the Third World that economic development can contribute to national security; an economically weak nation can be exploited or defeated more easily by foreign powers and may be exposed periodically to the violent wrath of dissatisfied citizens.

While most of the LDCs realize that there is little they can do alone militarily to protect themselves from determined security threats emanating from the superpowers, some LDCs feel more obligated than others to maintain relatively modern military forces to cope with internal insurgencies or potentially hostile neighbors. Those LDCs desiring sophisticated equipment for their forces traditionally have turned to the developed nations.

This dependency on foreign suppliers has upset nationalists, particularly those

---

[7] "Sugar: Unlikely Partners," *Latin America,* 20 July 1973, p. 1.

within the armed forces. The failure of France to deliver weapons to Israel after the 1967 Middle East war was a poignant reminder to the LDCs of the uncertainties involved in relying upon a single source for military hardware. This, and other factors, has led the LDCs to seek military supplies from a variety of sources, and, more importantly, it has led the larger LDCs to search for methods of producing their own weapons. Although this latter phenomenon is relatively new, as early as 1952 Argentina set out to produce an "all-Argentine" jet fighter, named the *Pulqui.*[8] India's recent development of a nuclear capability, through its own efforts, is of course the most dramatic example.

As was demonstrated by the Vietnam War, even the least industrialized LDCs have the capability of producing deadly weapons. However, the more technically advanced LDCs, such as Argentina and Brazil, now have the ability to build light tanks and armored cars, for example. To gain additional expertise, these countries are insisting that weapons purchased abroad be at least partly assembled in-country. This was the case, for instance, when Argentina and Brazil ordered guided missile destroyers from Britain recently. Licensing agreements with producers in the developed countries also are being obtained and are viewed as another means of transferring weapons technology.

The development and production of tanks, missiles, ships, and aircraft require large investments, and unit costs are likely to remain high since most LDCs have limited demands for this kind of equipment. In an effort to defray these expenses, LDC producers probably will search for buyers within the Third World. However, while such items as the Argentine designed *Pucara,* an antiguerrilla light plane, have aroused buying interest in Latin America, such sales will be difficult to conclude. At least during the 1970s, most LDC fabricated military equipment will remain more expensive and less sophisticated than that available from the developed countries. Moreover, LDCs dependent upon external sources no doubt will be just as chary about purchasing equipment from each other as they have been about their dependency upon the developed nations.

Although indigenous arms fabrication is not likely to have a great affect on South-South trade, with the possible exception of the sale of military vehicles, in the short term, weaker LDCs may turn increasingly to their more powerful LDC neighbors for military assistance in the form of training and donations of surplus or used arms. In Latin America, for example, Mexico has established training missions in Central America while Argentine and Brazilian military missions are operating in several of South America's smaller nations. Iran has been doing the same in the Persian Gulf area, and even has offered combat troops to suppress local insurgencies. These military assistance programs, it may be added, have received much less publicity in the United States than those sponsored by the more revolutionary LDCs such as Cuba, North Vietnam, and North Korea.

LDCs also have been financing development projects in other LDCs for

[8] For details, see H. Jon Rosenbaum, *Arms and Security in Latin America,* International Affairs Series 101 (Woodrow Wilson International Center for Scholars, December 1971), p. 90.

strategic reasons. It is well known, for instance, that the Arab combatants in the recent Middle East war have been receiving large financial donations from the wealthy Arab oil-producing states, particularly Saudi Arabia and Kuwait, for several years. These funds have been used to subsidize the domestic economies of the belligerents and have freed resources for the war effort. In Latin America, Argentina, Brazil, and Mexico all appear to be attempting to develop spheres of influence, and they have used limited foreign assistance of various kinds to further this goal.

In addition to military and developmental assistance, trade and investment are being utilized by certain LDCs for strategic purposes as well. Again, the result, if not the intention, is the formation of economic and political client-patron relationships. While aid, trade, and investment are treated in greater detail elsewhere in this article, it is appropriate to note here that the least developed countries are dubious about the merits of exchanging one dependency for another. Suspicions of Brazilian hegemonical ambitions are rife in Latin America at present, for example, and charges of Brazilian imperialism are reminiscent of those that traditionally have been aimed at the United States. However, the number of power contenders in the Third World gives the smaller countries some bargaining flexibility. The weakest Caribbean states, for instance, need no longer be dependent solely upon the United States and a former colonial ruler, for these countries are being wooed by at least four other nations: Brazil, Cuba, Mexico, and Venezuela. Naturally, this competition for the allegiance of the least developed countries is capable of resulting in conflict between the larger LDCs.

Conflict may also occur if the more powerful LDCs use economic policy as a political weapon to exact favorable decisions from each other. Direct confrontations of this kind have been rare to date but are likely to increase. Just recently, for example, the Nigerians intimated that they were prepared to ask the Arab oil producers to join them in an embargo against Brazil in order to force Brazil, a country that produces only 30 percent of its petroleum needs, to apply pressure on Portugal to grant independence to its African colonies.

In the past, the LDCs have not hesitated to castigate the developed nations when foreign economic policy has been used for strategic purposes. For instance, the Latin Americans complained bitterly in 1971 when the United States withheld foreign assistance from Ecuador in an attempt to maintain the right of American tuna fishermen to operate freely within the 200-mile territorial sea limit claimed by that country. So far the LDCs, however, have remained relatively silent when threatened economically by other LDCs. To cite the most obvious example, some LDCs currently are among those nations being harmed most seriously by the rise in oil prices and the curtailment of petroleum production. Uruguay, for instance, must import all of its fossil fuel, and the present crisis has severely aggravated the country's already substantial inflationary and balance-of-payments difficulties. India is facing famine due to the scarcity of petroleum-based fertilizers. Yet few official protests have been made,[9] and many of these countries even supported the

---

[9] A few countries, such as Kenya and Ghana, have issued protests.

Organization of Petroleum Exporting Countries (OPEC), and the call for "new OPECs," at the special session of the UN General Assembly in April 1974.

This attitude can be explained, in part, by fear. Understandably, the LDCs are reluctant to make accusations that might invite reprisals. Ideology is involved as well. The LDCs have been conditioned to believe that economic imperialism is something practiced exclusively by the industrialized nations. Finally, the reticence of the LDCs probably also is due to the vicarious sense of satisfaction they may be feeling from seeing the developed countries manipulated by other LDCs.

The recent oil crisis has caused the LDCs to be more concerned about the security of nonmilitary supplies. Similar apprehension was provoked by their difficulty in obtaining supplies during both world wars. During those hostilities the LDCs were forced to fend for themselves and develop local sources. This led to such steps as nationalizing certain areas of the economy, such as steel and petroleum in the case of Argentina. Current fears also may stimulate attempts to achieve greater economic autarky.

Just because those LDCs without oil have been relatively silent during the present petroleum crisis does not mean that they will not retaliate against other LDCs in the future should they feel that they are being mistreated. While extrapolation is not a completely adequate method for making forecasts, it is quite conceivable that as the local leviathans continue to invest and grant loans to the smaller LDCs, the leviathans will be susceptible to expropriation and debt repudiation.

A variety of disputes are likely to have an adverse effect on South-South cooperative efforts. Boundaries, population movements, and other issues probably will inhibit the voluntary formation of a coherent Southern bloc for either security or economic purposes. In addition, the LDCs have different internal political structures, attitudes, and objectives. Welfare, security, and status are all given different emphasis by individual LDCs. While the South is likely to act in concert in defending its options against certain threats originating in the North, it is not clear that a durable bloc can be developed in view of the inability of the LDCs to submerge their differing national political interests.

Growth and the nature of South-South relations

Concern with the hegemonical colonial and neo-colonial powers traditionally has dominated the foreign relations of the LDCs. This vertical relationship has had a hermetic character, and, with the exception of border disputes, relations among the LDCs have been of secondary importance and often of no significance at all. While costly diplomatic relations frequently have been maintained, they primarily have served to maintain domestic political systems by providing lucrative and prestigious employment to the upper classes, by coopting political opponents, and by exiling potential contestants for domestic political power. The developed countries have benefited to some extent from these hegemonical relations with the developing countries, since the LDCs have been precluded from effectively aggregating and pursuing their common interests. The divide-and-rule dictum has enabled the developed countries to enhance their bargaining position, to some extent, by dealing with the LDCs separately and playing them off against one another. This process has been facilitated by the nature of the LDC economies, which are, in general, more competitive than complementary.

While South-South relations were relatively weak in the past, in recent years these relations have become more significant. The growth of economic relations between these countries is particularly apparent. Total trade between the LDCs doubled between 1955 and 1971, while LDC manufactured exports to other LDCs more than tripled—although intra-LDC trade declined as a share of total LDC trade.[10] Regional trading blocs have been founded in Latin America, Central America, and east and west Africa, while regional development banks and United Nations economic commissions have been established and have flourished. Commodity agreements or arrangements between producers, usually developing countries, have been instituted for petroleum, coffee, copper, bauxite, and bananas. Regular meetings between government officials in responsible economic policy-making positions in the LDCs have occurred under the auspices of such varied international institutions as the International Monetary Fund (IMF), the United Nations Conference on Trade and Development (UNCTAD), the General Agreement on Tariffs and Trade (GATT), and the regional and more specialized organizations. While the sensitivity of economic transactions among the LDCs can still be considered low, especially when compared with their relations with the developed countries,[11] the interactions have been increasing in recent years.

Although economic issues are stressed in this article owing to the nature of the volume, other types of South-South interactions also have been growing. An intensification of relations among the LDCs has occurred in the political sphere both on a regional and a bilateral level, as was mentioned in the previous sections. In Latin America, for example, intraregional political transactions no longer are taking place primarily within the United States-dominated Organization of American States (OAS) but within the ad hoc CECLA (Special Economic Coordinating Commission for Latin America).[12] On a bilateral level, South-South interstate relations have expanded as certain key LDCs have assumed an increasingly hegemonical role, particularly within their own political subsystems. For example, Brazil has increasingly exercised its own leadership over other South American countries. Complementing these political and economic interactions in South-South relations is the growth of cultural and social interactions, such as student exchanges and tourism.

[10] See table 2 in this article.

[11] For a convincing analysis of the growing economic interdependence of the developed countries and a discussion of the high sensitivity in their economic transactions, see Richard N. Cooper, "Economic Interdependence and Foreign Policy in the Seventies," *World Politics* 24 (January 1972): 159-81. See also Cooper's *The Economics of Interdependence: Economic Policy in the Atlantic Community* (New York: McGraw-Hill, 1968), especially pp. 59-147.

[12] Weston H. Agor, "Latin American Inter-State Politics," *Inter-American Economic Affairs* 26 (Autumn 1972): 25-26.

In examining the nature of South-South relations, one can make a useful distinction between political subsystems, on the one hand, and dominant political systems, on the other. While political subsystems generally are regional in character, dominant political systems are global and may encompass one or more political subsystems. Indonesia, for example, currently belongs to both the Southeast Asian subsystem and the Western, or capitalist, political system. Relations between LDCs vary according to association with different political subsystems and dominant political systems. Table 1 presents a summary of these South-South relations according to the layer at which the interactions transpire. Clearly, the interactions between two LDCs of the same subsystem are the most varied and intense at present. Table 1 is an idealized summary and does not encompass the entire range of South-South relations; the types of countries and questions involved also determine the interactions. Also, specifically excluded from table 1 are region-to-region relations, normally conducted through regional organizations.

The recently developed concept of transnational relations is also useful in explaining the nature of South-South relations.[13] While classic interstate politics involve only the relations between governments, transnational politics include a consideration of other important actors coming from the societies of different nations but not always representing or supporting governmental policies. It has been postulated above that interstate politics among developing countries are weak relative to those existing between LDCs and developed or hegemonical powers. Similarly, the transnational interactions occurring among LDCs are also weak when compared to those on the North-South or North-North planes. The transnational interactions between great-power societies and LDCs, while intense, are generally unbalanced, with the LDCs demonstrating passivity in most cases. Developing country interactions with international organizations, depending of course on the institution in question, are in some ways similar in terms of intensity to North-South relations; they are more intense than bilateral interactions between individual LDCs. Figure 1 represents a simplified paradigm of North–South-South interstate politics and transnational interactions.[14] If indeed, as we have asserted, there exists a relative weakness in bilateral South-South interactions and a relative strength in LDC interactions with international organizations, then international organizations seem to represent a workable mode for intensifying South-South relations for the achievement of common ends.

[13] See Robert O. Keohane and Joseph S. Nye, eds., "Transnational Relations and World Politics," *International Organization* 25 (Summer 1971): entire special issue; Karl Kaiser, "Transnational Politics: Toward a Theory of Multinational Politics," *International Organization* 25 (Autumn 1971): 790-817; and Karl Kaiser, "The Interaction of Regional Subsystems: Some Preliminary Notes on Recurrent Patterns and the Role of Superpowers," *World Politics* 21 (October 1968).

[14] Figure 1 is an adaptation of similar diagrams found in Joseph S. Nye and Robert O. Keohane, "Transnational Relations and World Politics," *International Organization* 25 (Summer 1971): 333-34; and in Kaiser, "Transnational Politics: Toward a Theory of Multinational Politics," pp. 803-4.

Table 1. Layers of South–South relations

Layers of South-South relations for individual nation states	Example	Predominant types of interactions	Intensity of interactions	Institutional setting for interactions
Intrasubsystem and intra–dominant system	Brazil–Argentina	boundary conflicts	weak, but growing	classic interstate politics
		coordination of political response to hegemonical power(s)		regional economic, political, military, and cultural international organizations (governmental and extragovernmental)
		collaboration and conflict on matters of mutual economic interest		nonregional international organizations
		border trade		multinational corporations (generally through corporate head office)
		cultural and social interchange		
		some tourism		

Intrasubsystem but extra–dominant system	Brazil–Cuba	frequent ideological hostility but limited and covert economic collaboration	insignificant but exhibiting potential growth with diminution of hegemonical powers' influence	global international organizations third country diplomatic missions
Extrasubsystem but intra–dominant system	Brazil–Indonesia	collaboration and conflict on matters of mutual economic interest limited coordination of political response to hegemonical power(s)	insignificant but increasing	limited interstate politics global international organizations multinational corporations (almost always through corporate head office)
Extrasubsystem and extra–dominant system	Brazil–North Korea	frequent ideological hostility	insignificant	global international organizations

Figure 1. The effects of interstate politics and transnational interactions on the impact of the North on South-South relations

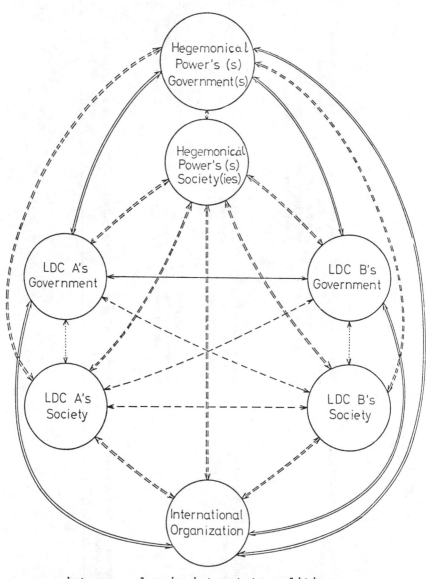

intense, classic interstate politics
relatively weak classic interstate politics
domestic politics
intense transnational interactions
relatively weak transnational interactions

Before turning to other matters, a note of clarification is necessary. While we have argued that the North has had great influence on South-South relations, despite the movement toward détente, the North cannot be viewed as a monolith in its relations with the South. Just as there were discernible differences in the manner in which the colonizers administered their holdings, there are qualitative differences in the way the developed countries behave toward the LDCs in the contemporary period. For instance, some former metropolitan countries continue to show great interest in their former colonies while exerting little influence on other LDCs. East-West relations as well as relations within the Eastern and Western blocs also have an effect on South-South relations. It is widely accepted among the LDCs that détente between the East and West and solidarity within the Eastern and Western camps would reduce the ability of LDCs to protect themselves from Northern penetration. However, shifting coalitions could give certain LDCs more influence on certain issues, and these occasions are likely to increase with the growth of multipolarity. In fact, on some issues the South may be able to exercise dominance or effective veto power. In the case of energy policy, some LDCs already have demonstrated this power. This has been made possible in part by the lack of solidarity on the part of the developed countries.

However, even considering the above qualifications, our basic premise, that North-South relations largely condition South-South relations, will arouse controversy. Nevertheless, we are not convinced that a single situation, the petroleum crisis, warrants an extreme reevaluation of our position. Southern influence may grow as the Southern haves discover that they possess certain bargaining advantages in their relations with the Northern have-nots, but this is unlikely to be a sudden process.

Domestic and international policy priorities

In discussing what they have termed the independent variables or policy objectives, Bergsten, Keohane, and Nye have enumerated and briefly discussed, in the first essay in this volume, the objectives of economic efficiency, growth, full employment, income distribution, price stability, the quality of life, and national and international security. We submit that it is misleading to consider these objectives in the same manner for the LDCs as they are frequently discussed when considering the developed countries. The Bergsten-Keohane-Nye analysis precludes a consideration of the more political and fundamental objectives, such as system maintenance, which we feel may have considerable importance in policy determination, and within which growth, full employment, etc. can be seen as instrumental variables. For the developed countries, blessed by relative political stability, the continuation of the established (and normally capitalistic) order is more or less assured. Discussion of policy objectives for those countries can thus proceed at a lower level of abstraction, i.e., full employment, price stability, growth, etc. For the LDCs, on the other hand, political stability is far less certain, capitalistic institutions are weaker, and the survival of an established, but fragile, economic, political, and social order is by no means always assured. The prime objective of any government is the preservation of the system in which its interests are vested. When that objective is assured, other objectives can be better considered on their own merits.

Another problem that arises when discussing policy priorities for the LDCs involves difficulties in generalization. Not only does there exist considerable heterogeneity among developing countries, but also within one country policy can undergo rapid change. Governments and ruling groups can change quickly in politically unstable developing countries, bringing about subsequent modifications of the weights given to different policy objectives. Furthermore, objectives are sometimes exogenously dictated by circumstances. National security, for example, becomes more important when, as in the case of Egypt, a country's security and territorial integrity are threatened. Similarly, it also can be contended that the political autonomy of the LDCs, and hence their ability to select policy priorities, is circumscribed by their dependence upon developed countries and upon international organizations controlled by developed countries (e.g., the IMF and the World Bank) for short-term and long-term economic assistance. At the same time, for example, that the World Bank was devoting much attention to lamenting the maldistribution of income in the LDCs, it refused to extend credits to Allende's Chile, although that government had done more than any other in Latin America, excepting Cuba, to redistribute incomes.[15]

This is not the place to discuss the compatibility and trade-offs between various policy objectives in the LDCs; the development literature is rich with such analyses, many of which relate to economic objectives.[16] As stated above, we feel that the maintenance of the system constitutes the main objective of LDC policy-makers. At the same time, the way in which this objective is approached varies from country to country and is partly dependent upon the nature of the government and other circumstances.

With an authoritarian military government, there is likely to be much explicit attention given to what is termed *national security,* although in practice this may be no more than a pretense for the suppression of all opposition. To legitimize and continue its rule, however, even authoritarian governments may have to rely on favorable economic performance in some cases. A good example is contemporary Brazil, where the attainment of growth objectives is considered by the country's military rulers to have the highest priority since it is viewed as crucial for the legitimization of the military form of government.[17]

---

[15] With the fall of the Allende government in September 1973, and the attendant radical modification of Chilean policy priorities, the World Bank has reinstituted activities in Chile.

[16] For a good general survey, see Derek T. Healey, "Development Policy: New Thinking about an Interpretation," *Journal of Economic Literature* 19 (September 1972): 757-97.

[17] For a discussion of the interplay of policy objectives and the political economy of recent Brazilian development, see the introduction to H. Jon Rosenbaum and William G. Tyler, eds., *Contemporary Brazil: Issues in Economic and Political Development* (New York: Praeger, 1972).

In a more well entrenched military or authoritarian type of government, or in more democratically inclined countries, such as India, growth objectives may not occupy such a high priority. When considering the growth objective, other economic and political demands, such as allocational efficiency and monetary stability, are likely to be considered as instrumental variables to attain growth. In countries with less emphasis on growth, economic policy is clearly discussed more in terms of its effects on other objectives.

It is notable, however, that while employment difficulties perhaps constitute the most dire and pressing problem for the LDCs, few developing countries, at least among those having capitalistic institutions, assign highest priority to the full-employment objective. Many LDCs also consider environmental destruction simply to be a necessary cost in attaining rapid economic growth and employment objectives.[18]

In considering the manner in which the policy priorities in different LDC's affect South-South relations, it is important to identify the benefits and effects of different policies and priorities on different groups. The authoritative decision makers may have policy preferences of their own, but only in those countries with apathetic populations are the governing elites entirely free to pursue their own inclinations. In most of the LDCs, a variety of demands must be considered and support from the population must be developed.[19] While a regime may seek to (1) cope with social and economic change, (2) induce social and economic change, (3) remain in authority, and (4) build the political and administrative infrastructure, other sectors of the society may be attempting to (1) maximize their well-being, status, and authority, (2) increase their productive capacity, and (3) achieve their respective ideological goals.[20]

South-South relations take place between elites, and to the extent that these actors possess similar interests, there is greater capacity for accommodation and consensus. Therefore, it is not surprising to observe that there has been greater understanding and cooperation between the present governments of Brazil and Bolivia than between Brazil and Péron's Argentina. The domestic interaction of different decision makers, as suggested by the concept of *bureaucratic politics,* also plays an important role in shaping policy priorities, both domestic and foreign. At times this may lead to internal disputes or to the pursuit of contradictory policies. At present, for example, the Brazilian military is concerned with the security of the South Atlantic and does not want to alienate South Africa and Portugal, while the foreign and finance ministries are interested in attracting new markets for Brazilian products and are busily courting the black African nations. The nature of South-

---

[18] For an American observer it is somewhat unsettling to see such a prestigious Brazilian newspaper as the *Estado de São Paulo,* for example, proudly proclaiming the Greater São Paulo industrial zone to be the world's most polluted area.

[19] Gabriel A. Almond and G. Bingham Powell, Jr., *Comparative Politics* (Boston: Little, Brown & Co., 1966), pp. 25-27.

[20] Warren E. Ilchman and Norman Thomas Uphoff, *The Political Economy of Change* (Berkeley: University of California Press, 1969), p. 58.

South relations, as discussed above, is also important in determining which policy objectives reflect common interests. With relatively little contact on security issues, except between neighboring LDCs, it is natural that economic issues and growth priorities emerge as common concerns among the LDCs and therefore dominate their relations.

International economic issues and South-South relations

In promoting and defending their economic interests, individually or in concert, the LDCs have had relatively little impact upon the international economic order. Developing countries to date have participated in the world economy only at its periphery, and their influence, mirroring their relatively minor economic importance, consequently has been minimal, with the exception of energy policy. Decisions dealing with international monetary reform, trading arrangements, investment decisions, and aid mechanisms have been in the hands of the more economically powerful developed country actors. In all four of these substantive areas of international economics and institutional change, the position of the LDCs, especially on an individual basis, continues, with few exceptions, to be analogous to that of a price taker in a functioning market; the LDCs have little control over the international economic order. As we show below, even in their relationships with other developing countries the LDCs are affected by external forces.

International monetary relations

In view of the limited economic interchange between LDCs, the monetary relations resulting from such interchange are also insubstantial. Yet the importance of the international monetary system to the developing countries in general cannot be emphasized too strongly. The LDCs are sensitive to changes in the international monetary system because of the unit-of-account function of developed country currencies. Many developing countries have defined their currencies in terms of developed country monetary units, hold their international reserves in developed country currencies, and have debt obligations denominated and payable in these currencies. The Indian rupee and many African currencies, defined in terms of British pounds, therefore are effectively devalued vis-à-vis third currencies when the pound is devalued, as are many Latin American currencies when the US dollar is devalued. For a developing country such as India, with an overvalued exchange rate and strong political pressures opposing devaluation, a domestic currency tied to a devaluing country's currency constitutes a politically advantageous way of effecting devaluation.[21] In general, the currency realignments resulting from the December 1971 Smithsonian Agreement have brought about a realignment in parities for the

---

[21] For a discussion of Indian exchange rate policy, see Ranadev Banerji, *Exports of Manufactures from India: A Prospective Appraisal of the Emerging Pattern* (Tübingen: J. C. B. Mohr, forthcoming in 1975).

LDCs that has affected their economic interactions with developed and developing countries alike. Paradoxically, this realignment of LDC currencies has largely taken place without the participation or consent of the developing countries;[22] the initial currency realignments were negotiated by the Group of Ten and were refined at the Smithsonian meeting.

Another consequence of the currency realignments for the developing countries has been the changes in the purchasing power of the foreign currency reserves that they hold. Since a large part of these LDC international reserves are held in American dollars, the real value of such reserves has decreased with the dollar's devaluation. At the same time, however, LDC debt obligations also have been affected by the post-1971 currency realignments. As a result, such debt service obligations have increased in real terms for many countries. Thus many LDCs, e.g., countries holding reserves in American dollars and possessing some debt in German marks, have been doubly injured by the post-1971 currency realignments; the real value of their international reserves has decreased while their debt service obligations have risen.

In addition to problems associated with the unit-of-account function of developed country currencies, the LDCs have been affected by the international monetary arrangements of the advanced countries in other, more important ways. It is clear that the LDCs as well as, or perhaps more than, the developed countries would benefit from a world economy with a more smoothly functioning, multilateral monetary system. In a system with freedom from undue adjustment burdens deriving from the nature of the system itself, with growing international reserves adequate to finance world trade expansion, and with the absence of a confidence problem for the principal reserve assets, the expansion of world trade would not be constrained by the international system. Benefits from decreased balance-of-payments adjustment burdens would accrue to the developing countries directly and indirectly—directly through greater adjustment ease for themselves, and indirectly because of increased adjustment ease for the developed countries, which would stimulate their imports from the LDCs. With improved international monetary arrangements, it is even conceivable that protectionist forces in the developed countries would be weakened. Furthermore, it can be contended that greater freedom would be allowed to capital movements, thus facilitating a greater transfer of such resources to the LDCs. Finally, freed from some of their pressing balance-of-payments adjustment problems, developed donor countries, such as the United States and Great Britain, could more easily expand their economic assistance to the developing countries.

Recognizing their stake in the world's international monetary system, the developing countries have begun to demand that their interests be considered more

---

[22] This is not to say that the developing countries that define their domestic currencies in terms of developed country currencies cannot redefine them. For example, Brazil, with its monetary unit tied to the US dollar, actually revalued by a nominal 3 percent in February 1973 after the dollar's devaluation.

seriously when new arrangements are being developed. It should be noted, however, that there has not been complete agreement among the LDCs about the reordering of the monetary system.

Consensual South-South relations have emerged on a number of international monetary topics.[23] First, there is widespread agreement among the developing countries that the discussions for international reform should include fuller participation by the LDCs. In fact, such expanded participation was a major topic at the UNCTAD III meetings in Santiago held during April and May of 1972.[24] Partly as a result of continuing UNCTAD recriminations, the Group of Ten has been expanded to include some developing countries and is now known as the Group of Twenty. At the same time, to ensure their greater participation in the discussion for reform, the LDCs have made efforts to restore the authority of the IMF in the decision-making process.[25] The LDCs also have been pressing for greater voting power in the IMF and in the World Bank, since they realize that discussions of alternative monetary arrangements within the IMF would permit them greater influence than they would have in any ad hoc group composed entirely, or almost entirely, of developed countries. At least in the forum provided by the IMF, the LDCs can articulate their positions on various international money matters. It also should be noted that any reform of the international monetary system involving a revision of the IMF's Articles of Agreement would require the support of more than one-third of the developing country membership.[26] Thus reform within the IMF framework is desirable from the LDC viewpoint; it is there that the bargaining power of the LDCs may be greatest.

A second international monetary issue generating widespread LDC agreement is the link between international reserve creation and the provision of economic assistance to the developing countries. This link, which originated in the old Stamp Plan, is designed to funnel additional real resources to the LDCs by providing them with larger shares of the IMF-created special drawing rights (SDRs). Under present arrangements, SDRs are distributed in accordance with IMF voting power, thus providing the developed countries with a disproportionately large share. Naturally, any proposal to give larger shares of the new SDRs to the developing countries has met with their enthusiastic approval. It is interesting to observe the gradually growing support of the developed countries for the link proposal, which can be attributed in part to the coordinated pressure and appeals of the LDCs.[27] Despite the opposition of some of the more important developed countries, most notably the United States, the link appears to be an idea whose time has come.

With the recent increases in petroleum prices, the liquid reserves of the oil-producing countries can be expected to increase further, especially for the Arab

---

[23] See also the discussion in this volume by Carlos Díaz-Alejandro.
[24] See Sidney Dell, "An Appraisal of UNCTAD III," *World Development* 1 (May 1973): 1-13.
[25] Ibid., p. 4.
[26] Ibid., p. 6.
[27] This growing support was readily apparent at the UNCTAD III meetings and at the IMF annual meeting in September 1973.

countries. As with all large liquid reserves, the existence of the Arab monetary reserves provides a certain amount of potential instability for the international monetary system. The capricious use of these reserves could no doubt be more detrimental to the industrialized countries than to the Arab countries. Whether the Arabs will use their newfound international monetary bargaining power to ensure greater representation of LDC interests in reform negotiations is yet to be seen but remains doubtful.

By emphasizing the growing South-South consensual relations on international monetary matters, we do not suggest that there is a North-South cleavage nor that all South-South relations are consensual on questions of international monetary reform. Different trading blocs possess different interests. Latin American positions on international monetary reform in many instances have coincided with the US position, whereas African positions have frequently corresponded with those of Europe. In many cases, the discussion of monetary topics parallels that of trade issues.

International trade and trade relations

Trade and trade arrangements are of vital importance to the economies of the developing countries. Not only are export to GNP ratios higher in the earlier stages of economic development, but most LDCs, unlike Brazil, India, Indonesia, and a few others, are small countries with small markets and therefore highly dependent upon trade for their present and future economic welfare. Of the four functional areas in the international economy—monetary, trade, investment, and aid—trade is currently the most significant factor in South-South relations. Many common interests exist, and trade between the developing countries has been growing. Yet, as table 2 demonstrates, it is important not to overestimate the importance of intra-LDC trade.

During the period from 1955 to 1971, total world exports, measured in current US dollars, increased at a compound annual rate of 8.6 percent, while LDC exports grew at a lower annual rate of 5.9 percent. Total LDC exports to other LDCs grew still more slowly—at an annual rate of 4.5 percent. Thus, during the 1955-71 period, not only did the LDC share of world trade decline (from 25.4 percent in 1955 to 17.0 percent in 1971) but the importance of LDC markets for LDC exports decreased as well. As seen in table 2, the share of LDC exports to other LDCs dropped from 24.4 percent in 1955 to 22.0 percent in 1962 and to 19.8 percent in 1971. Thus, at approximately 20 percent, LDC markets represent a relatively small and decreasing share of total LDC exports. The most important markets for developing countries are the developed nations, thus providing another indication of the relative importance of North-South economic relations for the developing countries.

In the case of manufactures, LDC markets are somewhat more important for LDC exports. Yet here again there has been a decrease, with the share of LDC manufactured exports going to other LDCs declining steadily from 32.0 percent in

Table 2. LDC exports and inter-LDC trade according to commodity group; 1955 and 1971

Commodity group	Total world exports (millions of US $)		LDC exports (millions of US $)		Share of LDC exports in total world exports (%)		LDC exports to LDCs (millions of US $)		Share of LDC exports to LDCs in total LDC exports (%)	
	1955	1971	1955	1971	1955	1971	1955	1971	1955	1971
Food, beverages, and tobacco (SITC 0-1)	18,400	45,250	7,720	13,120	42.0	29.0	1,460	2,150	18.9	16.4
Crude materials excl. fuels; oils and fats (SITC 2+4)	17,480	33,350	6,970	9,800	33.9	29.4	1,150	1,410	16.5	14.4
Mineral fuels and related materials (SITC 3)	10,270	35,780	5,990	23,320	58.3	65.2	2,160	4,630	36.1	19.9
Chemicals (SITC 5)	4,720	24,210	240	940	5.1	3.9	80	460	33.3	48.9
Machinery and transport equipment (SITC 7)	16,920	89,610	125	1,440	0.7	1.6	92	640	73.6	44.4
Other manufactured goods (SITC 6+8)	24,200	98,410	2,700	10,020	11.2	10.2	810	2,320	30.0	23.2
Total manufactures (SITC 5, 6, 7 + 8)	45,840	212,230	3,065	12,400	6.7	5.8	982	3,420	32.0	27.6
TOTAL	93,540	348,110	23,730	59,280	25.4	17.0	5,790	11,710	24.4	19.8
Percent of manufactures in total (%)	49.0	61.0	12.9	20.9	—	—	17.0	29.2	—	—

SOURCES: United Nations, *Monthly Bulletin of Statistics* 26, no. 7 (July 1972): xx-xxxvi; United Nations, *Monthly Bulletin of Statistics* 27, no. 7 (July 1973): xxii-xxxix; and UNCTAD, *Handbook of International Trade and Development Statistics–1972* (New York: United Nations, 1972): 46-363.

SITC = Standard International Trade Classification.

1955 to 27.6 percent in 1971. Only in the case of LDC chemical exports going to other LDCs does there appear to be a clear increase in the relative importance of LDC markets. For manufactured exports as a whole, however, it is apparent that the developed country markets not only are more important but are increasingly so. In relative terms, South-South trade relations have been actually decreasing in their significance.

To rapidly increase inter-LDC trade and to offset the tendency of the declining importance of LDC markets for LDC exports, a number of regional trading arrangements have been established by the developing countries. While the results of these arrangements, which range from loose trade associations to common market agreements, have been uneven, table 3 (at the end of this article) suggests that for the Latin American Free Trade Area (LAFTA), substantial relative increases in intraregional trade have been difficult to attain. From 1966 to 1970, the share of exports to LAFTA countries in relation to total LAFTA country exports increased only from 9.6 percent to 9.8 percent, although manufacturing exports rose from 15.7 percent in 1966 to 18.8 percent in 1970.

For individual key developing countries, the commodity and market composition figures are similar to the aggregate figures. Table 4 (at the end of this article) presents recent export data by Standard International Trade Classification (SITC) commodity group according to market destination for Brazil, Egypt, and India. Exports to LDCs represent 16.6 percent, 21.0 percent, and 19.2 percent, respectively, of total exports. For manufactured exports, LDC markets were more important for the three countries, representing 57 percent for Brazil, 27.7 percent for Egypt, and 28.1 percent for India of respective manufactured export sales. Comparing earlier figures with the later figures reported in table 4, it appears that the overall percentages of these three countries' exports going to developing countries have fallen.

As we have indicated, trade between LDCs is not as important presently, and perhaps even potentially, for the developing countries as their trade with developed countries. Thus South-South relations on trade matters have not been limited to the promotion of inter-LDC trade. Many LDCs confront similar problems in increasing their exports to the developed countries, and these problems and issues are increasingly of collective interest and concern in South-South relations. On the other hand, different LDCs compete with each other for the markets of the developed countries. Consequently, a pattern of consensual and conflictual relations on trade matters has grown out of more fundamental North-South trade relations.

As stated above, producers associations have been formed by some LDC primary producers. The purpose of such arrangements is to establish or exercise monopolistic strength in the international marketplace. As such, some exporters of primary products have found it attractive to collude in marketing their products, which are exported mostly to the developed countries. Conditions conducive to forming commodity arrangements include price inelasticity, growing demand owing to high income elasticity, the relative absence of production facilities in the principal consuming countries, and climatic or natural resource limitations on supply expansion. In addition, the fewer the number of producing countries, the fewer the political and organizational difficulties there will be in reaching a mutually advantageous restrictive agreement.[28]

Satisfying the above conditions, the most successful of all the existing commodity compacts among developing countries is OPEC.[29] Less success in forming and operating effective producers alliances has been experienced in the cases of coffee, cocoa, and tea.[30] A recent study of commodity agreements among LDC primary product producers has concluded that while some products (such as sugar, cotton, bananas, and citrus fruits) represent poor candidates for producers alliances, other products (notably coffee, cocoa, tea, pepper, and lumber) offer better prospects for LDC collusion.[31] To the list of good candidates might be added tin, bauxite, and copper. However, while there are only four major tin-producing countries, there are numerous substitutes for tin. The same is true of bauxite; rising prices would cause consumers to use lower-grade aluminum-bearing ores. In fact, for most mineral and agricultural products, the development of buffer stocks and substitutes as well as the production of these products in a large number of countries militates against the formation of successful commodity cartels.[32]

While there are persuasive economic reasons for the collusion of LDC producers, such behavior can also result in conflict among the supplying LDCs and between the supplying and consuming LDCs. The interactions within a producers cartel occur at the interstate level, and decisions such as those concerning production and export quotas are controversial in nature and invariably provoke conflict among the participating countries. For example, attempts to organize the tea market have been obstructed by conflict between the old producers, India and Sri Lanka, and the newer producers in west Africa. The organizational and political requirements for an effective collusive commodity agreement depend upon the

[28] See Stephen Krasner, "Oil is the Exception," Foreign Policy, no. 14 (Spring 1974): 68-83, for a complete listing of the key variables.

[29] For a description of the OPEC experience, see Abbas Alnaswari, "The Collective Bargaining Power of Oil Producing Countries," Journal of World Trade Law 7 (March-April 1973): 188-207. Given the rapidly growing world demand for petroleum products and the relatively low income elasticities for many other primary products, it can be argued that the petroleum industry presents far more favorable conditions for operating a producers alliance than most other products. It might also be argued that cultural and political similarities between the Arab oil-producing nations have facilitated reaching agreements.

[30] For discussion of the International Coffee Agreement, see Thomas L. Galloway, "The International Coffee Agreement," Journal of World Trade Law 7 (May-June 1973): 354-74; and Irving B. Kravis, "International Commodity Agreements to Promote Aid and Efficiency: The Case of Coffee," The Canadian Journal of Economics 1 (May 1968): 295-317. For an account of the attempts of developing countries to collaborate in the marketing of cocoa, see Ursula Wasserman, "The International Cocoa Agreement," Journal of World Trade Law 7 (January-February 1973): 129-34.

[31] Irfan Ul Hague, "The Producers' Alliances Among Developing Countries," Journal of World Trade Law 7 (September-October 1973): 511-26.

[32] See C. Fred Bergsten, "The Threat from the Third World," Foreign Policy, no. 11 (Summer 1973): 102-24, and "The Threat is Real," Foreign Policy, no. 14 (Spring 1974): 84-90, for a view that such arrangements are likely to be formed for numerous commodities.

suppression of discord in the interest of common gains. With the obvious success of OPEC, it seems certain that the developing countries will renew their attempts to form and operate effective producers alliances; however, their success, as we have suggested above, is not assured.

When success is achieved, there is no reason to expect that feelings of benevolence and obligation on the part of the LDCs participating in producers alliances will cause them to discriminate in favor of nonparticipating LDCs. As we have said elsewhere, some developing countries have been among the principal victims of the Arab oil embargo and the increase in oil prices. Remedies for the oil-consuming LDCs have been regional and incomplete in character. Prime Minister Eric Williams of Trinidad has promised to continue normal petroleum deliveries to other Caribbean states, and the Arab oil producers have vowed to make a loan of $200 million to the African countries and to form an Arab bank for African development. However, only Venezuela has suggested that it would consider the possibility of making a price distinction between the developed countries and the LDCs.

Besides forming arrangements limited to producing states, LDC suppliers of some commodities have worked together in seeking to negotiate commodity agreements jointly with consuming countries. Successful examples include the International Tin Agreement, which has been in existence for many years, and the International Coffee Agreement, which worked well for a while in the 1960s.

Another area of South-South trade relations concerns the common interest of the LDCs in combatting the import barriers of the developed countries. The protectionism the developing countries face when exporting their products to developed country markets is well documented,[33] and such trade restrictions appear to be greater for more labor-intensive products, in which the developing countries presumably have the greatest comparative advantages. Rather than dealing bilaterally with the developed countries in trade negotiations, it is clearly in the interests of the LDCs to work collectively toward the alleviation of trade barriers. UNCTAD has been the primary institutional embodiment of collective action among the developing countries.

A related question evoking widespread consensual interaction among the LDCs has concerned multilateral trade negotiations. Within UNCTAD, the consensus has been growing that special negotiating techniques and ground rules are necessary to ensure maximum benefits for the developing countries.[34] By having the LDCs present a unified position and bargain effectively in the proposed Tokyo Round, UNCTAD hopes to avoid a repetition of the Kennedy Round experience where the LDCs obtained few benefits relative to the large industrial countries.

To emphasize those trade matters relating to the larger issue of North-South trade is not to say, however, that all such interactions are consensual in nature.

[33] See, for example, Harry G. Johnson, *Economic Policies Toward Less Developed Countries* (Washington, D.C.: The Brookings Institution, 1967).
[34] See Sidney Dell, "An Appraisal of UNCTAD III," *World Development* 1 (May 1973): 7.

Serious differences between the less developed countries exist concerning trade preferences and negotiating strategy. The most common disagreements are: (1) between the LDCs associated with the European Economic Community (EEC) and those not associated with the EEC, especially those in Latin America, and (2) between the more developed LDCs and the less developed LDCs. Privileged access to the EEC and special trading privileges for the least developed of the LDCs constitute bones of contention among the LDCs.

Responding to the emphasis given to development problems in the mid-1960s, UNCTAD has been successful in focusing attention upon the trade problems of the LDCs and in negotiating tariff preferences for some LDC exports. At the urging of UNCTAD, schemes authorized by the Generalized System of Preferences have been instituted, at the time of this writing, in all the major developed countries with the exception of the United States and Canada. While there is some evidence that the concessions have not been as widespread or as helpful as anticipated,[35] tariff preferences have constituted an issue that has aroused considerable consensus and interaction among the developing countries.

The existence of the multinational firm raises additional problems. The manufacture and export of components requiring labor-intensive production has grown substantially in the LDCs in recent years.[36] Furthermore, foreign firms in many developing countries are important and increasingly significant exporters of manufactured goods. In Brazil, for example, 43 percent of the manufactured exports were produced by multinational firms in 1969—an increase from 34 percent in 1967. Again citing the Brazilian case, in 1969 a full 71 percent of multinational firm exports went to LAFTA countries while nationally owned Brazilian firms seemed to concentrate more on the markets of the developed countries.[37] Thus it would appear that not only are the multinational firms, which are normally based in the developed countries, important producers of LDC exports, especially manufactures, but that such firms may be even more important as participants in inter-LDC trade. As with other matters, here again South-South relations are overshadowed by what is essentially a North-South interaction—the operation of developed country firms in the developing countries.

International investment

While most multinational firms are based in the developed countries, and while at present there is relatively little direct private investment by LDCs in other

---

[35] See Tracy Murray, "How Helpful is the Generalized System of Preferences to Developing Countries," *Economic Journal* 83 (June 1973): 449-55.

[36] See Gerald K. Helleiner, "Manufactured Exports from Less Developed Countries and Multinational Firms," *Economic Journal* 83 (March 1973): 21-47.

[37] Fernando Fajnzylber, *Sistema Industrial e Exportacão de Manufaturados: Anàlise da Experiência Brasileria,* IPEA/INPES Relatorio de Pesquisa No. 7 (Rio de Janeiro: Ministério do Planejamento e Coordenação Geral, 1971), pp. 209, 238. In all fairness, it can be argued that the Brazilian example may not be representative in that many foreign firms are reported to have initiated or expanded their Brazilian operations with the hope of supplying the LAFTA market at least partially from Brazil.

LDCs, it appears that at least some of the more advanced developing countries are increasing these investments. Direct investments abroad are being made by some large Brazilian, Mexican, and Indian firms, although the magnitude of these investments must still be considered tiny. Thus the principal interactions between LDC business establishments are vertical in nature, taking place between the LDC subsidiary and the home office. To a lesser extent, there also may be some contact between a firm's subsidiaries in several developing countries. Yet even here the interactions are tempered by the fundamental North-South relationship.

In addition to interactions between business establishments, international investment relationships can take place on an interstate or a public-private level. Here again these interactions are primarily of a North-South character. Little direct public investment has been made by the LDCs in other developing countries, although there may be a slow but steady growth of such investments. Recently, for example, the Brazilian state oil company's international division, Braspetro, made a substantial investment in Iraq, and the Brazilians are increasing their public investments in such neighboring countries as Bolivia and Paraguay.

At present there are rather meager relations, with the exception of the Andean nations, between LDC governments concerned with the operation of multinational firms in their respective countries. To attract foreign investors, the LDCs usually have offered a host of inducements, including such incentives as tax rebates and exemptions, subsidized credit, and import privileges at overvalued exchange rates. Should the competition of the LDCs for foreign investment in foot-loose, export-oriented industries become more intense, there is a real risk that the developing countries will sacrifice a considerable part of the potential benefits that might be expected from such multinational firm operations. The value of cooperation among the LDCs is clear, but the obstacles to agreement are equally apparent.

As with producers alliances, the obstacles reflect the fact that intransigence on the part of an individual country may be more beneficial for it than collusion. As demonstrated by the UNCTAD III meetings, the growth of multinational firms in the LDCs has resulted in a growing concern and an increased interest among the LDCs in cooperating in their attempts to regulate the large firms based in their countries.[38] To stimulate such cooperation, some form of international or regional organization is required. Perhaps UNCTAD will prove to be the appropriate instrument, although regional cooperation may be easier to arrange at first. The Andean Group of LAFTA, for example, already has implemented common ground rules governing the treatment of foreign capital and the activities of foreign firms.[39]

Another subject capable of inspiring consensus among the developing countries relating to international investment and technological transfer concerns the

---

[38] For a discussion of UNCTAD III and the multinational firm, see Walter Krause, "The Implications of UNCTAD III for Multinational Enterprise," *Journal of Inter-American Studies and World Affairs* 15 (February 1973): 46-59.

[39] See "A Common Andean Group System for the Treatment of Foreign Capital," *Comercio Exterior de México* 17 (March 1971): 4-6.

\
regulation of patents. It is obvious that the developed countries in general, and the multinational firms in particular, derive benefits from the existing patent system. It is not clear, however, that the developing countries are beneficiaries of this system. Yet many developing countries belong to the International Union for the Protection of Industrial Property.[40] Greater cooperation on the part of the LDCs conceivably could be instrumental in obtaining greater benefits for the Third World as a whole through reform of the patent system.

Aid

Until recently the LDCs provided little economic assistance to each other. However, the more powerful developing countries have begun to use economic assistance to establish and maintain client-patron relationships in the areas that they consider to be their spheres of influence. Brazil has extended economic assistance to a large number of Latin American nations; Mexico has provided credits to several Central American countries; India has financed projects in Nepal; and Egypt has in the past given some assistance to the African countries.[41] In recent years, petroleum-producing Arab countries, bloated with oil revenues, have emerged as growing donor countries, but such assistance has mostly gone to other Arab countries. With the possible exception of the oil producers, South-South aid is largely of a token nature and is provided within a political subsystem.

Certainly this assistance is not very significant when compared to the aid provided by the developed nations and various international organizations. Yet this may not remain so. First, if the economic difficulties currently confronting many of the developed countries grow worse, economic assistance may be one of the first casualties, particularly if certain developing countries are blamed for these problems. Secondly, as some LDCs become wealthier they may wish to use their new riches to purchase status and political and strategic influence. This could be done, in part, through the provision of economic assistance. However, as stated previously, this will not ensure Third World harmony. The poorer LDCs surely will not be pleased if a redistribution of international income leaves them insolvent and causes them merely to exchange one patron for another.

To date most LDC donors have chosen to distribute their aid on a bilateral basis to neighboring countries. There does appear, however, to be some interest in the utilization of multilateral channels. Iran, for example, has pledged $1 billion for the purchase of World Bank bonds and for IMF short-term balance-of-payments

---

[40] For a presentation of some of the issues involved, see Edith Penrose, "International Patenting and the Less Developed Countries," *Economic Journal* 83 (September 1973): 768-86. As of the early 1970s, 42 members of the International Union for the Protection of Industrial Property were developing countries, representing over one-half of the total membership.

[41] Recently, however, Egypt has terminated its limited foreign aid program and has become a major recipient of aid from other LDCs, i.e., other Arab countries. This aid has been used to subsidize Egypt's war efforts and to defray losses inflicted by the war.

loans.[42] Nevertheless, the newly prosperous LDCs have been slow to recognize that they have a responsibility for nations outside their own regions.[43]

Given the nature of aid and the reason for which it is frequently given, the developing countries, while having a basis for consensual interactions among themselves, possess very little collective bargaining power to effectively extract increased assistance from the developed countries. Although the LDCs, using UNCTAD as a podium, for example, can forcefully argue that it is desirable for the developed countries to increase or maintain their present aid commitments, the provision of aid is really a question that will be decided ultimately by the developed countries themselves, and one that will be based on the domestic economic and political requirements of those countries as well as on foreign policy considerations. Naturally, if the more powerful LDCs demonstrate an unwillingness to assist their sister countries in a generous manner, it may become more difficult for certain developed countries to convince their populations of the desirability of providing even as much assistance as they are now donating to the LDCs.

Conclusions

While interactions among the LDCs are increasing steadily, they are still far less influential than North-South relations. Readers in the developed countries may find this assertion controversial; however, we believe that it accurately represents the view shared by the LDCs. Direct international monetary relations, investment flows, and aid transfers among the LDCs remain relatively small. Only in the case of trade is there significant direct interaction among the LDCs, and, as we have argued, even here the greatest present, and perhaps potential, exchange is North-South in character.

While direct South-South international economic relations remain very limited, direct inter-LDC relations constitute only one form of interactions among LDCs. There are many issues of substance and importance in their relations with developed countries that are amenable to inter-LDC discussion and agreement. These questions have been discussed by the LDCs, and joint positions have been assumed at times. In fact, a new pattern of South-South interactions, conflictual as

[42] Juan de Onis, "$ 1-Billion for Poor Lands is Pledged by Shah of Iran," *New York Times*, 22 February 1974, p. 1.
[43] A good expression of such an attitude is found in a recent statement by Mr. Mostafa Mansouri, director general of petroleum at the Iranian Ministry of Finance. When asked whether Iran would take measures to offset the higher cost of oil for the LDCs, he replied: "Industrial countries have to take care of those who are developing. . . . The fact that they [the LDCs] have no resources—that is not our fault." *New York Times*, 19 December 1973, p. 15. Kuwait has announced that most of its financial aid will be distributed to the Arab countries and other Moslem nations, particularly those in Africa. Mr. Abdel-Rahman Salem al-Atiki, Kuwait's minister of oil and finance, has stated: "Nobody looked at the Arabs before. Why does everybody expect us now to be the godfather?" See Juan de Onis, "Kuwait to Invest Riches in Arab Channels," *New York Times*, 7 March 1974, p. 1.

well as consensual, has been emerging in recent years as the LDCs have sought to improve their bargaining position vis-à-vis the industrialized countries.

Some LDCs are rapidly gaining wealth and status at present, and a few of them may join the ranks of the developed nations within this century. However, in the transitional period, some LDCs will seek alliances with the developed countries in an effort to prevent economic and political penetration by local leviathans, while others will attempt to benefit from the growing strength of their neighbors by accepting the role of client states.

A major cause of the growth of South-South relations has been the discovery by the LDCs that they confront common problems in their relations with the North. International and regional organizations have played a major role in aggregating LDC interests. Differences have been settled and joint positions articulated. Given the weakness of traditional bilateral interstate relations among the developing countries, these organizations may bear a still larger, and increasingly important, burden in the future conduct of South-South relations. Nevertheless, the situation is fluid. The LDCs are not immune from power politics, and bilateral arrangements may be preferred in some instances.

We have discussed South-South relations and the international economic system within the framework suggested in the first essay in this volume. While we do not feel that these relations are as important in today's world as many other observers do, we think South-South interactions will have increasing significance. Although a consideration of methodology is beyond the scope of this volume, the development of a methodological approach for the study of these interactions is necessary and an interdisciplinary effort is required.

The so-called new political economy of political scientists presents some possibilities for an appropriate interdisciplinary or supradisciplinary approach. It encompasses both analysis of the allocation and exchange of scarce resources (economic, social, and political) as well as consideration of the exercise of authority and the competition for authority.[44] Since South-South relations primarily concern the quest for authority and the redistribution of the world's resources, a consideration of these relations from the perspective of the new political economy may be particularly productive.

---

[44] Norman T. Uphoff and Warren F. Ilchman, eds., *The Political Economy of Development* (Berkeley: University of California Press, 1972), p. 1.

Table 3. Intra-LAFTA exports according to commodity group; 1966 and 1970

Commodity group	Total LAFTA country exports (millions of US $)		LAFTA country exports to LAFTA countries (millions of US $)		Share of exports to LAFTA countries in total LAFTA country exports (%)		LAFTA country share of total world exports (%)	
	1966	1970	1966	1970	1966	1970	1966	1970
Food, beverages, and tobacco (SITC 0-1)	3,720	4,760	320	390	8.6	8.2	11.4	11.5
Crude materials excl. fuels; oils and fats (SITC 2-4)	1,880	2,210	110	205	5.9	9.3	7.2	6.7
Mineral fuels and related materials (SITC 3)	2,670	3,170	220	185	8.2	5.8	14.3	11.0
Chemicals (SITC 5)	170	220	47	56	27.6	25.5	1.3	1.0
Machinery and transport equipment (SITC 7)	85	255	53	115	62.4	45.1	0.2	0.3
Other manufactured goods (SITC 6+8)	1,240	1,920	135	280	10.9	14.6	2.2	2.1
Total manufactures (SITC 5, 6, 7 + 8)	1,495	2,395	235	451	15.7	18.8	1.2	1.2
TOTAL	9,780	12,790	940	1,250	9.6	9.8	4.8	4.1
Percentage of manufactures in total (%)	15.3	18.7	25.0	36.1	–	–	–	–

SOURCE: United Nations, *Monthly Bulletin of Statistics* 26, no. 7 (July 1972): xx-xxxvi.
SITC = Standard International Trade Classification.

Table 4. Commodity and market structure of exports for Brazil, Egypt, and India (in millions of US dollars)

Commodity groups	Developed countries	Centrally planned economies	Developing countries	Total for commodity group
Brazil (1970)				
Total primary products (SITC 0-4)	2,009.4	121.3	275.7	2,406.3
Total manufactures (SITC 5-8)	128.7	3.0	174.8	306.3
Total exports	2,138.1	124.3	450.5	2,712.6
Egypt (1970)				
Total primary products (SITC 0-4)	148.1	305.1	10.0	554.3
Total manufactures (SITC 5-8)	27.0	141.9	64.7	233.7
Total exports	175.1	447.0	165.7	788.0
India (1968)				
Total primary products (SITC 0-4)	469.9	179.6	55.1	702.9
Total manufactures (SITC 5-8)	521.6	121.7	251.7	895.1
Total exports	991.5	301.3	306.8	1,598.0

SOURCES: SEEF, *Comércio Exterior do Brasil, 1970;* Maurice Girgis, "Sources of Industrial Growth in Egypt, 1950-1970," *Die Weltwirtschaft,* July 1973, in German; and Ranadev Banerji, *Exports of Manufactures from India: A Prospective Appraisal of the Emerging Pattern* (Tubingen: J.C.B. Mohr, forthcoming in 1975). The authors are grateful to Maurice Girgis and Ranadev Banerji for providing them with access to their worksheet data.
SITC = Standard International Trade Classification.

The economics and politics
of East-West relations

Franklyn D. Holzman and Robert Legvold

Conceived modestly, the idea of East-West interdependence offers a convenient framework for exploring the intersection of politics with economics, of national economic goals with international economic relations, and, ultimately, of East-West efforts to increase economic cooperation with Western efforts to restructure international economic institutions. By *interdependence* we do not mean to imply a decisive set of arrangements, capable of impinging on the most fundamental economic and political choices of the other party. Rather, we have in mind a lesser level of mutual dependence in which both or all parties view cooperation as a useful but not a decisive means for pursuing some or all of their essential economic goals. More simply, we use the term because, better than any other, it underscores the difference between an economic relationship imposed by political confrontation, and reflected in economic warfare and autarky, and an economic relationship benefiting from the easing of political tension, evident in a common recognition of gains, political as well as economic, to be had from cooperation.

Our primary focus is on the interaction of forces favoring and those obstructing a significant level of East-West economic cooperation—on the "dialectics" of interdependence. The first part of this essay introduces Soviet and East European reasons for wishing to increase their economic involvement with the West. Their eagerness to improve efficiency and growth by importing Western technology, capital, and technique constitutes a major, perhaps the major, *economic* impetus to interdependence. And it provides a justification, beyond the limitations of our individual expertise, for writing this article largely from the perspective of Soviet and East European interests.

In contrast, the second part weighs the fundamental impediments placed on the process of promoting interdependence by the organization and operation of the centrally planned economies. Again, our emphasis is on the Soviet Union and Eastern Europe, because we think that the techniques of central planning in these

Franklyn D. Holzman is a professor of economics at Tufts University and Robert Legvold is an associate professor of political science at Tufts University in Medford, Massachusetts.

economies ultimately raise the most significant *economic* obstacles to an extensive interdependence.

In the third and fourth parts of this essay, we turn our attention to the parallel political impulse to and limits on growing interdependence. Part three examines the effect of a changing international order on East-West economic cooperation; part four examines the obstacles still posed by East-West competition and expressed in terms of national security. In both, we have made an attempt to assess the way that these environmental forces and constraints are refracted through each side's foreign policymaking process. Although the approach is comparative in these two sections, the comparison features the Soviet-American relationship.

In the fifth part we broaden our approach somewhat. In order to deal with the politics or dynamics of interdependence, several questions need to be raised. The issues become: (1) the calculations and strategies by which each side draws the most advantage from interdependence, (2) the shape this is likely to give to interdependence, and (3) the impact of East-West interdependence on other dimensions, including the process of institutionalizing a more coherent and stable international economic system. This yields in part six to a discussion of the consequences of increased economic cooperation between East and West for general monetary and trade-supporting institutions and, conversely, the significance of new international economic institutions for a growing East-West economic cooperation.

Interdependence and communist domestic economic goals

One key to understanding the present Eastern interest in expanding trade and investment with the West is the potential relationship between this trade and investment and the domestic economic goals of these nations. The major domestic economic goals of the Eastern nations are much the same as those of the Western nations, although they differ in the relative weights attached to them and in the intensity with which they are pursued. The greater intensity with which the Eastern nations pursue most of their goals is partly a function of the fact that in centrally planned economies, the responsibility for national economic goals clearly lies with the governments (since there are no significant private enterprise sectors), which in turn usually employ more direct means of implementing these goals than do Western governments. In what follows, we distinguish six domestic economic goals, viz., rapid growth, efficiency, full employment, price stability, a fairly equitable income distribution, and quality of life. We argue that economic interdependence with the West is desired as a means of achieving the first two of these goals but that it is either irrelevant or secondary to the achievement of the last four.

The major goal of the USSR in the prewar period was rapid growth. After World War II, following the Soviets, the Eastern European nations all adopted rapid growth as their major goal. Typically, rapid growth has been equated with industrialization. When, in the Council of Mutual Economic Cooperation (COMECON), an attempt was made by the USSR around 1960 to substitute international division of labor for universal industrialization, Rumania rejected the proposal because it meant sacrificing rapid industrialization for the privilege of remaining an exporter of agricultural and other raw material products. Undoubtedly, Eastern Europe would have looked to the West in the postwar period for much of the machinery, equipment, and technology it needed had this been possible. It was, of course, largely precluded by the cold war and the virtual semiembargo by the West on trade with the East, especially trade in products that might contain advanced technology or have strategic significance.[1] A new division of labor developed among the COMECON nations, in which East Germany and Czechoslovakia became the major suppliers of machinery and equipment. Rapid growth through industrialization appeared to have been a successful strategy in the 1950s, for, as a group, the COMECON nations achieved an average annual growth of GNP of almost 6 percent.[2] The 1960s, however, were a different story. Even by official figures, the rate of growth of GNP declined relative to the 1950s by more than two percentage points on the average.[3]

Why have Eastern growth rates declined? The answers to this question may help us to understand Eastern motives in seeking greater East-West economic interdependence in the past decade. Economic growth in the 1950s was *extensive* rather than *intensive*. That is to say, it was due more to a rapid increase in employment and reallocation of factors of production than to an increase in the productivity of factors of production in the existing economic structure. Central planning authorities equipped with enormous powers put unemployed workers to work, moved underemployed peasants out of agriculture and into higher productivity industry, and generated very high rates of investment by reducing the share in GNP of consumption. (The less developed COMECON countries also gained by importing technology from the more advanced nations of the bloc.) However, the gains from reducing unemployment and from restructuring the economy are, of course, one-time gains; and, as Abram Bergson has demonstrated, it takes continually higher rates of investment, in the absence of changes in technology and the like, to achieve a given rate of growth as an economy develops.[4] Apparently, the exhaustion of possible large-scale gains from extensive growth was a major factor in the slowdown of the 1960s.

Evidence that intensive growth had not yet substituted for extensive growth is provided by data on changes in factor productivity. Labor productivity grew much more slowly in Eastern than in Western Europe and Japan, and capital

[1] Under Soviet pressure, the Eastern bloc was also consciously redirecting its trade inward. In our opinion, the pace of trade redirection in strategic products was dictated more by the West than by the East.

[2] Maurice Ernst, "Postwar Economic Growth in Eastern Europe," in US Congress, Joint Economic Committee, *New Directions in the Soviet Economy, Part IV,* 89th Cong., 2nd sess., 1966, p. 880.

[3] The average hides a wide variance, however, which ranges from a 6 pecentage point drop in the case of East Germany (10.4 to 4.4) to a ½ percent drop in the case of Hungary. Cited in Robert Campbell, *The Soviet-Type Economies: The Performance and Evolution,* 3rd ed. (Boston: Houghton Mifflin Co., 1974), p. 120.

[4] Abram Bergson, "Toward a New Growth Model," *Problems of Communism* 22 (March-April 1973): 1-9.

productivity actually *declined* in Eastern Europe from 1961 to 1967, a fact recognized and discussed by Eastern as well as Western economists.[5] Bergson estimates that Soviet increases in GNP per unit of labor and capital (total factor productivity) declined from 1.7 percent per year during 1950-58 to 0.7 percent during 1958-67.[6] In short, the Eastern nations have been unsuccessful at intensive growth—at raising productivity levels—because they are inefficient. Central planning with direct controls and without the use of effective prices and markets can achieve extensive growth but is relatively inefficient in promoting intensive growth.

To achieve intensive growth, the goals of growth and efficiency must be joined. In earlier years, efficiency was largely ignored as a goal.[7] Now that continued rapid growth appears to depend on increasing economic efficiency, particularly in the more advanced socialist nations, efficiency has come to the fore. Greater efficiency is what the reforms in Eastern Europe and the USSR of the past five to ten years have been all about. Greater efficiency encompasses many facets of the Eastern economies, such as insuring that supplies get delivered on time to the enterprises to which they have been allocated, reducing the number of unfinished investment projects, providing consumers not only with enough shoes but also with the right mix of styles and sizes, reducing the output of products no longer being purchased, improving the quality of products, obtaining reasonable gains from foreign trade, and so forth. More directly relevant to growth, greater efficiency also encompasses properly selecting investment projects, developing new technology, and, once having new technology available, getting enterprises to adopt it. We cannot stop at this point to explain all these problems in detail; some are discussed more fully in the next sections. We will say a few words about the question of technology, however, since it is important to our inquiry.

The major reason that plant managers did not introduce new technology in the prereform system was that they had no monetary incentive to do so. Their bonuses were tied to the achievement of output targets. If new technology increased the level of possible output, targets would be raised, leaving the manager no better off than before. Further, changes in technology were often risky—a learning period might be required during which bonuses would be sacrificed, and changes in supply channels might be involved (and these have often been difficult to arrange in a rigid supply system). As for the development of new technology in the first place, the problem has also been organizational. In the communist countries, there is a separation between research and development units and producing enterprises. Thus, there has been no constant feedback between the two as there is in most large Western enterprises. In fact, the research and development people in an industry

---

[5] Thad Alton, "Economic Structure and Growth in Eastern Europe," US Congress, Joint Economic Committee, *Economic Developments in Eastern Europe* 91st Cong., 2nd sess., 1970, pp. 63 and 42.

[6] See Bergson, "Toward a New Growth Model," p. 3.

[7] In fact, efficiency was sacrificed to the goal of growth in the USSR in the thirties and in Eastern Europe in the fifties. At one time or another, all of the socialist goals but full employment have been sacrificed to growth.

may be quite divorced from the problems of the industry and may be working on projects that are of little or no interest to the relevant enterprises.[8]

The reforms that have been partially directed at increasing innovation and encouraging adoption of new technology do not appear to be very successful. As we show later, with the exception of Hungary, the reforms are conservative in the sense that they have been mostly designed to improve the existing system of planning with direct controls rather than to change the system radically by introducing markets, prices, and decentralized decision making. They are conservative because a radical reform that substituted market for controls would, in effect, be substituting the market for many of the people who implement the controls, namely, the Party hierarchy. Moreover, allowing greater freedom of managerial decision making with reliance on market forces would undoubtedly threaten to spread to other sectors (e.g., If managers had more decision-making power, would not the unions attempt to increase their powers commensurately?) with an eventual possible impact on the nature of government control, the structure of power, and political freedom.

One other objective of the reforms needs to be mentioned here, namely, the desire to increase the static gains from trade. This has several facets, one of which is relevant to this section. One consequence of central planning with direct controls is that enterprises have little incentive to put out high quality products. This applies to intrabloc as well as to domestic trade. Thus, enterprises prefer to import from the West where possible rather than from Eastern partners, particularly those products whose quality can vary substantially and where the requirements of the importer can only be satisfied if the exporter takes special pains.

Interest in trade with the West, then, has increased partly because of dissatisfaction with intrabloc trade, but more importantly because of its potential contribution to growth and efficiency goals. This is particularly the case since the internal economic reforms for the most part are too conservative to remove deficiencies in the development and adoption of new technology. Even if they could be more successful, the socialist countries are sufficiently far behind the West in most sectors that importing technology makes good sense anyway. (A congressional study published in 1966 concluded that the USSR lagged behind the US by some 25 years in overall level of technology.[9]) Perhaps the import of technology is also, as we explore later, a means of avoiding more radical reform, at least for those entrenched elements that feel threatened by far-reaching reform. Finally, the Eastern nations are hopeful of financing imports of technology through credits in

---

[8] This portrayal of the difficulties that the socialist nations have in generating and absorbing new technology does not apply to high priority industries such as military and aerospace. In these industries, people in research and development and producers work closely together. Enterprises have no choice but to adopt whatever new technology is developed. Differences between technologies are often qualitatively important, and old technology is not acceptable. Plant managers in these industries do not have to worry about disruption of supplies with changed methods, since the industries have first priority on whatever materials are needed.

[9] Michael Boretsky, "Comparative Progress in Technology, Productivity, and Economic Efficiency: USSR versus USA," in US Congress, Joint Economic Committee, *New Directions in the Soviet Economy, Part II-A,* 89th Cong., 2nd sess., 1966, p. 149.

order to bridge both their "foreign exchange" and "savings" gaps. The foreign exchange gap is discussed in the next section; the savings gap stems in part from the fact that the output goals of the socialist nations are usually excessive, as well as from the declining marginal productivity of capital.

How much do the Eastern nations stand to gain from greater trade and investment with the West? The gains can come in four forms: increased efficiency of domestic industry stimulated by foreign competition, including further international division of labor; gains from the better quality and variety of products imported from the West; gains from the import of capital (i.e., borrowing); and gains from the import of technology. Unfortunately, none of these can be estimated very accurately. In order to suggest rough orders of magnitude, we present some mechanical calculations for the USSR. Before proceeding to these, it should be noted that it is not possible to measure the very important kinds of gains in domestic efficiency stimulated by foreign competition. However, it is hardly necessary to do so here, since, with the possible exception of Hungary, the central planners effectively protect domestic industries against competition from abroad and thereby exclude the possibilities of such gains. Only radical domestic reforms can change this situation. We turn now to some simple estimates.

Total Soviet trade is in the neighborhood of $15 billion each way, of which a little more than 20 percent, or $3 billion, is with the industrial West. Suppose that trade with the industrial West were to double (increase by $3 billion each way) at the expense of trade with Eastern Europe. Suppose that the gains from trade with Eastern Europe are 33.3 percent and that this were to double (or triple) by diverting trade to the industrial West. The total gain to the Soviets, under these favorable assumptions, would be $1 billion (or $2 billion) a year. These figures must be put in the perspective of an annual GNP of $600 billion.

Suppose now that the Soviet Union were able to obtain credits amounting to some $20 billion over a five-year period, or $4 billion a year. Since gross investment at present is roughly a little below $200 billion, these credits would increase investment by a little more than 2 percent. With GNP increasing by about $30 billion a year, a 2 percent increase in gross investment each year could be responsible for a maximum increase in output of $0.6 billion a year for each of five years and thereafter until depreciated (assuming no difference in the technology embodied in the investment financed by credit as compared to other investment). We say *maximum* because this calculation ignores the contribution to output of labor and other factors. Further, credit repayments would eventually have to be made out of the increments to output.

Suppose now that the credits involved, additionally, the introduction of new technology. Since the technology would have to be paid for out of the credits, the increment to investment would be reduced but the increase in output from each $1 million worth of investment would be greater. How much greater is anyone's guess. We can say no more than to point out that the prospective annual increase in output, taking account of all benefits and costs, would be somewhat greater than in the previous example. And an increase in output of, say, $1 billion a year implies an increase in growth rate from 5 percent ($30 billion/$600 billion) to 5.16 percent; an increase in output of $2 billion implies an increase in growth rate to 5.33 percent;[10] and so forth.

Under the assumed (favorable) conditions, it is clear that the projected gains to the USSR from more trade and investment with the West are substantial and very much worth striving for. A nation whose economy is always stretched taut and overcommitted will appreciate any additional resources that become available. On the other hand, a few billion dollars here or there is not going to make or break the USSR, nor will it substantially affect its declining rates of growth of output and of factor productivity.[11] As noted earlier, growth rates cannot be affected substantially by a small increase in the rate of investment. And while improvements in technology can affect growth rates, to do so on a significant scale requires more than just selected imports in particular industries; rather, what seems to be required, in our opinion, is a radical reform that not only would encourage indigenous development of all kinds of new technology but would also encourage the adoption of this technology by enterprises throughout the economy.

The smaller nations of Eastern Europe stand to gain somewhat more from increased economic interdependence with the West. This is because, being small nations, they all trade a much larger percentage of their GNPs than does the USSR. Further, being small nations, loans and technology from the West could conceivably be available on a more significant scale than is likely to be the case for the giant USSR. On the other hand, Western enterprises and governments may be more wary of making credit and technology available on a large scale to the smaller Eastern nations because, not having attractive exportables like oil and gas, they are not so good a long-run credit risk as the USSR.

What about the other goals? Full employment of labor and stable prices have always been very high priority goals of the socialist nations. These goals are much easier to achieve under socialism than under capitalism because of the greater power of the state to exercise direct controls—to employ the unemployed and to set wages and prices. Further, the socialist nations' achievement of these two goals is quite unrelated to the international sector. There is no temptation or need ever to resort to "beggar-thy-neighbor" devices to achieve full employment; nor is domestic employment ever threatened by imports, since domestic industries are thoroughly protected from competition. And, with the exception of Hungary, internal prices are not organically related to world prices, nor are they affected by trade in general as is the case under capitalism. However, it is important to note that the protection of domestic employment and internal prices from disturbance by external forces impedes radical reforms from opening the socialist economies to foreign competition and increased international interdependence.

---

[10] We have not considered the case of an import of technology without credits. In this case, the gains would come only from the increase in capital productivity; there would be no increase in the rate of investment. Note: examples in the preceding three paragraphs are based approximately on 1972.

[11] Soviet planners may, of course, have unrealistic perceptions (from our viewpoint) of the possible gains from East-West trade and investment.

A just distribution of income within and between nations is a more explicit goal of socialist than of capitalist nations. The distribution of income within the nation is a purely internal matter, and it is neither affected by nor does it affect economic relations with other nations. Within COMECON, the explicit goal is ultimate equalization of living standards between nations. While some equalization has taken place over the past twenty years, this appears to have resulted from the simple fact that developing countries tend to grow faster than more advanced nations, rather than from positive policies.

Some positive policies have been pursued, however. For many years, technology, blueprints, and the like were disseminated freely in COMECON, which means that they moved from the more advanced to the less advanced nations. There have also been capital flows between COMECON nations, but on a relatively small scale and not always from richer to poorer. These capital flows usually do contain an element of subsidy or aid, however, because of the very low interest rates charged—from 2 to 4 percent. It has been estimated that total loans granted among all socialist nations for 1945 to 1969 amounted to only $10 billion, or less than $500 million a year. This amounts to a very small fraction of 1 percent of donors' GNPs in comparison with official loans and grants by major Western nations of perhaps two-thirds of 1 percent. Further, the capital flows in COMECON appear to have been dictated as much by economic factors as by "justice." China, perhaps the poorest socialist nation, was the second largest lender.[12] To sum up, distributional equity appears to rank low as a motive for trade and investment by socialist nations.

Quality of life is certainly a socialist goal. It is difficult, however, to pin down its dimensions and the intensity with which it is pursued. If we look at crude proxies, it might be argued that the more equal distribution of income in socialist countries as well as their greater emphasis, at given levels of per capita GNP, on expenditures on health and education and on subsidization of the arts are indicators of greater concern with quality. On the other hand, the relatively high rates of investment, low ratios of consumption to GNP, and crowded urban living conditions are indicators in the opposite direction.

As far as specific quality factors, such as pollution, congestion, environmental destruction, and the like, are concerned, the socialist nations are in much better shape than the Western industrialized nations for at least two reasons. First, they are much less industrialized and also have not allowed mass ownership of private automobiles. Second, they believe in "keeping their streets clean" and have enough unemployed marginal workers to do this at almost no cost to society. On the other hand, socialism provides no automatic solutions to the environmental and pollution problems that industrialization generates, and every horror story in the West has its counterpart in the East. It turns out that the structure of incentives in socialist

---

[12] All Soviet bloc figures in this paragraph were estimated from Janos Horvath, "Grant Elements in Intra-Bloc Aid Programs," *The ASTE Bulletin* 13 (Fall 1971): 1-18. The Western estimates cited were for the 1962-65 period and were taken from Raymond Mikesell, *The Economics of Foreign Aid* (Chicago: Aldine Publishing Co., 1968), p. 241.

enterprises is such that socialist plant managers are no more motivated to stop polluting than are private entrepreneurs. And socialist governments have been no more effective than those in the West in applying corrective measures.[13]

Quality of life goals provide little or no Eastern incentive to greater East-West trade or investment. It is leading to East-West cooperation, however. In 1972, a US-USSR Joint Committee on Cooperation in the Field of Environmental Protection was formed with 30 joint projects; and a twelve-nation East-West International Institute of Applied Systems Analysis was established, which will investigate, among other things, pollution control.

Thus, the incentive for increased trade with the West is explained primarily by the desire of the Eastern nations to maintain growth rates and enhance efficiency through import of capital and technology, as well as to improve the quality of products they import in everyday commodity trade. The gains from trade that would be forthcoming from radical economic reforms, which would open the Eastern economies to foreign competition, are voluntarily forgone. In this regard, the goals of full employment and stable prices can be regarded as impediments to greater interdependence, although they are probably of less importance than factors relating to internal power politics.

Economic impediments to interdependence

In this section we explore the limits to interdependence posed by the economic mechanisms employed by the Eastern nations to run their economies. Some of these factors were alluded to above; here we consider them more systematically.

Stalinist model

The major difference between capitalist and communist economic mechanisms is the much greater reliance by communist states on direct controls rather than on market mechanisms in the allocation of resources. Before the economic reform movement of the late 1960s, output goals for major commodities of all the Eastern nations were established by the central authorities, individual output targets were set for enterprises or groups of enterprises, and supply plans specified to whom enterprises were to ship their outputs and from whom they were to procure their material (nonlabor) inputs. The difficulties in planning and coordinating flows of many hundreds, even thousands, of commodities between hundreds of thousands of enterprises cannot be exaggerated. Nor can we exaggerate the problems raised by errors in the plan or unforeseen events. For example, suppose it appears that the steel target will be underfulfilled by one million tons. To increase

[13] See, for example, Marshall Goldman, "The Convergence of Environmental Disruption," *Science,* 2 October 1970, pp. 37-42.

steel output, it is necessary to increase inputs (hence outputs) of coal, limestone, machinery, labor, and so forth. But more coal, limestone, and machinery require more steel, labor, etc.—and, again, more coal, limestone, and machinery, and so forth. Any error or shortfall in any single output or flow in the interrelated matrix of transactions affects many other sectors or flows and constitutes a nightmare for the planners.

Second, output and supply-planning problems have been exacerbated by the fact that, in practice, planning has chronically amounted to overfull employment planning. That is to say, the plans are drawn too taut, with insufficient allowance for reserves, errors, shortfalls in productivity, and so forth. The result is that output targets never can all be achieved with projected supplies of inputs and productivity changes; in effect, demand is greater than supply, as with inflation in a free-market economy. This condition, of and by itself, is serious. And, as noted, it complicates still further the coordination problems (described above) that are faced by the central planners.[14]

Third, commodity prices in the Eastern bloc nations are usually described as irrational. They are set by the planners, remain fixed for long periods of time, and are not usually market-clearing prices. Not only is demand largely ignored, but the cost or supply side is rendered a poor guide to price setting because of improper accounting for rent, interest, and profits (reflecting a lack of markets for nonlabor factors of production), extensive use of subsidies and sales taxes, and adherence to average rather than to marginal cost pricing. With prices so irrational, planners must, of course, use direct controls to allocate resources; conversely, prices are irrational partly because direct controls rather than decentralized markets are used in allocation.

Foreign trade behavior

From these three features of what might be called Stalinist central planning with direct controls, one can explain several major observable characteristics of the international trade and monetary relations of the communist nations. Later, we consider how the recent internal economic reforms might modify the picture.

Consider first the related problems of inconvertibility and bilateralism. A capitalist nation is forced into currency inconvertibility when its exchange rate is overvalued, causing its residents to want to buy more from other countries than the residents of other countries want to buy from it at the existing rate of exchange. As foreign exchange reserves become exhausted, import controls may be applied and/or residents may be prevented from converting domestic currency into foreign exchange for the purpose of spending abroad; that is to say, currency inconvertibility is introduced. One solution to this problem, of course, is to devalue the

---

[14] Some possible reasons why overfull employment planning is still practiced despite its obvious drawbacks are presented in Franklyn D. Holzman, "Overfull Employment Planning, Input-Output, and the Soviet Economic Reforms," *Soviet Studies* 22 (October 1970): 255-61.

currency, thereby bringing the nation's prices into line with the prices of other nations, and encouraging exports and discouraging imports. The communist nations undoubtedly suffer from this kind of inconvertibility because of overfull employment planning. This is obvious and we need not dwell on the point. They also suffer from another kind of inconvertibility, one that is quite specific to central planning with direct controls, and that yields less easily, if at all, to therapy. This is called *commodity inconvertibility.*

Commodity inconvertibility means not allowing foreigners to spend freely either their own currencies or your currency on commodities in your country. This does not refer, of course, to the consumer products and services purchased by tourists, embassies, foreign press, etc. It refers to the large mass of intermediate products (coal, oil, machinery) and investment goods directly allocated through the central plan. Commodity inconvertibility does not exist under capitalism. Almost everything that is produced and is movable is usually available for export. Central planners, on the other hand, cannot allow foreigners to import freely for two reasons. First, such imports would destroy the carefully drawn fabric of the central supply plan and would bring production to a halt in all enterprises and industries that found themselves deprived thereby of essential inputs. Second, since prices are irrational, allowing foreigners to shop around freely may lead to large national economic losses in the case of products that are, for one reason or another, priced too low. As a result, with the exception of products imported to meet emergency needs, exports and imports are confined largely to those planned in advance for foreign trade.

One consequence of this kind of inconvertibility is bilateralism. No socialist nation is willing to run a surplus with any other socialist nation because of the difficulties in spending the currency earned in either the country of issue or in any other socialist nation. As a result, each socialist nation plans for a bilateral balance in its trade with every other socialist nation. Rigid bilateralism in intrabloc trade substantially reduces the potential volume and efficiency of this trade. Attempts to introduce some multilateralism, such as the establishment of the International Bank for Economic Cooperation (IBEC) and its "transferable ruble," have all been unsuccessful.

The socialist nations are not, of course, bound to bilateralism in the East-West relations. In effect, they can and do spend the hard currencies earned through surpluses with some Western countries in other Western nations. In this respect, they are not significantly different from most smaller Western nations whose currencies are not used in trade. No socialist nation, however, is willing to use its hard currency earnings in intrabloc imports (which, in theory, could serve as a mechanism for multilateralism) because hard currency is usually worth so much more in terms of commodities imported from the West.

Related to inconvertibility and bilateralism are the twin facts that (1) the socialist nations conduct all of their trade, including intrabloc trade, at world prices rather than at their own prices, and (2) their exchange rates are not real prices but simply accounting units. These characteristics stem specifically from the irrationality of internal prices. With the internal prices of each bloc nation irrational, and irrational in differing ways, there exists within the bloc no consistent set of prices upon which the nations can agree for trading purposes. World trading prices are used to fill the gap. Since Western (rather than Eastern) currencies and prices are used in trade, exchange rates are clearly unnecessary: socialist currencies are never exchanged, and internal prices are not reflected through exchange rates in international trade. It is, in any event, impossible to have a meaningful exchange rate between the currencies of two countries where the prices in one or both nations are irrational.

Stemming directly from commodity inconvertibility, and perhaps just another way of looking at it, is what might be termed a *trade aversion* on the part of the socialist nations. There is a tendency on the part of the planners to avoid trade because they fear the disruptions to the plan that might result from possible disruptions to trade. One way of minimizing such disruptions is through the mechanism of annual and long-term trade agreements, and such agreements are part and parcel of the socialist technique of doing international business. This technique largely quiets planners' fears in intrabloc trade, because each party to a trade agreement programs the foreign trade into its annual plan and guarantees exports and imports. However, it does introduce a rigidity in trade which must be considered a drawback. On the other hand, while trade agreements are also made between the two governments in much of East-West trade, the agreements do not provide the planners with the same kind of security as in intrabloc trade. This is because while the Eastern nation stands ready to buy or sell per agreement, the Western government cannot commit its exporters or importers. The most it can do is to bring the parties together and guarantee that it will not place undue obstacles in the way of trade in the form of licenses, quotas, tariffs, etc.

Another consequence (for our purpose) of central planning with direct controls is the redundancy of tariffs. Since decisions regarding the size and composition of imports are part of the central planning process, and since prices are fixed and not necessarily at market-clearing levels, tariffs can affect the outcome no more than exchange rates can. Decisions to import are controlled, in effect, by what might be termed implicit quotas. The tariffs introduced by the socialist nations and used for most-favored-nation (MFN) purposes do not affect what is to be imported, but they may affect from whom the product is imported by discouraging imports from those nations that do not have MFN status.

Finally, an important consequence of Stalinist type central planning is that socialist nations are faced with persistent hard currency deficits and are deprived of the usual means of coming to grips with the problem in the absence of radical reforms. A major factor behind the deficits is the fact that the existing system of planning protects enterprises from the necessity of having to compete. In the first instance, this is due to overfull employment planning, which produces sellers markets. However, the competitive outlook would be blunted anyway in all intermediate product markets (interenterprise transactions) by the fact that products in these markets are not really sold; it is more accurate to say that they are distributed according to plan. Salesmanship is hardly necessary. The same is true of intrabloc foreign trade. As noted earlier, exports and imports conform to intergovernmental trade agreements, and enterprises find themselves delivering goods into predetermined and protected foreign markets. Further, there is rarely any contact between the exporter and the user of the product (hence little or no feedback) since most trade is conducted not by producers of exports and users of imports but by large foreign trade organizations, each representing hundreds of producers and users.

The end result of some twenty years of this collection of arrangements is a reduced ability to sell or compete on world markets, with the exception of relatively homogeneous raw materials. This inability expresses itself in difficulties in adapting to special requirements of Western buyers, and in low quality, poor packaging, poor servicing, poor marketing, inadequate advertising, and so forth. To have a comparative disadvantage in selling is much more of a problem than just having, as every nation does, a comparative disadvantage in a particular range of products, since selling affects virtually all manufactured products. The USSR has, of course, a wide range of raw materials that it can and does export to the West; the other socialist nations are raw material poor and suffer more intensely from the common socialist difficulty in exporting manufactured products.

A Western nation that found itself with balance-of-payments problems for the reason noted above or for any other reason could almost always improve its position by devaluing its currency. Devaluation would lower the prices of its products to foreign buyers and thereby encourage exports. It would also raise the prices of foreign products and would discourage imports. Unfortunately, this very important adjustment mechanism is not available to the socialist nations. As noted above, they trade with each other and with the rest of the world at world prices; their currencies are never exchanged for other currencies; and their exchange rates are not real prices but simply units of account. The obvious result is that a devaluation has absolutely no effect on either exports or imports.

The following question comes to mind: Can the socialist nations simulate a devaluation or its effects? Imports can, of course, always be reduced, but this is a negative solution and not in consonance with the goal of importing more from the West. The effect of a devaluation on exports can be simulated by simply lowering export prices, which would be equivalent to subsidizing the exports. This solution may work when the exports are not in competition with domestic industry in the importing nation. Where there is domestic competition, however, the Eastern nation may find that it has run afoul of Western antidumping regulations. Given their irrational prices and disequilibrium exchange rates, socialist nations cannot refute dumping charges even when subsidies are not being granted. In fact, partly because of the impossibility of refuting dumping charges, it is becoming common in East-West trade agreements, including the October 1972 Soviet-American arrangements, for the Eastern nations simply to agree to withdraw any export causing distress to local Western producers. This type of agreement legislates away the possibility of Eastern price competition in a large range of markets.

Economic reform

From the above, it is clear that Stalinist type central planning has a considerable impact on foreign trade behavior. The question arises as to how the recent planning reforms in Eastern Europe change this picture. Although inspired by similar problems, the nature of reform has varied from country to country as well as over time. The conservative reforms, which include those in all of the Eastern nations except for Hungary and pre-August 1968 Czechoslovakia, have not changed the essential nature of central planning. Prices have been reformed and rationalized somewhat, but they are still set by central planners, are fixed for long periods of time, and are not adjusted for shifts in supply and, especially, demand. Central planning of output and allocation of supplies still exist, even though management bonuses are based on sales rather than on output.[15] Managers have somewhat more flexibility in hiring workers than they had before and somewhat, though not much, more authority in investing retained profits; and part of the burden of central planning and allocation has been decentralized from the central planning boards and ministries to large associations or subministries (but not to enterprises). In effect, the purpose of these reforms has been not to change fundamentally the nature of central planning but rather to prop up the existing system and to make it work more effectively. The irrational prices, direct allocation of resources, and taut planning remain; so also, therefore, do commodity inconvertibility, bilateralism, functionless exchange rates, and convertible currency shortages.

The Hungarian reform (like the earlier Czech reform) is much more radical. Central planning of outputs and allocation of supplies have been eliminated and market forces have been assigned to take over these tasks. In principle, most prices are freely determined by these market forces, and enterprises are free to buy from or sell to other enterprises either in Hungary, in other socialist markets, or in the West—wherever profits are greatest. Profits from sales (purchases) in foreign markets are calculated by using the Hungarian exchange rates. We say exchange rates because, in view of the fact that Hungary must trade in two foreign markets, each with its own price system, it must necessarily convert the prices from each system into Hungarian forints at a different exchange rate.[16] Tariffs in this system presumably function in the same way as tariffs in a market economy. Not only do most-favored-nation rates give a favored nation a competitive advantage over one not so favored, but they also enable that nation's exporters to compete more favorably against Hungary's domestic producers.

Under these circumstances, one would expect the Hungarian economy to have broken the bonds of inconvertibility and bilateralism, and also to have shifted a substantial part of its trade from Eastern to Western partners as enterprise decisions based on market criteria were substituted for planners decisions. Why

---

[15] This was designed to prevent enterprises from producing goods that no one wants and to encourage better quality of output.

[16] This may seem to be in contradiction to our earlier statement that the socialist nations use world prices. In fact, while world prices provide the base for socialist market prices, they are adjusted by the socialist nations and, in general, are somewhat higher.

have these events not materialized? While a definitive explanation cannot be ventured, several possibilities come to mind.

The Hungarian economy operates under a number of serious constraints. Overfull employment still exists, although the method of its implementation is somewhat different. Continued existence of overfull employment probably reflects, at least in part, the importance of the socialist goal of guaranteed employment to all persons able to work. Each person views his job as *his* unless he voluntarily leaves for another job. This makes it very difficult for the Hungarians to free their trade to imports that are competitive with domestic products or, in general, to adapt their economy to foreign trade.

A second constraint, particularly serious in light of the full employment goal, is the apparent fear that no Hungarian government could survive inflation of more than a few percent a year. This view probably reflects the terrible experiences with inflation that Hungary suffered after both world wars, as well as the almost ideological predilection of communist countries for maintaining stable prices over long periods of time. One result of the need to preserve price stability, under what may be called inflationary conditions, has been the need for the government to control most prices despite the intent of the reform, or the New Economic Mechanism (NEM), which was eventually to free all or most prices. This mixture of free and controlled prices over several years of inflationary pressures, however, is likely to reduce the rationality of internal prices and, therefore, their utility in import and export decisions. At some point, a degree of commodity inconvertibility exists and exchange rates are not as "real" prices as they might be. It should also be noted that given overfull employment, Hungary should have the normal balance-of-payments and currency convertibility problems of the sort that beset capitalist nations suffering from inflationary pressures.

A third major constraint facing Hungary is the fact that, for one reason or another, most of its trade is with the other communist nations, all of which introduced very conservative economic reforms and, therefore, have no mechanisms for conducting trade any differently than before. This means that roughly 20 percent of what Hungary produces and consumes is committed to foreign trade by central planners rather than by plant managers. Enterprises, under NEM, cannot be forced or ordered to export or import from another socialist nation just because the government contracted to do so. The government, however, can induce cooperation by subsidies, tax rebates, and taxes—and this it does.[17] This constitutes a very substantial deviation from the principles of market operation.

Two possible explanations are offered for the continued dominance of socialist nations among Hungary's trading partners. First, it may be politically difficult for Hungary to break away more abruptly. Second, it may be very costly in economic terms for Hungary to shift the structure of its trade. Hungary depends

---

[17] Subsidies to exporters, particularly to the West, are also required by the fact that the hard-currency exchange rate (or *multiplier*, as it is called) was set at the average export rate rather than at the marginal export rate (which would have been equal to the marginal import rate in equilibrium).

very heavily on the USSR for energy and other raw material requirements. Under present COMECON pricing arrangements, these needs are met at very favorable prices. Given these favorable terms of trade, it may pay Hungary to continue to trade with socialist nations even though this involves a substantial compromise with the principles of NEM.

Ad hoc solutions

We have now sketched the negative consequences of both Stalinist central planning and the inadequate economic reforms for greater East-West economic interdependence. A full-blown economic reform that would eliminate central planning by direct controls, free prices to be determined in the market, make profits the goal of plant managers, and eliminate inflationary pressures would lead to the elimination of many, if not all, of the characteristics that impede East-West (not to mention intrabloc) trade. It would also, of course, eventually lead to a partial dissolution of COMECON as a tightly knit trading bloc, since many enterprises, free to seek the most advantageous market, would take their business to the West. This may not be possible at the moment for political reasons. Should it become possible at a later date because, say, the USSR wishes to sell its raw materials to the West, and should the other (internal) political obstacles to reform be reduced, then commodity convertibility, unreal exchange rates, and all the rest may die a natural death. This is not going to happen immediately, however, and attempts are being made to cope with these problems with what may be called second-best solutions.

Attempts to solve a number of these problems are embodied in the many different kinds of cooperative agreements that have been entered into by large capitalist enterprises, on the one hand, and by socialist state enterprises, on the other. Perhaps the simplest agreements are those in which the Western firm sells the Eastern firm a license to use its technology or a so-called turnkey plant. In the former, a package of technology is sold to the Eastern enterprise, along with whatever training of labor, etc., is required to use it. In the latter, not only the technology but the entire plant and equipment is put together in ready-to-operate form by the seller; all the purchaser has to do is "turn the key." Sales of franchises are similar, but here it is not so much the know-how that is desired as it is the name, e.g., Hilton or Pepsi-Cola. These three kinds of agreements are relatively simple because they automatically terminate with the completion of the plant or the successful transfer of technology.

More complicated are those agreements in which the participants collaborate in production, marketing, research, or any other industrial activity. At one end of the spectrum, the participants strictly maintain their separate identities and all interrelationships are specified by contract and in dollars and cents. At the other end of the spectrum are the true joint ventures in which Eastern and Western participants form a single new organization that encompasses their activities.[18] The

[18] It has been common to refer loosely to ordinary coproduction and comarketing arrangements as joint ventures.

new organization reflects joint ownership or pooling of assets, joint management, and a sharing of profits and losses. This kind of organization represents the most radical break with the past since it allows Western individuals an equity (always less than 50 percent) in an Eastern enterprise, in effect, private ownership of the means of production. So far, legislation permitting such arrangements has been passed only in Rumania, Hungary, and Yugoslavia. A major difference, it should be noted, between the cooperative agreements and joint ventures, on the one hand, and other forms of cooperation, on the other, is that the former are temporarily open-ended whereas the latter end with the completion of the single project.

Socialist countries enter into these agreements in order to get better access to Western technology and related production and to management know-how, in effect, to improve their hard-currency earning capacities and to obtain capital (credits), particularly hard-currency capital. Clearly, these various forms of collaboration do serve the purposes for which they have been intended by the East. And the coproduction arrangements and joint ventures have the special advantage of giving the Western partner a continuing interest in the efficiency, profitability, and success of the operation.[19] (Western motives can all be subsumed under expansion of profits. This is achieved by expansion of markets [either Eastern or Western], sale of technology already paid for, access to cheap labor supplies, and so forth.)

One other feature of these agreements deserves special mention, namely, the payments arrangements. Payments are always made either in hard currency or in commodities, usually the commodities produced by the venture.[20] Because of commodity inconvertibility, it seems highly unlikely that repayment could ever be in the local Eastern currency.

How successful are or can these arrangements be in meeting the economic needs of the socialist nations? This question cannot be answered with any precision, but it does appear at this juncture that the arrangements are very imperfect substitutes for real economic reforms. Ventures involving import of technology are likely to be the most successful in achieving the desired goals of socialist planners, particularly in the case of the smaller East European nations. Nations of this size must import a lot of technology, in any case, so that reform or no, they probably would not be able to do much better. On the other hand, problems relating to the adoption and spread of technology cannot be solved through international mechanisms but depend on domestic reform for solution. For the USSR, and perhaps for the larger Eastern European nations, import of sufficient technology to compensate for domestic shortcomings could be very expensive in terms of foreign exchange. Further, import of technology may not be feasible in foreign exchange terms in purely domestic industries that are likely to produce neither exportables nor import substitutes in terms of Western markets.

[19] Thus, for example, while a Western enterprise might sell a license for outdated technology to an Eastern country, it would not likely do so if the arrangement was in the form of a joint venture.

[20] An exception is the Pepsi Cola agreement in which payment to the West is, at least in part, in the form of vodka to be resold in the West.

The use of Western partners to assist in the preparation and marketing of products in hard-currency markets makes a lot of sense. However, it has its limitations. First of all, to the extent that Western marketing techniques and production advice must compensate for domestic deficiencies, the Eastern nations are, in effect, paying a high cost for these deficiencies. They lose both part of their profit and part of their potential hard-currency earnings. Second, because of the pervasiveness in the Eastern nations of an inability to produce and sell manufactured products to the West, it seems highly unlikely that cooperative marketing ventures could ever be on a large enough scale to fill the gap.

Finally, the coproduction and joint ventures do provide the Eastern nations with some Western capital. This is as it should be, since the Eastern nations are poorer than the most advanced Western nations and in the normal course of things would have experienced some capital inflow from the latter. "Things" have been abnormal, however, because of the cold war and inconvertibility, and the normal capital flow mechanism ceased functioning after World War II. It is too early to tell how much capital will flow under joint ventures. At the very least, capital flow will be inhibited, except perhaps into those industries that produce potential exportables to the West, such as oil. Moreover, the socialist nations presumably recognize that repayment in a commodity like oil is essentially repayment in hard currency, and, therefore, that the repayment of the capital is, in effect, competing with (or reducing) future hard-currency imports. Second, even the most radical Eastern joint ventures do not give the Western partner the kind of control that is possible for Western multinationals in many countries. This fact may also inhibit the flow of capital.

The great size of the USSR and its special needs for technology and capital raise questions regarding orders of magnitude. The large Siberian oil and gas projects envisage, as a starter, American investments of around $15 billion. The unprecedented size of these projected investments raises some economic issues, but more important it raises the political issue of whether the United States can afford to put so much "hostage" capital into a potential enemy nation. With this in mind, the question that immediately arises is whether it may not be as, or almost as, economical to devote the funds to developing alternative energy sources in the United States.

To sum up, the various ad hoc cooperative arrangements developed over the past decade to overcome the handicaps, both domestic and international, that the Eastern nations suffer as a result of their planning systems are clearly only second-best solutions and are not good substitutes for thoroughgoing reforms. The Eastern nations will continue to lag technologically, to have difficulties in selling manufactured products in the West, to be unable to devalue their currencies effectively, to find it difficult to trade up to the optimum with Western nations because of the planning rigidities, and so forth. On the other hand, so long as they cannot see their way clear to radical reforms, their problems are certainly ameliorated by the new arrangements.

The political impulse to interdependence

In the second part of this essay, we have argued that significant economic obstacles stand in the way of a profound East-West economic interdependence— that, for the moment, the limits to East-West economic interdependence are ultimately economic. If so, however, the reason these limits have never been remotely approached remains political. Politics—not the structure or the economic goals of centrally planned economies—have dictated the pattern and level of economic cooperation. And politics, as much as the economic advantages of increased cooperation, now dictate their change.

The next two sections try to explore the particular way that the economics of East-West relations yield to political considerations: first, by considering the re-alignment of circumstances retarding or promoting interdependence; second, by weighing against the movement toward interdependence the parallel political obstacles. In the first instance, the *political impulse* to interdependence, we are primarily concerned with the effect of the international environment on each side's stake in increased economic cooperation. In turn, the impact of the environment is to be judged both in macro terms (how the change in the environment has altered national preoccupations) and in micro terms (how it has altered the interplay of domestic forces influencing these preoccupations). In the second instance, the *political limits* to interdependence, our concern again has a macro dimension, that is, those sides to East-West relations working against cooperation, and a micro dimension, that is, those impediments added by the configuration of competing interests within each state.

Having pieced together the political context of interdependence, we can then turn to its political dynamics. How does the East or the West go about securing the advantages of interdependence and reducing its inconveniences or risks? How do the political and the economic imperatives, interests, and expectations of any nation interact? What impact does East-West interdependence have on intra-East or intra-West relations? With rudimentary answers to these questions, something can then be said of the kinds and degree of interdependence likely to emerge. Ulti-mately, our interest is in the effect that interdependence could (or should) have on the next generation of international economic institutions and, in turn, the poten-tial effect of these on it.

Few things are more striking about the stakes that the East and the West have in economic cooperation than their asymmetry. The West stresses the political advantages of economic cooperation, the East the economic advantages. At the moment, the West, particularly the United States, is inclined to view expanded trade and investment as a valuable part of the broader process by which the East and the West are to sort out their political relationship and put their signature on whatever international order replaces the bipolar world. The East, on the other hand, sees expanded trade and investment as a convenient way to augment its capital and technological resources.

The contrast, of course, oversimplifies. Neither side draws sharp distinctions between the political and economic advantages of cooperation, and certainly neither emphasizes one to the exclusion of the other. Moreover, the contrast grows more blurred the more dependent a country is on trade. Countries in the West that most rely on trade have usually most resisted subordinating economics to politics. (By this standard, it was natural for Khrushchev, the leader of a country whose imports were approximately 3 percent of national income, to say: "We value trade least for economic reasons and most for political purposes."[21] His successors have not changed their minds because this percentage has changed or will soon, but because they have developed a qualitatively different trade dependency.) Thus the West Europeans never enforced the postwar embargo on strategic goods with the same enthusiasm as the United States, and they were noticeably less thorough in composing their lists of strategic items. Today, while the political significance of East-West economic cooperation counts heavily with them, they are again less inclined than the United States to build a formal strategy around the connection between politics and economics.

Still, the difference exists. The so-called strategy of linkages associated with former President Nixon and Secretary Kissinger merely represents the clearest and most explicit attempt to exploit the East's (especially the Soviet Union's) desire for greater trade for political ends. Until menaced by Senator Jackson's own strategy of linkages, economic interdependence had served as an element—a most serviceable element—in a political strategy designed to induce the Soviet Union to deal comprehensively and systematically with issues capable of seriously disrupting the stability of great-power relations, notably the Middle East, Indochina, and the strategic arms race. For the Nixon administration, the Soviet interest in American technology and capital was the rough equivalent of the original Soviet interest in an antiballistic missile (ABM) agreement—that is, a negotiable item prized for the leverage it offered in the pursuit of a range of (artificially) interconnected political objectives. As Kissinger explained when introducing the Strategic Arms Limitation Talk (SALT) accords in June 1972: "We have . . . sought to move forward across a broad range of issues so that progress in one area would add momentum to the progress of other areas."[22]   Although its point is different, this approach represents the logical extension of economic warfare (and note how easily senators and congressmen turned it into economic warfare); both Secretary Kissinger and Senator Jackson feature the political instrumentalism of the East-West economic relationship, and both protect the subordination of economics to politics.[23]

---

[21] *New York Times,* 18 September 1955, quoted in J. Wilczynski, *The Economics and Politics of East-West Trade* (London: Macmillan, 1969), p. 237.
[22] Henry A. Kissinger, Congressional Briefing, White House, 15 June 1972, p. 3. (Mimeographed.)
[23] Indeed, the simplest version of the linkage principle, that is, using the prospect of MFN and Export-Import Bank credits as a more or less explicit bargaining chip in negotiations with the Soviet Union, is virtually identical with the hortatory side of economic warfare, that is, using aid and trade concessions as rewards for independent East European states, such as Yugoslavia, Rumania, and, once, Poland.

The Soviet Union, in contrast, has a certain incentive for keeping the two spheres apart. Obviously, Soviet leaders understand the interrelationship between political environment and economic cooperation. They continually emphasize the importance that increasing trade and technical cooperation has for reducing international tension and, in turn, the importance that reducing tension has for fostering increased trade and technical cooperation. But they have major benefits to secure from economic cooperation as such, and these may not necessarily be served by taxing efforts to promote interdependence with political objectives. They, therefore, seem more inclined to seek separately the considerable political advantages that they expect from East-West détente. Rather than conceive their ambitions (or, at least, the way to them) as a whole, Soviet leaders appear to prefer to break détente into its component parts: to pursue their European dream (a stable but divided Europe built around a divided Germany and a *Europe [Occidentale] des Patries*) by means of rather narrowly defined bilateral accords and an expeditious Conference on Security and Cooperation in Europe (CSCE); to regulate the strategic military balance, including many of its multilateral aspects, with the United States alone in SALT; to cope with the challenge of China by manipulating bilateral relations with Japan and the United States as well as by sponsoring an autonomous Asian security system; to facilitate East-West trade and the importation of Western capital, technology, and technique by clearing away the specific institutional and legal obstacles to increased cooperation and by negotiating a network of formal bilateral trade agreements; and to minimize the natural links that exist between virtually all of these concerns.

The difference between the two approaches carries significant implications for the interaction of détente and economic cooperation. That each side desires both tells but a portion of the story. It also matters that the United States chooses still to subordinate one to the other, treating economic interdependence basically as a means to an end; the Soviet Union, in this instance, has not established a similar hierarchy and is, therefore, bound to resist. Like Western Europe, the Soviet Union is opposed to American linkages—whether between the negotiations of mutual force reductions in Europe and CSCE, or between MFN and an interim agreement to limit offensive missile deployments.

Linkages are the natural preference of states whose advantages are in some but not in all the areas contested by others. By tying those areas in which the other side is clearly the *demandeur* with those in which the advantage is less clear, gains can be maximized and losses minimized. Tying the Soviet interest in East-West trade to progress in SALT, therefore, has much in common with tying Western Europe's security anxieties to the reordering of Atlantic commercial and monetary relationships. The United States hopes, thus, to squeeze the most from a favorably tilted triangle with Peking and Moscow, from the Soviet Union's greater intrinsic interest in East-West trade, and from the impatience of the East to have the West's formal blessing for what the East calls the "postwar European reality."

Failing a basic shift in the perspectives that the two dominant powers bring to the problem of East-West economic interdependence, the commitment of either to trade and to other forms of economic cooperation will be partially compromised by the different things that each wants from the *process* of promoting cooperation. The difference is fundamental: the United States wants the Soviet Union to get what it wants *conditionally;* the Soviet Union does not want the United States to get what it wants tactically. In turn, the things that each gets from (and yields to) the *process* will depend on: (1) the Soviet capacity for breaking linkages (which country turns out to have a greater stake in the process), (2) the reinforcement the environment provides in breaking linkages (a crisis-ridden environment tends to favor ad hoc solutions), and (3) the extent to which American leaders retain control over the rewards (MFN, export credits, the sacrifice of present or future weapons systems, etc.) around which linkages are built. It is the last variable that makes the American strategy the most vulnerable. It constitutes the chief hazard of a relatively pluralistic policymaking process. (If they could afford to, Soviet leaders should have an easier time putting politics ahead of economics.)

The asymmetry of stakes, however, does not diminish the critical fact that each side has come to have a stake in economic cooperation. Asymmetry influences each side's approach to economic cooperation, but obviously these differences depend first on both sides' interest in cooperating. That interest is the outcome or, more precisely, the beneficiary of significant change in the international political setting. On a number of past occasions—in 1952 at the Moscow Economic Conference, in 1959 at the time of Camp David, after 1966 with the Japanese—the Soviets have sought to enlarge their trade with the West. But not until Brandt's post-1969 *Ostpolitik* transformed the political character of East-West relations did they permit themselves to contemplate this trade as a significant part of the solution to their economic difficulties. Without the political hopes aroused by progress on the German problem, Soviet leaders would probably not have dared place so much emphasis on the utility of East-West economic cooperation. Without, however, the "normalization" of Soviet-American relations (as the Soviet press has described events since the May 1972 summit) this cooperation would have remained merely feasible, not lucrative. For the Soviet-American relationship is decisive in two respects: first, Soviet leaders know that American sanction is essential to any basic restructuring of East-West relations; second, only the Americans can provide capital and goods on the scale for which the Soviets are hoping. Thus, a modification in the premises of Soviet-American relations has very broad significance.

The mutual accommodation Soviet and American leaders seek to fashion rests, not on a failure to perceive the Soviet-American relationship as still fundamentally competitive nor on any real reconciliation with the nature of the opposing system, but, rather, on the prospect that each may be willing to cease striving for preemptive roles in areas other than those regarded as essential spheres of influence. For the Soviet Union, the United States has not and cannot outgrow its imperialist essence. But when Soviet leaders contend that circumstances have forced American policymakers to abandon their "aggressive globalism," they are acknowledging to themselves that the frustrations of recent American policy have produced a genuine revision in American conduct. For the United States, the Soviet Union remains its most ambitious rival, a rival motivated by an alien ideology. But American leaders, too, have been reassured by the problems posed for Soviet policy by an often intractable and sometimes downright unfriendly world. The American faith in the Sino-Soviet conflict, the imperatives of change in Eastern Europe, and Soviet setbacks in the Third World roughly equal the impact of Vietnam, disenchanted allies, and the domestic distractions on which Soviet leaders count to make the United States a sobered and safer adversary-partner.

Thus, in the first place, it is the limits of power together with an incipient faith in the other side's sensitivity to the limits of power that permits increased cooperation, whether in arms control, scientific research, or trade. The second element of change favoring cooperation is the Soviet Union's belated attainment of effective strategic parity. And the mixed character of Soviet success gives this factor even greater force. For while parity provides the confidence to promote interdependence, the Soviet Union's marked inferiority in other realms, some military and almost all economic, provides the reason for doing so. Third, economic cooperation simply extends a gradual movement toward interdependence occurring in other areas, where the transnational problems of pollution, environmental decay, and resource exploitation leave little choice.

The discussion to this point not only has simplified the number of nations that count in shaping East-West economic relations, but has also simplified the nature of those nations as they come to count; that is, it has ignored the interplay of forces determining the Soviet and American approaches to cooperation. Ultimately, however, the practical way that changes in the international environment work their effect on either's approach is in influencing the political setting and the politics of policymaking. There is, of course, an interplay between the two, since the domestic political process also affects the evolution of the international environment, but not so much as the environment conditions this process. Our argument is the superiority, not the irresponsiveness, of macropolitics to micropolitics.

Two somewhat simplifying shortcuts now need to be abandoned. First is the implicit notion that a nation's foreign policy represents the starting point of international politics. The second is that a nation's policy or, more generally, a nation's behavior can be equated with the preferences of the national leadership—in the United States, the president and his key advisers; in the Soviet Union, the general secretary and his principal political allies. It helps, in making order of basic international trends, to be able to work with "black boxes," and, when it comes time to give this abstraction life, to render the black box as Nixon (now Ford) and Kissinger or as Brezhnev and his lieutenants. Yet without rejecting the validity and the importance of the abstraction or the decisive role of the national leadership, an important part of reality remains concealed until a look is taken at what is happening within the black box. It has to be done, at a minimum, to understand the constraints that the local political context places on the policy of national leaderships.

Much progress has been made lately in developing a systematic theory of the politics of foreign policymaking, though less has been done on the interaction of politics with domestic settings.[24] To be shown the way, however, does not automatically make it possible to follow. Very considerable obstacles stand in the way of a rigorous and comprehensive exploration of the micropolitics of East-West economic interdependence. These boil down essentially to the two interrelated problems of access and scale. First, there is no conceivable way to penetrate adequately the politics of Soviet foreign policymaking. Soviet specialists (and even more so, Chinese specialists) simply do not have access to provide anything other than the most rudimentary speculative portrait of the interplay of political forces disgorging policy. Second, even if we had a better idea of what was going on within the black boxes, the task of dealing with the Soviet and American processes, plus the processes under way in all the other countries that matter to East-West economic cooperation, and in a context that is both dynamic and indeterminate, would require superhuman talents of integration.

Thus, the reader is warned that we offer a rather humble version of the way that domestic politics and setting relate to the course of East-West economic relations. Let us begin with our only conceptual device: a way of differentiating the participants in the foreign policymaking process. In the advanced systems of both the East and West, there are what may be termed direct, collateral, and indirect participants. The first are usually those distinctive structures whose functions are naturally associated with foreign policy, and that are often specialized in this area, that tend to initiate policy and sometimes to assume operating responsibility for policy, and that, however biased, tend to see policy integrally rather than particularistically. To use the United States as our Western example, in addition to the president, the direct participants are the State Department, the National Security Council, the Department of Defense, and various subagencies of each, the Central Intelligence Agency (CIA), representatives of each in ad hoc groupings, and, to a much lesser extent, the congressional armed services and foreign relations committees. To use the Soviet Union as our Eastern example, the equivalents would be the general secretary and his personal secretariat, the international affairs departments of the central committee, the Foreign Ministry, the Ministry of Defense, the Committee on State Security (KGB), and other members of the Politburo regularly consulted on foreign affairs.

By collateral participants we have in mind the other institutions and elements that impinge critically on policymaking, that may deal with foreign policy only as an extension of other concerns, that may not generally initiate or implement policy but that are capable of significantly altering its content, and that command the deference, wariness, or respect of the first group. This category is far more diffuse

---

[24] For the first, see Graham T. Allison, *The Essence of Decision* (Boston: Little, Brown & Co., 1970); and Graham T. Allison and Morton H. Halperin, "Bureaucratic Politics: A Paradigm and Some Policy Implications," in Raymond Tanter and Richard H. Ullman, eds., *Theory and Policy in International Relations* (Princeton, N.J.: Princeton University Press, 1972), pp. 40-79. For significant contributions in the second, more disappointing, area, see Henry A. Kissinger, "Domestic Structure and Foreign Policy," *Daedalus* 95 (Spring 1966): 503-29; and Gabriel A. Almond, *The American People and Foreign Policy* (New York: Harcourt, Brace & Co., 1950).

than the first, varying tremendously in the nature of its access to the policymaking process, its effectiveness, and, particularly, its place in the general political process. In the United States, examples may be as bureaucratic as the Departments of Commerce or Agriculture or as personal as a single prominent university specialist, as shapeless as a congressional bloc or as explicit as the Rand Corporation, as political as the American Federation of Labor–Congress of Industrial Organizations (AFL-CIO) or the International Longshoreman's Union or as aloof as the Council on Foreign Relations, as institutionalized as the House Ways and Means Committee or as informal as the anti-ABM lobby. In the Soviet Union, the range is also broad: from the Ministry of Trade and its trading organizations to such adjuncts of the Academy of Sciences as the Institute of World Economy and International Affairs and the Institute for the Study of the USA, from the State Committee on Science and Technology to the complex of military-industrial enterprises given direct representation in the Politburo.

Participants in the third category do not have direct access to foreign policymaking but may influence its course nonetheless. They do so either because those in the other two categories respond to their interests (or their importuning) or because they, the American media, in particular, play an important role in establishing the political setting. They are usually more difficult to identify in institutional terms, such as the Jewish voter in the United States or the economic reformer in the Soviet Union, more self-interested, such as the American business community or the middle-level *apparatchik*, and sometimes more remote from the system's center of gravity, such as the extreme right wing in the United States or dissident intellectuals in the Soviet Union.

Because our present theme is the impact of the environment on micropolitics, and because we will soon argue that this impact has been similar in the East (the Soviet Union) and in the West (the United States), we want to be careful to avoid leaving the impression that few differences exist in these participant categories between the United States and the Soviet Union. On the contrary, the fundamental structural differences in political and economic systems produce important distinctions. Most of these stem from the sharp contrast between levels of centralization (concentration of decision-making power), differentiation of political function (role specialization), and participation (access to the decision-making process). Thus, Soviet participants tend to be more consolidated, though not necessarily more monolithic, than American participants. The KGB, for example, has many more concerns than the CIA, since it also incorporates the work of the Federal Bureau of Investigation (FBI), the Customs Service, and, in the judicial system, even some of the work of the district attorney. As a participant in foreign policymaking, it brings all of these concerns, not merely those of the CIA, to bear. Second, the number of collateral participants in the Soviet Union is far smaller than in the United States, and the importance of indirect participants is much less striking. The first results, in general, from the monopolistic position of the Party, and the second, from its authoritarianism. Third, in contrast with the direct participants, the contribution of collateral participants in the Soviet Union appears to be far more compartmentalized than in the United States. International relations specialists in the Soviet Union interpret United States behavior. They do not offer approaches to arms control. That is the sphere of the military. The Committee on Science and Technology explains how much it means for improved planning to enlist the services of Control Data, but it does not worry about the political implications of getting involved with the major capitalist powers. That is the province of Agitprop and others in the Party hierarchy. Compare this circumstance with the broad expertise and influence to which the AFL-CIO pretends or the breadth of inquiry undertaken by Senator Jackson's subcommittees of the Government Operations Committee.

Later we will consider the potential effect of economic interdependence on these differences—whether interdependence is likely to generate pressures for system reform, say, economic decentralization, and whether interdependence can be used to encourage such reform. For the moment, however, we are more concerned with the effect of the environment on the way that the interplay of domestic political forces bears on economic interdependence.

The balance among these forces has shifted toward and perhaps is now in favor of interdependence. Without arguing the untenable—that all elements involved are committed to an unconditional economic partnership—it seems safe to say that a decisive portion of the spectrum has swung away from viewing Soviet-American relations as irretrievably hostile and economic cooperation as an unthinkable danger or betrayal. In both the United States and the Soviet Union, this change is reflected in two fundamental developments.

First, opinion favoring interdependence or, at least, opinion willing to tout the idea appears to prevail in all three categories of participants. But, more important, among the direct participants, those that we have been calling the national leadership now regularly declare their dedication to promoting interdependence. In the Soviet case, this seems to us more significant and, simultaneously, more perilous: more significant because first-category participants in the Soviet Union have a far stronger position vis-à-vis the other two categories than their American counterparts; more perilous because (1) the national leadership (Brezhnev and his allies) is less ascendent over other *first*-category participants than is the American president, and because (2) the issue of interdependence well may be one of the stakes of its uncertain ascendence.

Second, the spectrum has been extended in both countries. As the predominant view inches toward the possibility of interdependence, estimations more sanguine, more hopeful, than anything heard for a long time are now being expressed. Thus, Henry Kissinger may think of interdependence as merely a component of a grand political strategy, but others, some of them relatively frontline participants, place higher value on economic cooperation. The object, former Secretary of Commerce Peter Peterson has noted, is "to build in both countries a vested economic interest in the maintenance of an harmonious and enduring relationship."[25] Leonid Brezhnev may consider it a calculated risk that he

[25] See US Department of Commerce, *U.S.-Soviet Commerical Relationships in a New Era*, by Peter G. Peterson (Washington, D.C.: Department of Commerce, 1972), p. 3.

turn to the industrial nations of the West and, first among them, to the United States for help in addressing the shortcomings of the Soviet economy, but there is Georgi Arbatov, director of the Institute for the Study of the USA, telling him not to be anxious because the scales have shifted in the United States. Indeed, Arbatov has written in *Kommunist* that "the ruling American bourgeoisie" has come to recognize the arms race and military "adventures" as being a waste, as squandering a huge part of national resources and "only undermining its position in the competitive stuggle with other capitalist powers, dooming itself to monetary-financial shocks, and eroding the bases of its economic and political influence in the world."[26] Moreover, this is, according to him, a long-term, not an "episodic," trend, dictated by "objective conditions." Thus cooperation with the United States as an "acceptable partner" (he uses this term) can be something profound and relatively permanent.

Compared with the former secretary of commerce, Arbatov is merely a collateral participant in the policymaking process. But his role is no less interesting or illustrative. As a second-level participant, in one sense, his influence on decision makers at the top is much weaker than the most potent second-level participants in the United States. That is, he clearly participates at their deference and he clearly understands the range of ideas that will be tolerated. (Admittedly, someone like Peterson, too, must stay within the boundaries of good political taste; but the difference is that in the United States, the president determines those boundaries, whereas in the Soviet Union, the *relative strength* of the Soviet leader determines them.) It is difficult to imagine George Meany or Senator Jackson responding to the same constraints. Also, Arbatov tends to be a more effective participant the more he is the client of some part of the highest leadership. This is both a weakness and a strength: a weakness because it deprives him of autonomy, a strength because with the right kind of patronage his ideas acquire considerable currency. Arbatov has been the most fortunate of people in this sense because he has had the ear of the general secretary. His entrée is reportedly with Brezhnev's own personal secretariat, two of whom, Y. Alexandrov-Agentov and George Tsukanov, are emerging as prominent figures in the general secretary's foreign policy activities. He was also conspicuously part of the entourage accompanying Brezhnev to the United States in June 1973.[27] But presumably any group or individual in the second category seeks to have an input by the grace of one or two major participants.

Do not misunderstand. We are not suggesting that the evolution of the international environment now ensures the permanent triumph of elements favoring economic interdependence. Nor do we mean to slight the complicated butting and

---

[26] G. Arbatov, "O sovetsko-amerikanskikh otnosheniyakh," *Kommunist*, no. 3 (February 1973): 106. Here Arbatov is not merely the equivalent of a prominent American academic. Speaking through *Kommunist*, the chief theoretical organ of the Central Committee of the Communist Party of the Soviet Union, is not the same as speaking in *Foreign Affairs.*

[27] It is not likely that his influence is diminished by the presence at his institute of relatives of highly placed Soviet officials, such as Ludmila Gvishiani, Kosygin's daughter, or, until his recent posting to the Washington embassy, Gromyko's son, Anatoly.

grinding of interests by which each side comes to act. On the contrary, we devote the next section to the problems that the environment still poses and, more important, to the intricate and sometimes inauspicious struggle among viewpoints, interests, and institutions that the shadow of interdependence provokes.

But clearly the ground rules by which that struggle is being waged have changed. Most fundamentally, they have been changed by establishing East-West economic interdependence as a legitimate alternative. Senator Jackson's opposition to trade-facilitating measures is not based on principle, but is an expedient for compelling the Soviet leadership to alter objectionable domestic practices. And those who do oppose economic cooperation in principle, such as Ohio's Representative Charles Vanik, must today fashion their strategy around alliances with liberal congressmen, such as Ogden Reid, who, but for the plight of Soviet Jews, conceive Soviet-American relations quite differently.

Circumstances today resemble very little those of a decade ago. In 1962, George Kennan was abandoned by his administration at the first sign of a tussle, and he was left to wonder at Congress's decision to deprive Yugoslavia and Poland of most-favored-nation status. In the same year, Senator William Proxmire introduced an amendment to the foreign aid bill denying all forms of aid to Yugoslavia, an exclusion that was later amended to allow the shipment of surplus wheat, provided that the president determined that it was in the interest of national security and that the recipient was "not participating directly or indirectly in any policy or programs for the Communist conquest of the world."[28] So was the major East-West trade bill of 1966 a victim of Congress's deep-seated inability to imagine the Soviet Union and China as suitable trading partners. Whatever other burdens oppress efforts to advance trade with the East, a widely shared aversion to having truck with the enemy is no longer one of them.[29]

The political limits to interdependence

Relations between adversaries have mellowed over the last several years. Those between friends have in some ways hardened. The character of the international system, as a consequence (or as a tribute), has lost its precision. Foes, internally troubled and no more gifted than we at moulding the outside world, are no longer always foes. Friends sometimes are. The ambiguity makes economic interdependence between East and West plausible. But it does not mean that no one any longer has the ability or the reason to distinguish friend from foe. Rivalry between East and West, particularly between the Soviet Union and the United

---

[28] See George F. Kennan, *Memoirs: 1950-1963* (Boston: Little, Brown & Co., 1972), pp. 293-305. He did not wonder long. On precisely this score he left the diplomatic service once and for all.

[29] These burdens are obviously great, but, as the history of the Jackson-Vanik amendment indicates, their effect is not ultimately to preclude a steady growth in Soviet-American trade. In part, of course, this growth may require that the Soviet Union buy without the credit facilities for which it had hoped, but the basic idea of a growth in Soviet-American trade is no longer in question.

States, may be softened, but it remains a central feature of contemporary international politics. Thus, while the transformation of this rivalry permits a growing economic cooperation, the persistence of this rivalry places limits on its growth. (One of the basic questions that events must answer is how long these [political] limits will continue to intervene before the economic limits discussed in part two of this essay.)

Security, as Bergsten, Keohane, and Nye suggest in the first essay in this volume, is never very far removed from the problems of economic policy. In no dimension has security figured more explicitly or more integrally than in East-West relations. And, therefore, none provides a better illustration of their point about the three levels at which economic policy has been assumed to serve national security: (1) for the nation (by risk aversion), (2) for allies and potential victims or dupes of the other side (by economic assistance), and (3) against the other side (by economic denial). The illustration, of course, applies to a period when security had a narrower, more rigorous, and largely military connotation—when, as we have been saying, there was no political impulse to economic interdependence, only political limits. What happens when the limits no longer overwhelm the impulse to interdependence?

Concern for security still seems to us the best way to understand the political impediments to interdependence. Security now has a more diffuse and general sense, to suit a world in which not all challenges to national security are military. Yet, however redefined, it still lurks behind each side's apprehensions over economic cooperation with the other, over accepting an interdependence that one morning may turn out to be too much. *Too much,* reduced to its common essence, means an interdependent relationship in which the other side's net leverage is considerably greater than your own, an interdependent relationship that turns out to have spawned, or perhaps merely to have masked, a dependent relationship. The fear is everyone's. But the way each personalizes it varies significantly, not only between the United States and the Soviet Union, but within the West, and, to a lesser extent, within the East. Add to an asymmetry in the stakes of interdependence the asymmetry in the fears of interdependence.

For the Soviet Union, the concern is essentially that the integrity of its system may be prejudiced, that too much involvement with the advanced capitalist nations will lead to a serious erosion of empire together with a consistent and possibly noisome interference in Soviet domestic affairs. Soviet policymakers evidently spend a good deal of time worrying about the effect on their socialist allies of an economic opening to the West. Hence, the Soviets have made efforts to heighten the impression of COMECON integration since the summer of 1971, to come to terms with the European Economic Community (EEC) on a bloc-to-bloc basis, and to set something of an example of what they regard as an appropriate arrangement with Western traders and, particularly, investors (with Rumania, as always, the unruly pupil). The other care is even easier to see. In Sofia in September 1973, Brezhnev complained of those "naive" enough to believe that "since the Soviet Union and other socialist countries are expressing great interest in . . . devel-

oping political and economic cooperation," they can "bargain for various concessions."

The American concern strikes one as less imaginative. In basic respects it
prolongs the preoccupations of the earlier period. Thus, the worry that by trading
with or investing in the Soviet Union the United States is "helping the enemy"—
that is, permitting Soviet leaders to respond to consumer hopes and a lagging
technology without diminishing military spending—recalls the considerations behind the strategic embargo and the other measures of economic denial.[30] Other
fears resemble those that once prompted risk-averting policies. For example, some
worry that substantial investment in Soviet industrial development may provide the
Soviet Union with "hostage capital." Or, as Gregory Grossman has argued in a more
subtle variant of the same theme, the Soviet Union will develop through American
investors their own lobbyists in the American political process.[31] Conceivably,
Grossman has added, the Soviet Union will use the exposed position of American
investors to pressure the Americans into, say, restraining the growth of China trade
(a proposition not unlike Senator Richard Schweiker's efforts in 1973 to pass a bill
interrupting Soviet-American trade until the Arabs lifted their oil embargo, nor
unlike Representative Clarence Long's efforts to block expanded trade until a host
of foreign policy concessions had been secured). Finally, there is the apprehension
that too heavy an involvement in the development of Soviet natural gas may leave
the United States dangerously dependent on the Soviet Union for this strategic
good.

The Japanese have different concerns. What is for the United States a risk to
be averted is for them a way to avert a risk. For more than half a decade, the
Japanese have been attracted to the idea of helping the Soviet Union to develop its
petroleum and natural gas resources as a way to reduce their own dramatic
dependence on Middle Eastern oil.[32] In the short term, therefore, the Japanese
have a different, that is, a multilateral rather than bilateral, perspective on risk
aversion, though perhaps in the long term the differences are less. The Japanese also
have a different perspective on the problem of "helping the enemy," in this case a
historic as well as a contemporary adversary. They object not so much to the Soviet
Union drawing its fair share of advantages from a far more ambitious trade but
rather to it doing so before they have returned a part of the Kurile Islands.

The West Europeans fall somewhere in between. As the parties most sensitive
to the implications for security of recent changes in East-West relations, they

---

[30] The point is made by many people in many places. For one clear statement, see Walter
Laqueur's remarks in US Congress, Senate, Committee on Government Operations, *Hearings
before the Permanent Subcommittee on Investigations of the Committee on Government
Operations*, 93rd Cong., 1st sess., 17 April 1973, pp. 1-39.

[31] See US Congress, Joint Economic Committee, *Hearings before the Joint Economic Committee*, 93rd Cong., 1st sess., 17, 18, 19 July 1973, p. 143.

[32] Kiichi Saeki, "Toward Japanese Cooperation in Siberian Development," *Problems of
Communism* 21 (May-June 1972): 1-11. True, the Japanese do seem eager to involve the
Americans in their proposed Siberian natural gas projects for reasons that go beyond merely
mounting adequate economic resources.

presumably share American concerns. But, as for the Japanese, it is not so easy for them to frame the problem in simple risk-averting terms. Trade with the East means a great deal more to them—as much as ten times more as a percentage of GNP—and the challenge of maintaining energy supply is more like that of the Japanese than of the Americans. Second, in a practical sense, they have made a great deal over economic interdependence, perhaps in order to keep minds and hands off the central issue of European security—the military balance. That is, in order to prevent the Soviet Union and the United States, in particular, from turning too early and too casually to European security as arms control, there may be a natural tendency to busy East and West with other forms of détente. It is difficult, therefore, to hedge the prospect of increased economic cooperation with all kinds of doubts and reservations. On the other hand, as the Soviets, they also react to the possibilities that interdependence gives to the other side of interfering in their internal affairs, in this case, in the process of West European integration. The concern would be less troublesome were the economic and political integration of the Common Market further along or were all members equally bent on promoting integration.

In a phrase, one of the primary political limits to economic interdependence remains the powerful aftertaste of the postwar bipolar contest. But there is potentially another kind of political limit arising from the passing of this international circumstance: in a less neatly divided world, national leaderships can (and often feel compelled to) apply themselves to regulating the economic contact of former foes with former friends and even of foes with foes, where once their only option was to regulate the contact of friends with foes. No longer does China confine itself to fussing over the Soviet-American economic relationship Khrushchev evidently sought to launch in 1959; it now concentrates as well on influencing Japanese trade with the Soviet Union or with Taiwan.[33] And the United States goes about the more direct pursuit of its economic interests able to ignore the political implications of Great Britain selling buses to Cuba or of the Federal Republic of Germany underwriting a consortium's part in China's steel industry.

There is a third political limit to interdependence that, while partially a function of these broader environmental constraints, has a certain force of its own. The process by which any country, even the most autocratic, sets, or happens upon, its foreign policy course constitutes a lumbering, quasi-bureaucratic confusion on which no leader or school of thought can completely impose its will. Thus, while it may be that the changing quality of international politics has given the upper hand to people willing to contemplate a much grander trade between East and West, the domestic political process depreciates the meaning of that upper hand.

Take the Soviet Union, for example. At the center of the picture is Brezhnev, the architect of a *Westpolitik* predicated in part on a considerable increase in the

---

[33] Peking has more than once made it plain to the Japanese that their participation in the development of the Tyumen oil fields or the Druzhba pipeline will not help to expand Sino-Japanese trade. The Chinese have also refused to do business with Japanese trading firms that trade with Taiwan.

Soviet Union's economic involvement with the industrial states of the West. Arrayed at other points in the picture are supposedly colleagues and underlings who have little of Brezhnev's enthusiasm for mixing with Western investors and traders. Still elsewhere are presumably miscellaneous elements that, for their own reasons, would like to see this cooperation advance as far as possible, perhaps a good deal further than Brezhnev envisages. Brezhnev's policy emerges from this rather simple confrontation of interests as a moderate middle course whose very success owes to the avoidance of either extreme.

Reality is more complicated. It would be surprising if the lines were so simply and neatly drawn. In actuality, there is an extraordinary range of interests involved, often only obliquely or partially in conflict, and perhaps divided within themselves. In short, the ambiguities of policy correspond to the ambiguities of the process by which policy is formed and even at times to the ambiguities of key participants in the process.

Ambiguity is another way of expressing the third kind of limit to interdependence, i.e., the nature of the policymaking process. Mikhail Suslov, leader of the palace coup in 1964 and primary Party ideologue for more than a decade, is often identified as an opponent of détente and, by the same token, of the *Westpolitik.* To see him as such, however, doubtless distorts his contribution to policy. He is a traditionalist, a guardian of the Soviet Union's essential political values, and, therefore, probably not so much an opponent of détente and cooperation with the West as a cautioning voice. He does not reject economic involvement with the West but rather the tendency to rely too much on the outside in solving Soviet problems and too little on the traditional norms of self-reliance and socialist competition. He does not condemn the *Westpolitik,* not publicly, at least, but he does remind his peers of the need to counteract the infiltration of bourgeois ideas (and tastes) accompanying interdependence.[34] From most indicators, Brezhnev shares the same concerns. But Brezhnev appears to believe that enlisting the West in Soviet development is the surest way to protect the system from the pressures for reform, and, perhaps, this is how he sells the *Westpolitik* to his old colleague. Western technology, capital, and technique are intended as relief to, not from, central planning, a way to keep the planning system intact while the economy is finally shifted over from extensive to intensive growth.

Viewed in this light, the *Westpolitik*'s more natural opponent is Premier Kosygin, the Soviet leader most closely associated with economic reform. But Kosygin's position illustrates perfectly the multiple and sometimes competing concerns that motivate many of the major (direct) participants in policymaking. Thus, while Kosygin has defended much of what the reformers have urged since 1965, and while many of these people no doubt disapprove of the *Westpolitik* to the extent that it postpones critical choices, he also represents other interests with a different point of view. The influential State Committee for Science and Tech-

---

[34] See *Pravda,* 15 July 1973, p. 2, for his comprehensive statement on the seventieth anniversary of the Second Congress of the Russian Social Democratic Party.

nology, for example, has a heavy stake in acquiring the assistance of International Business Machines (IBM), Control Data, and others in developing the All-Union Automated System for Planning and Management, a giant computer network that is to serve as the backbone for automated central planning.[35] To complicate the issue furthur, Kosygin must also respond to the biases of Gosplan and, within Gosplan, to those who resent the rush to bring the computer to planning, the attack on comfortably familiar methods of planning, and the preoccupation with the quality of production and with catering to Soviet consumers. They have no particular interest in promoting vast levels of trade with the West. Presumably they make it easier for Kosygin to understand and communicate with Suslov. Thus, Kosygin brings to the question of East-West economic cooperation a complex and not always easily reconciled set of considerations. But so do most of the critical direct participants, and, for the same reason: they, as Kosygin, both lead and act on behalf of a variety of partially competing collateral participants.

In turn, a good many second-level participants are probably further divided within themselves over this issue. Say, for example, that Soviet Minister of Defense Andrei Grechko, a man bound by profession to be skeptical of East-West economic interdependence, listens to two voices: one maintains that détente is not only risky but a necessity only because the regime has given in to the consumer, that by chasing after Western goods and know-how the leadership is allowing itself to be pushed into an untimely arms control process; the other responds that without Western capital and technology, resources will surely be shifted from the military to other sectors, that, if carefully controlled, the process of arms control can help the Soviet Union to catch up in several of the areas where it lags. It is likely that these voices are each something less than a perfectly matched chorus. For example, those who most mistrust détente may differ in their assessment of East-West economic cooperation. The most reluctant, the navy perhaps, may resist any significant collaboration with the West. Some of its spokesmen have scarcely troubled themselves to conceal their impatience with the formulas of détente worked out by Brezhnev and Nixon.[36] Their fear is evidently that détente will complicate the task of keeping the leadership's attention on the gap between the navies of the two countries, and they know, whatever the current enthusiasm for expanding the Soviet navy, how great the gap is. Others, possibly close to the Strategic Rocket Forces, may have trouble identifying with people who see East-West cooperation as an essential way to acquire technology and other scarce goods. They have always been favored in both respects. But perhaps they perceive a more relaxed atmosphere, so long as nothing is sacrificed to it, as one means of restraining American defense efforts. Still others, perhaps some within the General Staff, may appreciate the benefits of eliminating the embargo on strategic items but worry about the influence of people too taken with the possibilities of Soviet-American cooperation.

---

[35] See Henry R. Lieberman in *New York Times,* 13 December 1973.
[36] See, for example, G. Svyatov and A. Kokoshin, *International Affairs* (Moscow), no. 4 (April 1973): 56-62.

There is not the space here to imagine the equivalent divisions within the other defense establishment viewpoint or within a third or a fourth, but we can be sure that they exist.

Thus, back through the process, differentiated interests, many of them far more intricate than our simple model, transform the issue of East-West economic interdependence into a subtly shaded maze of calculations. Rather than making policy formulation a clear-cut resolution of interests for and against increased economic cooperation, these encumbered calculations tend to complicate the process, to confuse its message, and, as a consequence, to modify the impulse to interdependence generated by changes in the international environment.

The same is true, with minor variations, in every country. Other nations may substitute relative chaos for the restricted and rather stylized interest articulation of the Soviet Union, but the effect is largely the same. American behavior (broader and more formidable than merely the administration's policy) is every bit as involved, internally inconsistent, and ambiguous. Indeed, more so.

This partially accounts for the remarkable symmetry in the configuration of Soviet and American attitudes toward economic interdependence. It may be true that the prevailing sentiment in both governments (in effect, the direct participants) favors increased economic cooperation. There may also be considerable support for the idea among collateral and indirect participants. But the relative strength of the idea, by definition, depends on the complete spectrum of opinion.

It seems to us that the symmetry in the present Soviet and American spectrums of opinion places a further restraint on the evolution toward greater East-West economic interdependence. It is not merely that the objective has its skeptics in both countries,[37] not to mention its opponents, public in the United States, less easily identified in the Soviet Union but no fewer, one assumes. Equally important, the balance of force *among* the proponents of economic interdependence appears to be less than ideal. Essentially, the role of vested interests with a purely economic stake in interdependence is too small. True, the number and, in some cases, the names of American firms interested in doing business with the Soviet Union are rather impressive, but even the most optimistic estimates do not suggest that American investments in the Soviet Union can in the next two decades amount to more than a small fraction of total American foreign investment. And the political impact of this comparatively small part of the American business community has been and will continue to be easily offset by other vested interests. In the Soviet Union, such elements are even weaker—an odd firm here and there, and 40 politically inconsequential trading organizations.

Second, functional interests with fundamental economic stake in East-West cooperation that might compensate for the weaknesses of vested interests also wield

---

[37] For the moment, we will disregard our categories of participants. It does not matter in this context whether the only Soviet skeptics with enough importance to impede the evolution toward interdependence are in the first category or whether American skeptics with the same clout can be and are in the second category. It only matters that there are such skeptics.

little influence. These are generally collateral participants. Thus, while the Soviet State Committee on Science and Technology is an important collateral participant, collateral participants occupy an inferior place in the Soviet policymaking process. In the United States, collateral participants have a greater impact on the policymaking process but those most interested in the economic benefits of East-West cooperation are among the least influential. When the director of the Office of East-West Trade urges expanded Soviet-American trade as one of the ways to build up substantial favorable trade balances by which some hope to rectify the American balance of payments, the input is coming from a lesser player.

This means that the momentum behind East-West economic interdependence depends even more than usual on participants whose calculations are primarily political. Classical economic liberalism, with its illusion of self-contained economic and political domains, has never had much to do with economic relations between East and West, and it is unlikely to come to have much more. Even the most enthusiastic advocates of East-West economic cooperation think in political terms: they supply the political reasons to explain why cooperation is safe, and they evaluate economic cooperation according to what are basically political advantages and disadvantages. The Americans ask: Is increased trade likely to create a vested interest in mutual restraint? Promote a liberalization of the Soviet system? Or give the Soviet Union leverage over the United States? The Soviets ask: Is increased trade likely to restore the Soviet Union's competitive position? Strengthen the political base of the regime? Or lead to a high level of external interference in Soviet domestic affairs? And, being realists, these advocates set the limits to economic cooperation in political terms: the West must not convince itself that the Soviet Union so wants Western technology and capital that it will be dictated to in its treatment of dissident intellectuals or Soviet Jews or whatever next comes to mind; the East must not be construed as something less than a powerful competitor or welcomed into the international economic community as one of us.

In both countries, the most important spokesmen for increased East-West economic interdependence present mirror-image arguments, and this, when it comes to these last matters, limits the level of economic interdependence they are willing to recommend. Nowhere is that more evident than among the key participants, the national leadership. In the third part of this essay we dealt with the heavy political stake that President Ford and Secretary Kissinger have in economic interdependence. Then we argued that the Soviet leadership has a more intrinsically economic stake in economic interdependence. But that stake is parochial. Brezhnev is not campaigning for expanded trade with the United States and its powerful capitalist friends because he wants to increase wealth all around. The thought that either country views East-West economic interdependence as the path to greater global efficiency and growth borders on the ridiculous—the claim of each notwithstanding.

Briefly then, a significant constraint on the political impulse to East-West economic interdependence derives from two related circumstances. The first is the error of Calvin Coolidge, of a good many contemporary conservatives fearful of continued American fascination with Moscow and Peking, and of a host of Soviet optimists in assuming that "the business of America is business." This is clearly not so, not, at least, in the East-West context. The second derives from the Soviet Union's failure ever to produce its own Calvin Coolidge.

The politics of interdependence

Broadly sketched, these seem to us to be the basic circumstances advancing and restraining East-West economic interdependence. The political impulse toward cooperation is, in terms of the postwar confrontation, a revolutionary development. But it is a nascent impulse and still far from self-sustaining or irresistible.

So far we have concentrated on the political context of economic interdependence without discussing the character of interdependence itself as it is likely to emerge over the remainder of the decade. We turn now to this other dimension—the political dynamics of interdependence, its impact on the behavior of the major East-West nations, its potential for stabilizing (or destabilizing) East-West relations, and, ultimately, its place in a reordered international economic system.

The two most fundamental trends in contemporary international politics, as common knowledge has it, are polycentrism—the fragmentation of (imperial) political power—and increasing interdependence—the loss of (national) political power. To what extent the two trends are related, however, is less well known. If they have a cause-and-effect relationship, it may be, with one exception, an essentially negative one. It is difficult to see what the collapse of two hegemonically ordered blocs has contributed to the exponential increase in American investments in Europe and, more recently, to the increase of Japanese and West European investments in the United States, or, secondarily, to environmental pollution, or now to some nations' desire to join forces in coping with long-term energy problems. But it is much less implausible to sense a connection between the frustrations of interdependence and the every-man-for-himself attitude increasingly displayed among the major Western nations. We return to this point in a moment.

The one exception is East-West relations, where cause and effect stand out more clearly. Polycentrism, by both demonstrating and reinforcing a more diffuse East-West rivalry, constitutes an obvious part of the environmental change encouraging the movement toward economic interdependence. In the process, it has significantly enlarged the role of transnationalism, a primary "carrier" of interdependence. Transnationalism, in turn, introduces a strange new dimension into East-West relations whose effects are already proving to be unpredictable. Not merely is there a new set, new at least since 1946, of transnational actors, such as Occidental Petroleum and the Texas Eastern Transmission Company, participating in East-West relations. Another, less conventional type of transnational actor, ironically more powerful in some ways than the businessman from whom he derives his influence, has also appeared: he is the prominent intellectual dissident, like Andre Sakharov (or the president of the American Academy of Sciences), who has sought to use the Soviet leadership's stake in East-West economic cooperation to internationalize the issue of Soviet human rights. One of the accomplishments of the cold war, Raymond Aron pointed out some years ago, was to interrupt transnational contact between nations in the two opposing camps.[38] The growth of interdependence will partially depend on the way the two sides come to terms with its restoration.

The growth of East-West economic interdependence will also partially depend on the shape interdependence takes in other contexts, notably, where it is the most highly developed, between Japan, Western Europe, and the United States. The disintegration of the primitively interdependent (capitalist) world economy created and sustained by American power and interests and the rise of, what Robert Gilpin called in his essay, the mercantilist model must exercise a critical influence on the level and nature of East-West interdependence.

Ironically, the character of West-West interdependence both spurs and sets the limits to East-West interdependence. On the one hand, Soviet and other communist leaderships are heartened by the antagonisms stimulated among the major capitalist powers by the economic burdens of their interdependence. The sudden increase in what communist leaderships perceive as "interimperialist contradictions" (or, in Gilpin's terms, a more "intense international economic competition for markets, investment outlets, and sources of raw materials") makes the West a less formidable economic entity, indeed, no entity at all, and East-West economic cooperation a less wrenching adventure.

On the other hand, the tensions of West-West interdependence remind both sides that extensive interinvolvement accentuates contending as well as common interests. The point has a double dimension. At one level, the socialist states would be the first to agree with Western economists who argue that a harmonious interdependent world economy must be "an imperial hierarchical system."[39] That is not the degree to which they care to see interdependence perfected nor, considering their general view of economic relations between and with capitalist states, is it a condition in which they would place much confidence. At a second, more practical level, neither East nor West can ignore the lessons of an economic interdependence that has been so easily politicized. The feature of interdependence among Western nations that gives pause, as Edward Morse has suggested, is not only the eruption of frequent international economic crises but also the conscious (political) manipulation of these crises by parties to the relationship.[40]

Therefore, if either or both sides learn from trends in the international economic relations of the West, trends fearfully duplicated in the oil diplomacy of the Arab states, East-West economic interdependence is bound to remain a rather stunted specimen. To the extent that either retains control over the process, prudence is bound to impose qualifications on interdependence. No country, at

---

[38] Raymond Aron, *Peace and War* (New York: Praeger, 1967), p. 105.

[39] Robert Gilpin, "Three Models of the Future," contained herein.

[40] Edward L. Morse, "Crisis Diplomacy, Interdependence, and the Politics of International Economic Relations," in Tanter and Ullman, *Theory and Policy in International Relations,* pp. 123-50.

least none that directs its own destiny, will blithely sanction, let alone aid, a pattern of trade or investment leaving it vulnerable to significant pressure from the *government* of a major opponent. This, it seems to us, means that economic interdependence will likely remain subnational, i.e., that it will not be permitted to impinge on national interests. Thus, while individual American petroleum companies may become deeply involved with the Soviet Union, it would be surprising if any American government would allow the United States to become heavily dependent on the Soviet Union for its oil. Now that an American president has committed the United States to basic self-sufficiency in this area, it seems more probable that the government will be increasingly torn between the economic and political elements of interdependence—between the pressures to underwrite large private deals, such as the $6.5 billion North Star natural gas project, for their salutary political effects and the pressures to spend the money off the California coast, in Alaska, or for coal research as a means of protecting other economic options.[41]

Similarly, the Soviet Union and most of the East European countries have made it plain that they are not going to give the multinational corporation the kind of authority it enjoys elsewhere. They have no intention of granting alien institutions the slightest influence over their administered economies. Nor are Soviet leaders prepared to leave their country dependent on trade, either by volume or by content. It is virtually inconceivable that trade with the West could exceed 1.5 percent of Soviet GNP over the next decade, or that foreign investments could exceed 3 percent of total investment. More important, the Soviet Union is not looking to the West for the long-term supply of basic goods or resources. The disruption of individual projects or the interruption of technological transfer would be inconvenient but scarcely fatal.

So, too, is the case in the United States. The Soviet Union already possesses the power to make life miserable for half a dozen major American chemical trading firms, and the number and variety of companies dependent on Soviet trade will surely double or triple. But that will still give the Soviet Union leverage over less than 3 percent of American trade, and, hence, over less than 0.15 percent of total GNP. Should American investments in the Soviet Union come close to the levels for which Soviet leaders are hoping ($15 to $20 billion over the next decade), the Soviet Union would acquire sizable "hostage capital." But even if one ignores the fact that it is not the Soviet style to renege on such agreements, it takes some imagination to see how Soviet leaders might bring this influence to bear, or, even more so, why they would employ what could be only marginal influence with considerable costs to themselves.

If, however, East-West economic interdependence is to be qualified, then the political uses to which it can be put are likely to be qualified as well. The notion that the United States may be able to "use" the Soviet stake in American capital

---

[41] North Star will supply at the most only 2 percent of the gas needs of the eastern United States.

and technology to induce system change does not make sense. This is not to say that the effect of a growing economic interdependence may not lead to internal adjustments, that, for example, the Soviet leadership will not gradually feel obliged to change in order to make the Soviet Union more competitive. But it does mean that the conscious manipulation of economic interdependence to secure political objectives that the other side judges dangerous is not likely to succeed. This expresses both the outer limits of the American strategy of linkages and, ironically, the reason why the United States has been successful in compromising Soviet policy on an issue like Jewish emigration. It is precisely the appearance that the administration is *not* trying to use economic cooperation against the Soviet Union but finds its hands tied by other elements that creates the pressure to which Brezhnev and his friends may have been willing to yield. (On how many other occasions Brezhnev will yield or tolerate the impression that he has yielded is a fair question.) In short, the Soviet leadership is at a certain disadvantage in the politics of economic interdependence because it cannot communicate the same lack of control over policy as the American administration can. Neither leadership, however, should expect to have the kind of leverage permitting it to dictate the other's behavior.

This is not to argue that economic relations will or should be less and less contaminated by political considerations. Nations on both sides or on all sides, if that is the way that international relations ought now to be viewed, will make political demands where they have a strong economic hand. But most often these are likely to be random quid pro quos, of fairly marginal political importance (such as the release of Japanese fishermen held by the Soviet Union, a place for France among the superpowers in a future Middle Eastern settlement, or formal recognition of the Common Market by the Chinese), and short of a systematic strategy for altering another country's foreign and domestic policies. Even here, the nation having something of an economic upper hand may find itself using it most of the time simply to protect its own economic interests. The Federal Republic of Germany, for example, may have trouble trading off future credits or technical cooperation against the exit of Volga Germans when these are essential to ensure prompt and full Soviet compliance with promised petroleum deliveries. In short, while both East and West will surely mix narrow political and economic initiatives, the scale of East-West interdependence is unlikely to tolerate linkages that, in broader concerns, do more than prod mutually acceptable political adjustments.

Finally, the peculiar asymmetries of polycentrism will give a special character to East-West economic interdependence. Because polycentrism will not soon produce genuine multipolarity—the discrepancies are too great in the power of Japan, Western Europe, China, and the two superpowers—interdependence will also have its discontinuities. For one, China, a prominent player in a polycentric world but no economic match for either superpower or for Japan, may play a much less significant role in the rapid expansion of East-West economic interdependence.

Second, to the extent that China figures in the growth of East-West economic interdependence, its importance is likely to be confined to Asia. Thus, while it is true that Sino-Japanese trade is nearly twice as large as Soviet-American trade and is likely to remain larger than Soviet-American trade for the rest of the decade, the political impact of the first is regional and of the second, global. Trade with the Soviet Union is at the intersection of East with West in the triple sense of geography, comparative politics, and the reach of power. Trade with China is essentially an Asian affair. Japan seeks a larger trade with China (beyond its economic benefits) in order to reduce the political risks of the enlarged trade that it seeks with the Soviet Union. Both in general and in particular, the Japanese view cooperation with China as a critical means of preserving the Asian balance. Thus, their aggregate trade has not only caught up with Soviet-Japanese trade, but Japanese leaders no doubt hope to lessen the political liability of the importance they attach to obtaining Soviet natural gas and oil by joining the Chinese in the development of their mainland and offshore petroleum. Similarly, China appears to value its trade with the United States and with Western Europe as a counterbalance to its trade with Japan. Unlike the Soviet Union, China does the greatest share (indeed, 80 percent) of its trading with noncommunist countries, but, more significantly, 23 or 24 percent of this is with its economically powerful neighbor. Thus, trade with the United States and with West European countries serves the function of permitting China to expand its trade without forcing the Japanese figure over 25 percent.

Third, the enormous power of the Soviet Union over Eastern Europe means that the level and nature of this region's contribution to East-West economic interdependence will be largely determined in Moscow. Fourth, the level and nature of economic interdependence sanctioned by the Soviet Union for itself and its allies will depend, in part, on its ability to contain other forms of interdependence, such as a freer interchange of ideas and tourists. And, fifth, because the scale of Soviet expectations is so much greater than those of other socialist countries, and because American resources for meeting Soviet expectations are so much greater than (or at least perceived as such by Soviet leaders) those of other capitalist countries, the shape of their economic relationship should fundamentally determine the course of East-West economic interdependence.

East-West interdependence and international economic institutions

In this essay, we have deliberately stressed the basic limits to East-West economic interdependence. We have done so not because we doubt the prospect of a marked increase in trade between East and West, particularly between the United States and the Soviet Union, and not because we dismiss the progress already achieved in reducing the economic and legal barriers to trade and investment. We have done so because our concern is with the potential relevance that increased East-West economic interdependence may have for the restructuring of international economic institutions. Should East-West trade double by 1980, as is perfectly conceivable, should United States–Soviet trade grow fifteenfold (from $200 million in 1971 to $3 billion by 1980), should Western investors sink billions of dollars,

yen, and deutschemarks into a wide array of joint ventures, should home governments provide additional billions in guarantees and credits, and should the Soviet
Union begin selling Ladas in New York and the United States begin constructing
Holiday Inns in Moscow, the impact on East-West relations will be considerable.
Economic cooperation can, indeed, become an important element in efforts to
build a more stable and productive East-West relationship. But, for reasons to which
we now turn, it need not be more than incidental to the process of fashioning new
international economic institutions.[42]

Poland, Rumania, and Hungary have each recently become full members of
the General Agreement on Tariffs and Trade (GATT). What does this do for
East-West trade? Presumably membership in the GATT should increase the East-
West trade of the three nations by putting trade on a most-favored-nation basis;
that is, the Western members reduce their tariffs and presumably also their quotas
on the products of the three nations to the low MFN levels, thus enabling an
increase in Eastern exports. Poland and Rumania, not having really meaningful
tariffs, must reciprocate in other ways. Poland has agreed to increase its imports
from the GATT nations by 7 percent a year, thereby stimulating a tariff or quota
reduction. Rumania has agreed to increase its imports from the GATT nations as
fast as total Rumanian imports increase. Hungary has insisted that its tariffs, under
the New Economic Mechanism, are really tariffs and presumably grants MFN
treatment via market mechanisms (i.e., through lowering tariffs) to other GATT
nations.

The increase in East-West trade that is likely to result through the GATT,
however, will probably be small. Some trade creation will undoubtedly occur as
Eastern and Western exports replace domestic production in Western and Eastern
nations, respectively. But sizable increments to East-West trade are unlikely to
occur unless there is trade diversion, particularly on the Eastern side—trade diversion that reverses, at least in part, the trade diversion of the immediate postwar
years. Before World War II, the COMECON nations conducted about 15 percent of
their trade with each other; the present figure averages over 60 percent. A substantial shift back toward the undistorted previous levels is undoubtedly justified on
commercial grounds and would go a long way toward restoring East-West trade to
more normal levels.

It seems highly dubious that this will happen. The main reason is that despite
GATT membership the members of COMECON continue to trade with each other
as before. Representatives of the ministry of foreign trade of each socialist nation
sit down with representatives of the ministry of every other socialist nation each
year and together work out the trading pattern for the year to come as well as

---

[42] We have not meant to slight the significance of China's role in a broader East-West
economic cooperation. On the contrary, we are merely assuming that the growth of the West's,
including Japan's, trade with China will ultimately be constrained by the same structural
limitations as Western trade with the Soviet bloc. In one respect, however, we are assuming a
more limited role for China—that is, in promoting East-West investment. Its role is likely to be
more, though not exclusively, concentrated in trade.

longer-run patterns. It is almost impossible, when large barter deals of this sort are negotiated, to view individual transactions strictly in terms of commercial consider-ations. Further, the commitments made under these deals are commitments that must be observed, since each nation's overall economic plan is geared to the foreign trade plan; failure to fulfill the latter, particularly imports, could have a serious impact on the former. This suggests that unless the Eastern GATT nations make a conscious decision to cut back their trade with other socialist nations, their East-West trade cannot increase any faster than before. This statement applies to Hungary as well as to Poland and Rumania, despite the fact that Hungarian enterprises, under the New Economic Mechanism, presumably are free—indeed, required—to buy and sell where the profits are highest. For the fact is that the Hungarian government is compelled to fulfill its obligations under trade agreements with other COMECON members, and, though in theory it cannot order an enter-prise to ship to or buy from, say, the USSR rather than to or from the West, it can and does induce appropriate behavior by various combinations of taxes and sub-sidies.

There are several factors that would appear to militate against any really substantial reduction in intrabloc trade and, hence, against an increase in East-West trade, at least in the medium run. First, it seems unlikely that radical economic reforms, of the kind projected but not quite achieved by Hungary, will be imple-mented. Reforms of this sort, which truly decentralize economic activity, including foreign trade, would undoubtedly lead to a sharp increase in trade with the West. In fact, however, over the last four years, Soviet leaders have been moving in the opposite direction. Far from building on the 1965 reform, they have successfully undone virtually everything promised in that timid venture, for two reasons. First, half-hearted reform does not make sense economically. Marginally improved mate-rial incentives and token decentralization within essentially the old setting, as Soviet leaders discovered, only compound problems. Second, and on the other hand, more than half-hearted reform has political risks that Soviet leaders refuse to run. Even before Czechoslovakia, they had sensed a link between economic and political decentralization. To sacrifice control in this one critical sector of political life endangers the Party's preeminence in all others. Soviet leaders believe too deeply in the monopolistic party as a guardian of the nation's purpose to allow any such erosion.[43]

It is a question not merely of keeping things together within the Soviet Union but also within the empire. Economic reform in the Soviet Union would be quickly and eagerly imitated in many of the East European countries. And economic reform in Eastern Europe, Soviet leaders justifiably fear, would create counterpres-sures against the economic interdependence of their alliance system.

Second, so long as substantial economic reforms are not undertaken by the

---

[43] Because trade forms such a small part of Soviet economic activity, at 2½ to 3 percent of GNP (a much smaller part than the trade of, say, Hungary, which may run as high as 25 percent), the importance of improving its efficiency is easily outweighed by political considerations.

bloc nations, they will be plagued by the "salesmanship" problems described earlier. The only Eastern nation not so severely restricted is the USSR with its large potential for raw material and energy resource exports that require almost no salesmanship ability. Therefore, with the possible exception of the USSR, increased East-West trade faces a salesmanship barrier.

While the USSR does have easily saleable exports, its appetite for hard-currency imports clearly exceeds its present hard-currency export potential. One factor handicapping the USSR in its attempt to achieve some kind of equilibrium in East-West trade is the fact that it stands as a supplier of oil, other raw materials, and grains to the nations of East Europe. The cost to the USSR in hard currency of this role in intrabloc trade is large indeed. Over the next decade, there will undoubtedly be a conflict between those who, for economic reasons, would like to divert Soviet exports from East Europe to the West and those who, for political reasons, will oppose such a diversion in order to preserve economic interdependence among the bloc nations. In the short run, the smaller bloc nations will suffer if they have to seek energy and raw material resources elsewhere, since Soviet prices have been very reasonable. Over the long run, they may gain if they take the opportunity provided to decentralize their economies and adjust themselves to Western markets.

To return to the GATT, until now Western nations have been willing to accept Eastern nations into the GATT so long as these nations reciprocate MFN in the ways indicated above. In so doing, however, they are overlooking the fact that the Eastern nations discriminate in favor of each other on an unprecedented scale. The 60 percent or so of trade that they conduct with each other is certainly excessive, as we have already noted. Can this be justified on economic grounds? Perhaps it can, in two ways.

First, it could be argued that the COMECON nations are a customs union and therefore are entitled under the GATT to grant each other preferential treatment. They do not consider themselves a customs union, however, nor do they feel that they grant each other preferential treatment; and they resent the fact that the members of the EEC are allowed, under the GATT, to grant each other preferential treatment. Nevertheless, this is one way the GATT can rationalize present COMECON practice, and has explicitly done so in the case of Hungary, whose COMECON trade is exempted from MFN treatment.

Second, and related to the first point, the current practice of Eastern European countries may be justified in order to redefine nondiscrimination for centrally planned economies. An important advantage that trade among centrally planned economies has is that they plan this trade in advance on a national scale and guarantee each other deliveries of large aggregations of goods. Given central planning, this feature of intrabloc trade can be viewed as a large positive value. When the Eastern nations argue that they do not grant each other preferential treatment, they may well have in mind the fact that only other Eastern nations are willing to deal with them on their preferred institutional terms, and that this is worth a lot of "price."

If this be the case, then we will have to face a future in which nondiscrimination is defined differently in East and West. This makes something of a mess of the rules of the game, but perhaps the West should not worry too much about it. For one thing, the rules have been breached many times over the years, and, with the recent international monetary crisis, the trend is increasing. Further, East-West trade is still very marginal.[44] Nevertheless, it is extremely important to recognize that so long as radical economic reforms are not undertaken by the Eastern nations, the GATT will not make a substantial contribution toward the increase of East-West trade unless it insists on nondiscrimination in the Western sense; that is to say, unless the GATT forces the Eastern nations to redirect more of their trade to the West. This may of course be impossible without decentralization, for reasons noted earlier, such as bloc export problems. If such reforms are implemented, the reforms themselves would be the important force in increasing East-West trade. The GATT would play a significant but a distinctly subsidiary role.[45]

We turn now to international financial matters—investment, balance-of-payments problems, exchange rates, and the role of the International Monetary Fund (IMF). Rumania has joined the IMF. Undoubtedly other Eastern nations will soon become members. There are advantages to IMF membership that cannot be overlooked. Membership in the IMF can lead to IMF credits, eligibility for World Bank loans, and the right to a share of new issues of special drawing rights—all very desirable, particularly to nations with serious hard-currency balance-of-payments problems. Aside from receiving "manna from heaven," however, it is not clear that membership confers further benefits on the centrally planned economies. Certainly, they do not appear to have much of a stake in the kind of rules of the game that the IMF was set up to insure some 30 years ago. Nor do they appear to have a stake in the future rules presently evolving.[46]

It is somewhat more difficult to understand why the IMF is interested, at this juncture, in encouraging the membership of centrally planned economies. The future framework of Western financial relations remains uncertain. To admit nations into the IMF with such different monetary systems and problems can complicate working out the new framework. To give such nations a vote, and the USSR would perforce have a significant vote were it admitted to the IMF, might encumber the future decision-making process without, in our opinion, adding a useful viewpoint. The fact of the matter is that, with the possible exception of Hungary, the COMECON nations are not in a position to aspire to any of the goals of the Western financial community. They are, in effect, nations without real international monetary systems. They trade with each other on a bilateral balance basis, their currencies are completely inconvertible into other currencies as well as

---

[44] Raymond Vernon, "Apparatchiks and Entrepreneurs," *Foreign Affairs* 52 (January 1974): 249-62, worries that a significant increase in East-West trade could have a very subversive impact on the rules of the game.
[45] COMECON devotes its efforts to promoting socialist integration. In this sense it serves an anti-interdependence role—like the EEC.
[46] We are referring here, of course, to commitments to achieve convertibility, to avoidance of trade controls for current balance-of-payments reasons, and to adjustable pegged exchange rates (now something between fixed and floating).

into commodities, their exchange rates are not real prices and serve no real function, and the prices at which they trade with each other are borrowed from the capitalist world. When they trade with the West, they are like visitors from another planet: they use the currencies, prices, and exchange rates of the West, but none of the financial magnitudes involved are organically related to their domestic economies. And when they trade with the West, they invariably want to buy more than they can sell, which is a problem that cannot be ameliorated by currency devaluation, the ultimate Western solution.

Before concluding this section, a brief comment is in order on the two COMECON banks, the International Bank for Economic Cooperation (IBEC) and the International Investment Bank (IIB). IBEC was established about a decade ago as a sort of European Payments Union for the socialist nations. Its primary purpose was to multilateralize intrabloc trade. (It also had short-term credit extension powers similar to those of the IMF, but these were secondary.) It was to accomplish this task by creating a "transferable ruble" for all intrabloc payments. Presumably, a surplus of transferable rubles earned with one country could be spent in another, thereby multilateralizing trade. In fact, however, given commodity inconvertibility, transferable rubles were no more capable of being spent on an ad hoc basis than zlotys or forints. No nation was willing to have an export surplus with another because it could not be sure that the rubles earned could be satisfactorily spent. As a result, no multilateralization took place. IBEC failed because it attempted to solve by an administrative device a profoundly economic problem. The International Investment Bank, established in 1971, is an institution designed to multilateralize and expand bloc investment. In principle it is similar to the World Bank, but it is actually more analogous to the investment funds established by the EEC.

IBEC seems to offer little in promoting greater East-West interdependence. Just as membership in the IMF by centrally planned economies, save possibly for Hungary, can only be token at this point, so is this also true of formal ties between the IMF and IBEC. On a small scale, IIB offers possibilities. At this point, however, if there were a formal tie between IIB and, say, the World Bank, it would primarily serve the function of funneling Western investment into the Eastern nations. This is already being accomplished by private business on an increasing scale, and IIB has borrowed money for this purpose in Western capital markets. At the moment, these seem to be more powerful forces for integration than IIB could ever be, just as in the West private capital flows dwarf those originating in intergovernmental institutions. Further, the major problems that serve to impede Western investment in the bloc—politics and currency inconvertibility—would be brought no closer to solution by linking IIB with Western financial organizations.

Greater economic interdependence between East and West has been fostered over the past decade by various kinds of ad hoc developments between private enterprises and socialist governments, rather than by international organizations. Joint ventures, coproduction agreements, comarketing agreements, repayments in kind, and the like have facilitated transfer of management know-how and technology, have made up for lack of marketing skills, have evaded problems of inconvertibility, and so forth. As noted earlier, all of these devices must be viewed as second-best strategies, designed to compensate for systemic deficiencies. As such, they are all suboptimal. Thus, paying a Western enterprise to market your products in the West earns hard currency but not so much as would have been earned if marketing skills were endemic. Or repaying long-term investments in gas and petroleum appears to get around the hard-currency problem, but only by repaying in commodities that are, in effect, the equivalent of hard currency.

Were the Soviet Union to institute major economic reforms and, hence, open the way to radical economic reform in Eastern Europe, then market-facilitating organizations like the GATT and the IMF would become more central to East-West economic cooperation. With radical reforms in all of the COMECON nations, internal markets would be decentralized and internal prices and exchange rates would have an organic relationship to world prices. They would become functional. In these circumstances, the Eastern nations could join the GATT on present Western terms. Eastern enterprises, basing their foreign trade decisions on market criteria and no longer constrained by governmental bilateral agreements, would begin to trade much more with the West. In less than a decade, the relative importance of East-West trade in total world trade could double or increase even more while intrabloc trade could decline, relatively, by a comparable percentage.

It is unlikely that East-West trade would reach prewar proportions, however, since the introduction of market socialism in COMECON would not necessarily mean the dissolution of COMECON nor the end of COMECON as a preferential trading area. In the absence of a drastic change in the political picture, it seems probable that the COMECON nations will continue to grant each other more preferential terms than they grant to the West, even as the nations of the EEC and the European Free Trade Association do. Certainly, however, the degree of preference would be less extreme than it is under the present state-trading system. Radical reforms would also end commodity inconvertibility, and membership in the IMF would become meaningful. Trade, and particularly credits and investment, would be facilitated and "normalized." No longer, for example, would there be an incentive on the part of Western investors to seek repayment in kind. In fact, many of the ad hoc arrangements discussed in the second part of this essay might well wither away.

It is, however, unlikely that political considerations will, in the near term, permit such far-reaching changes. Thus, East-West economic relations should remain essentially a political matter, produced and limited by politics. Their contribution—perhaps gradually a very meaningful contribution—will likely be primarily to the politics of East-West relations.

Section IV

Reflections on the economics and politics of international economic organizations

Lawrence B. Krause and Joseph S. Nye

International organizations, it is sometimes said, are always designed to prevent the last war. An analogous problem besets economic institutions. The inability of some existing international economic organizations to deal with the current problems in their domains is all too apparent. Two of the institutional pillars of the postwar Bretton Woods system, the International Monetary Fund (IMF) and the General Agreement on Tariffs and Trade (GATT), were shaken in 1971 and are still suffering from severe malaise. The political and economic conditions that led to their formation at the end of the Second World War have changed, calling into question the political and intellectual foundation upon which they were constructed. In the aftermath of the 1973 energy crisis, meetings of the United Nations Economic and Social Council (ECOSOC) and a special session of the General Assembly have been the scene of demands by poor countries for *a new economic order*, but the meaning of the phrase has been ambiguous and the formula has impeded rather than promoted agreement.[1]

The purpose of this volume and of this essay is not to design a new economic order. Rather, it is to bring together the elements of political and economic analysis that must inform constructive thought about a new economic order and the role that international organizations can play in it. The marriage is not an easy one. The tools of the dominant neoclassical economic paradigm are highly refined but better suited to comparative statics than to explaining social dynamics. The tools of political science are imprecise and in some cases overly constrained by narrow definitions of actors, goals, and instruments. Nonetheless, some effort at applying

Lawrence B. Krause is a senior fellow at the Brookings Institution in Washington, D.C., and is coeditor of this volume. Joseph S. Nye is a professor of political science at Harvard University in Cambridge, Massachusetts. The views in this essay are those of the authors and should not be attributed to any organization. A number of passages in this essay draw on ideas developed jointly with Robert O. Keohane. The authors are grateful for his comments on an earlier version as well as to C. Fred Bergsten, Benjamin J. Cohen, Richard Cooper, and Frank Holzman.

[1] At the 57th session of ECOSOC in July 1974, for example, agreement on the creation of a UN commission on multinational corporations was impeded by (among other things) disagreements over the verbal formula *a new economic order*.

both sets of tools, even if only at a primitive level, is important if thinking about new international economic organizations is not merely to prevent the last crisis.

The conception of world order that underlay postwar economic institutions grew out of the disorders of the 1930s. As individual countries attempted to improve their economic positions during the Great Depression, narrowly conceived self-interest led them to take actions that promised success only by making the conditions of other countries worse. Retaliation soon followed the introduction of new beggar-thy-neighbor policies, and as a result, world welfare was reduced. This was a classic case of a negative-sum game. The United States was an active participant in this destructive competition.

The postwar international economic institutions were designed to prevent a recurrence of this joint-loss situation. In the wake of depression and war, policy-makers in the United States began to take a more cosmopolitan or system-oriented view of US national interest. In economic terms, they foresaw American welfare being improved only if other countries also achieved welfare gains and the reverse if other countries retrogressed. In political terms, architects of the postwar economic institutions, such as Cordell Hull, regarded joint-loss situations as a major cause of political disorder and war. Economic liberalism was the path both to joint gains in welfare and to international peace. Thus the goals of the economic international organizations that were founded under United States and, to a lesser extent, British tutelage were the furthering of world welfare through greater international commerce. The challenge to welfare gains was perceived to be excessive and perverse governmental interference in private commerce. Over the past 25 years, these international organizations helped international commerce to expand by more than 7 percent per year to over $500 billion in 1973. To many economists, the liberal model represents the norm that should guide any restructuring of institutions.

Political scientists, on the other hand, tend to view world politics through models that assign far less importance to the welfare values of economic man that are basic to the liberal economic model. They point out that an international economic order presupposes a political structure or pattern of relations among states. This political structure is determined by the relative power of states and by their objectives, which include security, autonomy, and status as well as welfare. The success of the postwar liberal institutions was based not merely on their economic merits but on a favorable political structure.

Leadership plays an important part in the maintenance of a structure. Leadership involves the willingness of a state or states to forego short-term gains when this is necessary to preserve the structure. The advent of the cold war and of American leadership of a coalition concerned with security against Soviet military expansion enhanced the American incentive to strengthen the structure of the international economic order. For the first decade and a half of the postwar period after 1947, the sense of acute threat to military security tended to relegate economic disputes between allies to a secondary position, and led the US to accept, for example, rising Japanese imports or European discrimination against the dollar and to give aid to less developed countries. When the sense of threat slackened in the 1960s, the economic strains within the liberal world economy became more apparent.

The causes of the recent politicization of international economic relations and institutions are not quite as simple as this security determinism implies. Political scientists sometimes have a tendency to let their analysis become imprisoned by overly restrictive notions of national security in the same way that economists sometimes remain locked in the conceptual prison of economic efficiency and market optimality. In fact, the current disarray of international economic institutions reflects a mixture of political and economic causes. In addition to the shifts in the structure of the distribution of power described in the "Introduction" to this volume, there were problems created by the tremendous growth in economic interdependence among nations.

This interdependence was visible in product markets as international trade expanded faster than the growth of national economies, in money markets as substantial financial transfers across borders became a routine matter for financial institutions, and even in labor markets as significant amounts of temporary (and permanent) labor migration took place. Interdependence was particularly advanced through the actions of multinational corporations, which increased their direct investment activities to such an extent as to cause a qualitative change in international economic relations. This quantum jump in economic interdependence created in many countries fear and insecurity that a corporate decision to close a plant or restrict a market could cause severe unemployment problems and social distress for the country. Similarly, decisions made by other governments to disrupt trade could undermine the very pace of economic activity because of import dependence on raw materials. Finally, interdependence meant that countries could not effectively insulate themselves from world price developments and at times found themselves importing inflation with concomitant social unrest.

The political effects of rising economic interdependence are not always benign. One of the effects is to blur the traditional distinction between domestic and international politics. More groups have been affected and have become directly involved in international policy questions. More issues, once considered domestic, have begun to appear on the interstate agenda. Moreover, part of the natural political dynamics of rising economic interdependence has been the provocation of protectionist sentiments. As the integration of markets has progressed, immobile groups in societies, including large segments of labor, have pressed for governmental protection to redress their relative disadvantage in the competition with transnationally mobile competitors. The coherence of national policies has become more difficult to maintain.

These political problems generated by rising economic interdependence have taken place against a background of increased diversity of demands placed on governments. Among the advanced industrial societies, there has been an increase of concern for other values in addition to prosperity. This does not mean that citizen demands upon government for welfare have diminished, but that a broader range of goals is being factored into national foreign economic policies. Similarly among less developed countries, concern over the power of multinational firms and other foreign economic influences has led to demands for greater autonomy in addition to greater prosperity. Furthermore, an increased desire for status by some less developed countries commensurate with their growing prosperity has added to the complexity of their relations with developed countries and with other less developed countries as well. Thus, state goals in international economic institutions have become more diversified to include such concerns as pollution abatement, protection of endangered natural species, and the conduct of multinational firms.

The result of these changes has been to politicize the structural question of what rules and institutions should govern international economic relations. As Richard Cooper has argued, the postwar structure was a two-track (or multi-track) system in which various issues were kept relatively separate.[2] It is possible that this separation of security and economic issues at the process level was an anomaly in world politics, and depended upon a combination of US economic preponderance and military alliance leadership. As the "Introduction" to this volume argues, security and economic issues were linked *hierarchically* in the domestic politics of the leading state through rhetorical appeals to the symbol of national security. Now with changing circumstances, political rhetoric has begun to include appeals to the welfare gains from economic interdependence. But the structuring of economic institutions should not merely rest on rhetoric. Political and economic analysts must adapt their prevalent models to provide a better understanding of the politics of economic interdependence if international economic institutions are to rest on a firm foundation.

Models of the world

Political

Prevailing models of political analysis have tended to be based on three useful simplifying assumptions: (1) states are the only significant actors in world politics; (2) military force is their most useful and significant instrument; (3) military security and political status are their dominant objectives. The most powerful, though imprecisely specified, theoretical proposition in international political analysis is that states will act to maintain or create some balance of power, that is, that they will protect themselves by trying to limit or counteract the growth in the power of other states. The predictive power of balance of power theory depends upon the validity of the underlying assumptions. In economic issues, for example, states pursue a complex mixture of goals of which security and status are only a part. Insofar as welfare goals predominate, and there are absolute joint gains relative to the past to be shared, states may act to encourage rather than to limit the growth of another state's capabilities. Rising German GNP may diminish France's relative

---

[2] "Trade Policy Is Foreign Policy," *Foreign Policy* 9 (Winter 1972-73).

status in Europe, but given domestic pressures for increased welfare, the favorable effects to France through an increased market for French exports loom equally large in most politicians' minds.

The assumptions of traditional political analysis about goals and strategies not only sometimes lead to incorrect predictions about the politics of economic relations among states but the assumptions about actors and instruments tend to divert attention away from important aspects of the politics of international economic relations. There have been important changes in the relative utility of force and economic instruments of power, in the complexity of actors with significant power in many economic issue areas, and in the agenda of issues in world politics as a result of the increased sensitivity of societies to each other in areas that were formerly considered purely domestic.

The realism of traditional assumptions is a matter of degree and varies with situations and areas of world politics. The problem for analysis is knowing when to supplement traditional assumptions, not to discard them completely. A number of useful supplementary concepts had their origin in integration theory. Analysts concerned with explaining processes of regional integration noted that assumptions about force, security, and states as sole actors fit rather poorly with the politics among European states in the 1950s and 1960s. The conceptual impact of integration was somewhat limited by its own shortcomings of regional focus and teleological assumptions, but it has nonetheless left a legacy of concepts that have been as yet poorly assimilated into prevailing political paradigms: the use of economic interdependence as a political instrument, the variation of political processes by issue areas, the problem of linkage or separation of issue areas, the importance of transnational actors, and the roles of international institutions.[3]

Thus the design of a new international economic order must assume the continued existence of nation states, but also take into account important transnational actors. It must assume the continued importance of military power, and indeed the probable continuation of a bipolar distribution of power in the domain of nuclear deterrence, but it must take into account a greater dispersal of power in other issue areas and address itself to the problem of linkage and separation between issue areas. The order must take into account the broadening of state objectives and the growth of societal interdependence that has tended to abridge the distinction between domestic and international politics.

Economic

Economic models of world commerce historically were developed by liberal economists as an abstraction to give normative guidance to policymakers, not to explain behavior as it then existed. The paradigm was concerned with the inter-

---

[3] For elaboration, see Robert O. Keohane and Joseph S. Nye, "International Interdependence and Integration," in Fred Greenstein and Nelson Polsby, eds., *Handbook of Political Science* (Andover, Mass.: Addison-Wesley, 1975).

national trade of merchandise, but with appropriate adjustment was adapted as well to the movement of factors of production between countries. The classical tenet flowing from this analysis advocating free trade, although modified, has remained remarkably untouched by subsequent generations of economists. Since the low point of the 1930s, governments have moved toward more liberal commercial policies, but even the nonsocialist developed countries have stopped far short of endorsing free trade, and many less developed countries have hardly started down that road.

The critical features of the classical model that undermine its usefulness as the sole guide to policy relate to its acceptance of economic efficiency as the only goal of policy, to its reliance on comparative statics methodology, and to the inappropriateness of its assumptions concerning the competitive nature of markets and the political environment of policymaking. As discussed in the next section, economic efficiency has frequently been sacrificed in policy decisions to other policy objectives. Moreover, comparative statics methodology fails to highlight the difficulties involved in moving from one equilibrium situation to another and thus does not weight the adjustment costs involved. In real policymaking the adjustment process is of overwhelming importance, since it determines whether a policy will command support or not. Analytical proof that free trade could provide sufficient gains to society to compensate losers is not convincing as a policy argument unless the gains are immediately visible and the transfer mechanism is already in place, and even then it might not be convincing if a change of status is involved. Only a dynamic theory that traces the consequences of policy actions over time could provide the analytical basis for such an assurance, if one is possible.

A critical assumption of the classical model is that perfect competition, or at least workable competition, exists in product and factor markets. Without this assumption, there is no assurance that resource allocation will be appropriate or that the distribution of the gains from trade will be economically efficient or equitable. But markets are not perfectly competitive, and insufficient effort has been made to incorporate market imperfections into the analysis. Furthermore, the classical model was based on the implicit assumption that a stable political environment would be maintained. At a minimum, the model is defective in not analyzing the political disturbance that results directly from changes in commercial policy, and ideally the model should encompass other sources of political disturbance. In other words, political change must be considered endogenous in the model and cannot be assumed away.

The inadequacies of the classical model do not suggest necessarily that it should be discarded or replaced by another model, which might be equally inappropriate. Rather, the need is to broaden the vision and the coverage of the model so as to permit more realism. Adding period analysis, political actors, and a more sophisticated distributional determination will enormously complicate the model, one of whose virtues in the past has been clarity and simplicity. Nevertheless, the world is complex and models must reflect the essential ingredients of reality to be useful for policymaking. An important first step toward adjusting to reality is to go beyond simple two-value (welfare versus security) models of the goals that states pursue in their international political-economic relations.

Goals of nation states expressed in foreign relations

Neither economists nor political scientists can afford to be restricted by simple assumptions about the goals that nation states express in their foreign economic relations. Attention to these goals is required in order to envision a suitable structure for a new world order. Conceptually one can postulate that there exists a clear hierarchy of goals that motivate nations, yet recognize that some trade-offs are possible between them. One goal may be higher on the scale than another but be sacrificed to it if the marginal loss is sufficiently small relative to the expected marginal gain.

In general, economists have tended to stress the goal of economic efficiency in their considerations of international economic order. The desire for greater economic efficiency in international commerce translates into the promotion of factor price equalization and thereby achievement of maximum global welfare. The methods generally believed to implement this desire are the liberalization of goods transactions and factor flows between nations and the improvement of competition between and within countries.

Economists *expect* these policies to enhance economic growth and generally improve economic well-being. In reality, however, this goal, so dear to the hearts of economists, often appears low in the hierarchy of national goals. It must be recognized that for some countries, particularly for poorer countries, promoting economic growth is more important than implied here. Nevertheless, if one examines the preferences of nation states as revealed through their actions rather than their pronouncements, economic efficiency does not appear to be highly regarded. The list of illustrations of this point seems endless: prices of goods are frequently prevented from going either up or down; interest rate ceilings are placed on returns to savers; monopolies, monopsonies, and oligopolies are protected; investments (often foreign) are discouraged or distorted through tax subsidies; wasteful labor practices are permitted and sometimes required; international trade is restricted; and so on. Indeed, if it were not for a longer-term historical perspective, one could argue that the desire for economic efficiency is of secondary concern to nation states.

Economic efficiency is an instrumental value (not a *fundamental* goal) that enhances the prospects for achievement of welfare and other goals. Economists are generally aware that efficiency and welfare are traded off against other goals, the most important of which—national security—is frequently treated as an undifferentiated constraint. Political scientists, on the other hand, tend to think of national goals in terms of a hierarchy in which security dominates most decisions most of the time. Neither economists nor political scientists have paid enough attention to the complexity of the concept of security, including its *instrumental role* in the enhancement of other values.

Security is a frequently used word, yet the concept is more ambiguous than we first realize.[4] National security can be used to cover a wide range of goals and divergent, even contradictory, policies. In a sense, security is a negative goal—the absence of a sense of danger or threat. Narrowly defined, *security* means the absence of the possibility of a threat to survival. But survival is only rarely at stake. Most people want to feel secure in more than just survival. They wish to feel secure in their continued or future enjoyment of a number of other basic values. Since we can never be certain about the future, the problem of security is a question of degrees of uncertainty. How much are we willing to pay out of our current enjoyment for a little more certainty about future enjoyment?

Different people have different preferences for present versus future consumption, and different beliefs about which values are basic. Individual physical survival, for example, is a widely shared basic value, but many people have sacrificed it for the sake of group survival or for nontemporal religious values. Thus, the content of *security* is often a matter of contention. It is not fixed, but varies between peoples and over time. However, at a high level of abstraction, we can identify at least three basic clusters of values that nearly all peoples in today's world rank close to physical survival and that national security policies are designed to protect. These basic clusters of values are: (1) welfare—at least a minimal expected level of economic welfare; (2) independence—a certain political and social autonomy as a group; (3) prestige—a degree of political status as a group. Most national security policies in today's world are designed not merely to ensure the physical survival of the individuals within national boundaries but to ensure a certain minimal expected enjoyment of these other basic values as well.[5] Indeed, some national security policies may be said to actually increase the risks to physical survival in order to ensure greater certainty in the continued and future enjoyment of economic welfare, political status, and group autonomy.

In short, the political problem of security that confronts all states has important economic and social psychological aspects as well as the traditional military component. If we define *security* as the absence of acute threats to the minimal acceptable levels of the basic values that a people consider essential to its survival, then the economic dimension is important both as a potential instrument of threat to basic values and as one of the basic values itself.

Military security has traditionally been defined by the nature of the instruments, that is, the absence of threats based on military force. We find it more useful, however, to define economic security in terms of values rather than instruments. Economic security in this sense refers to the absence of threat of severe deprivation of economic welfare. Economic security as a goal becomes visible when a country consciously chooses to accept economic inefficiency to avoid

---

[4] Arnold Wolfers's "National Security as an Ambiguous Symbol" remains the classic analysis. See his collection of essays, *Discord and Collaboration* (Baltimore, Md.: The Johns Hopkins Press, 1962).

[5] The list is not exhaustive. Though we live in a secular age, some states (perhaps Saudi Arabia?) might rank promotion of religious values after survival.

becoming more vulnerable to economic impulses from abroad or when a country stresses national approaches at the expense of integration gains. Conventional international economic theory generally tends to criticize such a choice, but conventional theory does not properly value security of supply or adequately appraise the cost of economic disruption. The importance of economic security as a goal is positively related to prosperity. The more wealth that is achieved, the more likely the desire to protect what exists and the smaller the desire to risk for further gains. This may appear in the domestic choice to risk more unemployment rather than more inflation as the latter is more threatening to existing social structures. The goal may appear in efficiency-destroying controls and subsidies that both host and source countries place on the activities of multinational firms. Multinational corporations themselves recognize this goal when they stop well short of complete national sourcing for specialized parts and consciously maintain duplicative facilities.

The ways in which states trade off present consumption versus future security of such basic values as survival, welfare, autonomy, and status will have an important effect on the international economic order. Equally important are the trade-offs between these basic values and other basic values, such as promotion of ideological and religious beliefs. Such trade-offs affect the willingness of states to promote the instrumental values of economic efficiency and structural stability that loom so large in conventional economic and political analysis.

Collective economic security and principles for constructing institutions

This complexity of goals means that economic institutions will have to meet more basic principles than the instrumental value of efficiency. In particular, economic security has become a much more salient goal as a result of food and raw material shortages and the oil crisis. Countries are searching for instruments to increase their economic security. Thus, international economic institutions will have to be concerned not merely with global economic integration but with collective economic security. Broadly defined, *collective economic security* means governments' acceptance of international surveillance of their domestic and foreign economic policies, of criticism of the effects of their policies on the economic security of other countries, and of various forms of international presence in the operations of markets. In a domestic economic context, the economic security (and welfare) of all factors of production can be hurt by the instability of a wage-price spiral. Therefore, judicious government policies encouraging a halt to the fight over income shares can restore stability and improve economic security. Similarly, on the world scene, international organizations could be used to moderate conflicts over the distribution of the gains from trade and other economic relations and to improve the economic security of all participants.

While it is impossible at this point to catalog the full range of demands that will be made upon any institutions for the promotion of collective economic security, nonetheless it is possible to sketch some simple principles that will enable them to meet such demands more effectively.[6] Among the most important are: (1) the principle of joint gain, (2) the principle of optimizing rather than maximizing interdependence, (3) the principle of mixing market and organization methods, and (4) the principle of functional determination of scope and membership.

Joint gain

A basic principle for the construction of collective economic security should be the creation of conditions that encourage joint-gain situations, in which all parties are better off, and discourage joint-loss situations, where all parties are worse off, or fixed payoff situations, where one country's gains must result in another country's losses. One of the important aspects of economic issues is that they frequently involve a large component of joint gain. The task for institutionalizing an economic order is to ensure that this cooperative joint-gain aspect prevails. This basic principle represents an interpretation of collective economic security as a dynamic concept. Severe deprivation of welfare is most likely to be avoided under conditions of expanding joint gain.

The major obstacles to preservation of joint-gain situations may come from within the economic area or from linkage of economic issues and other values, such as military security or political status. Inside the economic area, there may be disruptive conflicts over distribution of gains. There are two dimensions to economic issues: joint gain and the distribution of gain. The joint gain may be reaped almost entirely by one party, or it may be shared more evenly between the parties. Where there is strong disagreement over distribution, the ensuing conflict can sometimes destroy the potential for joint gain, leaving one or both parties worse off. At any single point in time, the total gains from trade are fixed and conflicts over distribution can have negative results for the system as a whole. If the horizon of the participants can be lengthened to include the outcomes of future trade, however, then a joint-gain situation can be created. For example, a conflict over the price of copper between importers and exporters could be moderated if a longer horizon is accepted, since importers may agree to higher prices in return for assurances of price stability and adequacy of supply while exporters may accept lower prices in return for price stability and assurance of markets. The net gain to be divided between them would arise from avoiding market breakdowns and misallocation of investment in copper production or copper substitutes. Thus, a concern for principles of distribution is an important aspect of collective economic security.

Economic welfare does not exist in isolation from other values, and economic change can affect the relative military strength and sense of military security of different countries. States may sacrifice or forego the joint gain to be claimed from

---

[6] The concept of collective economic security is elaborated in Joseph S. Nye, "Collective Economic Security," *International Affairs*, Fall 1974.

trade or economic cooperation if they fear that a possible military opponent may improve its relative power as a result of its share of the joint gain.

Provision of national military security has been a classic dilemma of politics in a world of states that do not obey a common sovereign. States have tried to provide themselves with greater security by increasing their strength, either by investing in military forces or by joining alliances. But often this increased strength appears as a threat to other states, which take similar measures. The increases in military strength cancel each other out. The net result is often a loss of welfare (or autonomy) without any corresponding increase in security. All too often, the struggle to achieve national security has simply resulted in joint losses.

The search for military security need not lead to joint losses. The crucial factor is the intentions of the parties involved. If all important states are pursuing balance and stability rather than preponderance, and are able to communicate this to each other, then a sense of security can be achieved that leaves everyone better off. The problem, of course, has been being sure of other states' intentions. Thus, stability in international military balances and some relaxation of mistrust of political and military intentions are important if international economic welfare is to be made secure.

Issues of political status may also disrupt joint-gain situations. Concern for political status or hierarchical rank among states is a particularly difficult political value to accommodate, because (by definition) one country cannot improve its position without another country encountering a relative loss. Where economic issues and political status become closely intertwined, there is danger of conflict from which joint economic losses can ensue. However, it is possible that functional institutional arrangements that provide multiple hierarchies and different ways of measuring status may help to alleviate such situations.

The overall task for international institutions is to develop the framework within which the principle of cognizance or collective surveillance can be expanded in international economic affairs.[7] Economic policies are interdependent and thus the legitimate focus of an international dialogue. As states explain their policies and submit them to international discussion, mistrust of intentions that breeds insecurity may be diminished. For instance, advanced discussion of expected agricultural yields might have helped to reduce the harm caused by US restrictions on exports of soybeans to Japan in 1973. Other states will be able to formulate policies with greater knowledge and less uncertainty and sense of insecurity. This will help to focus attention on areas of joint gain and thus avoid disruptive conflicts that threaten economic welfare.

Optimizing interdependence

The principle of optimizing rather than maximizing interdependence entails the provision of opportunities for states to express and negotiate their preferences

---

[7] The concept of cognizance of *military* security policies is elaborated in Leonard Beaton, *The Reform of Power* (London: Chatto & Windus, 1972).

between basic values, if they value autonomy, for instance. In practice it means that institutions may be designed not simply to liberalize transactions but to curb and control economic interdependence.

Economic interdependence is a two-edged sword. As indicated above, it involves costs as well as benefits. Interdependence can be a source of political manipulation as well as a source of economic welfare. When states act to control international economic relations, they not only risk diminishing economic welfare but they also frequently create a new type of policy interdependence. Often the policy measures by which one government attempts to control transnational economic relations depend for their success upon the policy measures taken by other governments. Competitive tariffs, export subsidies, or exchange rate policies, for example, can lead to beggar-thy-neighbor cycles of retaliation, which leave everyone worse off. Where protective measures are necessary, attention should be paid to their relative effects on efficiency. For example, the Italian export deposit scheme of 1974 was less destructive of efficiency than alternatives would have been. If economic policy interdependence is to have positive effects rather than reduce welfare, a certain measure of international cognizance and rules are essential. This is the basis for the international collective role making economic welfare more secure.

International threats to economic welfare and economic security can come from three major sources: (1) from the intentional or unintentional actions of other governments, (2) from the intentional or unintentional actions of transnational organizations, such as multinational corporations or unions, (3) from natural causes, such as a crop failure. Threats to economic welfare arising from the intentional actions of other states or transnational organizations may be based upon the use of force, or may be based upon economic instruments of power. If we think of creating an international economic order that reduces economic insecurity, that is, reduces threats of deprivation of economic welfare, it is clear that a mixture of regimes and institutions will be required to deal with the variety of sources of threat.

Mixing market and organization methods

The principle of mixing market and organization methods is based on the comparative advantages of each in terms of different basic values. Market methods promote efficiency under appropriate circumstances, such as the absence of major externalities and indivisibilities, and they also depoliticize the myriad of day-to-day decisions in any allocative process. On the other hand, markets work within a given initial distribution of wealth. When that distribution is unacceptable to major participants, organizational devices involving representation and politicization of differing interests will be introduced into the process of allocation.

If the conditions for efficiency (including perfect competition and the absence of public goods) were present in the world, and if there were acceptance of the initial distribution, then international economic relations could be left to *market* determination. In reality, however, there are so many divergencies from these conditions that a serious question can be raised as to whether any important economic activity can be purely market determined.

Equally important, however, are the political effects of markets. By depersonalizing myriads of decisions, markets tend to depoliticize day-to-day economic processes. When an economic issue is technically arcane and does not have major distributional effects, as Cooper argues is the case with money, collective economic security may be best served by a regime that includes a large market component. On the other hand, the market power of buyers and sellers is affected by their "inherited" wealth and by nonmarket power levers such as diplomatic pressure. Where these are severe and arouse serious questions of distributional equity, depoliticization through market mechanisms is unlikely to be successful in the long run.

Markets not only tend to depoliticize issues, but under the right conditions, they may prove superior to organizations (private or public) in extending the range of choice and thus enhancing autonomy and status. Carlos Diaz-Alejandro argues that commodity markets, Eurocurrency markets, and arm's-length trade may be superior to commodity agreements, concessional aid, and multinational corporations in terms of the qualities of unintrusiveness, decomposability, and reversibility that are vital to the autonomy and status concerns of poorer countries. It has now become commonplace to realize that the ideology of free trade served British interests when its enterprises had market power relative to all others, and that there can be economic neo-colonialism or an "imperialism of free trade" (and investment). On the other hand, as D. C. M. Platt has pointed out, the difference between colonialism and neo-colonialism may be more important than the similarities.[8] Where force is not used to reinforce an institutional-legal structure, and where there is competition, albeit imperfect, between private actors in markets, the range of political alternatives available to the poorer countries is often considerable.

Functional determination of scope and membership

It is sometimes said that intergovernmental organizations operate according to "the law of inverse salience": the greater the political prominence of an issue, the less the operational autonomy of the organization. This law is sometimes used as a reason for limiting the scope of an organization's domain to a narrow range of issues that are more likely to be susceptible to technical than to broad political treatment. A related point is functionally specific sanctions. When sanctions are issue-specific, as in GATT provisions for the withdrawal of tariff concessions, there is less likelihood of the issue becoming politicized.

There are limits, however, to functional specificity. Not all narrowly defined issues are amenable to technical solutions, and even where they are, the experience of a number of functionally specific organizations has been that members without

---

[8] See J. Gallagher and R. Robinson, "The Imperialism of Free Trade," *Economic History Review*, March 1953. Also D. C. M. Platt, "Economic Imperialism and the Businessman: Britain and Latin America before 1914," in Roger Owen and Bob Sutcliffe, eds., *Studies in the Theory of Imperialism* (London: Longman, 1972).

technical concerns or competence may politicize the organizational process in pursuit of extra-organizational goals.[9] Attempts to curtail this behavior by restriction of membership cut across national goals of participation and status, as Cooper notes in his discussion of monetary organizations. Moreover, broad-based organizations can play a useful role in the exchange of information and in the establishment of basic principles of legitimacy.

Part of the answer to this problem lies in pluralism of organizations. Different organizations serve different needs. They complement and compete with each other. There is a role in trade for both the GATT and the United Nations Conference on Trade and Development (UNCTAD); in money, for the IMF, the Bank for International Settlements, and Working Party III of the Organization for Economic Cooperation and Development (OECD); in aid, both for the World Bank and regional banks. While this gives rise to administrative messiness and problems of overlap and underlap in organizational jurisdiction, organizational neatness is not necessarily a virtue from a political systemic point of view. Pluralism in organization can help to reserve some organizations for functionally specific tasks. The more an organization is concerned with detailed rules and operations, the more important is functional specificity and limited membership (or votes weighted by criteria relevant to the issue). If we lived in a "first-best" world, this untidy approach to international bureaucracy would be unnecessary. Its appropriateness derives from the large number of constraints that thwart first-best efforts to satisfy the diversity of preferences in the political world we live in.

Roles of international organization

Analyses drawn from domestic politics are frequently an impediment to understanding the political roles of international organizations. To think of international organizations as incipient world governments that hold supranational authority above states is to restrict attention to a small (and frequently trivial) aspect of their political roles. International organizations have latent roles as well as the manifest ones set forth in their charters. Both are relevant to the promotion of collective economic security. Three latent roles are those of arena, instrument, and actor.

Latent roles

Arena

Too little attention is paid to the political process by which agendas are set in world politics. The choice of organizational arena often has an important effect on

[9] See Robert Cox and Harold Jacobson, eds., *The Anatomy of Influence: Decision-Making in International Organizations* (New Haven, Conn.: Yale University Press, 1973).

setting the agenda. Moreover, the different jurisdictional scope and the differing composition of delegations to different organizations frequently result in quite different distributions of influence and outcomes. The same issue may come out quite differently in the GATT than in UNCTAD.[10] States try to steer issues to power arenas more favorable to their preferred outcomes. As indicated above, this "forum shopping" has its virtues, as well as shortcomings, and providing multiple forums is an important role of international organizations in the politics of international economic relations.

Instrument

Governments will frequently try to use international organizations to bring pressure upon other governments or transnational actors. Rosenbaum and Tyler describe how poor countries have used the United Nations to dramatize their feelings of insecurity vis-à-vis multinational corporations or to press for changes in the procedures of other organizations, such as the GATT and the IMF. Galtung characterizes the structure of world communications as "feudal," with horizontal communication between powerful states, vertical communication between powerful and poor states, and little horizontal communication between poor states. International organizations help poor states to escape this feudal communications structure.[11] On the other hand, rich countries have tried to use organizations such as the IMF to enforce fiscal constraints on borrowing countries, or the World Bank and the Inter-American Development Bank to bring pressure on governments like Peru to compensate for nationalization of corporate assets.

Actor and catalyst

With the growth of economic interdependence, more bureaucracies that were once considered domestic become involved in international affairs. Many bureaucracies and agencies of governments have similar interests. In some cases, the similarity of interests is greater across national lines than it is with competing domestic agencies and interests; witness Cooper's description of the common interest of financial officials in the Committee of Twenty.

From this perspective, one can envisage a considerable number of potential coalitions of functionally specific units in world politics. International organizations provide the physical contact and aura of legitimacy that translate some of these potential transgovernmental coalitions into active ones. The more functionally specific the organization, the more likely is this process to occur. These coalitions form not only through contacts in the countries but sometimes through an active role by secretariat officials.[12] Transgovernmental coordination and coali-

---

[10] Joseph S. Nye, "UNCTAD: Populist Pressure Group," in Cox and Jacobson.

[11] Johan Galtung, "A Structural Theory of Imperialism," *Journal of Peace Research*, 1971: 81-118.

[12] This argument is developed in Robert O. Keohane and Joseph S. Nye, "Transgovernmental Relations and International Organization," *World Politics*, October 1974.

tion building do not require a very elaborate organizational structure, but they are more than just curiosities. On the contrary, in a number of areas, they may play a significant role in the coordination of expectations and behavior that is important in the management of interdependence and is central to the concept of collective economic security.

Manifest roles

Even in their formal roles, there is wide variation between international organizations. Eugene Skolnikoff has suggested the following four-fold categorization:

1. Provision of information and minor services (includes data gathering and analysis, facilitation of interstate consultation, suggestions for coordination).
2. Legislation (creating rules and standards for regulation of activities and allocation of costs and benefits).
3. Regulation and adjudication (monitoring adherence to rules, possibly through inspection, mediation, conciliation, and management of specific sanctioning procedures).
4. Operations (large-scale research and development, operation of a technology or management of resources).

These manifest functions vary among organizations in money, trade, aid, and direct investment as described in the essays. From table 1 it can be seen that the highest operational levels have been reached in aid and money. Indeed, in aid the role of the multilateral institutions has increased from 18 percent of official development aid in 1963 to 42 percent a decade later. On the other hand, as Keohane and Ooms show, international organizations in the direct investment area have been limited largely to information, and only now are there efforts in the UN to move into the area of legislation. Trade, as described by Baldwin and Kay, falls in an intermediate category.

Conclusions: problems for the future

Fundamental institutional engineering, such as occurred at Bretton Woods, tends to follow a crisis. Even after the depression and war, however, the institutions that were created were limited in their operational authority. The late Bretton Woods system was not characterized by strong operational institutions. The broad authority of the proposed International Trade Organization was rejected in favor of a modest coordinating forum, the GATT. The powerful fund that Keynes had envisaged was not established. The IMF has exercised authority primarily in relation to weaker countries. In its relations with the stronger countries, it has been a follower rather than a leader, for example, on recent innovations such as special drawing rights and flexible exchange rates.

Table 1. Global economic organizations

	Information	Legislation	Regulation	Operation
Aid	various	UNCTAD United Nations General Assembly	World Bank regional consortia	World Bank United Nations Development Program
Money	various	IMF Group of Ten	IMF	IMF (minor) Bank for International Settlements
Trade	various	GATT UNCTAD	GATT	commodity agreements
Direct Investment	United Nations General Assembly OECD	–	–	–

NOTE: This table is illustrative, not exhaustive.

Given this view of the past, one should not expect current demands for a new economic order to lead to the establishment of new international economic institutions with broad operational authority. As we have indicated, however, an economic order based on the promotion of collective economic security requires new attitudes and policies but may or may not need new operational institutions. If one thinks of international organization in process terms rather than in formal structural terms, then elaborate organizational blueprints are not the only solution. This view is reflected in the essays in this volume.

One of the striking features of nearly all the essays in this volume is the limited nature of their specific suggestions for changes in international organizations. The specific suggestions in the essays are incremental rather than fundamental. In this they differ from the current conventional wisdom. They contrast strongly with the sense of crisis that has been prominent in the press and in the 1974 special session of the General Assembly or at the summer 1974 ECOSOC meeting. For example, look at the four functional essays. In aid, Frank and Baird want international organizations to become the prime source of humanitarian assistance and development aid, and also to provide economic operational assistance. In direct investment, Keohane and Ooms want to see the gradual growth of international controls on multinational corporations, but they are skeptical of any ambitious large-scale program. In trade, Baldwin and Kay want to see progress on nontariff barriers, domestic adjustment assistance, and GATT rules for export controls, but their suggestions are all incremental rather than fundamental. In money, Cooper advocates making special drawing rights the basis for world reserves, for gathering of information about the stability of Eurocurrency markets, and for cooperation between major states to insure that there is a lender of last resort in the event of crisis. But he advocates that this be done by evolutionary English constitutional procedures rather than by a formal constitutional assembly.

A similar attitude is found in the area-oriented essays. Legvold and Holzman foresee very limited prospects and limited benefits in bringing the centrally planned economies into the major economic organizations of the global economy. They do not advocate weakening the rules of global institutions to attract Eastern states into them. There is no need for an "Eastern countries' bypass" analogous to the "poor countries' bypass" in Chapter IV of the GATT. To the extent that special institutions are needed now, they are provided in large part by transnational corporations. Gilpin has little to suggest about institutional relations among advanced capitalist states. Rosenbaum and Tyler note the limited roles and prospects for economic organizations among poor countries.

At first glance, one might accuse the authors of complacency. But if there is complacency, it is not of the type that is usually associated with liberal economics, where the rational answers are all known, and the problem is merely one of coping with the "irrationality of politics." On the contrary, a number of the essays show a keen awareness of the importance of political values and the complexity of the trade-offs between values. In other words, the apparent complacency may reflect an appreciation of the complexity of the actors, issues, and goals of states in international economic affairs today, and of the feeling that the incremental changes to our existing range of second-best organizations may be the best way toward accommodating that diversity within the set of principles sketched in the fourth section of these conclusions.

At the same time, one *cannot* take the incremental nature of the authors' institutional suggestions as final evidence that there are no operational roles or that there is no need for new institutions. The individual authors have tended to focus on the difficulties in their functional areas. Viewed as a whole, however, problems not only cumulate, they interact with one another. This interaction, for example, of trade, aid, and direct investment, might require new institutional forms for the solution of problems. For instance, a new international bank for commodities from exhaustible resources might be desirable because markets for these products (1) are not perfectly competitive, (2) have evidenced price instability, (3) have been subject to supply interruptions, (4) have been questioned concerning their distribution of gains between exporters and importers, and (5) have raised concerns over the protection of future generations. A new institution with operating authority might be better placed than existing institutions to attempt to improve welfare, economic security, and distributional equity simultaneously. Formal structural solutions may (or may not) be the conclusion of an analysis that conceives of international organization in process terms.

The fact that a sense of crisis pervades the world economy in 1974 suggests that some appropriate role in resolving the situation may, indeed should, exist for international organizations. The crisis is not the result of the absence of the new economic order desired by some less developed countries. Rather, it is the result of the inability of existing mechanisms to handle the old problems of financing balance-of-payments disequilibria and of coordinating macroeconomic management. The magnitude of the disturbance affecting countries' balance of payments as a result of the sharp increase in oil prices means that immediate adjustment by oil importers would be inefficient, if not impossible, and that considerable financing of deficits over an extended period of time need be contemplated. Yet neither private commercial banks, existing swap facilities between central banks, the IMF, nor other international institutions as now constituted are adequate for the task. The IMF alone or jointly with the World Bank, however, could perform the intermediation function between oil exporters with surplus funds and oil importers in need of finance if special facilities were created, and this may well be the optimal solution for the recycling problem.

Similarly, the world economy need not be subjected to the disturbance that comes from having all industrial countries expand simultaneously as they did in 1972-73 and contract together as is threatened in 1974-75. Instability of commodity prices and general worldwide inflation necessarily result from such simultaneity. The immediate problem of a synchronized recession with the attendant risk of a real depression can be alleviated if those countries that have stronger balance-of-payments positions and better price performance (such as West Germany and the United States) lead the others in stimulating their economies for recovery. Such macroeconomic policy coordination has often been discussed within OECD, but the results have often been disappointing. The risks of uncoordinated policy responses, however, are now so great as to suggest that new efforts need be made to make OECD effective in this role.

In the realm of prediction and prescription, it is always safer to be a "viewer with alarm." The mistakes of alarmists are seldom held against them. Thus it is risky to suggest that there may be more stability in the system of international economic organizations than it is currently conventional to believe. Yet that is what the essays in this volume imply. The coming trade wars predicted in 1971 have not materialized. The failure of monetary reform has left a de facto system working tolerably well. This is not to suggest that there may not be immediate problems requiring governmental cooperation, particularly in maintaining the stability of the monetary and banking systems in the aftermath of the "oil crisis." Nor does it deny the importance of potential institutional developments, such as a food bank within the Food and Agriculture Organization, a UN commodity bank to stabilize prices, or a change in GATT rules to relate supply obligations to the concept of collective economic security. Nor does it deny the desirability of efforts to achieve redistribution of wealth and power in the long term. Rather, the argument is that even in time of crisis, the policy problem is less one of elaborate institutional engineering than one of developing greater policy coordination within a perspective of collective economic security. Taking into account both their latent and manifest functions, existing organizations may be sufficient to allow governments to cope with the crises—provided that there is perception of the need and that there is leadership.

Will leadership be forthcoming? Kindleberger has warned of the danger of leadership lag: the systemic perception on the part of leading states lags behind their growing strength by a critical and disastrous decade or two.[13] Thus the US was the de facto monetary and trade leader after the First World War, but failed to bear the costs of leadership until after the Second World War. Drawing on Kindleberger's views, and thinking of international organizations in traditional terms, Barraclough asks whether international organizations can fill the leadership role now that United States power has waned, and arrives at a negative conclusion and thus a gloomy prognosis for the future of the world economy.[14] But as the introductory essay in this volume indicates, the decline in US power has been greatly exaggerated. As the German chancellor has pointed out, with United States GNP five or six times greater than the next biggest Western country, and trade only 5 percent of GNP, the US can more easily withstand external disorder, and "it is hard to achieve anything fundamental without the cooperation of the United States."[15] Even in uncongenial institutions like UNCTAD, the US has considerable, albeit negative, influence.[16] The power resources for leadership in the international economy still exist.

One of the tasks of leadership is to behave in a way that lays a basis for a better economic order in the more distant future. One such long-term goal would be the greater integration of economic systems when the political cleavages underlying the current structure may have altered. A second goal would be redistributive—to construct a gradually rising floor under world poverty.[17] Yet another long-term goal would be to develop the sense of collective responsibility for economic security and to reinforce perceptions of the joint-gain aspects of economic relationships. In short, the fact that the essays do not propose beautiful blueprints for international economic order is not a cause for complacency. It means that efforts to improve our understanding and to improve our institutions must go hand in hand. The problem for international economic organizations in this decade is not a problem of major constitutional restructuring, but of ensuring far-sighted and systemic perceptions that make states willing to pay the price of leadership. A better understanding of the politics of economic interdependence may help to create such perceptions.

---

[13] Charles Kindleberger, *Power and Money* (New York: Basic Books, 1970).

[14] Geoffrey Barraclough, "The End of an Era," *The New York Review of Books,* 27 June 1974.

[15] "Excerpts from Interview with Chancellor Helmut Schmidt of West Germany," *New York Times,* 25 August 1974.

[16] Nye, "UNCTAD."

[17] Miriam Camps, *The Management of Interdependence* (New York: Council on Foreign Relations, 1974).

Selected bibliography of literature on world politics and international economics

The following bibliography is a selection of the major books, articles, and other documents to which the authors in this volume referred. It is not an exhaustive list. For example, newspaper articles, some general works on theory, and many government reports and United Nations documents are not included here. The reader should refer to the footnotes of the individual articles in this volume for additional reference material.

Books

Adler, John, ed. *Capital Movements and Economic Development*. London: Macmillan & Co., 1967; New York: St. Martin's Press, 1967.

Adler-Karlsson, Gunnar. *Western Economic Warfare, 1947-67*. Stockholm: Almquist & Wiksell, 1968.

Aliber, Robert Z. *Choices for the Dollar*. Washington, D.C.: National Planning Association, 1971.

_____, ed. *National Monetary Policy and the International Financial System*. Chicago: University of Chicago Press, 1974.

Allison, Graham T. *The Essence of Decision*. Boston: Little, Brown & Co., 1970.

Almond, Gabriel A. *The American People and Foreign Policy*. New York: Harcourt, Brace & Co., 1950.

Almond, Gabriel A., and Powell, G. Bingham, Jr. *Comparative Politics*. Boston: Little, Brown & Co., 1966.

Aron, Raymond. *Peace and War*. New York: Praeger, 1967.

Asher, Robert E. *Development Assistance in the Seventies; Alternatives for the United States*. Washington, D.C.: The Brookings Institution, 1970.

Avineri, Shlomo, ed. *Karl Marx on Colonialism and Modernization*. Garden City, N.Y.: Doubleday, 1968.

Balassa, Bela. *Trade Liberalization Among Industrial Countries*. New York: McGraw-Hill, 1967.

Baldwin, Robert E. *Non-Tariff Distortions of International Trade*. Washington, D.C.: The Brookings Institution, 1970.

Banfield, Edward C. *American Foreign Aid Doctrine*. Washington, D.C.: American Enterprise Institute for Public Policy Research, 1963.

Baran, Paul, and Sweezy, Paul. *Monopoly Capital—An Essay on the American Economic and Social Order*. New York: Monthly Review Press, 1966.

Bauer, Peter T. *Dissent on Development: Studies and Debates in Development Economics*. Cambridge, Mass.: Harvard University Press, 1972.

Behrman, Jack N. *National Interests and the Multinational Enterprise: Tensions Among the North Atlantic Countries*. Englewood Cliffs, N.J.: Prentice-Hall, 1970.

Bergsten, C. Fred. *Completing the GATT: Toward New International Rules to Govern Export Controls*. Washington, D.C.: British—North American Committee, November 1974.

_____. *The Dilemmas of the Dollar: The Economics and Politics of the United States International Monetary Policy*. New York: Council on Foreign Relations, forthcoming.

_____, ed. *The Future of the International Economic Order: An Agenda for Research*. Lexington, Mass.: D. C. Heath & Co., 1973.

_____, ed. *Toward a New World Trade Policy: The Maidenhead Papers.* Lexington, Mass.: D. C. Heath, 1975.

Bhagwati, Jagdish, ed. *Economics and World Order—From the 1970's to the 1990's.* New York: Macmillan Co., 1972.

Bhagwati, Jagdish N., et al., eds. *Trade, Balance of Payments and Growth: Papers in International Economics in Honor of Charles P. Kindleberger.* Amsterdam: North Holland Publishing Co., 1971.

Brash, Donald T. *American Investment in Australian Industry.* Cambridge, Mass.: Harvard University Press, 1966.

Calleo, David, and Rowland, Benjamin. *America and the World Political Economy.* Bloomington, Ind.: Indiana University Press, 1973.

Camps, Miriam. *The Management of Interdependence.* New York: Council on Foreign Relations, 1974.

Carr, Edward H. *The Twenty Years' Crisis, 1919-1939.* London: Macmillan & Co., 1951.

Cohen, Benjamin J. *The Question of Imperialism—The Political Economy of Dominance and Dependence.* New York: Basic Books, 1973.

Cohen, Stephen D. *International Monetary Reform, 1964-69: The Political Dimension.* New York: Praeger, 1970.

Cooper, Richard N. *The Economics of Interdependence: Economic Policy in the Atlantic Community.* New York: McGraw-Hill for the Council on Foreign Relations, 1968.

Cox, Robert, and Jacobson, Harold, eds. *The Anatomy of Influence: Decision-Making in International Organizations.* New Haven, Conn.: Yale University Press, 1973.

Dam, Kenneth W. *The GATT—Law and International Organization.* Chicago: University of Chicago Press, 1970.

Dunning, John H. *American Investment in British Manufacturing Industry.* London: Allen & Unwin, 1958.

_____, ed. *International Investment: Selected Readings.* Middlesex, Eng.: Penguin Books, 1972.

_____, ed. *The Multinational Enterprise.* New York: Praeger, 1971.

Einaudi, Luigi R., ed. *Beyond Cuba: Latin America Takes Charge of Its Future.* New York: Crane, Russak & Co., 1974.

Elmandjra, Mahdi. *The United Nations System: An Analysis.* Hamden, Conn.: Archon Books, 1973.

Esman, Milton J., and Cheever, Daniel S. *The Common Aid Effort: The Development Assistance Activities of the Organization for Economic Cooperation and Development.* Columbus, Ohio: Ohio State University Press, 1967.

Frank, Charles R., Jr. *Foreign Trade Regimes and Economic Development: South Korea.* New York: National Bureau of Economic Research, forthcoming.

Frank, Charles R., Jr.; Bhagwati, Jagdish N.; Shaw, Robert d'A; Malmgren, Harald. *Assisting Developing Countries: Problems of Debts, Burden Sharing, Jobs and Trade.* New York: Praeger for the Overseas Development Council, 1972.

Friedman, Irving S. *Inflation: World-Wide Disaster.* Boston: Houghton Mifflin Co., 1973.

Fulbright, J. William. *The Arrogance of Power.* New York: Random House, 1966.

Goldman, Marshall J. *Soviet Foreign Aid.* New York: Praeger, 1967.

Gould, J. D. *Economic Growth in History.* London: Methuen & Co., 1972.

Griffin, Keith. *Underdevelopment in Spanish America.* Cambridge, Mass.: Massachusetts Institute of Technology Press, 1969.

Hanreider, Wolfram, ed. *The United States and Western Europe.* Cambridge, Mass.: Winthrop, 1974.

Hayter, Teresa. *Aid as Imperialism.* London: Penguin Books, 1971.

Hirsch, Fred. *An SDR Standard: Impetus, Elements, and Impediments.* Princeton Essays in International Finance, no. 99. Princeton, N.J.: International Finance Section, Department of Economics, Princeton University, June 1973.

_____, *Money International.* Garden City, N.Y.: Doubleday, 1969.

Hirschman, Albert O. *How to Divest in Latin America and Why.* Princeton Essays in International Finance, no. 76. Princeton, N.J.: Department of Economics, Princeton University, November 1969.

Hirschman, Albert O., and Bird, Richard M. *Foreign Aid—A Critique and A Proposal.* Princeton Essays in International Finance, no. 69. Princeton, N.J.: Department of Economics, Princeton University, July 1968.

Hoffmann, Stanley. *Gulliver's Troubles, or The Setting of American Foreign Policy.* New York: McGraw-Hill, 1968.

Hughes, Helen, ed. *Prospects for Partnership.* Baltimore, Md.: The Johns Hopkins Press, 1973.

Hughes, Helen, and You Poh Seng, eds. *Foreign Investment and Industrialization in Singapore.* Madison, Wis.: University of Wisconsin Press, 1969.

Hunter, Robert, and Reilly, John E., eds. *Development Today; A New Look at U.S. Relations with Poor Countries.* New York: Praeger, 1972.

Hutcheson, Thomas L. *The Cost of Tying Aid: A Method and Some Colombian Estimates.* Princeton Essays in International Finance, no. 30. Princeton, N.J.: Department of Economics, Princeton University, March 1972.

Ilchman, Warren E., and Uphoff, Norman Thomas. *The Political Economy of Change.* Berkeley, Calif.: University of California Press, 1969.

Johnson, Harry G. *Comparative Cost and Commercial Policy Theory for a Developing World Economy.* Wicksell Lectures, 1968. Stockholm: Alquist & Wicksell, 1968.

_____. *Economic Policies Toward Less Developed Countries.* Washington, D.C.: The Brookings Institution, 1967.

_____. *International Economic Questions Facing Britain, the United States, and Canada in the 70's.* Washington, D.C.: British–North American Research Association, June 1970.

_____. *International Trade and Economic Growth: Studies in Pure Theory.* Cambridge, Mass.: Harvard University Press, 1967.

Johnson, Harry G., and Swoboda, A. K., eds. *The Economics of Common Currencies.* London: Allen & Unwin, 1973.

Jones, David. *Europe's Chosen Few: Policy and Practice of the EEC Aid Programme.* London: Overseas Development Institute, 1973.

Katz, Jorge M. *Patents, the Paris Convention and Less Developed Countries.* Yale Economic Growth Center Discussion Paper, no. 190. New Haven, Conn.: Yale University, November 1973.

Keohane, Robert O., and Nye, Joseph S., eds. *Transnational Relations and World Politics.* Cambridge, Mass.: Harvard University Press, 1972. Previously published as *International Organization* 25 (Summer 1971), special issue.

Kindleberger, Charles P. *American Business Abroad: Six Lectures on Direct Investment.* New Haven, Conn.: Yale University Press, 1969.

_____. *Power and Money.* New York: Basic Books, 1970.

_____, ed. *The International Corporation.* Cambridge, Mass.: Massachusetts Institute of Technology Press, 1970.

Kindleberger, Charles P., and Shonfield, A., eds. *North American and Western European Economic Policies.* London: Macmillan & Co., 1971; New York: St. Martin's Press, 1971.

Kolko, Joyce and Gabriel. *The Limits of Power: The World and United States Foreign Policy, 1945-54.* New York: Random House, 1972.

Kujawa, Duane, ed. *American Labor and the Multinational Corporation.* Praeger Special Studies in International Economics and Development. New York: Praeger, 1973.

Kuznets, Simon. *Modern Economic Growth.* New Haven, Conn.: Yale University Press, 1966.

Laudicina, Paul A. *World Poverty and Development: A Survey of American Opinion.* Monograph no. 8. Washington, D.C.: Overseas Development Council, October 1973.

Lewis, John P., and Kapur, Ishan, eds. *The World Bank Group: Multilateral Aid and the 1970's.* Lexington, Mass.: D. C. Heath & Co., 1973.

Machlup, Fritz. *Remaking the International Monetary System.* Baltimore, Md.: The Johns Hopkins Press, 1968.

Machlup, Fritz; Salant, Walter S.; Tarshis, Lorie; eds. *International Mobility and Movement of Capital.* New York: National Bureau of Economic Research, 1972.

McKinnon, Ronald I. *Money and Capital in Economic Development.* Washington, D.C.: The Brookings Institution, 1973.

_____. *Private and Official International Money: The Case for the Dollar.* Princeton Essays in International Finance, no. 74. Princeton, N.J.: Department of Economics, Princeton University, April 1969.

McNamara, Robert S. *One Hundred Countries, Two Billion People.* New York: Praeger, 1973.

Malmgren, Harald B., ed. *Pacific Basin Development: The American Interests.* Lexington, Mass.: D. C. Heath & Co. for the Overseas Development Council, 1972.

Mandel, Ernest. *Europe vs. America–Contradictions of Imperialism.* New York: Monthly Review Press, 1970.

Mason, Edward S., and Asher, Robert E. *The World Bank Since Bretton Woods.* Washington, D.C.: The Brookings Institution, 1973.

Mikesell, Raymond. *The Economics of Foreign Aid.* Chicago: Aldine Publishing Co., 1968.

Miller, J. D. B. *The Politics of the Third World.* London: Oxford University Press, 1967.

Millikan, Max F., and Rostow, Walter W. *A Proposal; Key to an Effective Foreign Policy.* New York: Harper & Brothers, 1957.

Mundell, Robert A. *International Economics.* New York: Macmillan Co.. 1968.

Mundell, Robert A., and Swoboda, A. K., eds. *Monetary Problems of the International Economy.* Chicago: University of Chicago Press, 1969.

Myint, Hla. *Theories of Welfare Economics.* New York: Sentry Press, 1965.

Nelson, Joan. *Aid, Influence and Foreign Policy.* New York: Macmillan Co., 1968.

Park, Y. S. *The Link Between Special Drawing Rights and Development Finance.* Essays in International Finance, no. 100. Princeton, N.J.: Department of Economics, Princeton University, September 1973.

Pen, Jan. *Income Distribution.* New York: Praeger, 1971.

Preeg, Ernest. *Economic Blocs and U.S. Foreign Policy.* Washington, D.C.: National Planning Association, 1974.

_____. *Traders and Diplomats.* Washington, D.C.: The Brookings Institution, 1970.

Reid, Escott. *Strengthening the World Bank.* Chicago: Adlai Stevenson Institute, 1973.

Robbins, Sidney M., and Stobaugh, Robert B. *Money in the Multinational Enterprise: A Study in Financial Policy.* New York: Basic Books, 1973.

Robinson, E. A. G., ed. *Problems of Economic Development.* London: Macmillan & Co., 1965; New York: St. Martin's Press, 1965.

Robock, Stefan H., and Simmonds, Kenneth. *International Business and Multinational Enterprises.* Homewood, Ill.: Richard D. Irwin, 1973.

Rosen, Steven, and Kurth, James, eds. *Testing Theories of Economic Imperialism.* Lexington, Mass.: D. C. Heath Lexington Books, 1974.

Rosenbaum, H. Jon. *Arms and Security in Latin America.* International Affairs Series 101. Woodrow Wilson International Center for Scholars, December 1971.

Safarian, A. E. *Foreign Ownership of Canadian Industry.* Toronto: McGraw-Hill Book Co. of Canada, 1966.

Samuelson, P. A., ed. *International Economic Relations.* London: Macmillan & Co., 1969.

Staley, Eugene. *World Economy in Transition.* New York: Council on Foreign Relations, 1939.

Stopford, John M., and Wells, Louis T., Jr. *Managing the Multinational Enterprise.* New York: Basic Books, 1972.

Strassmann, W. Paul. *Technological Change and Economic Development: The Manufacturing Experience of Mexico and Puerto Rico.* Ithaca, N.Y.: Cornell University Press, 1968.

Tinbergen, Jan. *On the Theory of Economic Policy.* 2nd ed. Amsterdam: North Holland Publishing Co., 1963.

Tugendhat, Christopher. *The Multinationals.* London: Eyre & Spottiswoode, 1971.

Uphoff, Norman T., and Ilchman, Warren F., eds. *The Political Economy of Development.* Berkeley, Calif.: University of California Press, 1972.

Vaitsos, Constantine V. *Intercountry Income Distribution and Transnational Enterprises.* Oxford University Press, forthcoming.

Vernon, Raymond. *Sovereignty at Bay: The Multinational Spread of U.S. Enterprises.* New York: Basic Books, 1971.

Von Neumann Whitman, Marina. *Government Risk-Sharing in Foreign Investment.* Princeton, N.J.: Princeton University Press, 1965.

Wallace, Don, Jr., and Ruof-Koch, Helga, eds. *International Control of Investment: The Dusseldorf Conference on Multinational Corporations.* New York: Praeger, 1974.

Ward, Barbara, et al., eds. *The Widening Gap; Development in the 1970's.* New York: Columbia University Press, 1971.

White, John. *Pledged to Development: A Study of International Consortia and the Strategy of Aid.* London: Overseas Development Institute, 1967.

_____. *Promotion of Economic Integration Through Development Finance Institutions: Three Cases.* Forthcoming.

_____. *Regional Development Banks.* New York: Praeger, 1972.
Winslow, E. M. *The Pattern of Imperialism.* New York: Columbia University Press, 1948.
Wolfers, Arnold. *Discord and Collaboration.* Baltimore, Md.: The Johns Hopkins Press, 1962.
Wynia, Gary W. *Politics and Planners: Economic Development Policy in Central America.* Madison, Wis.: University of Wisconsin Press, 1972.

Articles, and essays contained in larger works

Agor, Weston H., and Suarez, Andres. "The Emerging Latin American Political Subsystem." In Douglas A. Chalmers, ed., "Changing Latin America: New Interpretations of its Politics and Society." *Proceedings of the Academy of Political Science* 30 (August 1972): 153-66.
Allison, Graham T., and Halperin, Morton H. "Bureaucratic Politics: A Paradigm and Some Policy Implications." In *Theory and Policy in International Relations*, pp. 40-70. Edited by Raymond Tanter and Richard H. Ullman. Princeton, N.J.: Princeton University Press, 1972. (Brookings Reprint 246.)
Alnaswari, Abbas. "The Collective Bargaining Power of Oil Producing Countries." *Journal of World Trade Law* 7 (March-April 1973): 188-207.
Avery, William P., and Cochrane, James D. "Innovation in Latin American Regionalism: The Andean Common Market." *International Organization* 27 (Spring 1973): 181-224.
Bachrach, Peter, and Baratz, Morton. "Decisions and Nondecisions: An Analytical Framework." *American Political Science Review* 57 (1963): 632-42.
Ball, George W. "Cosmocorp: The Importance of Being Stateless." *Columbia Journal of World Business*, November-December 1967.
Ball, R., and Marwah, K. "The U.S. Demand for Imports: 1948-58." *Review of Economics and Statistics*, November 1962: 395-401.
Banfield, Edward C. *American Foreign Aid Doctrine.* Washington, D.C.: American Enterprise Institute for Public Policy Research, January 1963.
Barraclough, Geoffrey. "The End of an Era." *The New York Review of Books*, 27 June 1974.
Behrman, Jack N. "Sharing International Production Through the Multinational Enterprise and Sectoral Integration." *Law and Policy in International Business* 4, no. 1 (1972): 1-36.
Bergson, Abram. "Toward a New Growth Model." *Problems of Communism* 22 (March-April 1973): 1-9.
Bergsten, C. Fred. "Coming Investment Wars?" *Foreign Affairs*, October 1973: 135-52. (Brookings General Series Reprint 299.)
_____. "Crisis in U.S. Trade Policy." *Foreign Affairs*, July 1971: 619-35.
_____. "The Future of World Trade." In *The International Division of Labour: Problems and Perspectives*, pp. 543-54. Edited by Herbert Giersch. Tubingen: J.C.B. Mohr, 1974.
_____. "The New Economics and U.S. Foreign Policy." *Foreign Affairs* 50 (January 1972): 199-222. (Brookings Reprint 231.)
_____. "The New Era in World Commodity Markets." *Challenge*, September-October 1974: 32-39. (Brookings General Series Reprint 297.)
_____. "The Response to the Third World." *Foreign Policy*, no. 17 (Winter 1974-75).
_____. "The Threat from the Third World." *Foreign Policy*, no. 11 (Summer 1973): 102-24. (Brookings Reprint 268.)
Bienen, Henry. "An Ideology for Africa." *Foreign Affairs* 47 (April 1969): 545-59.
Binder, Leonard. "The Middle East as a Subordinate International System." *World Politics* 10 (April 1958): 316-33.
Blake, David H. "Trade Unions and the Challenge of the Multinational Corporation." *Annals of American Academy of Political and Social Science*, no. 403 (September 1972): 34-45.
Boffey, Philip. "Technology and World Trade: Is There Cause for Alarm?" *Science*, 2 April 1971.
Brecher, Michael. "The Subordinate State System of Southern Asia." *World Politics* 15 (January 1963): 213-35.
Calleo, David P. "American Foreign Policy and American European Studies: An Imperial Bias?" In *The United States and Western Europe.* Edited by Wolfram Hanreider. Cambridge, Mass.: Winthrop, 1974.

Caves, Richard E. "International Corporations: The Industrial Economics of Foreign Investment." *Economica* 38 (February 1971): 1-27.
Connor, Walker. "Nation-Building or Nation-Destroying?" *World Politics* 24 (April 1972): 319-55.
Cooper, Richard N. "Dollar Deficits and Postwar Economic Growth." *Review of Economics and Statistics* 46 (May 1964): 155-59.
_____. "Economic Interdependence and Foreign Policy in the Seventies." *World Politics* 24 (January 1972): 159-81.
_____. "Eurodollars, Reserve Dollars, and Asymmetries in the International Monetary System." *Journal of International Economics* 2 (September 1972): 325-44.
_____. "Macroeconomic Policy Adjustment in Interdependent Economies." *Quarterly Journal of Economics* 83 (February 1969): 1-24.
_____. "Trade Policy is Foreign Policy." *Foreign Policy*, no. 9 (Winter 1972-73).
Cooper, Richard N., and Truman, Edwin M. "An Analysis of the Role of International Capital Markets in Providing Funds to Developing Countries." *Weltwirtschaftliches Archiv*, no. 2 (June 1971): 153-82.
Dell, Sidney. "An Appraisal of UNCTAD III." *World Development* 1 (May 1973): 1-13.
Diaz, Ralph A. "The Andean Common Market: Challenge to Foreign Investors." *Columbia Journal of World Business*, July-August 1971, pp. 22-28.
Díaz-Alejandro, Carlos. "Some Characteristics of Recent Export Expansion in Latin America." In *The International Division of Labour: Problems and Perspectives*, pp. 215-36. Edited by Herbert Giersch. Tubingen: J.C.B. Mohr, 1974.
Diebold, John. "Multinational Corporations—Why be Scared of Them?" *Foreign Policy*, no. 12 (Fall 1973): 79-95.
Frank, Charles R., Jr. "Optimal Terms of Foreign Assistance." *Journal of Political Economy* 78 (September/October 1970): 1106-14.
Gabriel, Peter H. "MNCs in the Third World: Is Conflict Unavoidable?" *Harvard Business Review* 50 (July-August 1972): 93-102.
Gallagher, J., and Robinson, R. "The Imperialism of Free Trade." *Economic History Review*, March 1953.
Galloway, Thomas L. "The International Coffee Agreement." *Journal of World Trade Law* 7 (May-June 1973): 354-74.
Galtung, Johan. "A Structural Theory of Imperialism." *Journal of Peace Research*, 1971: 81-118.
Gilpin, Robert. "Integration and Disintegration on the North American Continent." *International Organization* 28 (Autumn 1974): 851-74.
_____. "The Politics of Transnational Economic Relations." *International Organization* 25 (Summer 1971): 398-419.
Goldberg, Paul M., and Kindleberger, Charles P. "Toward a GATT for Investment: A Proposal for Supervision of the International Corporation." *Law and Policy in International Business* 2 (Summer 1970): 295-323.
Goldman, Marshall. "The Convergence of Environmental Disruption." *Science,* 2 October 1970, pp. 37-42.
Griffin, Keith B. "Foreign Capital, Domestic Savings and Economic Development." *Bulletin, Oxford University, Institute of Economics and Statistics* 32 (May 1970): 99-122.
Griffin, Keith B., and Enos, John L. "Foreign Assistance: Objectives and Consequences." *Economic Development and Cultural Change* 18 (April 1970): 313-27.
Grubel, Herbert G. "The Distribution of Seigniorage from International Liquidity Creation." In *Monetary Problems of the International Economy*, pp. 269-82. Edited by R. A. Mundell and A. K. Swoboda. Chicago: University of Chicago Press, 1969.
_____. "The Theory of Optimum Currency Areas." *Canadian Journal of Economics* 3 (May 1970): 318-24.
Healey, Derek T. "Development Policy: New Thinking about an Interpretation." *Journal of Economic Literature* 19 (September 1972): 757-97.
Helleiner, Gerald K. "The Less Developed Countries and the International Monetary System." *Journal of Development Studies,* forthcoming.
_____. "Manufactured Exports from Less Developed Countries and Multinational Firms." *Economic Journal* 83 (March 1973): 21-47.

Holzman, Franklyn D. "Overfull Employment Planning, Input-Output, and the Soviet Economic Reforms." *Soviet Studies* 22 (October 1970): 255-61.

Huntington, Samuel P. "Transnational Organizations in World Politics." *World Politics* 25 (April 1973).

Hymer, Stephen. "The Efficiency (Contradictions) of Multinational Corporations." *The American Economic Review, Papers and Proceedings* 60 (May 1970).

――――. "The Multinational Corporation and the Law of Uneven Development." In *Economics and World Order―From the 1970's to the 1990's.* Edited by Jagdish Bhagwati. New York: Macmillan Co., 1972.

Johnson, Harry G. "A Note on Seigniorage and the Social Saving from Substituting Credit for Commodity Money." In *Monetary Problems of the International Economy,* pp. 323-29. Edited by R. A. Mundell and A. K. Swoboda. Chicago: University of Chicago Press, 1969.

――――. "Optimum Tariffs and Retaliation." In his *International Trade and Economic Growth.* Cambridge, Mass.: Harvard University Press, 1958.

Kaiser, Karl. "The Interaction of Regional Subsystems: Some Preliminary Notes on Recurrent Patterns and the Role of Superpowers." *World Politics* 21 (October 1968).

――――. "Transnational Politics: Toward a Theory of Multinational Politics." *International Organization* 25 (Autumn 1971): 790-817.

Kennan, George. "After the Cold War: American Foreign Policy in the 1970s." *Foreign Affairs,* October 1972: 210-27.

Keohane, Robert O. "The Big Influence of Small Allies." *Foreign Policy,* no. 2 (Spring 1971).

Keohane, Robert O., and Nye, Joseph S. "International Interdependence and Integration." In *Handbook of Political Science,* vol. 7. Edited by Nelson Polsby and Fred Greenstein. Andover, Ma.: Addison-Wesley, forthcoming.

Keohane, Robert O., and Nye, Joseph S. "Transgovernmental Relations and International Organization." *World Politics,* October 1974.

Keohane, Robert O., and Nye, Joseph S. "World Politics and the International Economic System." In *The Future of the International Economic Order: An Agenda for Research.* Edited by C. Fred Bergsten. Lexington, Mass.: D. C. Heath & Co., 1973.

Kindleberger, Charles P. "The Case for Fixed Exchange Rates, 1969." In *The International Adjustment Mechanism.* Boston: Federal Reserve Bank of Boston, 1970.

――――. "The International Monetary Politics of a Near-Great Power: Two French Episodes, 1926-1936 and 1960-1970." *Economic Notes* (Siena) 1, no. 2-3 (1972).

――――. "Less Developed Countries and the International Capital Market." In *Industrial Organization and Economic Development, In Honor of E. S. Mason,* pp. 337-49. Edited by Jesse W. Markham and Gustav V. Papanek. Boston: Houghton Mifflin, 1970.

Kissinger, Henry A. "Domestic Structure and Foreign Policy." *Daedalus* 95 (Spring 1966): 503-29.

Krasner, Stephen D. "Oil Is The Exception." *Foreign Policy,* no. 14 (Spring 1974): 68-83.

Krause, Walter. "The Implications of UNCTAD III for Multinational Enterprise." *Journal of Inter-American Studies and World Affairs* 15 (February 1973): 46-59.

Kravis, Irving B. "International Commodity Agreements to Promote Aid and Efficiency: The Case of Coffee." *The Canadian Journal of Economics* 1 (May 1968): 295-317.

MacDougall, G. D. A. "The Benefits and Costs of Private Investment from Abroad: A Theoretical Approach." *Economic Record* 36 (March 1960): 13-35.

Macrae, Norman. "The Future of International Business." *Economist,* 22 January 1972.

Mason, R. Hal. "Some Observations on the Choice of Technology by Multinational Firms in Developing Countries." *Review of Economics and Statistics* 60 (August 1973): 349-55.

Metzger, Stanley D. "American Foreign Trade and Investment Policy for the 1970's: The Williams Commission Report." *American Journal of International Law* 66, no. 3 (1972).

Mikdashi, Zuhayr. "Collusion Could Work." *Foreign Policy,* no. 14 (Spring 1974): 57-67.

――――. "Cooperation Among Oil Exporting Countries with Special Reference to Arab Countries: A Political Economy Analysis." *International Organization* 28 (Winter 1974): 1-30.

Mikesell, Raymond. "The ITO Charter." *American Economic Review* 37 (June 1947): 353-56.

Moran, Theodore H. "Foreign Expansion as an 'Institutional Necessity' for U.S. Corporate Capitalism: The Search for a Radical Model." *World Politics* 25 (April 1973): 369-86.

Morgenthau, Hans. "A Political Theory of Foreign Aid." *American Political Science Review* 56 (June 1962): 301-9.
____. "Western Values and Total War." *Commentary,* October 1961.
Morse, Edward. "Crisis Diplomacy, Interdependence, and the Politics of International Economic Relations." *World Politics* 24, supplement (Spring 1972): 123-50.
Müller, Ronald. "Poverty is the Product." *Foreign Policy,* no. 13 (Winter 1973-74): 71-102.
Mundell, Robert A. "Monetary Relations between Europe and America." In *North American and Western European Economic Policies.* Edited by Charles P. Kindleberger and A. Shonfield. London: Macmillan & Co., 1971; New York: St. Martin's Press, 1971.
Murray, Tracy. "How Helpful is the Generalized System of Preferences to Developing Countries." *Economic Journal* 83 (June 1973): 449-55.
Myint, Hla. "International Trade and the Developing Countries." In *International Economic Relations.* Edited by P. A. Samuelson. London: Macmillan & Co., 1969.
Nordhaus, William D. "The Allocation of Energy Resources." *Brookings Papers on Economic Activity,* no. 3 (1973): 529-70.
Nye, Joseph S. "Transnational Relations and Interstate Conflicts: An Empirical Analysis." *International Organization* 28 (Autumn 1974): 961-96.
O'Hare, P. K. "The Convention on the Settlement of Investment Disputes." *Stanford Journal of International Studies* 6 (1971).
Oliver, Covey T. "The Andean Foreign Investment Code: A New Phase in the Quest for Normative Order as to Direct Foreign Investment." *American Journal of International Law* 66 (October 1972).
Papanek, Gustav F. "Aid, Foreign Private Investment, and Growth in Less Developed Countries." *Journal of Political Economy* 81 (January/February 1973): 120-30.
____. "The Effect of Aid and Other Resource Transfers on Savings and Growth in Less Developed Countries." *Economic Journal* 82 (September 1972): 934-50.
Penrose, Edith. "International Patenting and the Less Developed Countries." *Economic Journal* 83 (September 1973): 768-86.
Platt, D. C. M. "Economic Imperialism and the Businessman: Britain and Latin America before 1914." In *Studies in the Theory of Imperialism.* Edited by Roger Owen and Bob Sutcliffe. London: Longman, 1972.
Rahman, Anisur. "The Welfare Economics of Foreign Aid." *Pakistan Development Review* 7 (Summer 1967): 141-59.
Reid, Escott. "McNamara's World Bank." *Foreign Affairs* 51 (July 1973): 794-810.
Ronfeldt, David F., and Einaudi, Luigi R. "Conflict and Cooperation among Latin American States." In *Beyond Cuba: Latin America Takes Charge of Its Future,* pp. 185-200. Edited by Luigi R. Einaudi. New York: Crane, Russak & Co., 1974.
Rosenbaum, H. Jon. "Argentine-Brazil Relations: A Critical Juncture." *World Today* 29 (December 1973): 537-42.
Rubin, Seymour J. "The Multinational Enterprise and National Sovereignty: A Skeptic's Analysis." *Law and Policy in International Business* 3, no. 1 (1971).
Schelling, Thomas C. "Hockey Helmets, Concealed Weapons, and Daylight Savings: A Study of Binary Choices with Externalities." *Journal of Conflict Resolution* 17 (September 1973): 381-427.
Schertz, Lyle P. "World Food: Prices and the Poor." *Foreign Affairs* 52 (April 1974): 511-37.
Schmidt, Helmut. "The Struggle for the Global Product." *Foreign Affairs* 52 (April 1974): 437-51.
Sunkel, Osvaldo. "Big Business and 'Dependencia': A Latin American View." *Foreign Affairs* 50 (April 1972): 517-32.
Szasz, Paul C. "Using the New International Centre for Settlement of Investment Disputes." *East African Law Journal* 7 (June 1971).
Tobin, James. "Europe and the Dollar." *Review of Economics and Statistics* 46 (May 1964).
Ul Hague, Irfan. "The Producers' Alliances Among Developing Countries." *Journal of World Trade Law* 7 (September-October 1973): 511-26.
Vernon, Raymond. "Apparatchiks and Entrepreneurs." *Foreign Affairs* 52 (January 1974): 249-62.
____. "Rogue Elephant in the Forest: An Appraisal of Transatlantic Relations." *Foreign Affairs* 51 (April 1973): 573-87.

____. "A Skeptic Looks at the Balance of Payments." *Foreign Policy,* no. 5 (Winter 1971-72).
Walters, Robert W. "International Organizations and the Multinational Corporation: An Overview and Observations." *Annals of American Academy of Political and Social Science,* no. 403 (September 1972): 127-38.
Wasserman, Ursula. "The International Cocoa Agreement." *Journal of World Trade Law* 7 (January-February 1973): 129-34.
Weisskopf, Thomas. "The Impact of Foreign Capital Inflow on Domestic Savings in Underdeveloped Countries." *Journal of International Economics* 2 (February 1972): 25-38.
Wionczek, Miguel S. "The Rise and the Decline of Latin American Economic Integration." *Journal of Common Market Studies* 9 (September 1970): 49-66.

United States and United Nations documents

Alton, Thad. "Economic Structure and Growth in Eastern Europe." In US Congress, Joint Economic Committee, *Economic Developments in Eastern Europe.* 91st Cong., 2nd sess., 1970.
Bhagwati, Jagdish. "The Tying of Aid." UNCTAD Secretariat, New York, 1966. Reprinted in UNCTAD Conference Proceedings (New Delhi), *Problems and Policies of Financing,* vol. 4, pp. 45-71. New York: United Nations, 1968.
Chudson, Walter A. *The International Transfer of Commercial Technology to Developing Countries.* UNITAR Research Report, no. 13. New York: United Nations Institute for Training and Research, 1971.
Colaco, Francis X. *Economic and Political Considerations and the Flow of Official Resources to Developing Countries.* Paris: Organization for Economic Cooperation and Development, 1973.
Ernst, M. "Postwar Economic Growth in Eastern Europe." In US Congress, Joint Economic Committee, *New Directions in the Soviet Economy, Part IV.* 89th Cong., 2nd sess., 1966.
Horsefield, Keith, et al. *The International Monetary Fund, 1945-1965.* 3 vols. Washington, D.C.: International Monetary Fund, 1969.
International Labour Organization. *Multinational Enterprises and Social Policy.* Studies and Reports. New Series, no. 79. Geneva: International Labour Organization, 1973.
Jackson, Sir Robert G. *A Study of the Capacity of the United Nations Development System.* 2 vols. Geneva: United Nations, 1969.
Ohlin, Goran. *Foreign Aid Policies Reconsidered.* Paris: Organization for Economic Cooperation and Development, 1966.
Organization for Economic Cooperation and Development. *Development Assistance: Efforts and Policies of the Development Assistance Committee.* Paris: Organization for Economic Cooperation and Development, 1969, 1971, 1973.
____. *Development Cooperation: Efforts and Policies of the Members of the Development Assistance Committee.* Paris: Organization for Economic Cooperation and Development, 1972 and 1973.
____. *Investing in Developing Countries; Facilities for the Promotion of Foreign Private Investment in Developing Countries.* Paris: Organization for Economic Cooperation and Development, 1972.
The OECD Observer 55 (December 1971).
Reuber, Grant L. *Private Foreign Investment in Development.* London: Oxford University Press for the Development Centre of the Organization for Economic Cooperation and Development, 1973.
Task Force on International Development. *U.S. Foreign Assistance in the 1970's: A New Approach.* Report to the President. Washington, D.C.: Government Printing Office, 4 March 1970. (Also known as Peterson Report.)
United Nations. Department of Social and Economic Affairs. *Multinational Corporations in World Development.* New York: United Nations, 1973.
US Congress. House. Committee on Foreign Affairs. *The United States and the Multilateral Development Banks.* Washington, D.C.: Government Printing Office, March 1974.
US Congress. Joint Economic Committee. *Hearings before the Joint Economic Committee.* 93rd Cong., 1st sess., 17, 18, 19 July 1973.

US Congress. Joint Economic Committee. Subcommittee on Foreign Economic Policy. *A Foreign Economic Policy for the 1970s, Hearings before the Subcommittee on Foreign Economic Policy of the Joint Economic Committee, Congress of the United States.* Part 4: *The Multinational Corporation and International Investment.* 91st Cong., 2d sess. Washington, D.C.: Government Printing Office, 1970.

US Congress. Senate. Committee on Finance. *Implications of Multinational Firms for World Trade and Investment and for U.S. Trade and Labor, Report to the Committee on Finance by the U.S. Tariff Commisssion.* 93rd Cong., 1st sess. Washington, D.C.: Government Printing Office, 1973.

US Congress. Senate. Committee on the Judiciary. Subcommittee on Antitrust and Monopoly. *International Aspects of Antitrust: Hearings before the Subcommittee on Antitrust and Monopoly of the Committee on the Judiciary.* 89th Cong., 2d sess. Washington, D.C.: Government Printing Office, 1966.

US Congress. Senate. Committee on Labor and Public Welfare. *The Multinational Corporation and the National Interest,* by Robert Gilpin. 93rd Cong., 1st sess. Washington, D.C.: Government Printing Office, 1973.

US Department of Commerce. *U.S.-Soviet Commercial Relations in a New Era,* by Peter G. Peterson. Washington, D.C.: Department of Commerce, 1972.

US Department of Commerce. Bureau of International Commerce. *The Multinational Corporation: Studies on U.S. Foreign Investment.* Washington, D.C.: Government Printing Office, 1972.

US Department of State. "The Scope and Distribution of United States Military and Economic Assistance Programs." Report to the President of the United States from the Committee to Strengthen the Security of the Free World (Clay Report), 20 March 1963.

Unpublished papers

Baird, Mary; Perkins, William; and Zook, Christopher. "The International Development Association: A Critical Analysis." Williams College, Williamstown, Massachusetts, 1973. (Mimeographed.)

Bhagwati, Jagdish, and Dallalfar, William. "The Brain Drain and Income Taxation: A Proposal." Working Paper No. 92, Massachusetts Institute of Technology, Department of Economics, September 1972.

Chenery, Hollis B. "Alternative Strategies for Development." Paper presented to the Rehovot Conference on Economic Growth and Developing Countries, September 1973.

Cline, William R. "The Role of Multilateral Lending Institutions in Development Finance." Paper presented to the Society of Government Economists, New York, 28 December 1973.

Cline, William R., and Sargen, Nicholas P. "Performance Criteria and Multilateral Aid Allocation." Washington, D.C., 1973. (Mimeographed.)

Cooper, Richard N. "Issues in the Balance of Payments Adjustment Process." Committee on Economic Development, New York, 1973. (Mimeographed.)

Hymer, Stephen H. "The International Operations of National Firms: A Study of Direct Investment." Ph. D. dissertation, Massachusetts Institute of Technology, 1960.

Leyton-Brown, David. "Governments of Developed Countries as Hosts to Multinational Enterprise: The Canadian, British and French Policy Experience." Ph.D. dissertation, Harvard University, 1973.

Russell, Robert W. "Public Policies Toward Private International Financial Flows." Paper prepared for the Fifteenth Annual Meeting of the International Studies Association, St. Louis, Missouri, March 1974.

Wallich, Henry. "Why Fixed Rates?" Committee for Economic Development, New York, 1973. (Mimeographed.)

Index

6- 2005
C. Sanders